# Praxis®
# Prep
# 2017–2018

## KAPLAN
### PUBLISHING
New York

© 2017 by Kaplan, Inc.

Published by Kaplan Publishing, a division of Kaplan, Inc.
750 Third Avenue
New York, NY 10017

10 9 8 7 6 5 4 3 2 1

ISBN: 978-1-5062-2876-1

Kaplan Publishing books are available at special quantity discounts to use for sales promotions, employee premiums, or educational purposes. For more information or to purchase books, please call the Simon & Schuster special sales department at 866-506-1949.

# Table of Contents

Additional resources available at www.kaptest.com/praxisbookresources

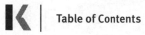

# Studying for the Praxis: Where Do I Start?

Studying for the Praxis means taking a big step toward embarking on a new and meaningful career as a teacher. But figuring out how to most effectively study for the exam can be stressful. Our goal is to give you the tools and strategies you need to feel calm and confident on test day.

You're not just getting the content in this book—as part of the Praxis package, you also have access to a wealth of practice and information through your online resources, including full-length computer-based tests that simulate the real online test environment. If you received this book as a component of Kaplan's Praxis Deluxe course, you also have video instruction and additional sets of practice questions in your online Study Plan.

These materials are customizable to your individual needs. You don't have to work through the book in the order it is written. If you are studying for any of the Praxis Core exams or for Praxis Principles of Learning and Teaching tests, you can start with an online pre-test to assess your strengths and weaknesses. Review your results: Which questions did you answer correctly? Is there a pattern to the ones you missed? In which content area or question style do you have the biggest opportunity to improve? Then dive into the chapters covering those tests, tackling your weakest areas first and working toward the areas of your biggest strengths.

Taking into account the information you learn from your pre-test, use the advice and study aids discussed below to make the most of your practice time.

# What's Included in my Praxis Study Plan?

### The Online Study Plan

Your online companion gives you access to additional content, including pre-tests for Chapters 1 through 4 and full-length practice tests for eight Praxis exams:

- Core Academic Skills for Educators: Reading
- Core Academic Skills for Educators: Mathematics
- Core Academic Skills for Educators: Writing
- Principles of Learning and Teaching (PLT) tests for grades K–6, 5–9, and 7–12
- Elementary Education: Content Knowledge
- Elementary Education: Curriculum, Instruction, and Assessment

Register your online companion using these simple steps:

1. Go to **kaptest.com/booksonline**.
2. Follow the on-screen directions. Have your copy of this book available.

Please note that access to the online portal is limited to the original owner of this book.

### Time-Tested Strategies for Every Question Type

Kaplan has spent decades researching the Praxis and teaching thousands of students the effective methods they need to succeed. This book contains detailed instruction on how to analyze and correctly answer the various question types you will encounter on the specific Praxis test for which you are studying.

### Pre-Tests For Chapters 1–4

Your online Study Plan also includes short pre-tests for the three Praxis Core exams (Reading, Mathematics, and Writing) and for the Praxis PLT tests. We recommend that you take these before you start working through the Kaplan Methods and strategies for the tests covered in these chapters. The pre-tests are accompanied by full explanations for each problem, and they break down your performance by content area to help you identify your strengths and opportunities. Having this information will let you work in an efficient and focused way.

### Practice Sets

Every chapter of this book contains sets of practice questions with the same format as questions you'll see on the computer-based practice tests and official exams. The explanations for these questions are in the book, immediately following the practice set. The practice questions provide an opportunity to check your skills after reading the material in the chapter, but before assessing your overall performance with a full-length online exam.

### Full-Length Practice Tests

As noted above, your online study plan contains full-length computer-based practice tests for eight Praxis exams. These computer-based practice tests are designed to replicate the official test day experience as closely as possible. You should treat these as if you were sitting for the actual exam: clear off your work space, turn off your cell phone, and remove any other distractions. The practice tests are timed in the same manner as the official tests, so make sure you have enough uninterrupted time to complete the test before you begin.

After you complete the test, you'll find complete answers and explanations for each question online. Moreover, you'll see an analysis of your strengths and weaknesses broken down by question type and content area in Kaplan's exclusive Smart Reports™ test analysis and reporting tool. Use this feedback to prioritize any area that needs significant improvement, and return early and often to study the relevant portions of this book.

## There's a Lot of Material to Review. How Will I Remember Everything I'll Need to Ace the Test?

In addition to providing you with the best practice questions and test strategies, Kaplan's team of learning scientists is dedicated to researching and testing the best methods for getting the most out of your study time. Here are our top five tips for improving retention.

### Start or End Each Study Session by Reviewing Practice Questions

Practice questions provide focus for each study session by showing what you still need to learn and by helping you draw connections between what you already know and what you will be studying. Studies show that students who test ahead of time score higher after studying than students who don't pre-test themselves. If your practice questions have explanations, be sure you take the time to read them carefully. Building familiarity with the structure of the questions and answers will help you feel more comfortable with the test itself.

### Review Multiple Topics in One Study Session

This may seem counterintuitive, as we're used to practicing one skill at a time in order to improve each skill separately. But research shows that weaving topics together leads to increased learning by creating semantic connections in long-term memory. Not only that, test makers often include more than one topic in a single question. Studying in an integrated manner is the most effective way to prepare for this test.

### Customize the Content

Drawing attention to difficult or critical content can ensure you don't overlook it as you read and re-read sections. The best way to do this is to make it more visual—highlight, make tabs, use stickies, whatever works. We recommend highlighting only the most important or difficult topics. Selective highlighting is great for emphasizing parts of the text, but over-highlighting can have the opposite effect.

### Repeat Topics over Time

Many people try to memorize concepts by repeating them over and over again in succession. Our research shows that retention is improved by spacing out the repeats over time (this technique is sometimes called spaced learning or boosting) and mixing up the order in which you study content. For example, try reading the chapters in a different order the second (or third!) time around. Revisit practice questions that you answered incorrectly in a new sequence. Often, information you reviewed more recently will help you better understand questions and solutions that you haven't seen in some time.

### Take a Moment to Reflect

When you finish reading a section for the first time, stop and think about what you read. Jot down a few thoughts about why the content is important or what topics came to mind when you read it. Thinking about what you've just learned activates a part of your memory called metacognition and can help long-term memories form more clearly. Associating new learning with a memory you already have is another fantastic way to retain information.

This also works when answering questions. After answering a question, take a moment to think through each step you took to arrive at a solution. What led you to the answer you chose, even if it wasn't correct? Understanding the steps you took will help you make good decisions when answering future questions.

## Are There Additional Resources Available to Me?

If you find that you would like more practice, more tests, more instruction, and more strategy, consider Kaplan's Praxis Deluxe program. Praxis Deluxe is a fully online, self-paced study program for students looking to maximize their scores. It includes video instruction from top teachers, eight additional full-length online practice tests, and additional practice questions for the exams covered in this book. Explore Praxis Deluxe and enroll at **kaptest.com/praxis** or find out more by calling 1-800-KAP-TEST.

Additionally, at the end of this book under Praxis Resources, there is information about furthering your occupation as a teacher. When you're done studying, make sure to read through the *Getting Started: Advice for New Teachers* section.

# The Praxis and You

First things first: Praxis isn't a single exam; it's a series of exams. This book, along with your online companion, provides preparation for several tests in the Praxis series. The first five chapters of the book are dedicated to eight of the most popular Praxis tests ("popular" in the sense that many aspiring educators must take them, not in the sense that they are necessarily well liked). Chapters 1–3 cover the three Core Academic Skills for Educators tests (one each for Reading, Mathematics, and Writing). Chapter 4 addresses the Principles of Learning and Teaching tests. Chapter 5 details two important Elementary Education tests (Content Knowledge and Curriculum, Instruction, and Assessment). Additionally, Chapters 6–9 outline several Praxis subject matter exams in the topic areas of Science, English Language Arts, Mathematics, and Social Studies. These chapters contain sets of practice questions that will help you evaluate your readiness and decide where you need further study.

It is essential that you know which tests are required in the state(s) in which you plan to teach before registering for the tests and beginning your preparation. Understanding these requirements will guide your use of this book and your online companion. To learn which tests you need to take, contact your state's department of education. You can find contact information and web addresses for each state in the State Certification Information table in the appendix of this book.

## The Tests and their Differences

### Praxis Core Academic Skills for Educators

The first part of this book deals with the Praxis Core, three tests covering basic reading (5712), mathematics (5732), and writing (5722) skills. These tests are often required for undergraduates entering education programs. Some states also require them for non–education major applicants seeking jobs in the classroom.

If you need to take tests from the Praxis Core series, then the first three chapters of this book will provide you with the content review you need. Each chapter in this part contains a set of practice questions for one of the three Core tests. Among your online materials, you'll find pre-tests for each of the Core exams, along with full-length tests to assess your performance.

### Praxis Principles of Learning and Teaching

The second part of the book is dedicated to the Praxis Principles of Learning and Teaching (PLT) tests. Chapter 4, which introduces the format and structure of the PLT tests, also contains subject matter information that is relevant to the Elementary Education: Curriculum, Instruction, and Assessment test covered in Part III of the book. In addition to the test review, Chapter 4 also contains three sets of practice questions, one each for three of the PLT tests: PLT: Grades K–6 (5622), Grades 5–9 (5623), and Grades 7–12 (5624). In addition, a PLT pre-test and three full-length PLT practice tests (again, one each for grades K–6, 5–9, and 7–12) are included in your online companion.

Refer to the requirements for the state in which you plan to teach to determine which of these tests you will need to take. You can find this information by looking at the table in the appendix.

### Praxis Elementary Education Tests

If you are required to take either of the tests listed below, then the third part of the book (Chapter 5) will provide valuable information about your exam(s).

- Elementary Education: Curriculum, Instruction, and Assessment (5017)
- Elementary Education: Content Knowledge (5018)

Chapter 5 provides an overview of these tests and their content, and contains sets of practice questions for each test. If you are studying for the Curriculum, Instruction, and Assessment exam, we recommend that you review Chapter 4: Principles of Learning and Teaching as well. In your online resources, you'll find full-length exams for both Elementary Education tests covered here. Use them to assess your overall performance after completing the chapter.

### Praxis Subject Assessments

There are literally dozens of subject assessments covered by the Praxis series, everything from Agriculture to Mandarin to Theater. Unfortunately, there aren't enough test takers in some subjects to warrant coverage in a general Praxis text like this. We have limited our coverage of the subject matter assessments to the four most commonly tested areas. In the fourth part of this book (Chapters 6–9), you'll find brief overviews of key English, science, social studies, and mathematics tests, followed by question sets testing content knowledge related to these fields.

If you are required to take any of the tests discussed in this section, these overviews and question banks provide helpful preparatory materials.

The Praxis tests can get confusing, and there's quite a bit of material contained in this book. It's up to you to determine which exams you need to take and which portions of the book and online companion will help you to make the most out of your preparation for the Praxis series of exams. If you have any questions regarding which tests you will need to take to teach in a given state, be sure to refer to the State Certification Information table at the back of this book.

## Computer-Delivered Tests

Aside from Braille Proficiency (0633), all Praxis tests are now offered exclusively via computer-delivered formats, and all of the full-length tests accompanying this book are now computer-delivered tests. The question sets in the printed book contain questions in formats that correspond to those you'll see on the computer-delivered exams.

Note: In the past, Praxis distinguished between computer-delivered tests (whose test numbers began with 5) and paper-based tests (whose test numbers began with 0). If you are using any Praxis materials or references more than a year or two old, you may see the same test referred to by both types of numbers, as paper-based testing persisted longer in some regions and on some tests. To make sure you are preparing for the most up-to-date test formats, visit **www.ets.org/praxis**.

## A Note about Scoring

A passing score on a Praxis test will vary depending on which state is requiring you to take the test. What's more, your state may change the passing score on a particular test from year to year. You can find passing score information by state at **ets.org/praxis/scores**; however, for the most up-to-date information about score requirements, please contact the state licensing board, organization, institution, or teacher-training program that will receive your scores.

## Registering for Praxis

The easiest way to register for Praxis tests is online at **www.ets.org/praxis/register**. You may also register by mail, by submitting a Test Authorization Voucher Request Form (download this PDF at the website), or by phone, by calling **1-800-772-9476**. There is a $35 fee if you use the phone registration service. If you are attempting to take a Praxis test outside of the United States, visit the registration website and follow the instructions you find there.

Depending on your method of registration, you either will be mailed a test admission ticket or will need to print out an e-ticket from the online registration site. Bring this ticket with you to the testing site—without it, you will not be allowed admission.

Whichever route you choose, be sure to check the test dates and locations and choose a location where you will feel the most comfortable. Also, look at up-to-date information about the state in which you plan to teach. A helpful list of relevant state addresses and websites appears in the appendix at the back of this book.

If you are a test taker who requires accommodations for a disability or other health-related issue, you will need to provide documentation to support your request. You can find official information about the process of submitting a request for accommodations at **ets.org/praxis/register/disabilities** or by contacting ETS.

Educational Testing Service
The Praxis Series
P.O. Box 6051
Princeton, NJ 08541-6051
Telephone: (609) 772-9476
Fax: (609) 530-0581
Website: **ets.org/praxis**

Please note that the information in this book is current as of the time of publication. It is recommended that you supplement your review with information from the Praxis website (**ets.org/praxis**), as test names, codes, content, and procedures are subject to change.

Good luck in your preparation for the Praxis series of exams!

# PRAXIS CORE ACADEMIC SKILLS FOR EDUCATORS

# Introducing the Praxis Core Academic Skills for Educators Tests

The Praxis Core Academic Skills for Educators tests (Core tests) consist of three exams: one in Reading, one in Mathematics, and one in Writing. These tests measure basic academic skills and are normally taken by undergraduates in education programs. Also, some non–education majors are required to take these exams to be certified to teach in some states.

In a nutshell, most teachers must pass the Core tests to be certified to teach.

This section is devoted to preparing you for the Praxis Core tests. The review sections and practice tests that follow provide comprehensive and thorough preparation for each of these tests. Be sure to understand your strengths and weaknesses as a test taker before working through these sections. You will need to pass all three tests to be certified to teach in many Praxis states. As a result, it's important to know where you need the most help so that you can focus your preparatory energies where they are most needed.

| Core Test | Questions | Time |
|-----------|-----------|------|
| Reading | 56 | 85 minutes |
| Mathematics | 56 | 85 minutes |
| Writing | 40<br>2 essays | 40 minutes<br>60 minutes |

# CHAPTER ONE

# Praxis Core Reading

## INTRODUCING PRAXIS CORE READING

Reading comprehension tests are the "bread and butter" of standardized tests, and the Praxis Core is no exception. According to ETS, the Praxis Core Reading test measures "academic skills in reading needed to prepare successfully for a career in education." That sounds straightforward enough. In fact, if you're reading this book, you're demonstrating "skills in reading." But success on this test is about more than just reading and comprehending. It's about reading to answer multiple-choice questions.

There are three basic components of this reading test: the passages, the questions, and the answer choices. Each component can be handled strategically—you can squeeze the test for all it's worth to get maximum points.

### LEARNING OBJECTIVES

By the end of this chapter, you will be able to:

- Describe the structure and format of the Praxis Core Reading test
- Outline and employ the Kaplan Method for Praxis Reading
- Apply Praxis Reading Strategies
- Use the Praxis Reading practice test to assess your performance

# KNOW WHAT TO EXPECT

## Test Format

The Praxis Core Reading test contains several passages of varying lengths. The lengthier passages are approximately 200 words, followed by four to seven questions. The shorter passages, about 100 words each, are followed by two or three questions. The test will include a set of paired passages on related topics, which total about 200 words, followed by four to seven questions. You will also encounter some brief statements, each followed by a single question. Finally, about three questions will accompany information presented in a chart or graph. Altogether, you will be required to answer 56 multiple-choice questions in 85 minutes. As with all Praxis exams, there is no penalty for incorrect answers, so be sure to answer every question, even if you have to guess.

| Praxis Core Reading |
| --- |
| Format: Computer-delivered |
| Number of Questions: 56<br>Time: 85 minutes |
| Question Types: multiple-choice (called "selected response" by the test maker)—one correct answer; multiple-choice—one or more correct answers. Questions will be based either on statements or passages or on a chart or graph. |
| Test may include pre-test questions that do not count toward your score |
| No penalty for incorrect answers |
| Scratch paper is available during the exam (it will be destroyed before you leave the testing center) |

Regardless of the length of the passage, the multiple-choice questions will be based exclusively on the passage's content. You will never be expected to bring any outside knowledge to bear on the questions. In fact, it can be dangerous to mentally add material to the passage, as doing so may make wrong answer choices seem more tempting. Keep your focus exclusively on what is stated in the passage. You may be required to make inferences or identify assumptions on the test, but even the answers to these questions will be based entirely on what is written in the passage and not on any outside knowledge you might have.

The vast majority of questions on the Praxis Core Reading test require you to select one answer from among five choices. Expect to see at least one question that requires you to choose all the answers that apply; to get credit for the question, you must select all the answers that are accurate, which could be anywhere from one to all of the choices. To indicate the difference, these questions will always include the special "Select all that apply" instruction and will have boxes, instead of ovals, in front of each answer choice.

The questions in Core Reading fall into one of three basic categories: Key Ideas and Details; Craft, Structure, and Language Skills; and Integration of Knowledge and Ideas. According to ETS, each category will comprise about a third of the questions on the Core Reading test, although Craft, Structure, and Language Skills will account for slightly fewer questions.

Key Ideas and Details questions require you to both understand the content of the passage itself and comprehend the implications of the passage's content. For instance, you may have to identify the main idea or purpose of the passage or identify a specific detail within the passage. Some of these questions are relatively straightforward; the challenge is to find the correct answer as quickly and efficiently as possible. The Kaplan Method for Reading and the Reading Strategies in the following pages will teach you how to do just that. Trick answers on these questions generally distort the meaning of the passage or focus on a scope that is broader or narrower than what appears in the passage. Additionally, Key Ideas and Details questions may ask you to apply your understanding of the passage's broad ideas and details by determining inferences that logically proceed from the passage content.

Craft, Structure, and Language Skills questions test your ability to understand the mechanics of a passage: how an author uses words, organization, and writing techniques to convey the passage's intended meaning. For instance, you may be asked what a particular word means in a given context or what a word reveals about the author's viewpoint or tone. You may have to provide an explanation of the structure of a passage. You may also be asked how the author uses information or writing techniques and what function they fulfill in achieving the author's purpose. Finally, these questions may ask what all these features of writing mechanics reveal about the author's particular viewpoint.

Integration of Knowledge and Ideas questions require you to pull together information from multiple sources, or multiple ideas from within one passage, and then interpret or apply that integrated information. Some of these questions will require the reading and interpreting of information presented visually in a chart or graph. Others will ask you to analyze the parts of an argument made in a passage, perhaps assessing the strengths, weaknesses, assumptions, evidence, and/or relevance of the argument. You may be asked to determine how ideas within a passage relate or to apply ideas from the passage to new situations. Finally, your ability to integrate ideas will be tested by requiring you to compare and contrast the approaches of different authors in paired passage sets.

Regardless of the nature of the material you encounter on your test, a systematic approach to handling the passages, questions, and answer choices will help you move through the test with confidence, efficiency, and accuracy.

# HOW TO APPROACH PRAXIS READING

As we already mentioned, you have 85 minutes to complete 56 questions about passages of varying lengths. That translates to about a minute and a half per question. When you consider the fact that while you are reading the passage, you are not answering questions, you quickly realize that this test does not give you a lot of time to work on each passage and question.

The lack of time makes it essential to move forward steadily on this test. Spending more than two or three minutes on a single question will jeopardize your ability to get a good look at every question. If a question gives you trouble, mark the question for review and move on. If you have time, return to the question, eliminate any answer choices you can, and guess. However, learn to let go of a question if needed, especially if there are other questions and passages you haven't seen yet.

Because there is no penalty for wrong answers on this exam, you should never leave any questions unanswered, even if that means taking random guesses at the end of the exam. Ideally, you will manage your time such that you get a decent look at every question and eliminate at least some wrong answer choices. However, if you are pressed for time, guessing is the best option.

Also, be aware that short passages are normally accompanied by a single question. Longer passages may have four or more questions associated with them. That means you should spend more time on the passages that translate to the most points. Short passages and passages with only one or two questions can be skimmed more quickly.

## How to Read for Points

The passages on the Praxis Core Reading test are drawn from a wide variety of topics—everything from art and science to business, politics, biography, and history. If you were reading them out of personal interest, you might take your time and re-read confusing portions or jargon. But on this test, you're reading for points, which is an entirely different proposition.

Almost all reading passages on the Praxis Core Reading test, no matter what the length or subject matter, share one important characteristic. Compared with typical reading material, these passages are extremely dense with information. This is one reason why they can be so difficult to slog through when you apply your usual reading skills. Not only is it useless to try to absorb everything you read on a Praxis reading passage; doing so is likely to slow you down and hurt your score.

## How Not to Read

1. Don't try to understand the passage thoroughly. Doing so is a waste of time.
2. Don't get caught up in the details.
3. Don't treat every part of the passage as equally important. Search for the answer you are looking for, find it, and move on.

Never forget that your goal in this section is to answer the questions correctly. You get absolutely no points for having an especially thorough understanding of the passage. To get the score you're aiming for, you need to develop a method for handling questions quickly without getting bogged down with your reading of the passages. In fact, you need to learn to spend less time reading the passages so that you can spend more time understanding the questions and finding the correct answers. Let's quickly take a look at the components of a typical Reading passage and question.

The Taj Mahal was built by the Mughal emperor Shah Jahan as a burial place for his favorite consort, Arjumand Banu Begum. She was known as Mumtaz Mahal, "the Elect of the Palace." Construction began
(5) soon after her death in 1631. The Taj Mahal and the surrounding complex of buildings and gardens were completed around 1653. However, the Taj Mahal is much more than an expression of love and loss. It's a breathtakingly symmetrical representation of heaven.

The passage is primarily concerned with

A. the Taj Mahal as an expression of love and loss
B. the history of the building of the Taj Mahal
C. the Taj Mahal as an architectural representation of heaven
D. the balance between the building and the gardens in the Taj Mahal complex
E. the importance of the Taj Mahal to the Mughal empire

This passage is full of dates, names, and all sorts of other information. All those details are not worth sweating over unless there is a question about them, in which case you'd zero in on the specific detail to answer the question. However, this question isn't focused on the details; this question asks about the passage as a whole.

Each of the wrong answer choices focuses too narrowly on a detail. Only choice (B) is broad enough to address the whole passage, which is about the history of the building of the Taj Mahal.

Now that we've covered the basics of how to read for points, it's time to look in detail at the Kaplan Method for Reading.

# THE KAPLAN FOUR-STEP METHOD FOR PRAXIS READING

If you approach every passage the same way, you will work your way through the Reading test efficiently.

| |
|---|
| **STEP 1**    **Read the passage** |
| **STEP 2**    **Decode the question** |
| **STEP 3**    **Research the detail** |
| **STEP 4**    **Predict the answer and evaluate the answer choices** |

The Kaplan Four-Step Method for Reading requires you to do most of your work before you actually get around to answering the questions. It's very tempting to read the questions and immediately jump to the answer choices. Don't do this. The work you do up front not only saves you time in the long run but increases your chances of avoiding the tempting wrong answers.

## Step 1. Read the Passage

The first thing you're going to do in most cases is read the passage itself. This should not come as a big surprise. It's important to realize that whereas you do not want to memorize or dissect the passage, you do need to read it. If you try to answer the questions without reading it, you're likely to waste time and make mistakes. Although you'll learn more about how to read the passages later in this chapter, keep in mind that the main things you're looking for when you read the passage are the Main Idea and the paragraph topics, both of which are often indicated by keywords.

For example, if you saw the following passage, here are some of the keywords and ideas you might want to note:

> The first detective stories, written by Edgar Allan Poe and Arthur Conan Doyle, emerged in the mid-19th century at a time when there was an enormous public interest in scientific progress.
> (5) The newspapers of the day continually publicized the latest scientific discoveries, and scientists were acclaimed as the heroes of the age. Poe and Conan Doyle shared this fascination with the step-by-step, logical approach used by scientists in their
> (10) experiments and instilled their detective heroes with outstanding powers of scientific reasoning.
> The character of Sherlock Holmes, for example, illustrates Conan Doyle's admiration for the scientific mind. In each case that Holmes
> (15) investigates, he is able to use the most insubstantial evidence to track down his opponent. Using only his restless eye and

**This passage is basically about detective stories and science.**

**Poe and Conan Doyle seem to be important.**

**Holmes is an example of a detective with a scientific mind.**

**Ways that Holmes uses a scientific approach.**

ingenious reasoning powers, Holmes pieces
together the identity of the villain from such
(20)    unremarkable details as the type of cigar
ashes left at the crime scene or the kind of ink
used in a handwritten letter. In fact, Holmes's
painstaking attention to detail often reminds the
reader of Charles Darwin's *On the Origin of Species,*
(25)    published some 20 years earlier.

**Author/Doyle think
Holmes is impressive.**

**Comparison between
Holmes and Darwin**

Again, you'll spend more time a little later learning how to read the passage. The point here is that the first thing you'll do is read through the entire passage, noting the major themes and a few details.

## Step 2. Decode the Question

The first thing you'll need to do with each question is to decode it. In other words, you need to figure out exactly what is being asked before you can answer the question. Basically, you need to make the question make sense to you.

> Which of the following is implied by the statement that Holmes was able to identify the villain based on "unremarkable details"?

Essentially, this question is asking what the author means by mentioning "unremarkable details." Looking at it in this way makes the answer more clear.

Exception: Check the instructions before reading a passage; if you see there is only one question (usually a short statement passage), read the question stem before reading the passage so you know precisely what you need to get out of the text. This will save time, because you can often skim or ignore portions of the passage as you search for only the information you need to answer the single question.

## Step 3. Research the Details

This does not mean that you should start re-reading the passage from the beginning to find the reference to "unremarkable details." Focus your research. Where does the author mention Holmes? You should have noted when you read the passage that the author discusses Holmes in the second paragraph. So scan the second paragraph for the reference to "unremarkable details." (Hint: you can find the reference in line 20.)

A common mistake to avoid is answering questions based on memory. Go back and do the research. Generally, if you can answer most questions correctly based on memory, you have spent too much time on the passage.

## Step 4. Predict the Answer and Evaluate the Answer Choices

When you find the detail in the passage, think about the purpose that it serves. What does the author mean by mentioning "unremarkable details"? If you read the lines surrounding the phrase, you should see that the author is discussing how amazing it is that Holmes can solve mysteries based on such little evidence (as he is "able to use the most insubstantial evidence to track down his opponent" in lines 15–17). Therefore, the reason the author mentions "unremarkable details" is to show how impressive Holmes is. Only after predicting an answer, scan your answer choices.

A. Holmes's enemies left no traces at the crime scene.
B. The character of Holmes was based on Charles Darwin.
C. Few real detectives would have been capable of solving Holmes's cases.
D. Holmes was particularly brilliant in powers of detection.
E. Criminal investigation often involves tedious, time-consuming tasks.

While you can quickly dismiss most of the answers because they do not match your prediction, choice (D) should leap out at you as a perfect match. Predicting an answer allows you to briskly eliminate incorrect answer choices, avoid tempting wrong answer choices, and zero in on the correct answer. Now that you've seen how to apply the Kaplan Method, it's time to back up a little and look more specifically at how to approach passages.

## THE PASSAGE

As you learned earlier, reading for points is not exactly like the reading that you do in school or at home. As a general rule, you read to learn or you read for pleasure. It's a pretty safe bet that you're not reading Praxis Reading passages for the fun of it. If you happen to enjoy it, that's a fabulous perk, but most people find these passages pretty dry. You should also be clear about the fact that you are not reading these passages to learn anything. You are reading these passages so that you can answer questions. That's it. Reading to answer a few questions is not the same thing as reading to learn.

The main difference between reading to learn and reading to answer questions is that the former is about knowledge and the latter is only about earning points. Anything that doesn't get you points is a waste of time for the purposes of the test. The Praxis Reading test is not a place to learn anything new. Therefore, your goal is to read in such a way that you maximize your chances of getting points on the questions. The questions will ask you about the Main Idea, a few details, a few inferences, and the author's writing strategy. You need to get enough out of the passage to deal with these questions.

## SEVEN PRAXIS READING STRATEGIES

### 1. Look for the Main Idea

The most important thing to pick up is the gist of the passage, i.e., the Main Idea and the paragraph topics. Praxis Reading passages are chosen because they are well organized; this means you will likely find the Main Idea very early in the passage text and the topic of each paragraph within the first one or two sentences of the paragraph. The remainder of a paragraph is likely to be more detail heavy. Remember that you can research the details as you need them later, using your paragraph notes to guide you to them.

### 2. Take Paragraph Notes

You are provided scratch paper, so use this to your advantage. Do not take a lot of notes, but do jot down a very brief paraphrase of each paragraph. If you do not take any notes, you are putting yourself at a disadvantage. These passages can be dull and difficult to remember. Make it easy to find the stuff you'll need to answer the questions.

### 3. Don't Sweat the Details

Don't waste time reading and re-reading parts you don't understand. As long as you have a general idea of where the details are, you don't have to really know what they are. Remember, if you don't get a question about a detail, you don't have to know it. Furthermore, as long as you have made a note of the paragraph topic, you should be able to go back and find the details. Details will always be consistent with the paragraph topics.

### 4. Find Structural Keywords

Within each paragraph, the most important words that reveal what you need to answer questions are ones that you might typically gloss over: Structural Keywords. These are words that indicate the structure and direction of the passage. For instance, keywords such as *but*, *however*, and *although* indicate a contrast is coming. *As*, *and*, and *moreover* signal the continuation of an idea. Keywords such as *because* and *resulting in* may indicate a cause-effect relationship. An author may also use keywords to indicate the passage's organization; these keywords include *first*, *next*, or *in conclusion*. While you might typically skim over these words, they are invaluable for answering Praxis questions because they reveal the structure of a passage and, therefore, the content of the paragraph notes you should take. Many Praxis questions center around Structural Keywords.

### 5. Locate Opinions

Some questions, including Global, Writer's View, and Connecting Ideas questions, will require you to understand the author's viewpoint. Therefore, it is important to note any opinions the author expresses in the passage. The most helpful indicator of the author's view is, again, keywords. Some Opinion Keywords—such as *excellent*, *remarkable*, or *horrifying*—obviously indicate a positive or negative view. Other Opinion Keywords are subtler, but if you practice looking out for words that signal the author's viewpoint, you will notice these too. Note that some passages may include the views of others (such as the views of people with whom the author disagrees), so be sure to keep viewpoints straight. Also be on the lookout for Emphasis Keywords (for instance, *enormous*, *outstanding*, and *ingenious* in the Holmes passage), which might not necessarily indicate an opinion but do signal important ideas in the passage.

### 6. Make It Simple

Sometimes you'll come across difficult language and technical jargon in the passages. As much as possible, try not to get bogged down by language you find confusing. The underlying topics are generally pretty straightforward. It can be very helpful to put confusing-sounding language into your own words. You don't have to understand every word in order to summarize or paraphrase. All you need is a general understanding.

### 7. Keep Moving

Aim to move quickly through each passage. Remember, just reading the passage doesn't get you any points.

# PRACTICE EXERCISE

Now it's time to see the Method put into action on a passage. As you read the following passage, keep in mind the Reading Strategies. Remember to not focus heavily on the details but on the Main Ideas. As you work through the passage, think about why particular words are underlined as keywords and read the accompanying paragraph notes.

The poems of the earliest Greeks, like those of other ancient societies, consisted of magical charms, mysterious predictions, prayers, and traditional songs of work and
(5) war. These poems were intended to be sung or recited, not written down, because they were created before the Greeks began to use writing for literary purposes. All that remains of them are fragments mentioned
(10) by later Greek writers. Homer, for example, quoted an ancient work song for harvesters, and Simonides adapted the ancient poetry of ritual lamentation, songs of mourning for the dead, in his writing.

(15) The different forms of early Greek poetry all had something in common: They described the way of life of a whole people. Poetry expressed ideas and feelings that were shared by everyone in a community—
(20) their folktales, their memories of historical events, and their religious speculation. The poems were wholly impersonal, with little emphasis on individual achievement. It never occurred to the earliest Greek poets
(25) to tell us their names or to try to create anything completely new.

In the "age of heroes," however, the content and purpose of Greek poetry changed. By this later period, Greek communities had
(30) become separated into classes of rulers and ruled. People living in the same community, therefore, had different, even opposed, interests; they shared fewer ideas and emotions. The particular outlook of the
(35) warlike upper class gave poetry a new content, one that focused on the lives of individuals. Poets were assigned a new task: to celebrate the accomplishments of outstanding characters, whether they were real or
(40) imaginary, rather than the activity and history of the community.

In the heroic age, poets became singers of tales who performed long poems about the fates of warriors and kings. One need only
(45) study Homer's *Iliad* and *Odyssey*, which are recorded examples of the epic poetry that was sung in the heroic age, to understand the influence that the upper class had on the poet's performance. Thus, the poetry of
(50) the heroic age can no longer be called a folk poetry. Nor was the poetry of the heroic age nameless, and in this period it lost much of its religious character.

1.  The passage is primarily concerned with

    A.  how the role of early Greek poetry changed

    B.  how Greek communities became separated into classes

    C.  the superiority of early Greek poetry

    D.  the origin of the *Iliad* and the *Odyssey*

    E.  why little is known about early Greek poets

2.  The author most likely mentions Homer and Simonides at the end of paragraph 1 in order to

    A.  provide examples of early Greek poets

    B.  demonstrate that such writers were ahead of their time

    C.  supply examples of quotes of early Greek poetry, which was generally unwritten

    D.  criticize the simplicity of some poets' styles in Greek oral poetry

    E.  honor two legendary Greek writers

3. Which of the following discoveries would strengthen the author's claims about Greek poetry in paragraph 2?

Select <u>all</u> that apply.

A. An early Greek poem about a village's collective praises to a god after a good harvest

B. An early Greek poem celebrating the exploits of the warrior Diocles

C. An undated Greek poem relaying an instructive fable

4. According to the passage, which of the following did poetry of the heroic age primarily celebrate?

A. Community life

B. Individuals

C. Religious beliefs

D. The value of work

E. Common people

5. Which of the following best describes the organization of the passage?

A. Two opposing views about poetry interpretation are presented, and one is rejected.

B. A claim about historical poetry is presented, then undermined with evidence.

C. The similarities among three historical periods are described.

D. The poetry of two historical periods is explained chronologically in order to show the contrasts.

E. The commonalities between the poems of two historical eras of the same culture are elucidated.

Notice that by using the Reading Strategies, you can answer many questions with the aid of your paragraph notes and the Main Idea you identified. Specific details should be researched only when needed. Practice using these Reading Strategies on every Praxis Reading passage you encounter to minimize the time you need to spend on each passage while maximizing your understanding of the material necessary to correctly answer questions.

# ANSWERS AND EXPLANATIONS

## Practice Exercise

### *Greek Poetry Passage*

**Main Idea:**      changes in ancient Gr. poetry

**Paragraph 1:**    intro early Gr. poetry, oral

**Paragraph 2:**    early: about community

**Paragraph 3:**    later: age of heroes, classes, individuals

**Paragraph 4:**    later cont'd: Homer, upper class, secular

Notice some of the keywords that signal the structure of this passage. "Earliest" in line 1 indicates the passage will begin by discussing early poetry, while "however" in line 27 indicates the switch to later poetry. Other keywords likewise signal the contrast between early and later Greek poetry: "rather than" in line 40 and "nor" in line 51.

Now let's see how the Reading Strategies will help with answering questions.

### 1.  A

Remember to predict an answer to the question before looking at the answer choices! In this case, the question asks for the Main Idea of the passage. You should not need to reread any of the passage text. Instead, look to the Main Idea identified in your notes. The Main Idea perfectly matches choice (A). (B) is outside the scope of this passage. (C) expresses an opinion that the author never expresses. (D) mentions the *Iliad* and the *Odyssey*, which are discussed only in paragraph 4. Likewise, (E) does not address the purpose of the entire passage.

### 2.  C

This question asks why the author decided to include a particular detail. Notice that the passage text includes the Structural Keywords "for example" in relation to these writers: questions often center around these types of keywords. This phrase indicates that the author included the writers as examples of "later Greek writers" who mentioned early Greek poetry. This matches choice (C). (A) distorts the intention of this detail, as Homer and Simonides are

not themselves early Greek poets. (B), (D), and (E) each misrepresent the author's viewpoint, which is objective throughout the passage (note the lack of any Opinion Keywords); the author never claims any poets were "ahead of their time," criticizes, or seeks to honor anyone.

### 3.  A

The question stem asks which discoveries would support the author's description of Greek poetry in the second paragraph. Rather than wasting time re-reading paragraph 2, check the paragraph note: it may contain all you need to answer the question. The note indicates the paragraph discusses early Greek poetry and its emphasis on the community. Therefore, (B) can be eliminated because it is about an individual person, and (C) can be eliminated because it cannot be attributed to early poetry. (A) is the only match and is therefore correct. Only if your paragraph note is insufficient to answer the question will you research the paragraph text for additional information, using the note as the foundation of your thinking.

### 4.  B

This question stem asks for the subject of poetry during the heroic age. The paragraph notes indicate the answer will be found in paragraph 3 or 4, and they state that poetry of the heroic period was about individuals, the upper classes, and secular material. This matches choice (B). Choices (A), (C), and (E) all reflect early Greek poetry as described in the first two paragraphs. Choice (D) is outside the scope of the passage.

### 5.  D

To review the structure of the overall passage, consult the paragraph notes. The first two paragraphs describe early Greek poetry, while the last two paragraphs describe late Greek poetry. This matches choice (D). The other answer choices either do not match the organization identified in the notes or miss the Main Idea of the passage. (A) incorrectly identifies two opposing views. Notice that there were no Opinion Keywords in the passage text; the passage never discusses opposing viewpoints, and thus the author never rejects one. Likewise, the passage only describes periods of poetry; it does not attempt to undermine a claim as in choice (B). (C) incorrectly identifies three periods instead of two. (E) focuses on the similarities rather than the differences between the passages.

# THE QUESTIONS

As you already know, Praxis Core Reading points come from answering the questions, not from absorbing everything in the passages. This doesn't mean that it is not important to approach the passage strategically—it is. However, if you do not answer the questions correctly, the passage hasn't done you much good.

Recall that there are three categories of question types on the Core Reading Test: Key Ideas and Details; Craft, Structure, and Language Skills; and Integration of Knowledge and Ideas. Before analyzing the types of questions you will encounter in each category, take three to four minutes to read the following passage. As always, read it with the goal of answering questions afterward: look for the Main Idea, take paragraph notes, locate keywords, and don't stress the details.

The <u>first</u> truly American art movement was formed by a group of landscape painters that emerged in the early 19th century called the Hudson River School.

(5) The first works in this style were created by Thomas Cole, Thomas Doughty, and Asher Durand, a trio of painters who worked during the 1820s in the Hudson River Valley and surrounding locations. Heavily

(10) influenced by European Romanticism, these painters set out to convey the remoteness and splendor of the American wilderness. The <u>strongly</u> nationalistic tone of their paintings caught the spirit of the times,

(15) and within a generation the movement had mushroomed to include landscape painters from all over the United States. Canvases <u>celebrating</u> such typically American scenes as Niagara Falls, Boston Harbor, and

(20) the expansion of the railroad into rural Pennsylvania were greeted with <u>enormous popular acclaim</u>.

<u>One factor</u> contributing to the success of the Hudson River School was the rapid

(25) growth of American nationalism in the early 19th century. The War of 1812 had given the United States a new sense of pride in its identity, and as the nation continued to grow, there was a desire to compete with

(30) Europe on both economic and cultural grounds. The vast panoramas of the Hudson River School fit the bill perfectly by providing a new movement in art that was <u>unmistakably</u> American in origin. The

(35) Hudson River School <u>also</u> arrived at a time when writers in the United States were turning their attention to the wilderness as a unique aspect of their nationality. The Hudson River School profited from

(40) this nostalgia because they effectively represented the continent the way it used to be. The view that the American character was formed by the frontier experience was widely held, and many writers were

(45) concerned about the future of a country that was becoming increasingly urbanized.

<u>In keeping</u> with this nationalistic spirit, <u>even</u> the painting style of the Hudson River School exhibited a strong sense of

(50) American identity. Although many of the artists studied in Europe, their paintings show a desire to be free of European artistic rules. Regarding the natural landscape as a direct manifestation of God, the Hudson

(55) River School painters attempted to record what they saw as accurately as possible. <u>Unlike</u> European painters, who brought to their canvases the styles and techniques of centuries, they sought neither to embellish

(60) nor to idealize their scenes, portraying nature with the care and attention to detail of naturalists.

**Main Idea:**    describe HRS subject, success, and style (Am. nationalism)

**Paragraph 1:**   describe HRS = 1st Am. art movement

**Paragraph 2:**   reason success = nationalism: pride identity & value frontier

**Paragraph 3:**   style = Am. identity; not Eur.

Hopefully, you caught that this passage was about why the Hudson River School became so successful. You should have also noted that the second paragraph addresses how American nationalism contributed to the success of the Hudson River School, and the third paragraph discusses how nationalist sentiment was evident in the Hudson River School painting style. Now use this passage to learn about the characteristics and strategies of each of the question types that appear on the Praxis Reading test.

# KEY IDEAS AND DETAILS QUESTIONS

## Global Questions

A Global question asks you to summarize the topic, theme, or purpose of the passage. Keywords such as *primary*, *purpose*, or *main idea* can signal a Global question. The key strategy for Global questions is to look for a choice that captures the entire passage. Usually, the test makers will try to distract you by having one or more answer choices focus on a detail or single paragraph. You need to recognize the choice that deals with the passage as a whole. As previously suggested, read every passage with the task of identifying the Main Idea in mind and include it in your notes; rarely, if ever, should you have to return to the passage text to answer a Global question.

The passage is primarily concerned with

A.  the history of American landscape painting

B.  why an art movement caught the public imagination

C.  how European painters influenced the Hudson River School

D.  why writers began to romanticize the American wilderness

E.  the origins of nationalism in the United States

Do you see which one of these answers describes the entire passage without being too broad or too narrow?

(A) is too broad, as is (E). The passage is not about *all* American landscape painting; it's about the Hudson River School. Nationalism in the United States is a much larger topic than the role of nationalism in a particular art movement. On the other hand, (C) and (D) are too narrow. European painters did influence the Hudson River School painters, but that isn't the point of the whole passage. Similarly, writers are mentioned in paragraph 2, but the passage is about an art movement. Only (B) captures the essence of the passage—it's about an art movement that caught the public imagination.

## Detail Questions

Detail questions are straightforward—all you have to do is locate the needed information in the passage. While Detail questions can be worded in various ways, the phrase *according to the passage* often signals a Detail question. The correct answer will be directly stated, though perhaps worded differently, in the passage text; you can put your finger on the information that answers the question. The key strategy is to use your notes to locate the relevant paragraph and research that portion of the text. Remember to predict an answer in your own words before looking at the answer choices.

> Which of the following is NOT mentioned as contributing to the success of the Hudson River School?
>
> A. American nationalism increased after the War of 1812.
> B. Americans were nostalgic about the frontier.
> C. Writers began to focus on the wilderness.
> D. The United States wanted to compete with Europe.
> E. City dwellers became concerned about environmental pollution.

Before reading the answer choices, paraphrase some of the reasons for the Hudson River School's success: nationalism, postwar pride, a desire to be equal with Europe, and the nostalgic appeal of the frontier. Four of the five answer choices are mentioned explicitly in the passage. (A) is mentioned in lines 23–31. (B) appears in line 40. (C) shows up in lines 35–42. (D) is mentioned in lines 26–31. Only (E) does not appear in the passage. Since we need the choice that is NOT mentioned, (E) is correct.

## Inference Questions

An Inference question, like a Detail question, asks you to find relevant information in the passage. However, once you've located the detail, you've got to go one step further to figure out the underlying meaning of a particular phrase or example. The correct answer will not be stated directly, but you can put your finger on evidence in the passage that directly supports the answer. The correct answer to an Inference question logically follows the information in the passage text. Wrong answer choices will often contain information beyond the subject matter of the passage. You can often spot Inference questions because they contain keywords such as *implies*, *suggests*, or *infers*.

> Which of the following best describes what is suggested by the statement that the Hudson River School paintings "fit the bill perfectly" (line 32)?
>
> A. The paintings depicted famous battle scenes.
> B. The paintings were very successful commercially.
> C. The paintings reflected a new pride in the United States.
> D. The paintings were favorably received in Europe.
> E. The paintings were accurate in their portrayal of nature.

The keyword "suggested" signals an Inference question. Remember that the answer will not be directly stated in the passage text, but you will use the evidence in the passage to predict what the author means by the phrase. First, read the lines surrounding the quote to put the quote in context. Paragraph 2 discusses the reason for the Hudson River School's success: its portrayal of American identity when Americans were highly nationalistic—that's why the paintings "fit the bill." The previous sentence refers to America's "new sense of pride in its identity" and "desire to compete with Europe on . . . cultural grounds." (C) summarizes the point nicely. Note that this question revolves around the interplay between the Main Idea of the passage and certain details within it. The detail in the question stem supports the topic of the paragraph—the growing sense of nationalism in America. (A) superficially relates to the War of 1812 but does not answer the question. (B) and (D) are way off base; (E) includes a detail that is found to be relevant later on in the passage, but it does not capture the gist of the inference.

# CRAFT, STRUCTURE, AND LANGUAGE SKILLS QUESTIONS

## Vocabulary-in-Context Questions

While Vocabulary-in-Context questions do require you to possess a college-level vocabulary, they are less about definitions and more about understanding how a word is used in the context of an overall passage-hence, Vocabulary-*in-Context* questions. The key strategy is to locate the word in the passage text, pretend the word is a blank, and then predict a word to substitute for the blank *before looking at the answer choices*. Base your prediction on the context of the surrounding text; sometimes you may need to re-read before and after the relevant sentence to truly understand the context. Sometimes, your prediction will actually match one of the choices; select it and you're done. Even if it doesn't exactly match an answer choice, making a prediction will still help you know what type of word you need. Trap answers on Vocabulary-in-Context questions are often common meanings of the word that do not fit the context of the passage. Therefore, take a moment to re-read your word choice back into the passage text to make sure it fits in context before selecting your answer choice.

> Which of the following words, if substituted for the word "celebrating" in line 18, would introduce the LEAST change in the meaning of the sentence?
>
> A. praising
> B. portraying
> C. worshipping
> D. observing
> E. partying

Remember the strategy: pretend the word is a blank and then predict a word to substitute for the blank. Consider the context: the paragraph describes how the Hudson River School paintings captured the "strongly nationalistic tone" (line 13) of the times, leading to their being received with "enormous popular acclaim" (lines 21–22). Some of these Emphasis Keywords may have stuck out to you when first reading the text. Since the word "celebrating" is used to describe how nationalistic scenes like Boston Harbor were depicted so that they were popularly received, predict that the word must mean *positively portraying*. This matches choice (A). Choices (B) and (D) are too neutral in tone for the contextual meaning of "celebrating." (C) is too extreme, while (E) uses a common meaning of the word that does not at all fit in context.

## Function Questions

Rather than asking you about the meaning of content in a passage, Function questions ask you about *how* the author uses elements of the passage. In other words, what *function* does something serve in the passage? Key phrases such as *the author mentions* and *in order to* often signal a Function question. Function questions may ask about the use of a particular word, phrase, paragraph, or writing device or even about the organization of the entire passage. The key strategy for Function questions is to locate the relevant portion of the text and use your notes to determine what role the text in question serves in the context of the entire passage. For instance, a portion of text could provide evidence, supply an example, provide a contrasting viewpoint, or contribute to an author's Main Idea. Trap answers may include an actual detail or point of the passage but not represent the function of the particular text in question. For Function questions that ask about the overall organization of the passage, use your notes to review the purpose of each paragraph and then find the answer choice that matches your prediction.

The passage most likely mentions the War of 1812 (line 26) in order to

A. refute the perceived inferiority of America

B. criticize European interference in America

C. provide an example of the Hudson River School's subject matter

D. identify a source of American nationalism

E. praise American nationalism

For Function questions, be sure to keep the author's overall purpose in mind: to describe the Hudson River School's subjects, success, and style. The correct function of a portion of the passage must be in line with the author's overall purpose. The cited text appears in paragraph 2, so use your notes to determine the purpose of this phrase in context. Paragraph 2 identifies the growth of American nationalism as contributing to the success of the Hudson River School and describes sources of this sentiment. The context around line 26 states that the War of 1812 "had given the United States a new sense of pride in its identity" (lines 26–28), so this must be the author's reason for mentioning the War of 1812: as a source of the growing nationalism. Choice (D) perfectly matches that prediction. Choices (A), (B), and (E) can be eliminated because they do not match the author's overall purpose: the author does not "refute" or "criticize," and while the author seems to have a positive view of the Hudson River School, it is not expressly "praised" in the passage. Choice (C) misrepresents the function of the cited phrase. Although the War of 1812 could have provided subject matter for the painters, it is not identified as such in the passage; its mention instead functions to identify a source of nationalism.

## Writer's View Questions

Writer's View questions require you to understand the nuances of the author's viewpoint and approach to the passage's subject matter. These questions may contain key phrases such as *author's attitude*, as they ask you about the attitude of the author toward a portion or Main Idea of the text. The key strategy for these questions is to develop an understanding of the author's view when first reading the passage, then predict and choose answers that match this viewpoint. To identify the author's view, remember to look for Opinion and Emphasis Keywords when reading the passage; these words will help you determine a Main Idea that aligns with the author's viewpoint. For instance, keywords may indicate that the author favors something, opposes something, is merely describing something, or perhaps takes a more nuanced view. Trap answers for Writer's View questions often misrepresent the author's attitude (for instance, stating the author favors a view while the author only reports on it objectively) or present the view of someone else in the passage.

> The author's attitude toward the Hudson River School can be described by which of the following statements?
>
> Select all that apply.
>
> A. Its artwork represents the best painting style to ever originate in America.
> B. Its style differed from the style of contemporary European artwork.
> C. It was artistically superior to contemporary European artwork.

It can be difficult to make specific predictions for questions that ask about the author's attitude, but keep in mind the author's overall purpose: to describe the subjects, success, and style of the Hudson River School. The correct answer will likely be similarly objective in tone, as the author does not express opinions about the art in the passage. With the overall view in mind, evaluate each answer choice. Eliminate (A), as the author never expresses a view about the superiority of the Hudson River School, saying only that it was the "first truly American art movement" (line 1). Use your notes to research choice (B). Paragraph 3 contrasts the Hudson River School style with the European style: though "influenced by European Romanticism" (line 10), the American "paintings show a desire to be free of European artistic rules" (lines 51–53) and the painters were "unlike European painters" (line 57). Therefore, the author would likely agree with (B). Evaluate (C) as well, as more than one answer could be correct. (C) can be eliminated for the same reason as (A); the author never claims the artwork is "superior." Therefore, (B) alone is correct.

# INTEGRATION OF KNOWLEDGE AND IDEAS

## Infographics Questions

One way you may be asked to integrate ideas is by reading and interpreting information presented in visual form in a graph, chart, or other diagram. Typically, an infographic will be accompanied by three questions. Some Infographics questions may simply ask you to read information from an infographic, while others may ask you to draw conclusions based on the information presented. When answering Infographics questions, pay careful attention to the labels and titles on the infographic; reading the infographic incorrectly will make it difficult, if not impossible, to correctly answer the related questions. Note that you may not need the entire infographic to answer a question, so focus only on the portion of the infographic required to answer the question. As on all Core Reading questions, predict the answer before looking at the answer choices. This will help you avoid trap answers that go farther than is warranted by the information presented in the infographic. Additionally, be careful not to confuse causation with mere correlation of data.

The Hudson River School emerged in the mid-1800s in America, and typically depicted natural American landscapes in such a way that celebrated America's unique national identity. The timeline below displays the names, dates, and artists of some famous Hudson River School paintings.

Selected Paintings of Hudson River School Artists

1836 *The Oxbow (The Connecticut River near Northampton)*, Thomas Cole

1857 *Niagara Falls*, Frederic Edwin Church

1859 *The Catskills*, Asher Brown Durand

1868 *Among the Sierra Nevada Mountains, California*, Albert Bierstadt

1869 *Mount Washington*, John Frederick Kensett

1872 *Great Canyon of the Sierra, Yosemite*, Thomas Hill

Which conclusion about the art of the Hudson River School is best supported by the data presented in the timeline above?

A. The majority of Hudson River School paintings were created in the 1850s.

B. Hudson River School paintings may depict mountains or water features.

C. Thomas Cole was the first Hudson River School painter.

D. Albert Bierstadt's paintings are the best examples of Hudson River School art.

E. The Hudson River School had fallen out of popularity by the 1880s.

Before reading the answer choices, remember to evaluate the infographic and make a general prediction if possible. The infographic is a timeline listing some Hudson River School paintings and artists. Don't skip the title of the timeline; the graphic only displays *selected* artists. This timeline does not contain every possible Hudson River School artwork, so keep that in mind when it comes to drawing conclusions about the infographic. Now evaluate the answer choices. Eliminate (A); although some paintings were created in the 1850s, this does not constitute the majority of paintings represented on the graphic, let alone the majority of *all* paintings. (B) seems more likely as it is supported by the names of the paintings. Additionally, the presence of the weaker word "may" makes this answer easier to support. Eliminate (C), as the timeline does not necessarily include *every* Hudson River School painting. Likewise, eliminate (E); if the timeline depicted the entirety of Hudson River School art, we might be able to draw this conclusion, but we do not know whether more paintings followed the one recorded in 1872. Also eliminate (D), as the timeline provides no viewpoints about Hudson River School art. Choice (B) is correct. Be careful that the answer you choose for an Infographics question can be fully supported by the information contained in the graphic.

## Logical Reasoning Questions

Logical Reasoning questions require you to both identify and evaluate the parts of arguments that appear in a passage. These questions may be identified by their use of argument-related terms in the question stem: *evidence, strengthen, weaken, assumption, conclusion, argument*, etc. Keep in mind that these questions are not asking for *your* opinion of the argument. Rather they require a logical analysis of the claim in question. For instance, you may be asked to evaluate whether given evidence is relevant to an argument's conclusion, what types of information could strengthen or weaken an argument, and what unstated assumptions may underlie the author's claim. These questions may also ask about additional conclusions that may logically be made from the passage's claims, such as identifying statements with which an author is "most likely to agree." For more complicated Logical Reasoning questions, it may be helpful to jot down the argument's components: the evidence, the conclusion, and the unstated assumption(s). When evaluating evidence, remember that it must be logically relevant to the argument's conclusion, while evidence that strengthens or weakens an argument must impact the likelihood of its assumptions being true. Trap answers will typically contain information that may be related to the overall subject matter but is logically irrelevant to the argument in question.

Which of the following, if true, would most strengthen the claims presented in the passage?

A. The subjects of many Hudson River School paintings were classical European landmarks.

B. Several renowned European painters were using the American West as the subject of their landscape paintings in the early 19th century.

C. During the time of the Hudson River School, poetry about living in American urban settings flourished.

D. The landscapes depicted in many Hudson River School paintings later became American national parks.

E. Based on the content of personal letters of the period, most Americans after the War of 1812 desired to emulate European culture.

While you cannot make a specific prediction for this question, review the author's claims before looking at the answer choices to determine the *type* of evidence that would strengthen the argument. While the author is not opinionated about the Hudson River School, the passage describes its subject matter (natural scenes depicting American nationalism), success (capturing the prevailing spirit of nationalism), and style (detailed depictions of nature). Use this prediction of the passage's purpose to evaluate the answer choices, looking for information that would provide further evidence for the author's claims. Eliminate choices that either weaken the argument or are irrelevant to the argument. Eliminate (A), as this would weaken, rather than strengthen, the author's claims that the Hudson River School depicted "the American wilderness" (line 12). Eliminate (B), as Europeans painting American scenes would not support the author's claims about the Hudson River School; this choice would perhaps undermine the claim that the movement "was unmistakably American in origin" (line 34). Likewise, (C) does not strengthen the author's claims about the Hudson River School's primarily natural subjects; rather, it weakens the claim that writers "were turning their attention to the wilderness" (lines 36–37) and "were concerned about the future of a country that was becoming increasingly urbanized" (lines 44–46). Choice (D) would strengthen the author's claims about the movement's subject matter, as scenes that "convey the remoteness and splendor of the American wilderness" (lines 11–12) would likely be valued as future national parks; (D) is therefore correct. Finally, choice (E) also weakens the author's claims that the prevailing American attitude was a "pride in its identity" and a "desire to compete with Europe" (lines 27–30).

## Connecting Ideas Questions

A final category of questions asks you to evaluate the various ways in which ideas may be related. For instance, since you must identify how the views and techniques of two authors compare/contrast, the questions that accompany paired passages fall into this category. Questions with paired passages may also ask you to identify how information from one passage relates to the other passage; for instance, perhaps one passage provides evidence for or against an idea in the other passage. Most questions that accompany paired passages are actually question types you have already encountered—Global, Inference, Function, etc.—but since they may ask about one or both passages, they require more careful attention to keeping the ideas straight.

Besides accompanying paired passages, Connecting Ideas questions may ask you to describe the relationship between ideas presented in a single passage (such as compare/contrast or cause/effect) or apply the information in the passage to a new situation. As always, make a strong prediction for Connecting Ideas questions before looking at the answer choices.

> According to the passage, European Romantic painters differed from American Romantic painters of the Hudson River School in that European Romantic painters
>
> A. desired to emulate naturalists
> B. ignored painting traditions
> C. might not depict scenes realistically
> D. rejected religious inspiration
> E. celebrated the nationalism of their homelands

Since it asks how two groups in the passage differ, this is a Connecting Ideas question. As always, use your notes to locate the relevant portion of the passage to research. Be especially careful to keep the characteristics of the different groups straight. Paragraph 3 discusses the contrasts between the American and European artists. The paragraph describes the Americans artists as desiring to be "free of European artistic rules" (lines 52–53), considering nature a "manifestation of God" (line 54), and painting realistically (lines 56 and 61–62). Since the Americans are described as being "unlike" the Europeans (line 57), by logical extension the Europeans are depicted as following "rules" and the "techniques of centuries" (lines 58–59), and willing to "embellish" and "idealize" their scenes (lines 59–60). Note that the question stem asks for a characteristic of *European* painters, so choice (C) is correct. The slightly weaker wording of (C), "might," makes the choice easier to support from the text and therefore more likely to be correct. Choices (A) and (B) are incorrect because they depict the behaviors of the Americans, who are said to be "unlike" the European painters. Choice (D) distorts the passage; the Americans are said to regard nature as "a direct manifestation of God," (lines 53–54), but the passage never states that Europeans differed in this practice. Finally, the passage never identifies the subject matter of the Europeans' art, so (E) is incorrect.

# PRACTICE

Now it's time to practice some Praxis Reading questions. Make sure to use Kaplan's Four-Step Method when working through this quiz.

**Questions 1–7**

The painter Georgia O'Keeffe was born in Wisconsin in 1887 and grew up on her family's farm. At 17, she decided she wanted to be an artist and left the farm for schools
(5) in Chicago and New York, but she never lost her bond with the land. Like most painters, O'Keeffe painted the things that were most important to her, and nearly all her works are simplified portrayals of nature.
(10) O'Keeffe became famous when her paintings were discovered and exhibited in New York by the photographer Alfred Stieglitz, whom she married in 1924. During a visit to New Mexico in 1929, O'Keeffe was
(15) so moved by the bleak landscape and broad skies of the Western desert that she began to paint its images. Cows' skulls and other bleached bones found in the desert figured prominently in her paintings. When her
(20) husband died in 1946, she moved to New Mexico permanently and used the horizon lines of the desert, colorful flowers, rocks, barren hills, and the sky as subjects for her paintings. Although O'Keeffe painted her
(25) best-known works in the 1920s, '30s, and '40s, she continued to produce tributes to the Western desert until her death in 1986.

O'Keeffe is widely considered to have been a pioneering American modernist
(30) painter. Whereas most early modern American artists were strongly influenced by European art, O'Keeffe's position was more independent. She established her own vision and preferred to view her painting
(35) as a private endeavor. Almost from the beginning, her work was more identifiably American than that of her contemporaries in its simplified and idealized treatment of color, light, space, and natural forms.

(40) Her paintings are generally considered "semi-abstract" because even though they depict recognizable images and objects, the paintings don't present those images in a very detailed or realistic way.
(45) Rather, the colors and shapes in her paintings are often so reduced and simplified that they begin to take on a life of their own, independent of the real-life objects from which they are taken.

1. Which of the following best states the main idea of the passage?

   A. O'Keeffe was the best painter of her generation.

   B. O'Keeffe was a distinctive modern American painter.

   C. O'Keeffe liked to paint only what was familiar to her.

   D. O'Keeffe never developed fully as an abstract artist.

   E. O'Keeffe used colors and shapes that are too reduced and simple.

2. The author most likely mentions "most early modern American artists" (lines 30–31) in order to

   A. demonstrate the superiority of O'Keeffe's landscape art

   B. explain that other American artists were influenced by Europeans

   C. show how O'Keeffe's inspiration and art were unique

   D. argue that O'Keeffe's American upbringing influenced her artistic style

   E. criticize O'Keeffe's contemporaries as artistically old-fashioned

3. The passage suggests that Stieglitz contributed to O'Keeffe's career by

   A. bringing her work to a wider audience
   B. supporting her financially for many years
   C. inspiring her to paint natural forms
   D. suggesting that she study the work of European artists
   E. requesting that she accompany him to New Mexico

4. Which of the following is most similar to O'Keeffe's relationship with nature as portrayed in the passage?

   A. A photographer's relationship with a model
   B. A writer's relationship with a publisher
   C. A student's relationship with a part-time job
   D. A sculptor's relationship with an art dealer
   E. A carpenter's relationship with a hammer

5. According to the passage, why have O'Keeffe's paintings been described as "semi-abstract" (line 41)?

   A. They involve a carefully realistic use of color and light.
   B. They depict common, everyday things.
   C. They show familiar scenes from nature.
   D. They depict recognizable things in an unfamiliar manner.
   E. They refer directly to real-life activities.

6. As used in line 46, "reduced" most nearly means

   A. decreased
   B. cheapened
   C. streamlined
   D. miniaturized
   E. humbled

7. The author would describe the "colors and shapes" (line 45) in O'Keeffe's paintings as

   A. dynamic
   B. realistic
   C. ornate
   D. unrecognizable
   E. abstract

**Questions 8–10**

Whether as a result of some mysterious tendency in the collective psyche or as a spontaneous reaction to their turbulent historical experience after the breakup of
(5) the Mycenaean world, the Greeks felt that to live with changing, unmeasured, seemingly random impressions—to live, in short, with what was expressed by the Greek word *chaos*—was to live in a state of constant
(10) anxiety.

If the apparent mutability of the human condition was a source of pain and bewilderment to the Greeks, the discovery of a permanent pattern or an unchanging
(15) substratum by which apparently chaotic experience could be measured and explained was a source of satisfaction, even joy, which had something of a religious nature.

8. The primary purpose of the passage is to

   A. evaluate conflicting viewpoints

   B. challenge an accepted opinion

   C. question philosophical principles

   D. enumerate historical facts

   E. describe a cultural phenomenon

9. The function of the first five lines in the passage ("Whether as a result. . . the Mycenaean world") is to

   A. supply a detailed context for the worldview of the ancient Greeks

   B. argue that the fragmentation of Mycenae led to the negative ancient Greek view of *chaos*

   C. describe the general mentality of the ancient Greek community

   D. present the religious underpinnings of the Greek view of *chaos*

   E. provide two possible explanations for the ancient Greek tendency to react to unpredictability with anxiety

10. Which of the following, if true, would most strengthen the argument presented in the passage?

    A. Ancient Greek artwork often depicted an admiration for the orderly movement of the constellations.

    B. The breakup of Mycenaean society actually resulted in the creation of a unique Greek cultural identity.

    C. Archaeologists discovered poems by numerous ancient Greek authors celebrating excitement associated with uncertainty about the future.

    D. The Greek work *chaos* means "quiet tranquility."

    E. An ancient Greek philosopher's determination that earthquakes could be attributed to three observable causes was met with widespread disdain and fear.

**Questions 11–13**

Katie spends some of her leisure time watching television. Last year, Katie decided to track her television viewing. The table below shows the time, in hours, Katie spent watching each of five television genres for each month. Katie watched no other television than what she recorded in the table, and she watched television programs only on her household television.

| Genre | J | F | M | A | M | J | J | A | S | O | N | D | Total |
|---|---|---|---|---|---|---|---|---|---|---|---|---|---|
| Comedy | 7 | 6 | 8 | 10 | 8 | 9 | 5 | 10 | 11 | 11 | 9 | 8 | 102 |
| Documentary | 3 | 4 | 4 | 3 | 5 | 2 | 3 | 5 | 6 | 2 | 3 | 5 | 45 |
| Drama | 5 | 5 | 6 | 4 | 5 | 6 | 2 | 4 | 6 | 3 | 7 | 5 | 58 |
| News | 12 | 12 | 12 | 12 | 12 | 12 | 12 | 12 | 12 | 12 | 12 | 12 | 144 |
| Reality | 4 | 5 | 4 | 0 | 1 | 2 | 2 | 2 | 8 | 9 | 9 | 3 | 49 |
| Total | 31 | 32 | 34 | 29 | 31 | 31 | 24 | 33 | 43 | 37 | 40 | 33 | 398 |

11. Which of the following television genres did Katie watch most during the first three months of last year?

    A. Comedy

    B. Documentary

    C. Drama

    D. Reality

    E. Katie watched all genres equally.

12. Given the information provided, which of the following best accounts for Katie's total hours of television watched last July and September?

    A. Katie's household television was broken in the month of July, but by September it was fixed.

    B. In July, Katie watched fewer hours of television in each genre than she averaged for previous months.

    C. Katie watched television programming as normal in July, but she increased her average television-viewing hours in every genre in September.

    D. Katie spent more hours of her leisure time in July on outdoor activities compared to other months, but in September she spent most of her leisure time watching new episodes of her favorite television shows.

    E. There were very few television programs that Katie wanted to watch in July and September.

13. Which of the following statements is best supported by the information provided?

    A. Katie watched a consistent amount of news programming every month last year.

    B. Katie watched more hours of documentary than of either comedy or drama last year.

    C. Katie watched the most hours of television last year in May.

    D. Katie watched a consistent number of reality program hours every month last year.

    E. Katie's favorite television genre is comedy.

**Questions 14–18**

Ever since the giant panda was discovered in the middle of the 19th century, a debate has raged over its relation to other species. Whereas the general public tends to view
(5) the panda as a kind of living teddy bear, biologists have not been sure how to classify this enigmatic animal. At different times, the panda has been placed alternately with bears in the Ursidae family, with raccoons
(10) in the Procyonidae family, and in its own Ailuropodidae family.

Biologists who classify animal species have tried to categorize the panda according to whether its traits are homologous or
(15) merely analogous to similar traits in other species. Homologous traits are those that species have in common because they have descended from a common ancestor. For instance, every species of cat has the
(20) homologous trait of possessing only four toes on its hind foot because every member of the cat family descended from a common feline ancestor. The greater number of such traits that two species share, the more
(25) closely they are related. An analogous trait is a trait that two species have in common not because they are descended from a common ancestor but because they have different ancestors that developed in similar
(30) ways in response to similar environmental pressures. A cat and a lion have more homologous traits between them than a cat and a human, for example. So cats and lions are more closely related than cats and
(35) humans. A whale and a fish have analogous tail fins because they both evolved in aquatic environments, not because they share a common ancestor. The questions surrounding the classification of the giant
(40) panda are linked to whether certain traits are homologous or simply analogous.

14. According to the passage, which of the following is true of the classification of the giant panda?

A. The correct classification of the giant panda is in the Ursidae family.

B. The classification of the giant panda is based on analogous traits.

C. The classification of the giant panda has changed because of the rapid evolution of the species.

D. The classification of the giant panda has proved difficult for biologists because of traits pandas share with several other types of animals.

E. The giant panda is best classified by biologists as a kind of giant teddy bear.

15. Which of the following is NOT possible using the homologous/analogous classification scheme?

A. Two species sharing more than one homologous trait

B. Two species sharing more than one analogous trait

C. Two species sharing an analogous trait but having no common ancestor

D. Two species sharing a homologous trait but having no common ancestor

E. Two species sharing no analogous or homologous traits

16. Which of the following best describes the organization of the second paragraph?

A. Two terms are defined using examples.

B. Two theories are contrasted.

C. A hypothesis is proven.

D. Two arguments are presented with evidence.

E. Examples of species are listed.

17. The author's attitude toward the panda classification debate can best be described as one of

    A. disdain

    B. incredulity

    C. objectivity

    D. elation

    E. concern

18. The passage suggests that which of the following is true about animal classification?

    Select all that apply.

    A. Giant pandas share traits with both bears and raccoons.

    B. Homologous traits are more significant for classification purposes than analogous traits.

    C. Cats and lions did not develop under similar environmental pressures.

19. Despite their amazing architectural and cultural achievements, including extensive roadway systems, none of the pre-Columbian civilizations of Mesoamerica developed a wheel used for transport. However, archeologists have discovered wheeled toys used by Mesoamerican children. Since they never applied wheel technology to vehicles, the Mesoamericans must not have had the need to carry heavy loads.

    Which of the following, if true, would suggest an alternative to the author's hypothesis?

    A. The wheeled toys used by Mesoamerican children often featured an animal pulling a toy wagon.

    B. The Mesoamericans' environment lacked any native animals capable of pulling heavy loads, so wheeled vehicles, such as carts, were unusable.

    C. The Mesoamericans did not engage in long-distance trade.

    D. Mesoamerican road systems connected villages only within the same geographic location.

    E. The Mesoamericans adopted the wheel for transport when it was later introduced by Europeans.

**Questions 20–23**
**Passage 1**

Stem cells are science's miracle cure. Since these undifferentiated cells have not yet chosen what type of cell to become, they can be nudged into becoming whatever type of cell is needed
(5)  to replace damaged cells in a person who has a degenerative disease or a serious injury.

Scientists obtain stem cells primarily from discarded embryos. Cells can also be obtained from the blood or organs from healthy adults,
(10)  but these are not as adaptable as embryonic stem cells. Embryonic stem cells can mean a revolutionary change in quality of life for patients suffering from debilitating diseases such as Parkinson's or Alzheimer's. With stem
(15)  cell research, the benefits for living, breathing, sentient people outweigh any debate regarding the origins of the cells themselves.

**Passage 2**

Stem cell research has the potential to assuage or completely halt the advance of
(20)  devastating diseases. However, scientists assault the dignity of life when they use embryonic stem cells for their work. By taking cells from discarded embryos, we begin treading on a slippery slope. It is all too easy
(25)  to transition from using discarded embryos to creating embryos solely for the purpose of stem cell medicine.

Since stem cells can be obtained from healthy adults with no cost to life, this is the
(30)  path on which we should be progressing. These stem cells, safely obtained, can have a life-changing impact on patients.

20.  The authors of both passages would most likely agree with which of the following statements about stem cell research?

  A.  The medical benefits of stem cell research outweigh ethical concerns.
  B.  Embryonic stem cells have greater potential than do adult stem cells.
  C.  Stem cell research could lead to benefits for human health.
  D.  Stem cell research is the only promising route to combat debilitating human diseases.
  E.  The benefits of stem cell research must be weighed against ethical concerns.

21.  The attitude of the author of Passage 2 toward the use of embryonic stem cells can best be described as one of

  A.  excitement
  B.  disapproval
  C.  indifference
  D.  uncertainty
  E.  ignorance

22.  Which best describes the relationship between Passage 1 and Passage 2?

  A.  Passage 1 recounts a narrative that is analyzed in Passage 2.
  B.  Passage 1 provides evidence that is undermined in Passage 2.
  C.  Passage 1 introduces a theory that is expanded upon in Passage 2.
  D.  Passage 1 proves an idea that is celebrated in Passage 2.
  E.  Passage 1 presents a viewpoint that is countered in Passage 2.

23.  Which of the following could be substituted for the word "assuage" in line 19 with the least change in meaning?

  A.  decrease
  B.  cure
  C.  heighten
  D.  satisfy
  E.  aggravate

# ANSWERS AND EXPLANATIONS

## Practice

### O'Keeffe Passage

**1. B**

**Global.** Use as your prediction the main idea you identified in your notes. The main idea here is that the passage describes the inspiration, subject matter, style, and uniqueness of O'Keeffe's art. This matches choice (B), which is both accurate and general enough without being so general that the meaning of the passage is lost—exactly the kind of answer you want on Global questions. (A) is incorrect because the author never claims O'Keeffe was the best painter of her generation. (C) is potentially tricky. It's true that O'Keeffe liked to paint things that were familiar to her (lines 6–9)—primarily certain nature images—but this is just one point about O'Keeffe discussed in the passage rather than the reason the passage was written. (D) is never suggested by the passage. (E), like (C), focuses too much on a detail. (E) also distorts the author's view, as O'Keeffe is never criticized.

**2. C**

**Function.** For Function Questions, research the context of the cited portion of the text while keeping in mind the author's purpose for both the relevant paragraph and the passage as a whole: the function of a particular part of the passage will always be to serve the purpose of the entire passage. The overall passage describes O'Keeffe's background and particular artistic style; paragraph 3 discusses O'Keeffe's particular legacy as a painter by differentiating her from other contemporary American artists. In the sentence in question, the Structural Keyword "whereas" indicates the author's intent to contrast O'Keeffe's "independent" position with the European influences of "most early modern American artists" (lines 30–33). This matches choice (C). Choices (D) and (E) incorrectly identify the author's purpose; while the author clearly takes a positive view of O'Keeffe's work, the author never goes so far as to "argue" or "criticize" anything. Likewise, the author identifies O'Keeffe's work as "pioneering" (line 29) but never claims it "superior" to any other

art; choice (A) is incorrect. Choice (B) correctly states the author's view that other American artists were influenced by "European art" (lines 31–32), but it does not identify the author's specific purpose for mentioning other artists, which is to show how O'Keeffe was unique.

**3. A**

**Inference.** Research Stieglitz: the first sentence of paragraph 2 states that O'Keeffe "became famous" when Stieglitz "discovered and exhibited" her work in New York City. You can infer, then, that Stieglitz helped O'Keeffe by introducing her work to more people, choice (A). Whatever financial arrangement, if any, existed between Stieglitz and O'Keeffe, (B) is not mentioned in the passage. Paragraph 1 strongly implies that O'Keefe was inspired to paint natural forms long before she met Stieglitz, making (C) inaccurate. Choice (D) contradicts paragraph 3, which states that O'Keeffe was not strongly influenced by European artists. Finally, (E) is incorrect because the circumstances leading to O'Keeffe's visit to New Mexico are not described.

**4. A**

**Connecting Ideas.** First, ask yourself what O'Keeffe's relationship to nature was. O'Keeffe painted from nature—it was the subject of her work. Of the choices offered, which is most similar to the relationship between a painter and her subject? Choice (A) is correct because a model is the subject of a photographer's work. (B) is incorrect because a publisher is not the subject of a writer's work; a publisher simply prints and distributes a writer's work. Similarly, (C) is out because a part-time job is not a student's subject. Choice (D) is incorrect because an art dealer buys and sells a sculptor's work, but the art dealer is not the subject of the sculptor's work. Finally, a hammer is simply a carpenter's tool; it doesn't provide a carpenter with a subject or model, so (E) is out.

**5. D**

**Detail.** Research around the cited reference to find the context of this potentially unfamiliar term. Note the Structural Keyword "because" in the sentence containing the term, which indicates that a cause-effect relationship will be explained: her work is considered "semi-abstract" *because* it depicts "recognizable images" in a way that is not "very detailed or realistic." Choice (D) simply restates this idea. Choice (A) is incorrect because it refers to "realistic" qualities, contradicting the passage's definition of *semi-abstract*. Choices (B) and (E) can both refer to a component of the semi-abstract style—its portrayal of "recognizable" subjects—but neither accounts for the unrealistic depiction of such subjects that constitutes the other component of semi-abstract art. Choice (C) accurately describes the subject matter of O'Keeffe's work, but it is not a reason for her style being classified as semi-abstract.

## 6. C

**Vocab-in-Context.** Read the surrounding lines for context and then predict a word that could be substituted for the cited word. The relevant sentence begins with the Structural Keyword "rather," which indicates the contrast between presenting "images in a very detailed or realistic way" and the "reduced and simplified" style of O'Keeffe. Notice that the word in question must therefore contrast with "detailed" and be a synonym for "simplified"; predict a word like *minimal*. Choice (C) matches this prediction. Choices (A) and (D) are both words that mean "small in size," which is not suggested by the context. Choice (B) incorrectly refers to either low monetary value or a negative view of O'Keeffe's art, neither of which is indicated by the author. Choice (E) does not fit in context, as it does not make sense that "colors and shapes" could be "humbled."

## 7. A

**Writer's View.** Research the context of the cited phrase. Your paragraph notes should indicate that in the fourth paragraph, the author identifies O'Keeffe's "colors and shapes" as "simplified" and taking "on a life of their own" (lines 47–48). The previous paragraph provides more clues: the author refers to O'Keeffe's art as "semi-abstract" depictions of regular things in unrealistic ways (lines 40–44). The "color" and "space" are again referred to as "simplified and idealized" (line 38). Use these references as your prediction for how the author describes the

"colors and shapes." This matches choice (A), which reflects the author's description of the features as taking "on a life of their own" (lines 47–48). Choices (B), (C), and (D) are all the opposite of the author's description of O'Keeffe's paintings. Choice (E) distorts the author's view, as O'Keeffe's work (and not her colors and shapes in particular) is instead described as "*semi*-abstract."

### Chaos Passage

## 8. E

**Global.** There is only one answer choice that captures the purpose of the two paragraphs. This passage is simply a description of a cultural phenomenon—the desire to seek out order and avoid chaos—that was prevalent in ancient Greece. Choice (E) fits right in line with the Main Idea.

(A) misses the point of the passage because the author does not mention any conflicting viewpoints. Instead, two aspects of a single cultural phenomenon are described. (B) and (C) are out because the passage is not challenging or questioning anything. It simply attempts to describe a perspective on Ancient Greek culture. Finally, (D) is out because it misses the point. This passage is less concerned with delineating historical facts than with the overall zeitgeist or collective spirit of a society.

## 9. E

**Function.** Consider how the first five lines in particular serve the author's purpose for the overall passage: to describe the ancient Greek culture's collective drive to avoid chaos and seek order. The lines in question include the Structural Keywords "as a result," indicating the cited lines provide a reason for what follows (the Greeks viewing "*chaos*" with "anxiety"). The first five lines also include the Structural Keywords "whether . . . or," indicating two possible reasons. So the first lines of the passage present two possible explanations for the Greek view of chaos, which matches choice (E). The first lines do not provide a "detailed context," so choice (A) is incorrect. Choice (B) inappropriately identifies the author's purpose as argumentative, and also misrepresents the author's statement that there were *two* possibilities (not only the fragmentation of Mycenae) that led to the Greek view of chaos. Choice (C) is incorrect, as the lines in question provide *reasons* for the Greek view, not a description of the mentality itself. Choice (D) is incorrect because the lines include no mention of "religious underpinnings."

## 10. A

**Logical Reasoning.** Before looking at the answer choices, paraphrase the author's argument: the ancient Greeks collectively viewed perceived chaos with anxiety and valued order. An answer choice that provides evidence that would strengthen this argument will be correct; eliminate answers that either weaken or are irrelevant to the argument. Choice (A) is correct because it provides an example of the Greek tendency, described in lines 13–19, to view the discovery of order positively. Although the passage does mention the breakup of Mycenae, as in choice (B), the passage does not argue that the Greek viewpoint described was "unique." Nor does this fact provide evidence to support the passage's main claim. Choices (C) and (D) would weaken, rather than strengthen, the author's argument that the Greeks viewed uncertainty with "constant anxiety" (lines 9–10). Choice (E) would also weaken the author's argument that "the discovery of a permanent pattern" would be met with "satisfaction, even joy" (lines 13–14, 17–18).

## *Infographic*

## 11. A

**Infographic.** Research only the relevant portions of the table, making a prediction before looking at the answer choices. To determine the number of hours watched, you will need to add together the hours listed for January, February, and March across the row for each genre. A quick assessment of the table reveals that the most hours were watched for news, but since this is not an answer choice, evaluate the other genres. Exact numbers are not necessary; since comedy has the highest number of hours for each month, comedy was the most watched. Choice (A) is therefore correct.

## 12. D

**Infographic.** Before looking at the answer choices, research the relevant portions of the table. Katie's total hours watching television were the lowest for the entire year in July and highest in September. These trends also held true for individual genres (for the most part), with the notable exception of news programs, which held steady at 12 hours a month for the entire year. With this information in mind, evaluate the answer choices. Choice (A) is incorrect because Katie still watched television in July, and the paragraph before the table indicates she only watches programs on her household television. Choice (B) is incorrect because Katie watched the same number of news programming hours as previous months. Choice (C) is incorrect because, while Katie did increase her television viewing in September, her total hours in July were lower. Choice (D) could account for the lower than average total hours in July and the higher than average total hours in September, so (D) is correct. Choice (E) is incorrect because it does not describe Katie's viewing in September.

## 13. A

**Infographic.** Although you cannot make a specific prediction, keep in mind the overall trends of the table when evaluating the answer choices. Choice (A) is correct; Katie watched 12 hours of news programming every month of last year. Select choice (A) and move on to the next question. Choice (B) is incorrect because Katie watched more hours of comedy and of drama than she did of documentary. Choice (C) is incorrect because Katie watched the most total hours in September. (D) is incorrect because Katie's hours spent watching reality programs varied from month to month. Choice (E) is incorrect because even if Katie had watched more hours of comedy than anything else, you could not reach the conclusion that Katie's favorite genre necessarily corresponds with whichever one she watched the most.

*Panda Passage*

**14. D**

**Detail.** Check your paragraph notes for the location of this detail. The classification of the giant panda is discussed in the first paragraph. The answer to this question can be found in the second sentence of the first paragraph. According to this sentence, "biologists have not been sure how to classify this enigmatic animal." This is right in line with (D).

(A) contradicts the passage because the author never states which classification is correct. (B) is also incorrect because classification should be based on homologous, not analogous traits. (C) is never discussed in the passage. (E) is a comical distortion of the passage. Although the passage does state that the general public may view the panda as a giant teddy bear, that does not correspond to the biological classification of the animal, which is the focus of this question.

**15. D**

**Connecting Ideas.** Homologous and analogous traits are discussed in depth in the second paragraph. The second sentence of the second paragraph defines homologous traits as those linked to a common ancestor. Consequently, (D) is the correct answer here because two species with a homologous trait by definition possess a common ancestor.

(A), (B), (C), and (E) are all possible based on the description given in the second paragraph. Two species can share numerous homologous traits, choice (A). That would simply mean that they inherited multiple traits from a common ancestor. Similarly, two species can share numerous analogous traits, choice (B). This would simply mean that they did not share a common ancestor but developed under similar environmental pressures. Choice (C) is consistent with the definition of analogous traits, so it can be eliminated. Finally, (E) can be eliminated because nowhere in the passage is it stated that two species must have analogous or homologous traits. (E) is therefore possible and can be eliminated.

**16. A**

**Function.** Check your paragraph notes and paraphrase the organization before looking at the answer choices. The second paragraph explains the difference between homologous and analogous traits, using examples of various animals to illustrate the definitions, and concludes that panda classification is difficult because it is uncertain what types of traits this animal exhibits. This matches choice (A). Choices (B), (C), and (D) are incorrect because the paragraph never presents any theories, hypotheses, or arguments; rather, the passage merely explains why it is difficult to classify the panda due to the ambiguity of its traits. (E) is incorrect because although the paragraph does list examples of animals, the paragraph organization and purpose center around explaining the two categories of traits.

**17. C**

**Writer's View.** Review the purpose and Main Idea of the passage before looking at the answer choices. Does the author express an opinion regarding the panda debate? The author acknowledges the debate in paragraph 1 and concludes the passage by stating that the classification is questionable due to the uncertainty regarding the panda's traits. Therefore, predict that the author thinks the debate is legitimate, but does not take a particular side. This matches choice (C); the author objectively explains the debate. Choices (A) and (D) are incorrect because they present the author as either rejecting or rejoicing over the debate; neither of these views is presented in the passage. Choice (B) is also incorrect; the author does not question the legitimacy of the debate but rather acknowledges it by concluding that the panda classification is questionable. The author never expresses concerns about the debate, so (E) is also incorrect.

**18. A, B**

**Inference.** It is not possible to make a specific prediction for some Inference questions, but keep in mind the overall Main Idea of the passage when evaluating the answer choices. The first paragraph states that pandas have been classified with both bears and raccoons; the second paragraph states that classification can be based on shared traits, so the panda must share at least some traits with both bears and raccoons. (A) is therefore correct. Evaluate the remaining answer choices, as the question asks you to select all that apply. Choice (B) is also correct; the passage concludes that "the questions surrounding the classification of the giant panda are linked to whether certain traits are homologous or simply analogous" (lines 38–41). Choice (C), however, is incorrect; although the passage explains in lines 31–35 that cats and lions share homologous traits (and therefore, by definition, a common ancestor), nothing is stated about the environments in which they developed. They may have developed in similar or differing situations, and the passage makes no claim about either possibility.

## 19. B

**Logical Reasoning.** Be sure to identify the components of the author's argument and make a prediction of what could constitute an alternate hypothesis before looking at the answer choices. The author concludes that the Mesoamericans did not have a need to carry heavy loads based on the evidence that wheels were used for toys but not for transport vehicles. The author makes the assumption that the only reason the Mesoamericans would not have applied wheel technology to transport vehicles is that there was no need to carry heavy loads. Predict that an alternate hypothesis would be a different reason for not applying wheel technology to transport. This matches choice (B), as it provides another reason for not applying the wheel technology: lack of animals capable of pulling a heavy wheeled vehicle. Choice (A) is incorrect because it provides information about the children's toys but does not give an alternate hypothesis for not applying wheel technology to transport. Choice (C) is incorrect because there could be other possible reasons for using the wheel for transport (such as farming or short-distance trade) besides just long-distance trade. Choice (D) is irrelevant as a reason for not applying the wheel for transport. Choice (E) only serves as a potential weakener to the author's original hypothesis, rather than providing a potential alternate hypothesis, in its suggestion that the Mesoamericans actually did have a need for carrying heavy loads using the wheel.

## Stem Cells: Paired Passage Set

## 20. C

**Connecting Ideas/Logical Reasoning.** Be sure to predict before reading the answer choices. The correct answer must be quite general, since the two authors disagree. Author 1 argues that the use of embryonic stem cells will likely help combat disease, while author 2 claims adult cells should be used. On what point do the authors agree? Stem cell research (regardless of the stem cell origin) can significantly aid the fight against disease; this matches choice (C). Be careful of answer choices that only represent one of the two authors. Choices (A) and (B) represent author 1's view, while (E) reflects author 2. While both authors consider stem cell research promising, neither go so far as to claim it is the "only" possible route to combating disease as in choice (D).

## 21. B

**Connecting Ideas/Writer's View.** Carefully consider only the attitude of the author of Passage 2. The author strongly disapproves of using embryonic stem cells, stating that when scientists do so, they "assault the dignity of life" (line 21) and "begin treading on a slippery slope" (line 23–24). This prediction matches choice (B). Choice (A) incorrectly provides the opposite of the author's view. Choice (C) incorrectly indicates the author lacks an opinion, while (D) and (E) convey, respectively, that the author's position is ambivalent or nonexistent; the author is firmly against the use of embryonic stem cells.

## 22. E

**Connecting Ideas/Global.** Paraphrase the Main Idea of each passage before evaluating the answer choices. Passage 1 claims stem cells are a "miracle cure" (line 1) and argues for the superiority of using embryonic stem cells, despite any possible debate about the cells' origin. Passage 2 also praises the use of stem cell research, but argues the cells should be obtained from adults due to ethical concerns. This prediction matches choice (E). Choice (A) misrepresents Passage 1, which is not a "narrative." Passage 1 provides some evidence concerning the use of embryonic stem cells as superior to those obtained from adults, and while Passage 2 disagrees with Passage 1's conclusion, the evidence concerning the superiority of embryonic stem cells is never countered in Passage 2; (B) is incorrect. For choice (C), Passage 1 could be said to introduce the theory that stem cells are a "miracle cure," but Passage 2 does not so much "expand" the theory as affirm it but disagree about how to act on it. Choice (D) is incorrect because while Passage 1 makes claims and provides some evidence, it does not actually "prove" anything; moreover, Passage 2 certainly does not "celebrate" the claim of Passage 1.

### 23. A

**Connecting Ideas/Vocabulary-in-Context.** Remember to predict a word to substitute for the word in context. The first sentence of Passage 2 claims "stem cell research has the potential to *assuage* or completely halt the advance of devastating diseases." "Assuage" must mean something related to stopping the ad-

vance of diseases, but less than "*completely* halting" them. Predict a word like *reduce*. This matches choice (A). Choice (B) is incorrect because it is too extreme, being too close in meaning to "completely halt." Choices (C) and (E) have the opposite of the intended meaning and make no sense in context. Choice (D) also does not work in context; "assuage" can mean "satisfy" in some contexts (as in "assuaging hunger"), but it does not make sense that the "advance of . . . diseases" can be "satisfied."

# CHAPTER TWO

# Praxis Core Mathematics

## INTRODUCING PRAXIS CORE MATHEMATICS

Few people are neutral on the subject of mathematics. Math tests generate strong reactions, both from students in school and from Praxis test takers. Whether you are looking forward to the Praxis Core Mathematics Test or dreading it, there is good news: becoming familiar with the test's structure and format, along with doing some solid review of math fundamentals, will put you in position to succeed.

The subject matter of the Praxis Core Mathematics test should be familiar. The test covers arithmetic, simple data and statistics (such as charts and averages), and middle school–level algebra and geometry. For those who feel hazy or out of practice with this material, this chapter contains a substantial math review section. Start by taking the Core Math Pre-Test to identify the topic areas in which you need a refresher.

Even those who feel rock solid with their math skill set can benefit from practice on Praxis Core Mathematics questions. That's because the standardized test format rewards those who can answer questions quickly *and* accurately. A large majority of the questions on the Praxis Core Mathematics test are multiple-choice questions. This format has two important implications.

First, you need not show your work. In some cases, it may be faster to work backward, by testing the answer choices, than to work forward by doing lengthy calculations. This chapter will show you how to spot such cases to improve your efficiency.

Second, the presence of wrong answer choices can lead to mistakes, especially for a math whiz. Imagine a simple algebra problem that asks you to solve for the value of $2x$. You might dive right in, set up the equation, and determine that $x = 4$. You glance at the answer choices and see that the first one is 4. "Piece of cake," you think. But, be careful. The question asked you to solve for $2x$, so the choice you must select is 8. Success on Praxis Core Mathematics requires learning to avoid careless errors like that one, even when you have no trouble completing the math.

In this chapter, we'll show you an approach to test taking that takes advantage of the nature of the Praxis test's format to increase your score.

## LEARNING OBJECTIVES

By the end of this chapter, you will be able to:

- Describe the structure and format of the Praxis Core Academic Skills for Educators: Mathematics test
- Outline and employ the Kaplan Method for Praxis Mathematics
- Apply Praxis Mathematics strategies
- Refresh basic math concepts and rules
- Use the Praxis Core Mathematics practice test to assess your performance

# KNOW WHAT TO EXPECT

## Test Format

The Praxis Core Mathematics test covers a wide range of math topics. More on that shortly. First, here are the basics of the test format.

| Praxis Core Mathematics |
| --- |
| Format: Computer-delivered |
| Number of Questions: 56<br>Time: 85 minutes |
| Question Types: multiple-choice (called "selected response" by the test maker)—one correct answer; multiple-choice—one or more correct answers; numeric entry (the test taker enters the correct answer in a blank box on the screen) |
| On-screen four-function calculator available |
| Test may include pre-test questions that do not count toward your score |
| No penalty for incorrect answers |
| Scratch paper is available during the exam (it will be destroyed before you leave the testing center) |

There are a few ways in which you can take advantage of the test format to improve your score.

- Manage your time effectively. With 56 questions in 85 minutes, you have just over $1\frac{1}{2}$ minutes per question. Make sure to give yourself time to see every question.
- Guess strategically. There is no penalty for selecting a wrong answer. If a question has you thoroughly confused, or if you feel that it will take you too long to answer, eliminate any clearly incorrect answer choices, select your best guess, and move on. The next question may be one you can answer quickly and confidently.
- You can answer questions in any order. You should plan to move through the test more or less in order, but you may skip or guess on a question that is confusing or threatens to take too much time. Be sure to note any questions you skip or guess on so that you can return to them if you have time left at the end of the section.

## Test Content

According to ETS, the Praxis Core Mathematics exam "measures academic skills in mathematics needed to prepare successfully for a career in education." While the test covers a range of math subjects, most of the content will be familiar. The test draws primarily from math content that corresponds to material you learned in eighth- or ninth-grade math classes. For some test takers, that's great news. For those of you who haven't looked at these concepts since middle school, the *Mathematics Content Review* section of this chapter will allow you to reacquaint yourself with the basics and practice with this content as it is tested on the Praxis Core Mathematics exam.

The following table provides a quick breakdown of the math content that appears on the Praxis Core Mathematics test. It shows the approximate number of questions per content area and the percentage of the test they represent.

| Praxis Core Mathematics Content | |
| --- | --- |
| Number and Quantity | 17 questions: 30% |
| Algebra and Functions | 17 questions: 30% |
| Geometry | 11 questions: 20% |
| Statistics and Probability | 11 questions: 20% |

While the content is familiar, the question types on the Praxis Core Mathematics exam are different from the questions you remember from math tests you took in school. Rather than asking you to show your work and demonstrate mastery of concepts, Praxis Core Mathematics is all about results. You don't have to show your work, and you're not graded on how you approach the problems—all that matters is that you get to the correct answer, and get there quickly.

In short, Praxis Core Mathematics is a standardized exam, largely composed of multiple-choice questions. That means that there will be opportunities throughout the test to use the answer choices to help you solve problems, especially when you're in a pinch. Since there is no penalty for incorrect answers, you have a one-in-five chance of selecting the right answer, even without reading the question. After reading the question and plugging in an answer or two, you're well on your way to finding the correct answer, even on questions that cause you trouble. We'll discuss how to make the most of these "backdoor" strategies later in the chapter.

As you work through this chapter, pay attention to the material with which you are already comfortable and those topics that give you any difficulty. For questions you have a natural knack for, it makes sense to work out your answers in a more straightforward fashion. For questions in areas that give you trouble, think about using the answer choices and working backward. Praxis Core Mathematics is all about results, and the only results that matter are correct answer choices.

## Question Types

On Praxis Core Mathematics, you'll see three question types: Multiple-Choice Single-Select, Multiple-Choice Select-One-or-More Answer Choices, and Numeric Entry. Let's take a look at an example of each.

**Multiple-Choice Single-Select.** By far the most common is the familiar multiple-choice question with five answer choices and one correct answer. Of the 56 questions on the test, approximately 49 will be of this type.

**Answer the following question by selecting the correct response.**

The town of Spartaville is 500 km away from the town of Pleasantville. A map is drawn of the county to a scale of 1 cm = 2.5 km. How many centimeters apart are the two towns on the map?

A.  50

B.  200

C.  250

D.  1,000

E.  2,500

To solve this problem, you can use a proportion to determine the distance on the map. The relationship between map and actual kilometers is given in the scale 1 cm = 2.5 km. The ratio is always the same. So $\dfrac{1\,cm}{2.5\,km} = \dfrac{x\,cm}{500\,km}$ . Cross multiply and solve for the number of centimeters, 200.

Choice **(B)** is correct. Notice that you can also solve this problem by testing the answer choices. Choice (A) would give you 50 × 2.5 = 125. That's too small. Choice (B) gives 200 × 2.5 = 500. Correct. It's now clear that the remaining choices would all be too large. You'll see more about how to use "backsolving" strategies like this in the next section.

**Multiple-Choice Select-One-or-More Answer Choices.** Occasionally, the test maker will give you a multiple-choice question in which more than one answer choice may be correct. Sometimes, a question of this type will ask you to choose the "correct response(s)," meaning that one or more answer choices may work. You get credit for a question of this type only if you select all of the correct answer choices and none of the incorrect ones. At other times, the instructions for a question of this type may specify the number of correct answer choices. If, for example, a question gives you four answer choices and tells you to click on "two correct responses," you will get credit for that question only if you select the two correct choices and neither of the incorrect ones. While the instructions may sound a little complicated, you will get used to these questions with a little practice. Moreover, you are unlikely to see more than three or four questions of this type on the test.

**Answer the following question by selecting the correct response(s).**

Which of the following values are equal to 760?

Indicate <u>all</u> such values.

A.  $0.76 \times 10^{3}$

B.  $7.6 \times 10^{2}$

C.  $7.6 \times 10^{3}$

D.  $7,600 \times 10^{-1}$

E.  $7,600 \times 10^{-2}$

This question tests your knowledge of exponents. When multiplying by powers of 10, simply move the decimal point the number of places indicated in the exponent of 10 to the left if the exponent is negative and to the right if the exponent is positive. Convert the values this way:

(A) $0.76 \times 10^3 = 760$; (B) $7.6 \times 10^2 = 760$; (C) $7.6 \times 10^3 = 7{,}600$; (D) $7{,}600 \times 10^{-1} = 760$; (E) $7{,}600 \times 10^{-2} = 76$

Because you are asked to select all of the applicable choices, answers **(A)**, **(B)**, and **(D)** must be selected, and (C) and (E) not selected, to get credit for this question.

**Numeric Entry.** The third question type you'll see on the Praxis Core Mathematics test is the one that is most like the typical questions on math tests in school. These problems present you with a question and then a box in which to type your answer. If the answer is meant to be a fraction, you'll see two boxes, one for the numerator and one for the denominator. Although there are no answer choices to select, you still don't have to show your work. You may do your work on scratch paper and type in your answer. If you use the on-screen calculator, it has a button marked "Transfer Display" that will automatically enter whatever is on the calculator screen into the answer box. (If you use that feature, make sure you are at your final answer before clicking "Transfer Display.")

**Enter the correct answer in the box.**

Donald's daily commute is 20 miles. Marta's daily commute is 24 miles. What percent longer is Marta's daily commute than Donald's daily commute?

Marta's commute is ⬚ % longer than Donald's commute.

To solve this problem, you need to find the difference between Marta's and Donald's commutes and then determine what percent of Donald's commute that difference represents. The formula you'll use here is:

$$percent\ greater = \frac{higher\ value - lower\ value}{lower\ value} \times 100\%$$

Apply the numbers from the story problem to this formula.

$$\frac{24 - 20}{20} \times 100\% = \frac{4}{20} \times 100\% = \frac{1}{5} \times 100\% = 20\%$$

So, to get this problem correct, enter **20** into the blank box.

## Calculator

For the Praxis Core Mathematics test, you will have access to an on-screen four-function calculator. This calculator has buttons for the primary arithmetic operations, parentheses, square root, and positive/negative numbers. As previously mentioned, it also has a button labeled "Transfer Display" that will enter the number on the calculator screen into the blank box for numeric entry questions.

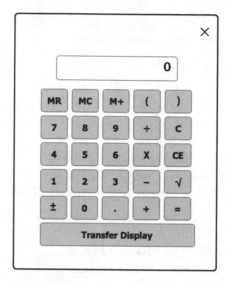

You will have the opportunity to work with a calculator that has the same functionality when you are doing the practice tests or exercises in this book's online Study Plan.

While the calculator may be helpful and save you time on some questions, don't use the calculator unnecessarily. Here are a few tips to make the most of the calculator:

- Most of the questions on Praxis Core Mathematics will not require the calculator.
- The calculator is most helpful on questions that require lengthy calculations or those that contain large numbers.
- The calculator will display fractions as numbers with decimal points. You might have to translate the result to a fraction to answer some multiple-choice and numeric entry questions.
- Opening the calculator and typing in numbers could actually cost you time if the calculations are simple enough to do in your head or on scratch paper, so be judicious with your calculator use.

One caution: Some Praxis tests, such as Mathematics: Content Knowledge (5161) and Algebra I (5162), provide scientific and graphing calculators that have additional functionality. For any test in the Praxis series that contains mathematics, check **www.ets.org/praxis/test_day/policies/calculators** for information about the type of calculator provided or permitted, for tutorials on their use, and for tips on using the appropriate calculator efficiently and effectively.

# HOW TO APPROACH PRAXIS CORE MATHEMATICS

The two most important things to remember when it comes to Praxis Mathematics are that Praxis Mathematics is not high-school mathematics and that you should never leave a question unanswered.

If you have not taken the Praxis Core Mathematics Pre-Test, do so now. Completing the pre-test and reviewing your results will give you a sense of the content areas with which you are most comfortable and those that give you trouble. You'll be able to refresh your familiarity with those content areas in the *Mathematics Content Review* section of this chapter.

## Managing Your Time

Once you know your strengths and weaknesses, you can make more strategic use of your time on the test. If a question looks like one you can readily handle using a straightforward "textbook approach," work through it in a straightforward manner. But be on the lookout also for alternative, time-saving approaches, such as using the answer choices to work backward or estimating to avoid lengthy calculations.

Plan to work through the section more or less in order. If you are strong with the math content on this test and have completed sufficient practice, you may be able to complete all of the questions with time remaining. If so, use the extra time to double-check any questions on which you were not entirely confident. You can mark questions within the test interface or keep a list on your scratch paper of questions you'll revisit, time permitting.

While rolling through the entire test quickly and confidently is the ideal goal, chances are that most test takers will feel some degree of time pressure and will run into a handful of questions that cause them some doubt or confusion. If you fall into this latter group, what follows can have a big impact on your score.

## Skip and guess strategically

To take full advantage of the test format, keep three things in mind:

- With 56 questions in 85 minutes, you have approximately a minute and a half per question.
- Your goal is to answer as many questions correctly as possible.
- There is no wrong answer penalty.

All of this means that mismanaging just two or three questions can impact your score. If you confront a very difficult or confusing question and respond by taking two (or three, or four, or more) minutes to solve it, you have eaten up the time that you could have used to get two or three or more questions correct. That trade-off is bad for your score (even if finally getting that tough question is psychologically satisfying).

Great test takers follow a few simple guidelines to skip questions and guess strategically to improve their scores.

- When you encounter a question you know you are unlikely to answer correctly (or is likely to take you more than a minute and a half to answer), skip it immediately.

- When you skip a question, mark it in the test interface (and/or on your scratch paper) so that you can return to it after answering all other questions.

- Before skipping to the next question, select an answer. You don't want to inadvertently run out of time and leave a question blank. Even a random guess gives you a chance of getting the question right.

- If there are some answer choices you can eliminate through estimation or critical thinking (e.g., "I know that the right answer will be a positive number, but (D) and (E) are negative"), do so. Then guess from among the choices that remain.

Following those tips will help you maintain control of the test. If you allow a question to cost you time and increase your frustration, you sacrifice that control. A good way to think about it is this: "I won't guess because I fail and give up; I will guess when it is the smart and strategic thing for me to do to improve my score." Sometimes, when you skip a question and come back to it at the end, you discover that it was simpler than you had thought at first. That's great. Even if you still find it hard or confusing, you'll be happy that you managed the test in a way that allowed you to get to all of the easiest questions with time to answer them, and you'll know you've done your level best throughout.

## THE KAPLAN THREE-STEP METHOD FOR PRAXIS MATHEMATICS
**STEP 1.  Read through the question**
**STEP 2.  Do it now or guess**
**STEP 3.  Look for the fastest approach**

## Step 1. Read Through the Question

This step may sound comically obvious. "Of course, I'm going to read through the question. How else can I solve the problem?" In reality, this step is not as self-evident as it seems. Many test takers will start doing calculations after reading the first part of the question's first sentence. Expert test takers, however, read the entire question carefully before they start solving the problem. Doing this helps them spot the most efficient approach to the question, and helps them avoid careless mistakes. Consider the following problem:

At Blinky Burgers restaurant, two hamburgers and five orders of french fries cost the same as four hamburgers and two orders of french fries. If the restaurant charges $1.50 for a single order of french fries, how much does it charge for two hamburgers?

A.  $2.25

B.  $3.00

C.  $4.50

D.  $5.00

E.  $6.00

Pay close attention to what the question is asking. This question contains a pitfall for test takers who don't read carefully. Can you spot it?

The question asks for the cost of two hamburgers, not one. Many students will get this question wrong by finding the price for one hamburger and then forgetting to double it. It's a careless mistake to make, but it's easy to be careless when you're working quickly. Always make sure you know what's being asked.

## Step 2. Do it Now or Guess

Another reason to read carefully before answering is that you probably shouldn't solve every problem on your first pass. As discussed previously, taking control of your Praxis test experience involves deciding which problems to answer and which ones to guess on and come back to later.

Before you try to solve the problem, decide whether you want to do it now. In our sample problem about Blinky Burgers, this will likely depend on how comfortable you are setting up algebraic equations or, possibly, whether you've spotted an alternative approach to the problem. If you have no idea how to solve the problem, or if you think the problem will take a long time to solve, take your best guess, mark the question, and make note of it on your scratch paper. After you've answered the remaining questions, you can return to the questions you've marked and spend more time on them.

Don't worry about the "ones that got away." It feels good to try to answer every question on a test, but if you end up not getting back to a question or two, don't feel bad. Take quick, strategic guesses, bank your time, and let go. By spending more of your time on the questions you can answer, you're more likely to get a great score.

## Step 3. Look For the Fastest Approach

Once you've understood what a question is asking and have decided to tackle it, look for any alternative approaches that may be more efficient. Sometimes the "obvious" or "classroom" way of solving a problem is the long way. Take another look at the Blinky Burgers problem.

> At Blinky Burgers restaurant, two hamburgers and five orders of french fries cost the same as four hamburgers and two orders of french fries. If the restaurant charges $1.50 for a single order of french fries, how much does it charge for two hamburgers?
>
> A. $2.25
> B. $3.00
> C. $4.50
> D. $5.00
> E. $6.00

Here many students would turn this word problem into two algebraic equations: $2h + 5f = 4h + 2f$ and $f = 1.50$. From there, they will substitute 1.50 for $f$ in the first equation and solve for $h$. Finally, they must remember to multiply that answer by 2 to identify the correct answer choice. There is nothing wrong with that algebraic approach, and it will definitely produce the correct answer.

With a little critical thinking, however, you may spot an even faster approach here. Since the story problem tells you that two hamburgers and five orders of fries cost the same as four hamburgers and two orders of fries. Take away all of the like items from the two orders, and you're left with a helpful equation: three orders of fries cost the same as two hamburgers. Because one order of fries costs $1.50, three orders cost $4.50, so $4.50 must also be the cost of two hamburgers. You can select correct answer **(C)** with confidence, and you didn't even have to set up any algebraic equations.

## Textbook Approaches Versus Backdoor Strategies

We've mentioned a few times that the Praxis Core Mathematics test is not like the math tests you took in high school. That's because on most high school tests, you were expected to show your work to demonstrate the ability to work step-by-step from the information given to the correct answer.

Praxis Core Mathematics doesn't work like that. While you're welcome to work through a problem in a straightforward way, you are by no means required to do so. Frequently, in fact, it pays to use an alternative approach. Let's apply the Kaplan Method for Praxis Core Mathematics to a few practice problems to see alternative strategies in action.

The questions that make up the Praxis Mathematics test contain many word problems with five answer choices containing numbers: integers, percents, or fractions. Praxis Core Mathematics also tests basic algebra, so occasionally the answer choices will contain variables. In either case, it's important to note that the answer is right in front of you—you just have to find it.

Two methods in particular are extremely useful when you don't see how to use—or would rather not use—the textbook approach to solving the question. We call these strategies Backsolving and Picking Numbers. These strategies can help to make confusing problems more concrete. But even when you know how to solve using the "traditional approach," solving strategically may be faster.

### Backsolving

Backsolving is a strategy that you can use on questions in which all of the answer choices contain nothing except numbers (no variables and no operations). In questions like these, it is sometimes easier to work backward from the answer choices than to work forward from the question.

Here's how Backsolving works. Once you note that all of the answer choices are exclusively numbers, note whether they are arranged from smallest to largest (more common) or from largest to smallest (less common). In either case, start with choice (C). If that number works when you plug it into the problem, then that's the correct answer, and you're done. If choice (C) does not work, then you can usually see whether it was too large or too small. If choice (C) is too large, try the next smallest choice. In other words, if the choices are arranged from smallest to largest, you would next test choice (B). If it is correct, you're done. If choice (B) is still too large, you know that choice (A) must be correct, and again, you're done. If you use Backsolving strategically, you usually don't have to try out more than two answer choices before zeroing in on the correct answer. To make this idea concrete, apply the strategy to the following problem.

In a certain school, the ratio of boys to girls is 3:7. If there are 84 more girls than boys in the school, how many boys are there in the school?

A. 48

B. 54

C. 63

D. 84

E. 147

The correct answer should yield a ratio of boys to girls of 3:7. Note that the answer choices are arranged from smallest to largest and begin by testing out choice (C).

If there are 63 boys, there are 63 + 84 = 147 girls, so the ratio of boys to girls is $\frac{63}{147} = \frac{9}{21} = \frac{3}{7}$, which is correct. You're done.

With choice **(C)** as the correct answer, this question took almost no time at all. Even if (C) weren't correct, this question illustrates how Backsolving can make your work more concrete by giving you a number to plug in.

Of course, the answer isn't always the first choice you pick. But usually, when you start with (C) and that answer doesn't work, you'll know which direction to go. Choice (C) will be too big or too small, leaving you with only two answers that could possibly be correct.

Try another one.

A tailor has 20 yards of shirt fabric. How many shirts can she make if each shirt requires $2\frac{3}{4}$ yards of fabric?

A. 6

B. 7

C. 8

D. 10

E. 14

You can, of course, find the correct answer by dividing 20 by $2\frac{3}{4}$. If that calculation gives you pause, Backsolving can get you to the correct answer efficiently and effectively. Note that the answer choices are arranged from smallest to largest. Now, start by testing choice (C). If the tailor could make 8 shirts, that would require at least $2\frac{3}{4} = \frac{11}{4} \times 8 = 22$ yards of fabric. That's too much fabric, so the correct answer must be less than 8. Eliminate (C), (D), and (E). You could multiply $2\frac{3}{4}$ by 7 at this point, or you could reason out the problem. If 8 shirts require 22 yards of fabric, and each shirt takes $2\frac{3}{4}$ yards, you know that 7 shirts would take less than 20 yards of fabric because $22 - 2\frac{3}{4}$ would be less than 20. **(B)** is correct.

Let's quickly recap the steps involved in Backsolving:

Step 1: Start with choice (C) and plug it in. If the numbers work out, choose (C) and move on.

Step 2: If (C) doesn't work, eliminate it along with other choices you know are too big or too small.

Step 3: Keep going until you find the choice that works.

**Picking Numbers**

Some problems on the Praxis Core Mathematics test may initially strike you as vague or abstract, particularly when they contain variables or test the properties of numbers. Picking a number to stand in for a variable can make questions of this type far more concrete. Just make sure that the number you pick meets the criteria described in the question. Consider the following example, which tests remainders.

> When $n$ is divided by 14, the remainder is 10. What is the remainder when $n$ is divided by 7?
>
> A.  1
> B.  2
> C.  3
> D.  4
> E.  5

To pick a number that can stand in for $n$ in this problem, add the remainder given in the problem to the divisor given in the problem and substitute that number for $n$. Because $14 + 10 = 24$, substitute 24 for $n$. Now, divide 24 by 7: $24 \div 7 = 3r3$ (in other words, "3 with a remainder of 3"). Thus, the answer is **(C)**.

Note, too, that Backsolving would not have provided any help in the preceding problem. That's because the problem was about the properties of an unknown number. As you practice, take note of the characteristics of problems for which various strategies are or are not useful so that you can spot those cases when you're taking the official exam.

Another case in which Picking Numbers can be helpful is on questions in which the answer choices contain variables. This is great news because, for some test takers, these problems are among the most confusing on the Praxis Core Mathematics test. Give the following example a try:

> Four years from now, Ron will be twice as old as his sister will be then. If Ron is now $R$ years old, how many years old is his sister now?
>
> A.  $\dfrac{R-4}{2}$
> B.  $R-4$
> C.  $\dfrac{R+4}{2}$
> D.  $R-2$
> E.  $R+2$

If you are comfortable translating word problems into algebra, you may be confident tackling this problem with the "classroom approach." Keep in mind, however, that Picking Numbers can be easier and quicker on questions like this one. Here's how you would pick numbers in this case. Begin by picking a number for $R$, Ron's age now. Choose a simple number that is easy to add to, subtract from, and divide. We'll use $R = 10$. Now, substitute 10 for $R$ in the question and the answer choices, and you're left with the following, much simpler problem:

Four years from now, Ron will be twice as old as his sister will be then. If Ron is now 10 years old, how many years old is his sister now?

A. $\dfrac{10 - 4}{2}$, or 3

B. $10 - 4$, or 6

C. $\dfrac{10 + 4}{2}$, or 7

D. $10 - 2$, or 8

E. $10 + 2$, or 12

Now let's see. Ron is now 10 years old, so in four years, he'll be 14, which means his sister will be 7 years old *then*. Because she'll be 7 in four years, that means she must be 3 years old *now*. The correct answer is **(A)**.

Percent questions that do not specify a value are another instance in which Picking Numbers is an effective strategy. In these questions, pick 100 as your value because it is easy to calculate percents of 100.

Give this question a try:

The value of a certain stock rose by 30 percent from March to April and then decreased by 20 percent from April to May. The stock's value in May was what percent of its value in March?

A. 90%

B. 100%

C. 104%

D. 110%

E. 124%

Notice that while the question involves the value of a certain stock, that value is never given. Picking a number to stand in for the initial value of the stock will make the question more concrete and manageable. Since you are asked to determine a percent of the initial value, use 100 to stand in for the initial value of the stock. If the stock price was initially $100 per share, then after it rose by 30 percent from March to April, its value in April was $130. When that value decreased by 20 percent in May, that decrease was 0.20 × $130 = $26. Subtract $26 from $130 to find the value of the stock in May: $130 − $26 = $104. Because the March value was $100, the May value of $104 is 104% of the March value. Choice **(C)** is correct.

These examples show how Backsolving and Picking Numbers can come in handy on Praxis Core Mathematics questions. Get comfortable with these strategies and be flexible in your approach to new problems. It's essential that you figure out which techniques work best for you for the wide range of problems you'll see on the test.

The next section of this chapter provides a review of the basic mathematical concepts that are tested on the Praxis Core Mathematics test. Use your results from the pre-test to help you determine which areas are especially important for you to review, but don't hesitate to work through the entire *Content Review* section. After that, the chapter closes with a practice set of questions in the formats you'll see on test day. You may choose to refresh your memory on the Backsolving and Picking Numbers strategies before you work through that set.

## INTRODUCING THE MATHEMATICS CONTENT REVIEW

Now that you've learned the Kaplan Method for the questions on the Praxis Core Mathematics test, let's review the math concepts and rules that you are expected to know for the exam before we practice these questions in format. Keep a few things in mind as you work through the content review.

First, quite a bit of content is covered in this review. Depending on your strengths and weaknesses, you may be able to move quickly through some areas but may need to slow down and focus on others that give you trouble.

Second, before working through this review, be sure that you have taken the Praxis Core Mathematics pre-test to note the areas in which you have the greatest difficulty.

Finally, although this is a content review, you may find a few questions for which the strategies we covered earlier in this chapter are helpful. If you can use Backsolving or Picking Numbers to get to a correct answer in a multiple-choice question, that's great. Don't, however, overlook the content covered in the example. You'll have additional opportunities to practice using strategic approaches in the Practice Set at the end of the chapter. First, shore up your content weaknesses so that you'll be ready to play to your strengths when test day rolls around.

# THE DECIMAL SYSTEM

**Decimals** are numbers that use place value to show amounts less than 1. You already use decimals when working with money. For example, in the amount $10.25, you know that the digits to the right of the **decimal point** represent cents, or hundredths of a dollar.

The first four decimal place values are labeled on the chart below.

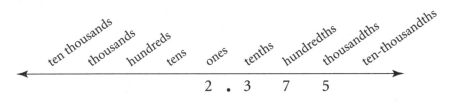

The number 2.375 is shown on the chart. When reading a decimal out loud or in your head, read *and* in the place of the decimal point. After reading the decimal part, say the place value of the last decimal digit. This number would be read, "Two *and* three hundred seventy-five *thousandths*."

## Comparing and Ordering

Comparing decimals is similar to comparing whole numbers.

Matt ran the 400-meter race in 45.8 seconds. Alonzo ran the same race in 45.66 seconds. Which runner had the faster time?

- Line up the decimal points. Add a zero at the end of 45.8 so that both times have the same number of digits after the decimal.

  45.80
  45.66

- Since the whole numbers are the same, now compare the decimal parts of the numbers as though they were whole numbers. **Alonzo's time was faster.**

  80 is greater than 66, so 45.8 is greater than 45.66

When you compare more than two numbers, it is helpful to compare one place-value column at a time, working left to right.

Arrange the numbers 0.85, 1.8, 0.8, and 0.819 in order from greatest to least.

- Write the numbers in a column, lining up the decimal points. Add zeros so that the numbers have the same number of decimal places.

  0.850
  1.800
  0.800
  0.819

- Compare the digits, working from left to right. Only 1.8 has a whole number part—a number greater than zero to the left of the decimal point—so it is the greatest. The remaining numbers each have 8 in the tenths column. Looking at the hundredths column, 0.85 is next, followed by 0.819. The least number is 0.8.

  In order:
  1.8
  0.85
  0.819
  0.8

# DECIMAL OPERATIONS

## Addition and Subtraction

Adding decimals is much like adding whole numbers. The trick is to make sure you have lined up the place-value columns correctly. You can do this by writing the numbers in a column and carefully lining up the decimal points.

Add 0.37 + 13.5 + 2.638.

- Write the numbers in a column, lining up the decimal points.

- You may add placeholder zeros so that the decimals have the same number of decimal places.

$$\begin{array}{r} 0.370 \\ 13.500 \\ +2.638 \\ \hline \end{array}$$

- Add. Starting on the right, add each column. Regroup, or carry, as you would with whole numbers.

- Place the decimal point in the answer directly below the decimal points in the problem.

$$\begin{array}{r} {}^{1}\phantom{0}{}^{1}\phantom{00} \\ 0.370 \\ 13.500 \\ +2.638 \\ \hline 16.508 \end{array}$$

To subtract decimals, write the numbers in a column with the greater number on top. Make sure the decimal points are in a line.

Find the difference between 14.512 and 8.7.

- Write the numbers in a column, lining up the decimal points. Add placeholder zeros so that the numbers have the same number of decimal places.

$$\begin{array}{r} 14.512 \\ -8.700 \\ \hline \end{array}$$

- Subtract. Regroup, or borrow, as needed. Place the decimal point in the answer directly in line with the decimal points in the problem.

$$\begin{array}{r} {}^{13}\phantom{0}{}^{15} \\ \cancel{1}\cancel{4}.\cancel{5}12 \\ -8.700 \\ \hline 5.812 \end{array}$$

The greater number may have fewer or no decimal places. In the next example, a decimal is subtracted from a whole number.

What does 9 minus 3.604 equal?

- Line up the place-value columns. Put a decimal point after the whole number 9 and add placeholder zeros.

$$\begin{array}{r} 9.000 \\ -3.604 \\ \hline \end{array}$$

- Subtract, regrouping as needed. Place the decimal point in the answer directly below the decimal points in the problem.

$$\begin{array}{r} {}^{8}\phantom{0}{}^{9}\phantom{0}{}^{9}{}^{10} \\ \cancel{9}.\cancel{0}\cancel{0}\cancel{0} \\ -3.604 \\ \hline 5.396 \end{array}$$

## Multiplication and Division

The rules you use to multiply whole numbers can be used to multiply decimals. You don't have to line up the decimal points. You will wait until you are finished multiplying before you place the decimal point in the answer. The number of decimal places in the answer equals the sum of the number of decimal places in the numbers you are multiplying.

Find the product of 2.6 and 0.45.

- Set up the problem as though you were multiplying the whole numbers 26 and 45.

$$\begin{array}{r} 2.6 \\ \times\, 0.45 \\ \hline \end{array}$$

- Ignore the decimal points while you multiply.

- Now count the decimal places in the numbers you multiplied. The number 2.6 has one decimal place, and 0.45 has two decimal places, for a total of three.

- Starting from the right, count three decimal places to the left and insert the decimal point.

$$\begin{array}{r} 2.6 \\ \times\, 0.45 \\ \hline 130 \\ 1040 \\ \hline 1.170 \end{array}$$

When you divide decimals, you must figure out where the decimal point will go in the answer before you divide.

Divide 14.4 by 6.

- Set up the problem. Because the divisor (the number you are dividing by) is a whole number, place the decimal point in the answer directly above the decimal point in the dividend (the number you are dividing).
- Divide. Use the rules you learned for dividing whole numbers.

$$\begin{array}{r} 2.4 \\ 6\overline{)14.4} \\ -12\phantom{.} \\ \hline 24 \\ -24 \\ \hline 0 \end{array}$$

If the divisor is also a decimal, you must move the decimal points in both the divisor and the dividend before you divide.

Divide 4.9 by 0.35.

- Set up the problem. There are two decimal places in the divisor, which is 0.35. Move the decimal point in both the divisor and the dividend, 4.9, two places to the right. Note that you need to add a zero in the dividend to move the decimal two places.

$$0.35\overline{)4.90}$$

- Place the decimal point in the quotient directly above the decimal point in the dividend.
- Divide.

$$\begin{array}{r} 14.\phantom{0} \\ 35\overline{)490.} \\ -35\phantom{0.} \\ \hline 140 \\ -140 \\ \hline 0 \end{array}$$

# FRACTIONS

A fraction uses two numbers to represent part of a whole. The bottom number, called the **denominator,** indicates how many equal parts are in the whole group or the number of parts into which one item is divided. The top number, called the **numerator,** indicates how many parts you are working with.

- There are 4 equal parts in this rectangle. Because 3 are shaded, we say that $\frac{3}{4}$ of the rectangle is shaded.

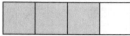

In a proper fraction, the numerator is less than the denominator. A **proper fraction** represents a quantity less than 1. An **improper fraction** is equal to or greater than 1.

- There are 6 equal parts in the figure below, and 6 are shaded; therefore, $\frac{6}{6}$ of the figure is shaded: $\frac{6}{6} = 1$

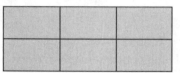

- In this grouping, each figure is divided into 2 equal parts or halves, so the denominator of the fraction is 2. A total of 3 parts are shaded, so the fraction of the shaded area of the figures is $\frac{3}{2}$.

A **mixed number** is another way to show an amount greater than 1. It consists of a whole number and a proper fraction. Another name for the shaded portion in the last figure is $1\frac{1}{2}$. The improper fraction $\frac{3}{2}$ equals the mixed number $1\frac{1}{2}$.

You can also change an improper fraction to a whole number or mixed number.

Change $\frac{16}{5}$ to a mixed number.

- Divide the numerator (16) by the denominator (5). Because 16 is not evenly divisible by 5, there is a remainder. In this case, the remainder is 1.

  $16 \div 5 = 3r1$

- The answer becomes the whole number, and the remainder becomes the numerator of the proper fraction. The denominator is the same as that of the original fraction.

  $\frac{16}{5} = 3\frac{1}{5}$

You can also change a mixed number to an improper fraction.

Change $7\dfrac{2}{3}$ to an improper fraction.

- Multiply the whole number (7) by the denominator of the fraction (3). Then add the numerator (2).

$$7 \times 3 = 21$$
$$21 + 2 = 23$$

- Write the sum over the denominator of the original fraction.

$$7\dfrac{2}{3} = \dfrac{23}{3}$$

To perform operations with fractions, you need to be able to write equal fractions in higher or lower terms. The terms are the numerator and the denominator. A fraction is **reduced to lowest terms** when the two terms do not have any common factor except 1.

- To **raise** a fraction, multiply both terms by the same number:

$$\dfrac{3}{4} = \dfrac{3 \times 3}{4 \times 3} = \dfrac{9}{12}$$

- To **reduce** a fraction, divide both terms by the same number:

$$\dfrac{10}{15} = \dfrac{10 \div 5}{15 \div 5} = \dfrac{2}{3}$$

# FRACTION OPERATIONS

## Addition and Subtraction

You can add or subtract **like fractions**. Like fractions have a **common denominator**. In other words, the numbers below the fraction bar are the same.

Add $\dfrac{3}{10} + \dfrac{5}{10}$.

- Because the denominators are the same, add the numerators.

$$\dfrac{3}{10} + \dfrac{5}{10} = \dfrac{8}{10}$$

- Reduce the answer to lowest terms.

$$\dfrac{8}{10} = \dfrac{8 \div 2}{10 \div 2} = \dfrac{4}{5}$$

Subtract $\dfrac{2}{9}$ from $\dfrac{7}{9}$.

- Subtract the numerators. The answer is already in lowest terms.

$$\dfrac{7}{9} - \dfrac{2}{9} = \dfrac{5}{9}$$

If the denominators are not the same, convert one or both fractions to equivalent fractions so that they become like fractions.

Add $\dfrac{5}{6} + \dfrac{1}{4}$.

- One way to find a common denominator is to list some multiples of both denominators.
  Multiples of 6: 6, $\boxed{12}$, 18
  Multiples of 4: 4, 8, $\boxed{12}$, 16
  The lowest common multiple of the denominators is 12.

  $\dfrac{5 \times 2}{6 \times 2} = \dfrac{10}{12}, \dfrac{1 \times 3}{4 \times 3} = \dfrac{3}{12}$

- Convert each fraction to an equivalent fraction with a denominator of 12.

  $\dfrac{10}{12} + \dfrac{3}{12} = \dfrac{13}{12}$

- Add the like fractions.

## Multiplication and Division

It is not necessary to find a common denominator to multiply and divide fractions. To multiply fractions, simply multiply the numerators and then the denominators. Reduce the answer to lowest terms, if necessary.

What is the product of $\dfrac{7}{8}$ and $\dfrac{1}{2}$?

- Multiply the numerators together and then multiply the denominators.

  $\dfrac{7}{8} \times \dfrac{1}{2} = \dfrac{7 \times 1}{8 \times 2} = \dfrac{7}{16}$

Before multiplying a mixed number, change it to an improper fraction.

What is $\dfrac{1}{3}$ of $3\dfrac{3}{4}$?

- Change $3\dfrac{3}{4}$ to an improper fraction.

  $3\dfrac{3}{4} = \dfrac{15}{4}$

- Multiply the numerators and the denominators.

  $\dfrac{1}{3} \times \dfrac{15}{4} = \dfrac{1 \times 15}{3 \times 4} = \dfrac{15}{12}$

- Change to a mixed number and reduce to lowest terms.

  $\dfrac{15}{12} = 1\dfrac{3}{12} = 1\dfrac{1}{4}$

To divide fractions, **invert** the divisor (the fraction you are dividing by) by switching its numerator and denominator. Then, multiply the fractions.

Jim has an 8-pound bag of nuts. He wants to fill smaller, $\frac{1}{2}$-pound bags using the nuts. How many $\frac{1}{2}$-pound bags can he fill?

- Divide 8 by $\frac{1}{2}$. Set up the division problem. Always write the whole or mixed numbers as improper fractions.

$$8 \div \frac{1}{2} = \frac{8}{1} \div \frac{1}{2} =$$

- Invert the fraction you are dividing by and change the operation sign to multiplication. Multiply, following the rules for multiplying fractions. **Jim can fill 16 small bags.**

$$\frac{8}{1} \times \frac{2}{1} = \frac{16}{1} = 16$$

## RATIOS

Ratios represent the proportion of one quantity to another.

Ratios are usually written in the form $c:d$. A ratio does not, by itself, tell you the number of each item present.

The ratio of blue marbles to green marbles in a bag is 5:3.

This does *not* necessarily mean that there are 5 blue marbles and 3 green marbles in the bag. All it means is that for every 5 blue marbles, there are 3 green marbles. It is possible that there are 10 blue marbles and 6 green marbles, 50 blue marbles and 30 green marbles, or any other combination in which the proportion of blue marbles to green marbles is 5:3.

Ratios can also be written as fractions. To write a ratio as a fraction, put the number associated with the word *of* in the numerator (on top) and put the number associated with the word *to* in the denominator (on the bottom) and reduce.

The ratio of 20 apples to 12 oranges is $\frac{20}{12}$, which reduces to $\frac{5}{3}$, or 5:3 when expressed as a ratio.

## Part-to-Part Ratios Versus Part-to-Whole Ratios

A ratio can either express the relationship of a part to the whole of which it is a part, or it can express the relationship of a part to another part of the same whole.

The previous examples both express part-to-part ratios. In the case of the marbles, there are two parts: blue marbles and green marbles. If all marbles in the bag are either blue or green, they make up the whole, that is, all the marbles in the bag. If we wanted to express the ratio of blue marbles to all the marbles in the bag, we would have to add the blue and green marbles together.

If the ratio of blue marbles to green marbles in a bag is $\frac{5}{3}$, then the ratio of blue marbles to all marbles is $\frac{5}{3+5} = \frac{5}{8}$.

# PROPORTIONS

A **proportion** is an equation that shows that two ratios are equal. The cross products in a true proportion are equal. In other words, when you multiply diagonally across the equal sign, the products are equal.

The directions on a can of powdered drink mix say to add 3 cups of water to every 2 scoops of drink mix. Mike adds 12 cups of water to 8 scoops of drink mix. Did he make the drink correctly?

- Write the proportion, making sure the terms of the ratios are in the same order.

$$\frac{\text{cups}}{\text{scoops}} = \frac{3}{2} = \frac{12}{8}$$

- Cross multiply and compare the products. Because the products are the same, the ratios are equal. **Mike made the drink correctly**.

$$3 \times 8 = 24$$
$$2 \times 12 = 24$$

In most proportion problems, you are asked to solve for a missing term.

A map scale says that 2 inches = 150 miles. What actual distance would a map distance of 5 inches represent?

- Write a proportion with both ratios in the same form: inches to miles. The variable $x$ represents the unknown distance in miles.

$$\frac{\text{inches}}{\text{miles}} = \frac{2}{150} = \frac{5}{x}$$

- Locate the term in the first ratio that is diagonal from the known term in the second ratio. Cross multiply.

$$\frac{2}{150} = \frac{5}{x}$$
$$150 \times 5 = 750$$

- Divide the result by the remaining known term to find the value of $x$.

$$x = 750 \div 2 = 375$$

## RATES

Some proportion problems ask you to find a **rate**. A rate compares the number of units of one item to one unit of another item. When a rate is written in fraction form, its denominator is always one unit. In word form, rates are often expressed using the word *per*.

Connie drove 276 miles on 12 gallons of gasoline. How many miles per gallon did she get on the trip?

- Gas mileage is one kind of rate. You need to find how many miles Connie drove on 1 gallon of gasoline.

$$\frac{\text{miles}}{\text{gallons}} = \frac{276}{12} = \frac{x}{1}$$

- Solve. **Connie got 23 miles per gallon on the trip.**

$$(276)(1) = 12x$$
$$x = 276 \div 12 = 23$$

## PERCENTS

*Percent* means "per hundred" or "out of one hundred." For example, if you have $100 and you spend $25, you spent $25 of $100 or 25% of your money.

Because a percentage is a way of showing part of a whole, it has much in common with fractions, decimals, and ratios. In fact, percentages are just a specific type of fraction, one in which the denominator is 100.

To convert a percent to a fraction, write the percent over 100 and reduce. To convert percents to decimals, drop the percent symbol and move the decimal point two places to the left.

| **Percent to Fraction** | **Percent to Decimal** |
|---|---|
| $25\% = \dfrac{25}{100} = \dfrac{1}{4}$ | $25\% = 0.25$ |

In any percent problem, there are three elements: the whole, the part, and the percent. The **whole** is the amount that the problem is about. The **part** is a portion of the whole. The **percent** is a number followed by the percent symbol (%).

At a restaurant, Janice's bill is $20. She gives the waiter a tip of $3, which is 15% of her bill. Identify the whole, part, and percent in this situation.

- The entire bill of $20 is the whole. The $3 tip is the part, and the percent is 15%.

- One way to think of a percent problem is as a proportion. In this example, there are two ratios. The $3 tip is figured as a part of the $20, and 15% is the same as $\dfrac{15}{100}$. Because the two ratios are equal, they can be written as a proportion.

$$\frac{\text{part}}{\text{whole}} = \frac{3}{20} = \frac{15}{100}$$

- Cross multiply to prove that the ratios are equal.

$$20 \times 15 = 300$$
$$3 \times 100 = 300$$

You can solve percent problems by using the equation $\text{percent} = \dfrac{\text{part}}{\text{whole}}$ and solving for the missing element. Sometimes you will want to use the equation in the form part = percent × whole. Just remember to express the percent as a fraction with percent value over 100, or as a decimal.

At a plant that manufactures lighting fixtures, it is expected that approximately 2% of the fixtures assembled each day will have some type of defect. If 900 fixtures are completed in one day, how many of these are expected to be defective?

- We are given the percent and the whole, and we want to find the part. So we will use the equation part = percent × whole. Here, 2% = 0.02.
- Find the part: 2% of 900 = 0.02 × 900 = 18. **The company can expect to have 18 defective fixtures.**

# PROBABILITY

The numerical representation of the likelihood of an event or events occurring is termed **probability**.

Probability is the ratio of the number of favorable outcomes possible to the total number of possible outcomes or, in fractional form,

$$\text{probability (event)} = \frac{\text{\# of favorable outcomes possible}}{\text{\# of total possible outcomes}}$$

If you flip a coin, what are the odds that it will fall with the heads side up?

- The probability that the coin will land heads up is $\dfrac{1}{2}$, because there is one outcome favorable to your result (heads up) and there are two possible outcomes (heads or tails).

# FACTORS, PRIMES, AND DIVISIBILITY

## Multiples

An integer that is divisible by another integer with no remainder is a **multiple** of that integer.

- 12 is a multiple of 3 because 12 is divisible by 3; $\dfrac{12}{3} = 4$.

The multiples of a number can be thought of as those numbers that you would get if you "counted" by that number. For example, if you counted by 6, you would get 6, 12, 18, 24, 30, 36, 42, 48, and so on. All of these numbers, including 6, are multiples of 6.

## Remainders

The **remainder** is what is left over in a division problem. A remainder is always smaller than the number you are dividing by.

- 17 divided by 3 is 5 with a remainder of 2.

This means that you can divide 17 into 5 equal parts, all of which have 3 units, plus 2 leftover units.

## Factors

The **factors** of a number are the positive integers that evenly divide into that number.

- 36 has nine factors: 1, 2, 3, 4, 6, 9, 12, 18, and 36.

These factors can be grouped into pairs:

$$1 \times 36 = 2 \times 18 = 3 \times 12 = 4 \times 9 = 6 \times 6$$

## Divisibility Tests

There are several tests to determine whether a number is divisible by 2, 3, 4, 5, 6, or 9.

A number is divisible by 2 if its last digit is divisible by 2.

- 138 is divisible by 2 because 8 is divisible by 2.

A number is divisible by 3 if the sum of its digits is divisible by 3.

- 4,317 is divisible by 3 because $4 + 3 + 1 + 7 = 15$ and 15 is divisible by 3.
- 239 is *not* divisible by 3 because $2 + 3 + 9 = 14$ and 14 is not divisible by 3.

A number is divisible by 4 if its last two digits are divisible by 4.

- 1,748 is divisible by 4 because 48 is divisible by 4.

A number is divisible by 5 if its last digit is 0 or 5.

- 2,635 is divisible by 5, but 5,052 is *not* divisible by 5.

A number is divisible by 6 if it is divisible by both 2 and 3.

- 4,326 is divisible by 6 because it is divisible by 2 (last digit is 6) and by 3 ($4 + 3 + 2 + 6 = 15$).

A number is divisible by 9 if the sum of its digits is divisible by 9.

- 22,428 is divisible by 9 because $2 + 2 + 4 + 2 + 8 = 18$, and 18 is divisible by 9.

## Prime Number

A **prime number** is an integer greater than 1 that has no factors other than 1 and itself. The number 1 is not considered a prime. The number 2 is the first prime number and the only even prime. (This is fairly evident. Every other even number is divisible by 2 and therefore is not prime.) The first ten prime numbers are 2, 3, 5, 7, 11, 13, 17, 19, 23, and 29.

# THE COORDINATE PLANE

A coordinate grid is a way of locating points that lie in a **plane** or flat surface. The grid is formed by two intersecting lines: an x-axis and a y-axis. The x-axis is actually a horizontal number line y, and the y-axis is a vertical number line. The point at which the two axes intersect is called the **origin**.

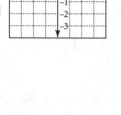

Each point on the grid can be named using a set of two numbers called an **ordered pair**. The first number is the distance from the origin along the x-axis. The second number is the distance from the origin along the y-axis. The numbers are written in parentheses and are separated by a comma: (x, y).

Write the ordered pairs for points M and P.

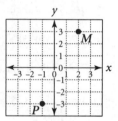

- Point M lies 2 spaces to the right of the origin along the x-axis and 3 spaces above the origin along the y-axis. The coordinates are (2, 3).
- Point P lies 1 space to the left along the x-axis and 3 spaces down along the y-axis. The coordinates are (−1, −3).

To plot points on the grid, use the number lines located at the axes. Remember that right and up are the directions for positive numbers, while left and down are the directions for negative numbers.

Point A is located at (−2, 1), and point B is located at (3, −2). Plot these points on a coordinate grid.

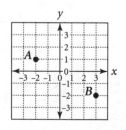

- To plot A, start at the origin. Count 2 spaces left along the x-axis. Count 1 space up along the y-axis.
- To plot point B, start at the origin. Count 3 spaces right along the x-axis. Count 2 spaces down along the y-axis.

## Review One Practice

Round these numbers as directed.

1. Round 3.75 to the tenths place.

2. Round 5.908 to the ones place.

Which number is greater?

3. 0.45 or 0.449

4. 0.008 or 0.08

Write these numbers in order from least to greatest.

5. 5.6  5.08  5.8  5.802

6. 0.1136  0.12  0.2  0.115

Solve.

7. $\begin{array}{r} 4.025 \\ +3.971 \\ \hline \end{array}$

8. $\begin{array}{r} 8.5 \\ -1.074 \\ \hline \end{array}$

9. $\begin{array}{r} 17.52 \\ +3.8 \\ \hline \end{array}$

10. James ran three miles. His times for the individual miles were 7.2 minutes, 6.8 minutes, and 8.25 minutes. How long did it take him, in minutes, to run the three-mile distance?

   A. 9.65
   B. 22.25
   C. 22.7
   D. 23.35
   E. 96.5

11. $\begin{array}{r} 5.3 \\ \times 0.5 \\ \hline \end{array}$

12. $8\overline{)28.8}$

13. $\begin{array}{r} 9.62 \\ \times 1.005 \\ \hline \end{array}$

14. One container of floor cleaner holds 3.79 liters. If Zachary bought 4 containers, how many liters of cleaner did he buy?

    A. 0.9475

    B. 7.79

    C. 9.48

    D. 12.83

    E. 15.16

Write the proper fraction for the shaded portion of each figure.

15.     16.

Write an improper fraction and a mixed number for the shaded portion of each group of figures.

17.      18.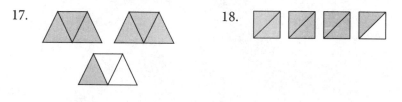

Write improper fractions as mixed numbers and mixed numbers as improper fractions.

19. $\dfrac{17}{3} =$

20. $2\dfrac{5}{12} =$

Write an equal fraction with the given denominator.

21. $\dfrac{3}{4} = \dfrac{}{16}$

22. $\dfrac{3}{8} = \dfrac{}{40}$

Reduce each fraction to lowest terms.

23. $\dfrac{21}{28} =$

24. $\dfrac{4}{24} =$

25. Eighteen of every 24 people surveyed say they went to at least one movie in December. What fraction of the people surveyed went to a movie in December?

  A. $\dfrac{3}{4}$

  B. $\dfrac{2}{3}$

  C. $\dfrac{1}{2}$

  D. $\dfrac{1}{3}$

  E. $\dfrac{1}{4}$

Express the correct answer as a mixed number.

26. $5\dfrac{5}{6} + 2\dfrac{2}{3} =$

27. $\dfrac{3}{8} + \dfrac{7}{12} + 1\dfrac{2}{3} =$

28. To make the top of a dining room table, Craig glued a piece of oak that is $\dfrac{5}{16}$ inch thick to a piece of pine that is $\dfrac{7}{8}$ inch thick. What is the total thickness, in inches, of the tabletop?

  A. $\dfrac{1}{2}$

  B. $\dfrac{9}{16}$

  C. $1\dfrac{3}{16}$

  D. $1\dfrac{1}{4}$

  E. $1\dfrac{9}{16}$

29. $\dfrac{2}{3} \times \dfrac{1}{4} =$

30. $2\dfrac{1}{3} \times 3\dfrac{2}{5} =$

31. A pygmy kangaroo needs to cross a highway that is 10 meters across. If the kangaroo covers exactly $1\frac{1}{4}$ meters each time it hops, how many hops would it take for the kangaroo to cross the highway?

    A. 5
    B. 6
    C. 7
    D. 8
    E. 9

Write each ratio as a fraction in lowest terms.

32. Stan made 24 sales in 6 hours. What is the ratio of sales to hours?

33. Carol's monthly take-home pay is $1,500. She spends $250 a month on food. What is the ratio of her food cost to her take-home pay?

34. A toy rocket travels 180 feet in 15 seconds. What is the rocket's speed expressed in feet per second?

35. Soan made a $400 down payment on a washer and dryer that cost a total of $1,200. What is the ratio of the down payment to the balance Soan owed after making the down payment?

    A. 1 to 4
    B. 1 to 3
    C. 1 to 2
    D. 2 to 3
    E. 3 to 4

Find the value of the variable that completes the ratio.

36. $\dfrac{2}{3} = \dfrac{x}{18}$

37. $\dfrac{4}{\$2.12} = \dfrac{7}{x}$

38. The Bay City Cardinals have won 5 of 8 games. At the same rate, how many games will they have to play to win 60 games?

    A. 190
    B. 180
    C. 120
    D. 96
    E. 12

39. What is 20% of $25?

40. Find 90% of 200.

41. Pat called 120 customers to offer a software upgrade. Of those he called, 72 purchased the upgrade. What percentage of the customers that Pat called agreed to the purchase?

    A. 6%
    B. 40%
    C. 48%
    D. 60%
    E. 66%

For each situation, identify and label the whole, part, and percent.

42. Victor owes his uncle $1,000. Recently, he gave his uncle $200. The payment was 20% of the money he owes.

43. On a test with 80 problems, Sophie got 72 problems correct. In other words, she answered 90% of the problems correctly.

For each situation, express probability as a fraction, a decimal, and a percent.

44. A game has 50 wooden tiles. Players draw tiles to spell words. If 20 of the tiles are marked with vowels, what is the probability of drawing a vowel from the tiles?

45. There are four red, four blue, and two green marbles in a bag. If one marble is chosen from the bag, what is the probability that the marble will be green?

46. What is the greatest integer that will divide evenly into both 36 and 54?
    A. 6
    B. 9
    C. 12
    D. 18
    E. 27

47. Which of the following is NOT a factor of 168?
    A. 21
    B. 24
    C. 28
    D. 32
    E. 42

Write the ordered pair for each point.

48.   Point *A*

49.   Point *B*

50.   Point *C*

51.   Point *D*

52.   Point *E*

53.   Point *F*

54.   Point *G*

55.   Point *H*

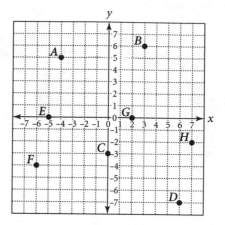

Plot the points on the coordinate grid.

56.   Plot the following points:

    *J* at (−3, −2)

    *K* at (4, 0)

    *L* at (1, −3)

    *M* at (−4, 2)

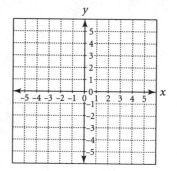

# ANSWERS AND EXPLANATIONS

## Review One Practice

1. 3.8

2. 6

3. 0.45

4. 0.08

5. 5.08, 5.6, 5.8, 5.802

6. 0.1136, 0.115, 0.12, 0.2

7. 7.996

8. 7.426

9. 21.32

10. B

Add the times: 7.2 + 6.8 + 8.25 = 22.25 minutes. You do not need to use the three-mile distance to solve the problem, as the problem only asks about the time taken to run that distance.

11. 2.65

12. 3.6

13. 9.6681

14. E

Multiply 3.79 liters by 4: 3.79 × 4 = 15.16 liters.

15. $\frac{3}{5}$

16. $\frac{2}{4}$, or $\frac{1}{2}$

17. $\frac{7}{3}$, or $2\frac{1}{3}$

18. $\frac{7}{2}$, or $3\frac{1}{2}$

19. $5\frac{2}{3}$

20. $\frac{29}{12}$

21. $\frac{12}{16}$

22. $\frac{15}{40}$

23. $\frac{3}{4}$

24. $\frac{1}{6}$

25. A

Of those surveyed, $\frac{18}{24}$ went to at least one movie.

Reduce the fraction to lowest terms: $\frac{18 \div 6}{24 \div 6} = \frac{3}{4}$.

26. $8\frac{1}{2}$

27. $2\frac{5}{8}$

28. C

Add to find the total.

$\frac{5}{16} + \frac{7}{8} = \frac{5}{16} + \frac{14}{16} = \frac{19}{16} = 1\frac{3}{16}$ inches.

29. $\frac{1}{6}$

30. $7\frac{14}{15}$

31. D

Divide 10 by $1\frac{1}{4}$ because the kangaroo needs to cover 10 meters with a series of jumps each $1\frac{1}{4}$ meters in length. When dividing by a mixed number like $1\frac{1}{4}$, it's easier to work with an improper fraction: $1\frac{1}{4} = \frac{5}{4}$, so divide 10 by $\frac{5}{4}$. Remember, when dividing by a fraction, you flip the divisor and then multiply. So, $10 \div \frac{5}{4} = 10 \times \frac{4}{5} = \frac{40}{5} = 8$. It would take the kangaroo exactly 8 hops to cross the highway, making choice (D) correct.

32. $\frac{24}{6} = \frac{4}{1}$

In other words, Stan made an average of four sales per hour.

**33.** $\dfrac{\$250}{\$1,500} = \dfrac{1}{6}$

**34.** $\dfrac{180}{15} = \dfrac{12}{1}$

**35. C**

Subtract to find the amount owed: $1,200 − $400 = $800. Write the ratio and reduce: 400 to 800 = 1 to 2.

**36.** 12

**37.** $3.71

**38. D**

Set up the proportion: $\dfrac{5}{8} = \dfrac{60}{x}$. Then solve for $x$: 8 × 60 ÷ 5 = 96.

**39. $5**

**40. 180**

**41. D**

72 ÷ 120 = 0.6 = 60%.

**42.** whole = $1,000; part = $200; percent = 20%

**43.** whole = 80; part = 72; percent = 90%

**44.** $\dfrac{2}{5}$, 0.4, 40%

**45.** $\dfrac{1}{5}$, 0.2, 20%

**46. D**

Since you are looking for the greatest common factor of 36 and 54, start with the largest answer choice and test out the choices until you find the correct answer.

**47. D**

You need to find the answer choice that does *not* divide evenly into 168. Test out each answer and eliminate those that produce an integer result when you divide into 168.

**48. (−4, 5)**

**49. (3, 6)**

**50. (0, −3)**

**51. (6, −7)**

**52. (−5, 0)**

**53. (−6, −4)**

**54. (2, 0)**

**55. (7, −2)**

**56.**

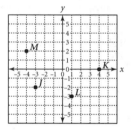

| Review Two |
| --- |

# THE ORDER OF OPERATIONS

When a mathematical expression contains more than one operation, its value may depend on the order in which the operations are performed. To avoid confusion, mathematicians have agreed to perform operations in a certain order.

## The Order of Operations

1. Parentheses or any other grouping symbols that enclose operations

2. Exponents and roots

3. Multiplication and division, working from left to right

4. Addition and subtraction, working from left to right

Study the following example to see how to apply the order of operations. Notice that parentheses are used in two places in the expression; however, only the first set of parentheses encloses an operation.

Evaluate the expression $\dfrac{(5+3)^2}{4} + 3(-1)$.

- Perform the addition in parentheses. $\qquad$ $\dfrac{(8)^2}{4} + 3(-1)$

- Raise 8 to exponent 2. $\qquad$ $\dfrac{64}{4} + 3(-1)$

- Divide, then multiply. $\qquad$ $16 + (-3)$

- Add. $\qquad$ $13$

The value of the expression $\dfrac{(5+3)^2}{4} + 3(-1)$ is 13.

The fraction bar is also a grouping symbol. Before you divide, perform any operations shown above and below the bar.

Evaluate the expression $\dfrac{15+25}{2(5)} + 6$.

- Perform the operations above and below the fraction bar. $\qquad$ $\dfrac{15+25}{2(5)} + 6$

- Divide, then add. $\qquad$ $\dfrac{40}{10} + 6$

$\qquad$ $4 + 6 = 10$

## ALGEBRAIC EXPRESSIONS

An **algebraic expression** uses numbers, operations, and variables to show number relationships. **Variables** are letters (such as $x$ and $y$) that represent unknown numbers. Each time the same letter is used within the same expression, it represents the same number.

Here are some examples of algebraic expressions in both words and symbols:

| Algebraic expressions in words | In symbols |
|---|---|
| the product of 5 and a number | $5x$ |
| a number decreased by 12 | $x - 12$ |
| the sum of 3 and the square of a number | $3 + x^2$ |
| 6 less than the quotient of a number and 2 | $\dfrac{x}{2} - 6$ |
| one-half a number increased by 15 | $\dfrac{1}{2}x + 15$ |
| 4 times the difference of −3 and a number | $4(-3 - x)$ |
| a number less another number | $x - y$ |
| 10 less the square root of a number, plus 3 | $10 - \sqrt{x} + 3$ |

## SIMPLIFYING AND EVALUATING EXPRESSIONS

**Simplifying an expression** means performing all the operations you can within an expression. When working with variables, you must remember an important rule: you can add or subtract like terms only.

A **term** is a number, a variable, or the product or quotient of numbers and variables. A term cannot include a sum or a difference.

$$5x \quad 3y^2 \quad 13 \quad x^3 \quad \frac{x}{2}$$

**Like terms** have the same variable raised to the same power. For example, $3x^2$ and $5x^2$ are like terms; $8y$ and $4y$ are also like terms. However, $4x$ and $4y$ are not like terms because they contain different variables. Likewise, $6x$ and $2x^2$ are not like terms because the variables are not raised to the same exponent.

To simplify an expression, combine like terms.

- Simplify $2x - 5 + 4x^2 - 8 + 6x$.

    In the result, it is customary to write the term with the greatest exponent first and to continue in descending order.

$$
\begin{aligned}
2x &- 5 + 4x^2 - 8 + 6x \\
&= (2x + 6x) + (-5 + (-8)) + 4x^2 \\
&= 8x + (-13) + 4x^2 \\
&= 4x^2 + 8x - 13
\end{aligned}
$$

The **distributive property** allows you to remove grouping symbols to simplify expressions. We can state the distributive property using symbols.

$$a(b + c) = ab + ac \text{ and } a(b - c) = ab - ac$$

In other words, each term inside the parentheses is multiplied by the term outside the parentheses, and the results are added or subtracted depending on the operation inside the parentheses. The next example applies the distributive property.

Simplify $4x - 3(x + 9) + 15$.

- Change the subtraction of $3(x + 9)$ to the addition of a negative number.
- Use the distributive property. Multiply $-3$ by each term in the parentheses.
- Combine like terms. (*Note:* $1x$ means $x$.)

$$4x - 3(x + 9) + 15$$
$$= 4x + \left[-3(x + 9)\right] + 15$$
$$= 4x + (-3x) + (-3)(9) + 15$$
$$= 4x + (-3x) + (-27) + 15$$
$$= (4x + -3x) + (-27 + 15)$$
$$= 1x - 12$$
$$= x - 12$$

**Evaluating** an expression means finding its value. To evaluate an expression, substitute a given number for each variable.

Find the value of the expression $\dfrac{3x + 2y}{4}$ when $x = 6$ and $y = 5$.

- Replace the variables with the corresponding values given in the problem.

$$\frac{3x + 2y}{4} = \frac{3(6) + 2(5)}{4}$$

- Perform the operations above the fraction bar.

$$\frac{3(6) + 2(5)}{4} = \frac{18 + 10}{4} = \frac{28}{4} = 7$$

*Note:* To remove parentheses from an operation that follows a minus sign, imagine that the parentheses are preceded by $-1$. Then use the distributive property.

Simplify $-(2x + 3)$.

$$-(2x + 3)$$
$$= -1(2x + 3)$$
$$= -1(2x) + (-1)(3)$$
$$= -2x + (-3) \text{ or } -2x - 3$$

# EQUATIONS

An **equation** is a mathematical statement that two expressions are equal.

$$3 + 5 = 4 \times 2 \qquad 10 - 1 = 3^2 \qquad 5(3 + 5) = 40$$

An equation can contain one or more variables. Solving an equation means finding a value for each variable that will make the equation true.

$$4 + x = 11 \qquad 3x = 24 \qquad x - 5 = -2$$
$$x = 7 \qquad x = 8 \qquad x = 3$$

The basic strategy in solving an equation is to isolate the variable on one side of the equation. You can do this by performing **inverse**, or opposite, operations. However, you must always follow one basic rule: whatever you do to one side of the equation, you must also do to the other side.

Solve $x - 23 = 45$.

On the left side of the equation, the number 23 is subtracted from $x$. The inverse of subtraction is addition. Add 23 to both sides of the equation.

$$x - 23 = 45$$
$$x - 23 + 23 = 45 + 23$$
$$x = 68$$

To check your work, replace the variable with your solution and simplify. When $x = 68$, the equation is true.

Check:
$$x - 23 = 45$$
$$68 - 23 = 45$$
$$45 = 45$$

The following examples use the inverse operations of multiplication and division. Solve $\frac{x}{2} = 17$.

The variable $x$ is divided by 2. Because multiplication is the inverse of division, you must multiply each side of the equation by 2.

$$\frac{x}{2} = 17$$
$$2\left(\frac{x}{2}\right) = 2(17)$$
$$x = 34$$

To check your work, replace the variable with your solution and simplify.

When $x = 34$, the equation is true.

Check:
$$\frac{34}{2} = 17$$
$$17 = 17$$

Solve $5x = 75$.

Because the variable $x$ is multiplied by 5, divide both sides of the equation by 5.

$$5x = 75$$
$$\frac{5x}{5} = \frac{75}{5}$$
$$x = 15$$

# ALGEBRA WORD PROBLEMS

Algebra problems describe how several numbers are related. One number is the unknown, represented by a variable. Using the relationships described in the problem, you can write an equation and solve for the variable.

There are twice as many women as men in a class on auto repair. If there are 24 students in the class, how many are women?

- Express the numbers in the problem in terms of the *same* variable. Let $x$ represent the number of men. Because there are twice as many women, let $2x$ represent the number of women.

- Write and then solve an equation. The total number of men and women is 24, so $x + 2x = 24$. Solve:

$$x + 2x = 24$$
$$3x = 24$$
$$x = 8$$

Because $x = 8$, $2x = 2(8) = 16$. There are 8 men and 16 women in the class.

**Consecutive integers** are numbers that are evenly spaced and follow in the counting order. For example, 1, 2, and 3 are consecutive integers. The numbers 2, 4, and 6 are consecutive even integers, and 1, 3, and 5 are consecutive odd integers.

The sum of three consecutive integers is 105. What is the greatest of the three numbers?

- Let $x$ represent the first number and $x + 1$ and $x + 2$ represent the other numbers.

- Write an equation and solve for $x$.

- Find the answer. The variable $x$ represents the first number in the sequence, so the three numbers are 34, 35, and 36. The problem asks for the greatest number, which is 36.

$$x + (x + 1) + (x + 2) = 105$$
$$3x + 3 = 105$$
$$3x = 102$$
$$x = 34$$

# PATTERNS AND FUNCTIONS

A **pattern** is a series of numbers or objects whose sequence is determined by a particular rule. You can figure out what rule has been used by studying the terms you are given. Think: What operation or sequence of operations will always result in the next term in the series? Once you know the rule, you can continue the pattern.

Find the seventh term in the sequence: 1, 2, 4, 8, 16, …

- Determine the rule. Each number in the sequence is two times the number before it.
- Apply the rule. You have been given five terms and must find the seventh. Continue the pattern. The sixth term will be 16 × 2 = 32, and the seventh term will be 32 × 2 = 64.

A **function** is an algebraic rule that shows how the terms in one sequence of numbers are related to the terms in another sequence. For example, a sidewalk vendor charges $1.50 for a slice of pizza. The chart below shows how much it would cost to buy one to six slices.

| Number of Pizza Slices | 1 | 2 | 3 | 4 | 5 | 6 |
|---|---|---|---|---|---|---|
| Cost | $1.50 | $3.00 | $4.50 | $6.00 | $7.50 | $9.00 |

Each number of slices in the first row corresponds to a price in the second row. We could say that the amount a customer will pay is a function of (or depends on) the number of slices the customer orders. This function could be written as follows:

Cost = number of slices × $1.50, or $C = n(\$1.50)$.

If you know the function and a number in the first set of numbers, you can solve for its corresponding number in the second set.

Using the function $y = 3x + 5$, what is the value of $y$ when $x = -3$?

- Substitute the given value of $x$.
- Solve for $y$.

$$y = 3(-3) + 5$$
$$y = -9 + 5$$
$$y = -4$$

Using the function $n = 100 - 4(3 + m)$, what is the value of $n$ when $m = 6$?

- Substitute the given value of $m$.
- Solve for $n$.

$$n = 100 - 4(3 + 6)$$
$$n = 100 - 4(9)$$
$$n = 100 - 36$$
$$n = 64$$

## Solving Function Word Problems

Functions are used in many business applications. For instance, they can be used to calculate profits, costs, employee wages, and taxes.

Anderson Advertising is finishing a series of print ads for a client. Finishing the project will cost $2,000 per day for the first seven days and $3,500 per day after seven days. When finishing the project takes seven days or longer, the finishing costs can be found using the function $C = \$2{,}000d + \$1{,}500(d - 7)$, where $C$ = the cost of finishing the project and $d$ = the number of days. If the project takes 12 days to complete, what will the project cost?

Use the function to solve the problem.

$$
\begin{aligned}
C &= \$2{,}000d + \$1{,}500\left(d - 7\right) \\
&= \$2{,}000(12) + \$1{,}500\left(12 - 7\right) \\
&= \$24{,}000 + \$1{,}500(5) \\
&= \$24{,}000 + \$7{,}500 \\
&= \$31{,}500
\end{aligned}
$$

Nita decides to join a health club. She gets brochures from two health clubs and compares the plans. No Sweat Fitness charges a one-time membership fee of $250 and $8 per month. Freedom Health Center charges $25 per month. At both health clubs, the price ($P$) Nita will pay is a function of the number of months ($m$) she attends the club. The functions are as follows:

No Sweat Fitness $\qquad\qquad\qquad\qquad\qquad$ $P = \$250 + \$8m$

Freedom Health Center $\qquad\qquad\qquad\qquad$ $P = \$25m$

Nita plans to move in 18 months. If she attends a health club until she moves, which one offers the better price?

- Find the price at No Sweat Fitness.

$$
\begin{aligned}
P &= \$250 + \$8m \\
&= \$250 + \$8(18) \\
&= \$250 + \$144 \\
&= \$394
\end{aligned}
$$

- Find the price at Freedom Health Center.

$$
\begin{aligned}
P &= \$25m \\
&= \$25(18) \\
&= \$450
\end{aligned}
$$

- Compare the results. Even though Nita will have to pay a large amount up front, **No Sweat Fitness** offers the better price for 18 months of membership.

# MEAN, MEDIAN, AND MODE

Suppose you were asked how much money you usually spend on groceries in a week. Some weeks you may spend a great deal; other weeks, much less. You would probably choose an amount in the middle to represent what you typically spend. This middle value is called a **measure of central tendency.**

The most common measure of central tendency is the **mean,** or the arithmetic average.

In five football games, a team scored 14, 21, 3, 20, and 10 points. What is the mean, or average, score per game?

- Add the values.
- Divide by the number of items in the data set.

$14 + 21 + 3 + 20 + 10 = 68$

$68 \div 5 = 13.6$ points per game

Although it is impossible for a football team to score 13.6 points in one game, the number represents the average of the scores from the five games.

Another measure of central tendency is the median. The **median** is the middle number in a list of data when the number of items in the list is odd.

During a seven-hour period, a bookstore recorded the following numbers of sales. Find the median number of sales.

| Hour 1 | Hour 2 | Hour 3 | Hour 4 | Hour 5 | Hour 6 | Hour 7 |
|--------|--------|--------|--------|--------|--------|--------|
| 43 | 28 | 24 | 36 | 32 | 37 | 48 |

- Arrange the values in ascending order.
- Find the middle number.

24, 28, 32, 36, 37, 43, 48

24, 28, 32, 36, 37, 43, 48

If there is an even number of values, the median is the mean of the two middle values.

Robert has the following test scores in his math class: 90, 72, 88, 94, 91, and 80.

- Arrange the values in ascending order and find the middle.
- Find the mean of the two middle values. The median score is 89.

72, 80, 88, 90, 91, 94

Add: $88 + 90 = 178$
Divide by 2: $178 \div 2 = 89$

The **mode** is the value that occurs most often in a set of data. A set of data could have more than one mode if two or more items occur the same number of times and these items occur more often than any other items. If each item of data occurs only once, there is no mode.

Six weather stations recorded the following temperatures at 3:00 PM: 45°, 44°, 45°, 47°, 46°, and 45°. What is the mode of the data?

The temperature 45° occurs the most often (three times), so the mode is 45°.

# TABLES AND PICTOGRAPHS

**Data** are facts and information. By analyzing data, we can make predictions, draw conclusions, and solve problems. To be useful, data must be organized in some way. A **table** organizes data in columns and rows. The labels on the table help you understand what the data means.

The table below shows population figures for selected counties in 2000 and 2010 and the land area in square miles for each county.

| County | Adams | Bell | Cook | Davis | Evans |
|---|---|---|---|---|---|
| **2000 Pop.** | 11,128 | 25,199 | 6,532 | 82,204 | 139,519 |
| **2010 Pop.** | 15,295 | 22,707 | 6,518 | 90,834 | 130,748 |
| **Land Area in Sq. Miles** | 4,255 | 2,532 | 2,398 | 1,139 | 321 |

Which county showed the greatest percent increase in population from 2000 to 2010?

- **Read the labels.** The first row shows the county names. The second and third rows show population figures. The fourth row shows land area data. You do not need the land area data to answer this question.

- **Analyze the data.** Only Adams and Davis counties show increases from 2000 to 2010.

- Use the data. Find the percent increase for Adams and Davis counties.

  Adams: $\dfrac{15{,}295 - 11{,}128}{11{,}128} \approx 0.374 \approx 37\%$     Davis: $\dfrac{90{,}834 - 82{,}204}{82{,}204} \approx 0.105 \approx 10\%$

**Adams County** shows the greatest percent increase in population from 2000 to 2010.

A **pictograph** is another way to display data. Pictographs use symbols to compare data. A key shows what value each symbol represents.

A city has three public library branches. A librarian kept track of the numbers of books checked out from each branch in a week. He used the data to create the pictograph below.

| Branches | Books checked out from 3/4 to 3/10 |
|---|---|
| **North** | ▱ ▱ ▱ ▱ ▱ ▱ ▱ |
| **South** | ▱ ▱ ▱ ▱ ▱ |
| **West** | ▱ ▱ ▱ ▱ ▱ ▱ ▱ ▱ ▱ |
| Key: ▱ = 150 books | |

From March 4 to March 10, how many books were checked out from the South and West branches combined?

- There are $4\frac{1}{2}$ symbols for the South branch and 9 symbols for the West branch. Add.

  $4\frac{1}{2} + 9 = 13\frac{1}{2}$ symbols

- Find the value of the symbols. The key states that each symbol equals 150 books. Multiply $13\frac{1}{2}$ by 150.

  $13\frac{1}{2} \times 150 = 2{,}025$ books

## Review Two Practice

1.   $4(3) - 2 + (6 + 4 \times 2)$

2.   $5^2 - (5 - 7)(2)$

3.   In the expression $5 + 2 \left[ 7 \left( \dfrac{10^2}{10} \right) + (6 - 2)(3) \right]$, what is the last operation you should perform to find the value of the expression?

   A.   Multiply by 3.
   B.   Subtract 2 from 6.
   C.   Add 5.
   D.   Multiply by 2.
   E.   Find the square of 10.

Write an algebraic expression for each description. Use the variables $x$ and $y$.

4.   A number decreased by seven

5.   The product of 3 and the square of a number, increased by that number

6.   The amount by which $-3$ multiplied by a number is greater than the product of 2 and another number

7.   A Minor League Baseball team is giving a local charity the sum of $1,500 and $0.50 for each ticket over 2,000 sold for one game. Let $x$ represent the number of tickets sold, where $x > 2,000$. Which of the following expressions could be used to find the amount of the donation?

   A.   $1,500 + $0.50x$
   B.   $1,500 + $0.50(2,000)$
   C.   $1,500 + $0.50(2,000 - x)$
   D.   $1,500 + $0.50(x - 2,000)$
   E.   $1,500(2,000 - x)($0.50)$

Simplify the following expressions.

8.   $5 + x^2 - 3 + 3x$

9.   $2y + 5 + 17y + 8$

Evaluate each expression as directed.

10.   Find the value of $6(x + 2) + 7$ when $x = 2$.

11.   Find the value of $3x^2 + 3(x + 4)$ when $x = 3$.

12. Which of the following expressions is equal to $3x^2 + 3(x - 3) + x + 10$?

    A. $x^2 + 9x + 1$

    B. $3x^2 + 4x + 19$

    C. $3x^2 + 2x - 19$

    D. $3x^2 - 2x + 19$

    E. $3x^2 + 4x + 1$

Solve for the variable in each equation.

13. $7x = 63$

14. $23 + m = 51$

15. $-13 = y - 12$

16. $\dfrac{x}{4} = -16$

17. When a number is divided by 4, the result is 32. What is the number?

    A. 8

    B. 28

    C. 36

    D. 128

    E. 512

18. Two houses are for sale on the same street. The second house has 1,000 square feet less than twice the square feet of the first house. Together the houses have 4,400 square feet. What is the square footage of the first house?

19. The Bulldogs won twice as many games as they lost. If they played a total of 36 games, how many did they win?

20. Sylvia scored 10 points better than Wiley on their science exam. Greg scored 6 points less than Wiley. Altogether the students earned 226 points. How many points did Sylvia earn?

    A. 68

    B. 74

    C. 78

    D. 84

    E. 94

21. Which number should come next in the following pattern?

    $-12, -9, -6, -3,$ _____

22. Each term in the second row is determined by the function $y = 2x - 1$.

| $x$ | 1 | 2 | 3 | 4 | 5 | ... | 12 |
|---|---|---|---|---|---|---|---|
| $y$ | 1 | 3 | 5 | 7 | 9 | ... | |

What number belongs in the shaded box?

23. The price per scarf is a function of the number of scarves purchased. The original price per scarf, $5.00, is reduced by 25 cents with each scarf purchased, starting with the second scarf. The table shows the price per scarf for purchases of up to four scarves.

| Number ($n$) of scarves | 1 | 2 | 3 | 4 |
|---|---|---|---|---|
| Cost ($c$) per scarf | $5.00 | $4.75 | $4.50 | $4.25 |

Which of the following was used to determine the prices shown in the table?

A. $c = n(\$5.00 - \$0.25)$

B. $c = \$5.00 - \$0.25(n - 1)$

C. $c = \$5.00 - \$0.25n$

D. $c = \$5.00n - \$0.25$

E. $c = \$5.00n - \$0.25n$

Questions 24–25 refer to the following information.

The Chimney Sweep charges $25 for a chimney inspection. If the customer purchases additional services, $15 of the inspection fee is deducted. Let $s$ = the cost of any additional services. The total cost ($C$) of an inspection and services can be determined by the function $C = \$25 + (s - \$15)$.

24. Jan has her chimney inspected and purchases a smoke guard for $89. How much will she be charged?

25. After an inspection, Ahmed decides to have a new damper installed for $255. How much will he pay?

26. Alicia is considering three job opportunities. At all three jobs, weekly pay ($P$) is a function of the number of hours ($h$) worked during the week. The functions are shown below:

Job 1:     $P = \$9.75h$

Job 2:     $P = \$70 + \$8.40h$

Job 3:     $P = \$380 \times \dfrac{h}{38}$

If Alicia works 30 hours in a week, how much more will she earn at Job 2 than at Job 1?

A. $5.33

B. $29.50

C. $40.50

D. $59.00

E. Not enough information is given.

For each data set in questions 27 and 28, find the mean, median, and mode. Round calculations to the nearest hundredth or cent.

27. Golf scores for 18 holes: 76, 82, 75, 87, 80, 82, and 79

28. Sales totals for 6 weeks: $5,624; $10,380; $8,102; $6,494; $12,008; and $8,315

29. What is the median value of $268; $1,258; $654; $1,258; $900; $1,588; and $852?

    A. $1,258
    B. $960
    C. $900
    D. $913
    E. $852

Use the following table to answer questions 30 and 31.

| County | Adams | Bell | Cook | Davis | Evans |
|---|---|---|---|---|---|
| 2000 Pop. | 11,128 | 25,199 | 6,532 | 82,204 | 139,519 |
| 2010 Pop. | 15,295 | 22,707 | 6,518 | 90,834 | 130,748 |
| Land Area in Sq. Miles | 4,255 | 2,532 | 2,398 | 1,139 | 321 |

30. On average, how many people were there per square mile in Bell County in 2010? (Round your answer to the nearest integer.)

31. To the nearest percent, what was the percent decrease in Evans County's population from 2000 to 2010?

Question 32 refers to the following table.

32.

| Percentage of three-year-old children with school-readiness skills for the years 2004 and 2010 | | |
|---|---|---|
| | 2004 | 2010 |
| Recognizes all letters | 13% | 15% |
| Counts to 20 or higher | 37% | 41% |
| Writes own name | 22% | 24% |
| Reads or pretends to read | 68% | 70% |

A community had 350 three-year-old children in 2010. Based on the table, how many were able to write their own names?

    A. 22
    B. 77
    C. 84
    D. 140
    E. 273

# ANSWERS AND EXPLANATIONS

## Review Two Practice

1.  **24**

2.  **29**

3.  **C**

The operations in the brackets must be performed first. Once these are completed, you would multiply by 2 and then add 5. Notice that it is not necessary to find the value of the expression to answer the question.

4.  $x - 7$

5.  $3x^2 + x$

6.  $-3x - 2y$

7.  **D**

Here, $x$ represents the number of tickets sold. The expression $x - 2,000$ is the number of tickets over 2,000 sold. Multiply this expression by \$0.50 to find the amount donated based on ticket sales. Add \$1,500 to this product. Only choice (D) performs these operations.

8.  $x^2 + 3x + 2$

9.  $19y + 13$

10. **31**

11. **48**

12. **E**

Simplify the expression.

$$3x^2 + 3(x - 3) + x + 10$$
$$= 3x^2 + 3x - 9 + x + 10$$
$$= 3x^2 + 4x + 1$$

13. $x = 9$

14. $m = 28$

15. $y = -1$

16. $x = -64$

17. **D**

When $x$ is divided by 4, the result is 32. Solve for $x$.

$$\frac{x}{4} = 32$$
$$4 \cdot \frac{x}{4} = 4 \times 32$$
$$x = 128$$

18. **1,800 sq ft**

Call the first house $f$ and the second house $s$. Set up two equations with the information given: the first equation is $2f - 1,000 = s$, and the second equation is $f + s = 4,400$. Isolate $s$ in the second equation: $s = 4,400 - f$. Now take the two expressions that are equal to $s$ and set them equal to each other: $2f - 1,000 = 4,400 - f$. Add $f$ and 1,000 to each side to get $3f = 5,400$. Finally, divide both sides by 3 to get $f = 1,800$.

19. **24 games**

Label the number of games that the Bulldogs lost as $x$ and the number of games that they won as $2x$. The total number of games played was 36, so $x + 2x = 36$. Combine like terms to get $3x = 36$. Divide both sides by 3 to get $x = 12$. The number of games won equals $2x$, and $2(12) = 24$.

20. **D**

Let $x$ = Wiley's points, $x + 10$ = Sylvia's points, and $x - 6$ = Greg's points. Write and solve an equation:

$$x + x + 10 + x - 6 = 226$$
$$3x + 4 = 226$$
$$3x = 222$$
$$x = 74$$

The question asks for Sylvia's points, so $x + 10 = 74 + 10 = 84$.

**21.** 0

**22.** 23

We're looking for the $y$ value when $x$ is 12. Plug 12 into the given equation and solve for $y$.

**23.** B

The price per scarf starts at $5.00 and decreases by $0.25 for every scarf after the first one. Represent this decrease as $0.25(n − 1)$, where $n$ is the number of scarves being sold. Subtract this amount from the starting point, which is $5.00: $c = \$5.00 − \$0.25(n − 1)$.

**24.** $99

Simplifying the equation $C = \$25 + (s − \$15)$ yields $C = \$10 + s$. To find Jan's cost, add $10 to the service cost of $89.

**25.** $265

Again, work with the simplified equation $C = \$10 + s$. To find Ahmed's cost, add $10 to the service cost of $255.

**26.** B

Use the functions for the two jobs, substituting 30 hours for $h$.

Job 1:  $P = \$9.75h$
   $= \$9.75(30)$
   $= \$292.50$

Job 2:  $P = \$70 + \$8.40h$
   $= \$70 + \$8.40(30)$
   $= \$70 + \$252$
   $= \$322$

Subtract:  $\$322 − \$292.50 = \$29.50$.

**27.** mean: 80.14; median: 80; mode: 82

**28.** mean: $8,487.17; median: $8,208.50; mode: none

**29.** C

The median is the middle number. Arrange the amounts in order and find the middle value.

**30.** 9

Divide Bell County's 2010 population by its land area: $22{,}707 ÷ 2{,}532 \approx 9$.

**31.** 6%

Find the difference in population from 2000 − 2010 and divide it by the original (2000) population: $(139{,}529−130{,}768) ÷ 139{,}519 \approx 0.06$. That's approximately 6%.

**32.** C

In 2010, 24% of three-year-old children could write their own name. Find 24% of 350: $0.24 × 350 = 84$.

## Review Three

# INTERPRETATION OF GRAPHS

## Bar Graphs

A **bar graph** uses bars to represent values. Bar graphs have two axis lines. One line shows a number scale, and the other shows labels for the bars. By comparing the length of a bar to the scale, you can estimate what value the bar represents.

A national corporation made a bar graph (shown below) to show the number of discrimination complaints made by employees during a six-year period. About how many more complaints were made in 1999 than in 1998?

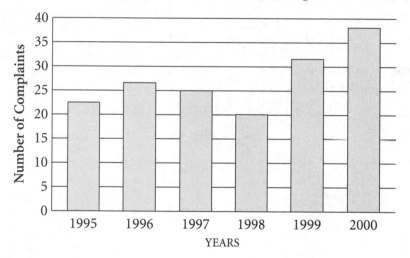

Employee Discrimination Complaints

- **Read the labels.** Each bar represents the number of complaints made within a year. The years are shown beneath the bars.

- **Analyze the data.** Compare the bars for 1998 and 1999 to the scale. There were 20 complaints in 1998 and about 32 complaints in 1999.

- **Use the data.** Subtract: 32 − 20 = 12. There were about 12 more complaints in 1999 than in 1998.

A **double-bar graph** compares more than one type of data.

A studio released four films in one year. The graph below compares the cost of making each movie to its box office receipts, or ticket sales. Film B's cost is approximately what percent of its box office receipts?

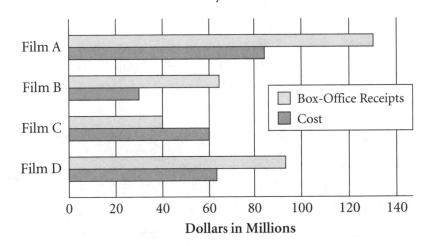

Profit Analysis for Four Films

- **Read the labels.** Read the key to find the meaning of the bars. Notice that the scale represents millions of dollars.

- **Analyze the data.** Film B's cost is about $30 million. It brought in about $65 million in receipts.

- **Use the data.** Find what percent $30 is of $65.

The percent that $30 is of $65 is
$$\frac{\$30}{\$65} = 0.462 \approx 46\%$$

# LINE GRAPHS

A **line graph** is useful for showing changes over time. By analyzing the rise and fall of the line, you can tell whether a value is increasing, decreasing, or staying the same. Like a bar graph, a line graph has two axis lines. One is marked with a scale; the other is (usually) marked in regular time intervals.

The graph below shows the number of patients who visited an emergency room for the treatment of scooter-related injuries.

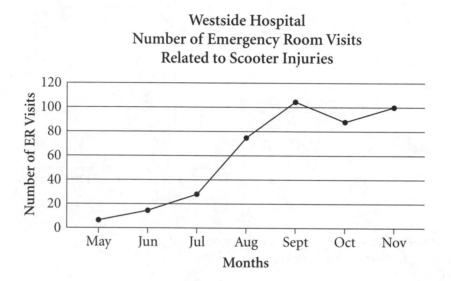

**Westside Hospital**
**Number of Emergency Room Visits**
**Related to Scooter Injuries**

During what month was there a decrease in the number of emergency room visits for scooter-related injuries from the previous month?

The points on the graph are positioned above the months, which are arranged in calendar order. By examining the line that connects the points, you can tell whether there was an increase or decrease from one month to the next.

You can tell a lot about the information in a line graph even if you don't look at the exact values. Because the scale on the vertical axis increases from bottom to top, a line that slopes up from left to right shows an increase over time. Likewise, a line that slopes down from left to right shows a decrease during that period of time.

In this graph, there is only one segment that does not slope up from left to right—the segment from September to October. This means that there was a decrease in scooter-related injuries in **October** from September.

The steepness of a line can also be informative. A steeper line indicates a faster rate of change than a flatter line. In this graph, the line from July to August is the steepest, indicating that the largest one-month increase occurred during that period. (This can be confirmed by actually reading the values and comparing them.)

If a line graph has more than one line, a key will tell you what each line represents.

The graph below shows the changes in ticket prices for two amusement parks.

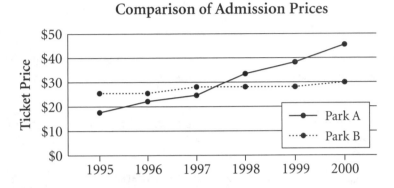

**Comparison of Admission Prices**

What was the last year in which the admission price to Park B was greater than the admission price to Park A?

- The admission prices for Park A are represented by a solid line. Park B's prices are shown with a dotted line. The graph begins in 1995. In 1995, Park B's ticket price is greater than Park A's. Follow the two lines to the right. Between 1997 and 1998, the lines cross, and Park A's prices climb higher than Park B's. **The year 1997** was the last time that Park B charged more than Park A for a ticket.

# CIRCLE GRAPHS

A **circle graph,** or **pie chart,** is used to show how a whole amount is broken into parts. The sections of a circle graph are often labeled with percents. The size of each section corresponds to the fraction it represents. For example, a section labeled 25% will be $\frac{1}{4}$ of the circle.

A graph below shows how a children's sports camp spends its weekly budget.

**Sports Camp Weekly Budget = $2,250**

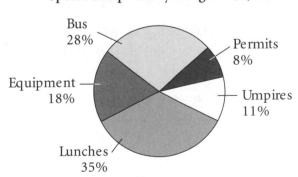

How much does the sports camp spend on lunches each week?

- **Analyze the graph.** According to the heading, the entire circle represents the camp's weekly budget of $2,250. Find the section labeled "lunches." According to the section label, lunches make up 35% of the weekly budget.
- **Use the data.** To find the amount spent on lunches, find 35% of $2,250: $2,250 × 0.35 = **$787.50**.

A circle graph may also be labeled using fractions or decimals. One common kind of circle graph labels each section in cents to show how a dollar is used.

According to the graph, what percentage of the average energy bill is spent on drying clothes, lighting, and heating water?

**Where Do Your Energy Dollars Go?**

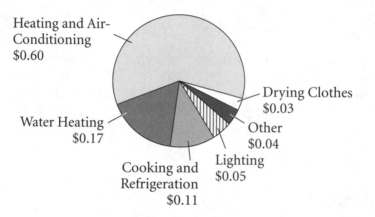

- **Analyze the graph.** The entire circle represents $1. The amounts in the sections mentioned in the problem are $0.03, $0.05, and $0.17.
- **Use the data.** Add the amounts: $0.03 + $0.05 + $0.17 = $0.25. Because $0.25 is 25% of a dollar, **25%** of an average bill is spent on these items.

# THE NUMBER LINE AND SIGNED NUMBERS

**Signed numbers** include zero, all positive numbers, and all negative numbers. Zero is neither positive nor negative. On a number line, the positive numbers are shown to the right of zero, and the negative numbers are shown to the left.

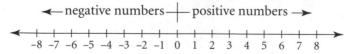

A positive number may be written with a plus (+) sign. If a number has no symbol, it is assumed to be positive. A negative number *must* be preceded by a minus (–) sign.

A signed number provides two important facts. The sign indicates the direction from zero on a number line, and the number indicates the distance from zero. For example, −5 lies five spaces to the left of zero, and +4 lies four spaces to the right of zero.

## Adding and Subtracting Signed Numbers

You can use a number line to model the addition of signed numbers.

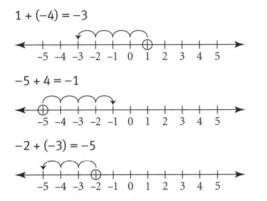

$1 + (−4) = −3$

Begin at +1; move 4 units in a negative direction (left).

$−5 + 4 = −1$

Begin at −5; move 4 units in a positive direction (right).

$−2 + (−3) = −5$

Begin at −2; move 3 units in a negative direction (left).

To add without a number line, follow these steps:

- If numbers have like signs, add the numbers and keep the same sign.
- If the numbers have unlike signs, find the positive difference between the two numbers and use the sign of the larger number.

Add $15 + (−25)$.

- Because the numbers have unlike signs, subtract: $25 − 15 = 10$.
- Use the sign from the larger number: $15 + (−25) = −10$.

Subtraction is the opposite of addition. To rewrite a subtraction problem as an addition problem, change the operation symbol to addition and change the sign on the number you are subtracting. Then apply the rules for adding signed numbers.

Subtract $3 − 8$.

- Change the operation and the sign of the number you are subtracting. So, $3 − 8$ becomes $3 + (−8)$.
- Add: $3 + (−8) = −5$.

# POWERS AND ROOTS

**Powers** are a special way to show repeated multiplication. For example, suppose you need to multiply $5 \times 5 \times 5 \times 5$. This series of operations can be expressed as "five raised to the fourth power." In other words, the number 5 appears in the expression 4 times.

We can write these operations using **exponents**. In the expression $5 \times 5 \times 5 \times 5$, the number 5 is the base. The exponent, a number written slightly above and to the right of the base, indicates how many times the base is repeated: $5 \times 5 \times 5 \times 5 = 5^4$.

To evaluate an expression, perform the multiplication indicated by the exponent.

Find the value of $2^5$.

Write the base out the number of times indicated by the exponent and multiply.

$2^5 = 2 \times 2 \times 2 \times 2 \times 2 = 32$

There are certain instances of exponents to make note of:

1. A number raised to the exponent 1 equals itself. For example, $8^1 = 8$.
2. A number other than zero raised to the exponent zero equals 1. Example: $6^0 = 1$.
3. A number raised to a negative exponent is equal to a fraction with a numerator of 1 and the term with a positive exponent in the denominator. Example:

$$4^{-2} = \frac{1}{4^2} = \frac{1}{4 \times 4} = \frac{1}{16}$$

A square root of a number $n$ is a number that, when squared, equals the number $n$. Every positive number has two square roots. One square root of a positive number is positive, and one square root of a positive number is negative. For example, the square roots of 25 are 5 and −5. This is because $5^2 = 25$ and $(-5)^2 = 25$. The number 0 has only one square root, 0.

By convention, if $x$ is positive, $\sqrt{x}$ means the positive square root of $x$. Whenever there is a $\sqrt{\phantom{x}}$ symbol, this means the positive square root. We have mentioned that 25 has two square roots, which are 5 and −5. However, $\sqrt{25}$ is unambiguous; it means the positive square root of 25. Therefore, we write $\sqrt{25} = 5$.

Find the value of $\sqrt{144}$.

- We know that $12 \times 12 = 144$.
- So $\sqrt{144} = 12$.
- Note that $\sqrt{144}$ is unambiguous. It means 12.

# INEQUALITIES

An **inequality** is a mathematical statement that connects two unequal expressions. Here are the inequality symbols and their meanings:

$>$ greater than $\qquad$ $\geq$ greater than or equal to

$<$ less than $\qquad$ $\leq$ less than or equal to

An inequality is solved much like an equation. Use inverse operations to isolate the variable.

Solve for $x$ in the inequality $3x + 2 < 8$.

- Subtract 2 from both sides.
- Divide both sides by 3.

$$3x + 2 < 8$$
$$3x < 6$$
$$x < 2$$

The solution $x < 2$ states that any number less than 2 makes the inequality true. Check by substituting 1 (a number less than 2) for $x$: $3(1) + 2 < 8$, which simplifies to $5 < 8$, a true statement.

Note that if an inequality is multiplied or divided by a negative number, the direction of the inequality is reversed. For instance, if both sides of the inequality $-3x < 2$ are multiplied by $-1$, the result is $3x > -2$.

# PERIMETER, AREA, AND VOLUME

**Perimeter** is the distance around a figure. To find the perimeter, simply add the lengths of the sides. For common figures, you can apply a formula to find the perimeter.

| square | Perimeter = 4 × side | $P = 4s$ |
|---|---|---|
| rectangle | Perimeter = 2 × length + 2 × width | $P = 2l + 2w$ |
| triangle | Perimeter = side$_1$ + side$_2$ + side$_3$ | $P = a + b + c$ |

A rectangle is 16 inches long and 9 inches wide. What is the perimeter of the rectangle?

Use the formula:

Perimeter = 2 × length + 2 × width

$\qquad$ = 2 × 16 + 2 × 9

$\qquad$ = 32 + 18

$\qquad$ = 50 inches

**Area** is the measure of the space inside a flat figure. Area is measured in square units. For example, if the sides of a figure are measured in inches, its area will be measured in square inches. The formulas for finding area are shown below.

| | | |
|---|---|---|
| square | Area = side$^2$ | $A = s^2$ |
| rectangle | Area = length × width | $A = lw$ |
| parallelogram | Area = base × height | $A = bh$ |
| triangle | Area = $\frac{1}{2}$ × base × height | $A = \frac{1}{2}bh$ |
| trapezoid | Area = $\frac{1}{2}$(base$_1$ + base$_2$) × height | $A = \frac{1}{2}(b_1 + b_2)h$ |

Three of the formulas mention two new measures: base and height. The **base** is one side of the figure. The **height** is the length from a vertex to the base, forming a right angle to the base.

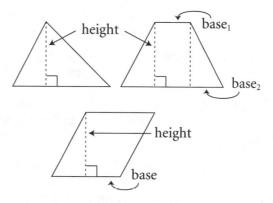

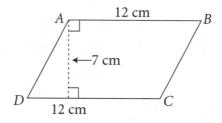

Find the area of polygon *ABCD*.

- Identify the figure. *ABCD* is a parallelogram.
- Find the data that you need. To use the formula for finding the area of a parallelogram, you need to know the height and the length of the base. You do not need to know the length of sides *BC* or *AD*.

- Use the formula: area = base × height.

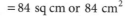

Area = 12 × 7

= 84 sq cm or 84 cm$^2$

# CIRCLES: CIRCUMFERENCE AND AREA

A **circle** is a closed, linear figure all of whose points are the same distance from a single point, the center of the circle. The **circumference** of a circle is its perimeter, or the distance around the circle. The area of a circle is the space inside the circle.

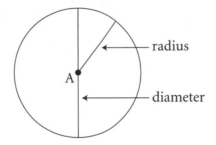

To find the circumference and area of a circle, you need to know certain measurements of the circle. The **diameter** is a line segment with endpoints on the circle that passes through the center of the circle. The **radius** is a line segment that connects the center of the circle to a point on the circle. The radius is one-half the diameter.

The formulas for the circumference and area of a circle use a special quantity called pi ($\pi$). Pi is the ratio of the circumference to the diameter. Pi is approximately 3.14. The formula for the circumference $C$ of a circle is $C = \pi \times$ diameter, or $C = \pi d$. The circumference of a circle is related to the radius $r$ of the circle by $C = 2\pi r$. The formula for the area $A$ of a circle is $A = \pi \times$ radius$^2$, or $A = \pi r^2$.

A china plate has a gold rim. If the plate's diameter is 10.5 inches, what is the distance around the rim to the nearest tenth of an inch?

- The diameter of the circle is 10.5 in.
- Use the formula $C = \pi d$:

$$C = \pi d$$
$$\approx 3.14(10.5)$$
$$= 32.97, \text{ or about 33 inches}$$

The circular surface of a satellite component must be covered with heat-resistant tiles. If the radius of the circular surface is 4 meters, what is the area of the circular surface in square meters?

- The radius of the circle is 4 m.
- Use the formula $A = \pi r^2$:

$$A = \pi r^2$$
$$= 3.14\left(4^2\right)$$
$$= 3.14(16)$$
$$= 50.24 \text{ square meters}$$

What is the circumference of circle *B* to the nearest tenth of a centimeter?

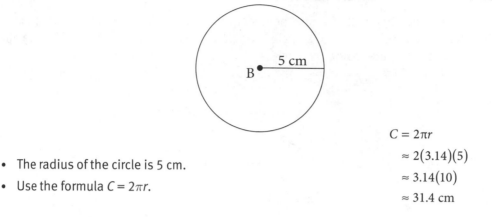

- The radius of the circle is 5 cm.
- Use the formula $C = 2\pi r$.

$$C = 2\pi r$$
$$\approx 2(3.14)(5)$$
$$\approx 3.14(10)$$
$$\approx 31.4 \text{ cm}$$

# VOLUME

**Volume** is the measure of space inside a three-dimensional object. Volume is measured in cubic units. For example, if the sides of an object are measured in inches, the volume is the number of cubes with an edge of one inch that would be needed to fill the object.

Many common three-dimensional objects have at least two identical and parallel faces. Think of a cereal box or soup can. Both objects have identical faces at the top and bottom. Either of these faces can be called the base of the object. To find the volume of any container with identical bases, multiply the area of one base by the height of the object: volume = area of base × height.

Another way to find the volume of an object is to use the formula that applies specifically to that object. Three common regular solids are rectangular solids, cubes, and cylinders.

| rectangular solid | Volume = length × width × height | $V = lwh$ |
| cube | Volume = edge$^3$ | $V = e^3$ |
| cylinder | Volume = $\pi$ × radius$^2$ × height | $V = \pi r^2 h$ |

A **rectangular solid** has two identical rectangular bases. The remaining sides of the solid are also rectangles.

A cardboard box has the dimensions shown in the diagram. What is the volume of the box in cubic feet?

- Use the formula $V = lwh$:

$$V = lwh$$
$$= 5(4)(3) = 60 \text{ cubic feet}$$

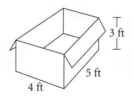

A cube is a rectangular solid with six identical faces. In a cube, each edge is the same length.

A wood block measures 2 inches on each edge. What is the volume of the block?

- Use the formula $V = e^3$:

$$V = e^3$$
$$= 2^3 = 2 \times 2 \times 2 = 8 \text{ cubic inches}$$

A **cylinder** has two circular bases. The bases are connected by a curved surface. Cans, barrels, and storage tanks are often in the shape of cylinders.

A storage tank has a radius of 1.5 meters. What is the volume of the tank to the nearest cubic meter?

- Use the formula $V = \pi r^2 h$:

$$V = \pi r^2 h$$
$$\approx 3.14(1.5^2)(3) = 21.195 \text{ m}^3,$$

which rounds to 21 cubic meters

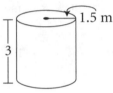

## WORKING WITH IRREGULAR FIGURES

An irregular figure combines geometric figures to form a new shape. To find the perimeter of an irregular figure, simply add the lengths of all the sides. You may need to deduce the lengths of some of the sides using the measures given for the other sides.

A family room has the dimensions shown in the diagram. All measurements are in feet. What is the perimeter of the room?

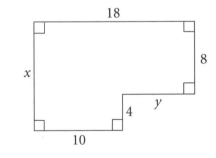

- Find the missing measurements. Measurement $x$ equals the combined lengths of the two opposite walls: $x = 8 + 4 = 12$ ft. You also know that $18 - 10 = y$, so $y = 8$ ft.
- Add all the distances to find the perimeter: $12 + 18 + 8 + 8 + 4 + 10 = 60$ ft.

To find the area of an irregular figure, break the figure into parts. Then apply the correct formula to each part.

What is the area of this figure in square centimeters?

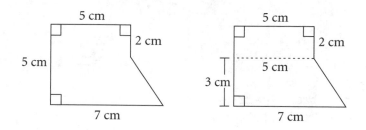

- Divide the figure into two shapes and find any missing measurements. Here, the figure is divided into a trapezoid and a rectangle.

- Calculate the area of each shape.

  Rectangle: $A = lw$

  $$= 2(5) = 10 \text{ sq cm}$$

  Trapezoid: $A = \dfrac{1}{2}(b_1 + b_2)h$

  $$= \dfrac{1}{2}(5+7)(3) = \dfrac{1}{2}(12)(3)$$
  $$= 6 \times 3 = 18 \text{ sq cm}$$

- Combine: $10 + 18 = 28$ sq cm.

## Review Three Practice

Questions 1 and 2 refer to the following graph.

1. To the nearest ten, how many employee discrimination complaints were there in 1995 and 1996 combined?

2. About how many more complaints were there in 2000 than in 1995?

Questions 3 and 4 refer to the following graph.

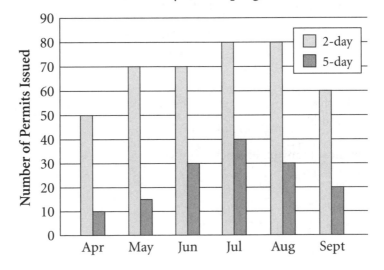

3. In May, what was the ratio of the number of 2-day permits to the number of 5-day permits?

    A. 2:5

    B. 3:14

    C. 3:17

    D. 14:3

    E. 14:17

4. In which month was a total of 80 permits issued?

    A. May

    B. June

    C. July

    D. August

    E. September

Questions 5 and 6 refer to the following graph.

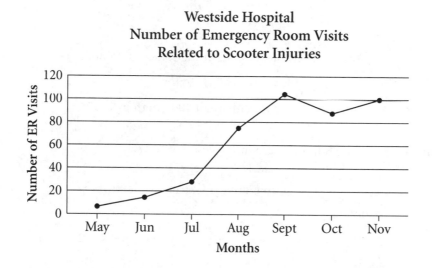

5. In which month did the number of scooter-related injuries increase by the greatest amount over the previous month?

6. To the nearest ten, how many emergency room visits were caused by scooter injuries in August, September, and October?

Questions 7 and 8 refer to the following graph.

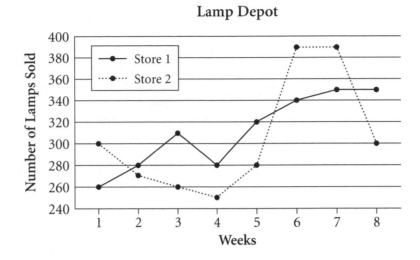

7. About how many more lamps were sold at Store 2 than at Store 1 in week 6?

   A. 110

   B. 50

   C. 40

   D. 25

   E. 20

8. During which week did Store 1 experience the greatest increase in sales over the week immediately before?

   A. Week 2

   B. Week 3

   C. Week 4

   D. Week 5

   E. Week 6

Question 9 refers to the following graph.

**Sports Camp Weekly Budget = $2,250**

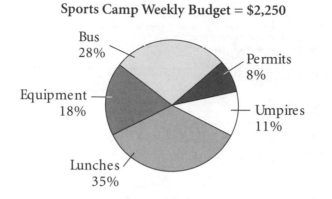

9.     What percentage of the total sports camp budget is spent on equipment and umpires?

Question 10 refers to the following graph.

**Where Do Your Energy Dollars Go?**

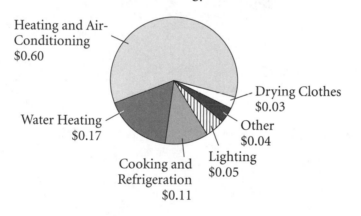

10.     Which expense is more than 50% of an energy dollar?

Question 11 refers to the following graph.

The employees of National Bank are given the following graph to explain how their retirement fund is invested.

**How Your Retirement Dollar Is Invested**

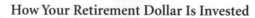

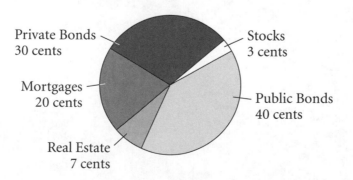

11. What percentage of each retirement dollar is invested in real estate and stocks?

    A. 4%
    B. 10%
    C. 40%
    D. 90%
    E. 100%

For questions 12–14, simplify the expressions.

12. $8 + (-3)$

13. $-1 + 2$

14. $6 - (-3) + (-5) + 8$

15. At noon, the temperature in the high desert was 92°F. A scientist observed the following temperature changes over the course of the next two hours: +12°, −5°, +6°, −3°, and +13°. What was the temperature at the end of the two-hour period?

    A. 53°
    B. 95°
    C. 103°
    D. 115°
    E. 131°

For questions 16–18, simplify each expression.

16. $3^2$

17. $4^1$

18. $\sqrt{49}$

19. A cube has an edge length of 6 inches. Which of the following expressions represents the volume of the cube?

    A. $6^2$
    B. $6(12)$
    C. $6(4^2)$
    D. $6^3$
    E. $3(6^3)$

For questions 20–22, simplify the inequalities.

20. $3x - 7 > 5$

21. $\dfrac{4 + x}{5} > 8$

22. $-4(x + 2) < 24$

23. Three added to the product of $-4$ and a number $x$ is less than 5 added to the product of $-3$ and the number. Which of the following is a graph of the solution set of $x$?

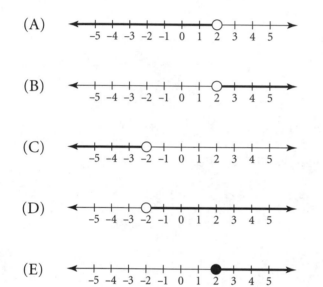

(A)

(B)

(C)

(D)

(E)

For questions 24 and 25, find the area and perimeter of each figure.

24.

25.

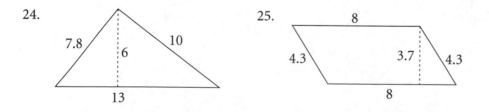

26. The four sides of a parallelogram measure 9 feet, 6 feet, 9 feet, and 6 feet. What is the area of the parallelogram in square feet?

   A. 30

   B. 36

   C. 54

   D. 81

   E. Not enough information is given.

Find the approximate circumference and area of the circle. Round answers to the nearest whole number.

27.

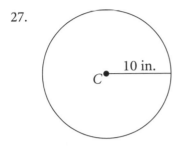

Question 28 refers to the following drawing.

28. If workers lay a tile border around the edge of the fountain shown in the diagram, how many feet long will the border be to the nearest foot?

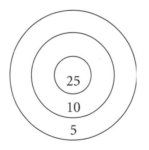 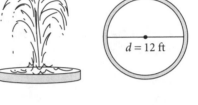

A. 19
B. 36
C. 38
D. 57
E. 113

29. On the target below, the 5- and 10-point bands are each 2 inches wide, and the inner circle has a diameter of 2 inches.

To the nearest inch, what is the outer circumference of the 10-point band?

A. 6
B. 13
C. 19
D. 25
E. Not enough information is given.

For questions 30 and 31, find the volume of each object to the nearest whole unit.

30.

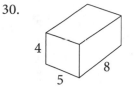

31.

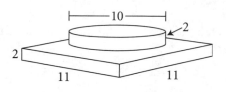

32. A wooden crate measures 5 feet along each edge. What is the crate's volume in cubic feet?

   A. 15
   B. 25
   C. 125
   D. 150
   E. Not enough information is given.

33. Find the volume of the entire figure to the nearest cubic unit.

# ANSWERS AND EXPLANATIONS

## Review Three Practice

1. **50**

2. **About 15**

3. **D**

Write a ratio and simplify: $\dfrac{70}{15} = \dfrac{14}{3}$ .

4. **E**

Add the 2-day and 5-day permits for each month. Only September's permits equal 80: 60 + 20 = 80 permits.

5. **August**

6. **270**

7. **B**

There were 390 sales in Store 2 and 340 sales in Store 1 in the sixth week. So, 390 − 340 = 50.

8. **D**

The steepest line segment is for the time period for week 4 (between week 4 and week 5), an increase of 40 sales.

9. **29%**

10. **Heating and air-conditioning**

11. **B**

Add: 3 cents + 7 cents = 10 cents. Then 10 cents out of 100 cents is $\dfrac{10}{100}$ , or 10%.

12. **5**

13. **1**

14. **12**

15. **D**

Begin with 92°. Then perform the following operations: 92° + 12° − 5° + 6° − 3° + 13° = 115°.

16. **9**

17. **4**

18. **7**

19. **D**

The volume of a cube is the length of an edge cubed. The volume of this cube is $6^3$.

20. $x > 4$

21. $x > 36$

22. $x > -8$

Always remember to flip the direction of an inequality when you multiply or divide both sides by a negative number.

23. **D**

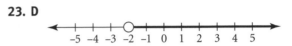

Solve the inequality:

$$-4x + 3 < -3x + 5$$
$$-x < 2$$
$$x > -2$$

To graph the solution $x > -2$, place an open circle at −2 because −2 is not included in the solution. Then extend the line to the right to include all values greater than −2.

24. **area: 39 sq units; perimeter: 30.8 units**

Area of a triangle: $\dfrac{1}{2}$ (base)(height). Perimeter: sum of the lengths of all sides.

25. **area: 29.6 sq units; perimeter: 24.6 units**

Area of a parallelogram: (base)(height)

26. **E**

The formula for the area of a parallelogram uses the base and height of the figure. From the measures of the sides, you cannot determine the height of the parallelogram.

27. $C = 63$ **in.,** $A = 314$ **in.**$^2$

$A = \pi r^2$
$C = 2\pi r$

28. **C**

Use the formula $C = \pi d$, where $d = 12$. Then 12(3.14) $\approx 37.7 \approx 38$.

**29. C**

You need to find the circumference of the 10-point band. First, find the diameter that passes through the circle that includes the 10-point band (but not the outer 5-point band). Add the width of the 10-point band twice and the diameter of the inner circle: 2 + 2 + 2 = 6 inches. Now use the formula for circumference to get 6(3.14) = 18.84, which rounds to 19 inches.

**30. 160 cubic units**

$V = length \times width \times height$

**31. 236 cubic units**

$V = \pi r^2 h$

**32. C**

If each edge measures 5 feet, then the figure is a cube. Use $V = e^3$, so $V = 5^3 = 125$.

**33. $V \approx$ 399 cubic units**

Calculate the volume of the top solid (cylinder) and the bottom solid (rectangular solid) and add the volumes:

$$V_{cyl} = \pi r^2 h = \pi(5)^2(2) \approx 157$$
$$V_{rect} = lwh = (11)(11)(2) = 242$$
Total volume $\approx$ 157 + 242 = 399

Review Four

# POINTS, LINES, AND ANGLES

A **point** is a single location in space. We assign a name to a point by writing a letter next to it. A **plane** is a two-dimensional flat surface. In the drawing, point *A* lies in plane *P*.

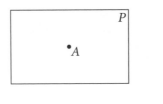

A **line** is a one-dimensional straight path that extends indefinitely in two directions. A line may be named by a single letter or by two points on the line.

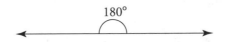
line *s* or $\overleftrightarrow{CD}$

A **ray** is part of a line that begins at the endpoint and extends indefinitely in one direction. A portion of a line with two endpoints is called a **line segment.** Both rays and line segments are named using two points.

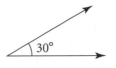
ray: $\overrightarrow{FG}$     segment: $\overline{FG}$

When two rays share an endpoint, they form an **angle**. The shared endpoint is the vertex of the angle. An angle can be named in different ways: by a number or letter written inside the angle, by the name of the vertex, or by the vertex and a point on each ray. The symbol ∠ means angle.

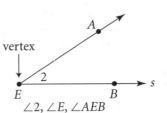
∠2, ∠E, ∠AEB

Angles are measured in degrees, indicated by a number and the degree symbol (°).

A **right angle** forms a square corner and measures 90°. A right angle is often identified by a small square drawn inside it.

right angle symbol

An **obtuse angle** is greater than 90° but less than 180°.

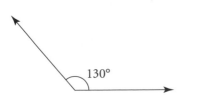
130°

An **acute angle** is less than 90°.

30°

A **straight angle** measures 180°.

180°

A **reflex angle** has a measure greater than 180° but less than 360°.

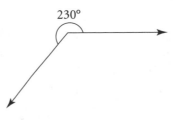
230°

When the sum of two angles is 90°, the angles are **complementary.** When the sum of two angles is 180°, the angles are **supplementary.** You can use this information to solve for a missing angle measure.

In the drawing, $\angle AOB$ and $\angle BOC$ are complementary. What is the measure of $\angle AOB$?

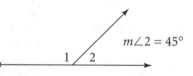

- The measure of angle *BOC* is given as 23°, or $m\angle BOC = 23°$. The sum of the angles is 90°. Therefore, $\angle AOB$ measures 67°.

$$m\angle AOB + 23° = 90°$$
$$m\angle AOB = 90° - 23°$$
$$m\angle AOB = 67°$$

In the drawing, $\angle 1$ and $\angle 2$ are supplementary. What is the measure of $\angle 1$?

- It's given that $\angle 2$ measures 45°. The sum of the angles is 180°. Thus, $\angle 1$ measures 180° − 45° = 135°.

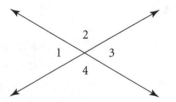

$$m\angle 2 = 45°$$

# PARALLEL LINES AND TRANSVERSALS

When two lines intersect, they form two pairs of vertical angles. **Vertical angles** have the same angle measure. In the drawing, $\angle 1$ and $\angle 3$ are vertical angles, as are $\angle 2$ and $\angle 4$.

Intersecting lines also form adjacent angles. **Adjacent angles** share a common ray. For example, $\angle 1$ and $\angle 2$ are adjacent angles. The adjacent angles in this figure are supplementary angles because their sum is the measure of a straight angle.

If you know the measure of one angle, you can find the measure of the other three angles.

In the figure above, $m\angle 1 = 35°$. What are the measures of $\angle 2$, $\angle 3$, and $\angle 4$?

- Because $\angle 1$ and $\angle 2$ are supplementary, their sum equals 180°. Solve for $\angle 2$.

$$m\angle 2 + 35° = 180°$$
$$m\angle 2 = 145°$$

- Angles 1 and 3 are vertical, so both measure 35°. Angles 2 and 4 are vertical, so both measure 145°.

**Parallel lines** are lines that never intersect. This means that their distance from each other remains constant. The symbol for parallel is ||. A **transversal** is a line that intersects two or more other lines. When a transversal intersects two parallel lines, special angle relationships are formed.

In the drawing, *M*||*N*. The transversal, line *P*, forms eight angles.

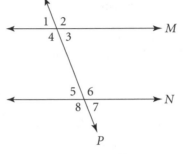

Each angle matches another angle in the same position on the transversal. These angles, called **corresponding angles**, always have the same measure. The corresponding angles are ∠1 and ∠5, ∠2 and ∠6, ∠3 and ∠7, and ∠4 and ∠8.

**Alternate exterior angles**, which are also equal in measure, are on opposite sides of the transversal and are on the outside of the parallel lines. One pair of alternate exterior angles is ∠1 and ∠7, and the other is ∠2 and ∠8.

**Alternate interior angles** are on opposite sides of the transversal and are inside the parallel lines. One pair of alternate interior angles is ∠3 and ∠5; the other is ∠4 and ∠6. Alternate interior angles are always equal in measure.

In the figure, *C*||*D*. If $m\angle 4 = 48°$, what is the measure of ∠5?

- There are many ways to solve the problem. Here is one way: ∠4 and ∠8 are corresponding angles, so $m\angle 8 = 48°$.

- Then ∠8 and ∠5 are supplementary angles, so $m\angle 5 + 48° = 180°$, and $m\angle 5 = 132°$.

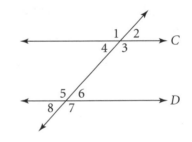

# TRIANGLES

A **triangle** is a closed three-sided figure. From the definition, we can infer other properties. Because a triangle has three sides, it must also have three interior angles and three vertices.

A triangle is named by writing its vertices in any order. The triangle shown here could be named Δ*DEF*. Its sides are *DE*, *EF*, and *DF*.

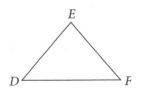

Triangles can be classified by the lengths of their sides and by the measures of their angles. In the triangles in this section, sides with the same number of marks are equal.

## Triangles Classified by Side Lengths

**Equilateral triangle:** All sides are equal in length. Note that the angles are equal as well.

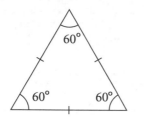

**Isosceles triangle:** Exactly two sides are equal in length. Note that the two angles opposite these sides are equal.

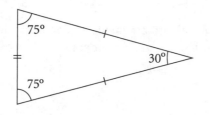

**Scalene triangle:** No sides are equal in length, and no angles are equal.

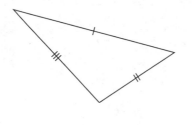

## Triangles Classified by Angle Measures

**Right triangle:** One angle measures 90°.

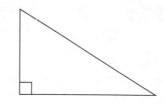

**Acute triangle:** All angles measure less than 90°.

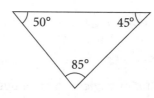

**Obtuse triangle:** One angle is greater than 90°.

Each triangle can be classified in two ways.

What kind of triangle is $\triangle PQR$?

- Classify by its sides: Two sides have the same length, so $\triangle PQR$ is an isosceles triangle.
- Classify by its angles: $\angle P$ is a right angle, so $\triangle PQR$ is a right triangle.

$\triangle PQR$ is a **right isosceles triangle**.

The sum of the measures of the interior angles for any triangle is 180°. We can use this fact to solve for a missing angle.

In $\triangle ABC$, $\angle A$ measures 55° and $\angle B$ measures 100°. What is the measure of $\angle C$?

- Write an equation and solve.

$$55° + 100° + \angle C = 180°$$
$$155° + \angle C = 180°$$
$$\angle C = 25°$$

The measure of $\angle C$ is 25°.

# COMPARING TRIANGLES

Figures are **congruent** (indicated by the symbol ≅) when they have exactly the same size and shape. In other words, two figures are congruent if their corresponding parts (the angles and sides) are congruent. You can often tell that two geometric shapes are congruent by sight. However, in geometry, you must be able to prove that figures are congruent.

Two triangles are congruent if the following corresponding parts are congruent:

**Side-Side-Side (SSS)**     The side measures for both triangles are the same.

**Side-Angle-Side (SAS)**     Two sides and the angle between them are the same.

**Angle-Side-Angle (ASA)**     Two angles and the side between them are the same.

Are triangles $ABD$ and $BCD$ congruent?

- Find the known corresponding parts: $\angle ABD \cong \angle CBD$ and $\angle ADB \cong \angle CDB$. Both triangles share side $BD$.
- Is this enough information to prove that the triangles are congruent? Yes, two angles and the side between them are equal. Using the ASA rule, $\triangle ABD \cong \triangle BCD$.

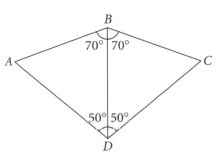

# UNDERSTANDING SIMILARITY

Figures are **similar** (shown by the symbol ~) when the corresponding angles are congruent and the corresponding sides are in proportion. In other words, similar figures always have the same shape, but they do not have to be the same size.

There are two rules that you can use to prove that two triangles are similar:

**Rule 1:** If two angle measures in the first triangle are equal to two angle measures in the second triangle, the triangles are similar.

**Rule 2:** If all corresponding sides have the same ratio, the triangles are similar.

Are triangles *JKL* and *MNO* similar?

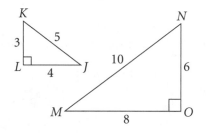

- Compare corresponding angles. Because only one angle measure is given, you cannot use Rule 1 to prove that the triangles are similar.

- Write ratios comparing the sides in the first triangle to the corresponding sides in the second triangle. Each ratio is equal to $\frac{1}{2}$.

$$\frac{\triangle JKL}{\triangle MNO} = \frac{3}{6} = \frac{4}{8} = \frac{5}{10} = \frac{1}{2}$$

Because the ratios are equal, the triangles are similar: $\triangle JKL \sim \triangle MNO$.

# QUADRILATERALS

A **quadrilateral** is a closed shape with four sides.

A **rectangle** is a four-sided figure with four right angles. The opposite sides (sides across from each other) are the same length, and they are parallel.

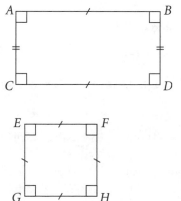

A **square** is actually a kind of rectangle. It, too, has four right angles with parallel opposite sides. However, a square has one additional property: its four sides are all the same length.

A **parallelogram** is a four-sided figure whose opposite sides are parallel and the same length. In addition, its opposite angles (the angles diagonally across from each other) are also equal in measure. A special parallelogram, called a **rhombus** (not shown), has four sides of equal length.

A **trapezoid** (not shown) is a four-sided figure with only two parallel sides.

All quadrilaterals have one important property in common. The sum of the measures of the interior angles is 360°. You can use this fact to find a missing angle measure.

In figure *ABCD,* the opposite sides are parallel. What is the measure of $\angle A$?

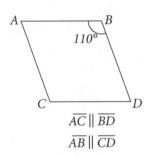

- Identify the figure. Because the opposite sides are parallel, the figure is a parallelogram.

- Find the measure of $\angle C$. The opposite angles of a parallelogram are equal in measure; therefore, $m\angle C = m\angle B$. Both $\angle B$ and $\angle C$ measure 110°.

- Because all of the angles in the figure must total 360° and $\angle A$ and $\angle D$ are equal, you can solve for $\angle A$.

$$\overline{AC} \parallel \overline{BD}$$
$$\overline{AB} \parallel \overline{CD}$$

$$2 \times m\angle A + 110° + 110° = 360°$$
$$2 \times m\angle A = 140°$$
$$m\angle A = 70°$$

# THE ENGLISH SYSTEM OF MEASUREMENT

Measurements are used to describe an object's length, weight, or volume. We also use measurement to describe a quantity of time. The United States uses the English, or standard, system of measurement. Study the lists below to learn the common standard units and their abbreviations.

### Measurement Equivalencies

**Length**

1 foot (ft) = 12 inches (in.)

1 yard (yd) = 3 ft

**Volume**

1 cup (c) = 8 fluid ounces (fl oz)

1 pint (pt) = 2 c

1 quart (qt) = 2 pt

1 gallon (gal) = 4 qt

**Weight**

1 pound (lb) = 16 ounces (oz)

1 ton (t) = 2,000 lb

To change a larger unit of measurement to a smaller one, you need to multiply.

A picture frame is 3 feet 8 inches long. What is the length of the frame in inches?

- Change 3 feet to inches using the fact that 1 foot = 12 inches.          $3 \text{ ft} \times 12 = 36 \text{ in.}$
- Add the remaining 8 inches. The picture frame is 44 inches in length.          $36 + 8 = 44 \text{ in.}$

To change a smaller unit of measure to a larger one, divide using the appropriate measurement equivalency.

A package weighs 84 ounces. What is the weight of the package in pounds?

- Change 84 ounces to pounds. Because 1 pound = 16 ounces, divide by 16.
- The remainder is in ounces, the same unit you started with. Therefore, the package weighs 5 lb 4 oz. You can also express the remainder as a fraction:

$$16 \overline{)84} \quad \begin{matrix} 5 \\ -80 \\ \hline 4 \end{matrix}$$

$$5\frac{4 \text{ oz}}{16 \text{ oz}} = 5\frac{1}{4} \text{ lb}$$

In a measurement problem, you may need to add, subtract, multiply, or divide measurements. When finding a sum or a difference, remember that you can only add or subtract like measurement units.

A deck requires pieces of railing that are 5 feet 9 inches, 15 feet 4 inches, and 8 feet 6 inches. What is the total length of railing needed?

- Write the measurements in a column, aligning like units of measure.
- Add like units.
- Simplify the answer. Change 19 inches to 1 feet 7 inches and add this result to 28 feet. The deck requires 29 feet 7 inches of railing.

$$\begin{matrix} 5 \text{ ft} & 9 \text{ in.} \\ 15 \text{ ft} & 4 \text{ in.} \\ +8 \text{ ft} & 6 \text{ in.} \\ \hline 28 \text{ ft} & 19 \text{ in.} \end{matrix}$$

When you subtract, you may need to regroup, or borrow.

How much more is 4 pounds 3 ounces than 2 pounds 8 ounces?

- Align the values in the problem. Because you cannot subtract 8 ounces from 3 ounces, regroup 1 pound from the pounds column and add it to the ounces column as 16 ounces.
- Subtract. The difference is 1 pound 11 ounces.

$$\begin{matrix} & 3 & & 19 \\ & \cancel{4} \text{ lb} & & \cancel{3} \text{ oz} \\ -2 & \text{lb} & 8 & \text{oz} \\ \hline 1 & \text{lb} & 11 & \text{oz} \end{matrix}$$

To multiply a measurement by a whole number, multiply the units of measure separately. Then simplify the result.

Tony has five lengths of plastic pipe, each measuring 6 feet 10 inches. What is the combined length of the five pieces of pipe?

- Multiply each part of the measurement by 5.
- Simplify using the fact 1 feet = 12 inches. The combined length is 34 feet 2 inches.

$$
\begin{array}{r}
6\text{ ft }10\text{ in} \\
\times \quad 5 \\
\hline
\end{array}
$$

30 ft 50 in =

30 ft + 4 ft 2 in =

34 ft 2 in

To divide a measurement, you can divide each part of the measurement and then add the results. However, it will usually be faster to rewrite the measurement in terms of the smallest unit of measure. Then divide and simplify.

John has 1 pint 5 fluid ounces of liquid lawn fertilizer. He plans to mix one-third of the liquid with two gallons of water and apply it to his lawn. How many fluid ounces of fertilizer will he use?

- Change the amount to ounces.

1 pt = 2 c = 16 fl oz

1 pt + 5 fl oz = (16 + 5) fl oz = 21 fl oz

- To find one-third, divide by 3. John will use 7 fluid ounces of lawn fertilizer.

21 fl oz ÷ 3 = 7 fl oz

## THE METRIC SYSTEM

The **metric system** is the measurement system used in most countries of the world. The main unit of length in the metric system is the **meter** (m). The **gram** (g) is the basic metric measure of mass (or weight). The basic unit of volume is called the **liter** (l).

The units of measurement in the metric system are named by adding prefixes to the basic units. The prefixes have specific meanings:

*milli-* means one-thousandth         *deka* or *deca-* means ten

*centi-* means one-hundredth          *hecto-* means hundred

*deci-* means one-tenth               *kilo-* means thousand

Therefore, a kilometer (km) equals 1,000 meters, a milligram (mg) equals a one-thousandth gram, and a centiliter (cl) equals a one-hundredth liter.

As in the decimal place-value system, each column on the chart below is 10 times the column to its right. To convert between metric units, count the number of times that you must move to the right or left from the unit you are converting from to the unit you are converting to. Then move the decimal point that number of place values in the same direction.

| kilo- (km) 1,000 m | hecto- (hm) 100 m | deka- (dam) 10 m | meter (m) 1 m | deci- (dm) 0.1 m | centi- (cm) 0.01 m | milli- (mm) 0.001 m |
|---|---|---|---|---|---|---|

*Note:* Although the chart uses the meter as the basic unit, the chart can also be used with liters and grams.

How many millimeters (mm) are equal to 3 centimeters (cm)?

- Find *milli-* and *centi-* on the chart. The prefix *milli-* is one place to the right of the prefix *centi-*; therefore, you need to move the decimal point one place to the right to convert from centimeters to millimeters.
- So, 3 cm = 3.0 cm = 30 mm.

How many grams (g) are equal to 6,400 (mg)?

- Start in the *milli-* column. The basic unit is three columns to the left. Move the decimal point three place-value columns to the left.
- So, 6,400 mg = 6.4 g.

Metric measurements are written as decimal numbers. Therefore, you can perform operations with metric measurements using the rules for adding, subtracting, multiplying, and dividing decimals.

Three metal rods measure 1.5 meters, 1.85 meters, and 450 centimeters. What is the total length of the rods in meters?

- The first two measures are in meters. Convert the third measure to meters: 450 cm = 4.5 m.
- Use the rules for adding decimals. The total is 7.85 meters.

$$\begin{array}{r} \overset{1}{1.5} \\ 1.85 \\ +\,4.5 \\ \hline 7.85 \end{array}$$

Follow the same steps to subtract.

Tanya is jogging in a city park. The park has a path for joggers that is 2 kilometers in length. When she reaches the 750-meter checkpoint, how many kilometers does she have left to run?

- Change 750 meters to kilometers: 750 m = 0.75 km.
- Subtract using the rules for subtracting decimals. Tanya has 1.25 kilometers left to run.

$$\begin{array}{r} \overset{1\ \ 9\ 10}{2.\cancel{0}\cancel{0}} \\ -0.75 \\ \hline 1.25 \end{array}$$

Multiplying and dividing is easy in the metric system. Follow the rules for multiplying and dividing decimals.

Alex is a buyer at Rugs Plus. He plans to order 25 acrylic rugs to sell in the store. The shipping weight for each rug is 7.8 kilograms. What is the shipping weight in kilograms of the entire order?

- Multiply the weight of one rug (7.8 kg) by 25.
- The weight of 25 rugs is 195 kilograms. Notice that the answer has the same unit of measure as the number you multiplied.

$$
\begin{array}{r}
7.8 \\
\times\ 25 \\
\hline
390 \\
1560 \\
\hline
195.0
\end{array}
$$

At a food-processing plant, a storage tank holds 92.4 liters of a fruit drink. It takes three hours for a machine to empty the tank into small containers. How many liters of fruit drink are processed per hour?

- To find the number per hour, divide 92.4 liters by 3.
- The machine can process 30.8 liters per hour.

$$
\begin{array}{r}
30.8 \\
3{\overline{\smash{\big)}\,92.4}} \\
\underline{9\phantom{2.4}} \\
24 \\
\underline{-24} \\
0
\end{array}
$$

# ESTIMATION

Some questions ask for an **estimate** rather than an exact value. Here are some estimation techniques to practice.

Approximately how many people attended the three-game series if attendance at the games was 33,541, 35,045, and 34,092, respectively?

- The problem asks for the *approximate* number of people; therefore, you can estimate. Notice that all three amounts are close to 35,000.

  $33,541 \approx 35,000$

  $35,045 \approx 35,000$

  $34,095 \approx 35,000$

- Multiply 35,000 by 3 to find that the approximate attendance for the three-game series was 105,000.

  $35,000 \times 3 = 105,000$

If Ambrose wants to save enough money to make a $1,159 purchase a year from now, approximately how much should he save per month?

- The problem asks for the *approximate* amount; therefore, you can estimate. Divide to find how many equal parts are in the total money to be saved. Because 1 year = 12 months, divide $1,159 by 12.

- Round one or both of the numbers so that they are easy to divide. Here, rounding $1,159 to $1,200 makes the division simple. Ambrose needs to save about $100 a month.

  $1,200 ÷ 12 = $100 per month

Estimation can also be used to help you narrow down answer choices in multiple-choice questions or to check your calculations.

Souvenir sales are $389, $205, and $276 at each of three booths. What is the total amount in sales?

A.  $615
B.  $870
C.  $999
D.  $1,523
E.  $2,621

## Strategy 1

You can estimate an answer by rounding values to the nearest hundred. The closest option to $900 is (B) $870.

$400 + $200 + $300 = $900

## Strategy 2

You can calculate an answer and then check it against an estimate to see whether your answer makes sense. The solution (B) $870 is close to an estimate of $900.

$389 + $205 + $276 = $870

## Review Four Practice

For questions 1 and 2, classify each angle based on its angle measure.

1. 55°

2. 270°

Questions 3 and 4 refer to the figure provided.

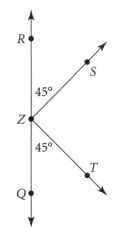

3. ∠QZR is a straight angle. What is the measure of ∠QZS?
   A. 135°
   B. 125°
   C. 90°
   D. 60°
   E. 45°

4. What kind of angle is ∠SZT?
   A. Acute
   B. Obtuse
   C. Right
   D. Straight
   E. Reflex

Questions 5 and 6 refer to the figure provided.

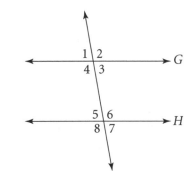

5. List one pair of alternate interior angles.

6. Which angle corresponds to ∠7?

7. Which of the following is a true statement about corresponding angles?
   A. They are also vertical angles.
   B. They are also supplementary angles.
   C. They are in the same position with respect to the parallel lines.
   D. They are also alternate interior angles.
   E. They are also alternate exterior angles.

Question 8 refers to the following figure.

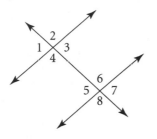

8. The measure of ∠7 is 115°. What is the measure of ∠4?

   A.  25°

   B.  65°

   C.  115°

   D.  245°

   E.  Not enough information is given.

Classify the triangle in two ways.

9.

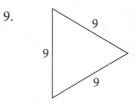

Find the measure of the unknown angle in the triangle.

10.

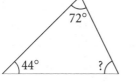

Decide whether the pairs of triangles are congruent. Write Yes, No, or Not Enough Information.

11.

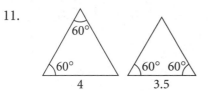

12.

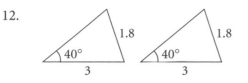

Question 13 refers to the figure provided.

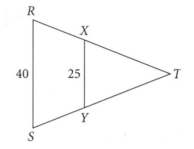

13. If $XY \parallel RS$, $m\angle S = 68°$, and $m\angle T = 48°$, then what is the measure of $m\angle TXY$?

    A. 48°

    B. 64°

    C. 68°

    D. 116°

    E. 135°

List the names of quadrilaterals with the following properties. Write None if no quadrilateral has the given property.

14. Four right angles

15. Opposite sides are equal in length

16. Exactly one pair of parallel sides

Question 17 refers to the figure provided.

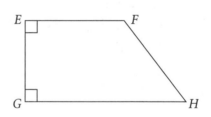

17. $\angle F$ is 20° more than three times the measure of $\angle H$. What is the measure of $\angle F$?

    A. 40°

    B. 60°

    C. 120°

    D. 140°

    E. 180°

18. How many inches are equal to 4 feet?

19. How many minutes are equal to 420 seconds?

Question 20 refers to the following information.

| Portable Air Cooler |
| --- |
| Duracool R612 |
| 3.75 gallon capacity |
| Runs 6 hours without refilling |
| Width: 27 in.; depth: 16 in. |
| Height: $13\frac{13}{4}$ in. |
| Shipping weight: 26 lb |

20. Bob wants to buy an air cooler. He knows the capacity of several other models in quarts. Which of the following expressions could he use to find the capacity for this model in quarts?

    A. $3.75 \times 2$

    B. $3.75 \div 2$

    C. $3.75 \times 4$

    D. $3.75 \div 4$

    E. $3.75 \times 8$

21.    3 hr 30 min

       4 hr 20 min

    +2 hr 45 min
    _____

22.    3 gal 1 qt

    −1 gal 3 qt
    _____

23. Nydia works in a photo lab. She uses 1 pint 6 fluid ounces of film developer from a full container. If the capacity of the container is 3 quarts, how much developer is left in the container?

    A. 2 qt 10 fl oz

    B. 2 qt 6 fl oz

    C. 2 qt 2 fl oz

    D. 2 qt

    E. 1 qt 10 fl oz

24. How many meters equal 5 kilometers?

25. Six hundred centimeters equal how many meters?

26.  How many milligrams equal 4 grams?

27.  In a vitamin supplement, each capsule contains 500 milligrams of vitamins. How many grams of vitamins are found in each capsule?

A.  5,000
B.  500
C.  50
D.  5
E.  0.5

Solve questions 28 and 29 as directed. Pay special attention to the label given for each answer.

28.  5.4 cm + 19 cm + 2.85 cm = _____ cm

29.  12 kg + 10.5 kg + 120 g = _____ g

30.  To make a carbonated punch, Kay Lynn adds six cans of club soda to 2 liters of cranberry juice. If each can holds 355 milliliters, how many liters of punch has Kay Lynn made?

A.  4.13
B.  4.26
C.  5.55
D.  23.3
E.  37.5

# ANSWERS AND EXPLANATIONS

## Review Four Practice

1. **Acute**
2. **Reflex**
3. **A**

$m\angle RZS + m\angle QZS = 180°$. Because $\angle RZS$ measures 45°, $\angle QZS$ must measure 135°.

4. **C**

Because $m\angle RZQ = 180°$, subtract the two known angles to find the measure of $\angle SZT$: $180° - 45° - 45° = 90°$. Because $\angle SZT$ measures 90°, it is a right angle.

5. **∠4 and ∠6, ∠3 and ∠5**
6. **∠3**
7. **C**
8. **B**

$\angle 7$ and $\angle 3$ are corresponding angles, so $m\angle 7 = m\angle 3$; therefore, $m\angle 3 = 115°$. $\angle 3$ and $\angle 4$ are adjacent angles, which means that $115° + m\angle 4 = 180°$. $m\angle 4 = 65°$

9. **equilateral, acute**
10. **64°**
11. **No**

The angles in the two triangles are equal but the sides are not.

12. **Not enough information**

This is Angle, Side, Side, which is not one of the congruent structures; the triangles may or may not be congruent.

13. **B**

Because $XY$ is parallel to $RS$ and $m\angle S = 68°$, then $m\angle TYX = 68°$. $m\angle TYX + m\angle T + m\angle TXY = 180°$. Substitute and solve. $68° + 48° + m\angle TXY = 180°$ and $m\angle TXY = 64°$.

14. **Rectangle, square**
15. **Parallelogram, rectangle, square, rhombus**
16. **trapezoid**
17. **D**

Let $x$ = the measure of $\angle H$. $3x + 20° = m\angle F$. The sum of the angles of a quadrilateral is 360°, so $3x + 20° + x + 90° + 90° = 360°$. Solve the equation.

$$4x + 200° = 360°$$
$$4x = 160°$$
$$x = 40°$$

so $3x + 20° = 140°$.

18. **48 in.**
19. **7 min**
20. **C**

4 qt = 1 gal, so multiply the number of gallons by 4 to find the number of quarts.

21. **10 hr 35 min**
22. **1 gal 2 qt**
23. **A**

3 qt = 2 qt 2 pt = 2 qt 1 pt 16 fl oz

Subtract.

```
  2 qt 1 pt 16 fl oz
−      1 pt  6 fl oz
  ─────────────────
  2 qt      10 fl oz
```

**24. 5,000 m**

**25. 6 m**

**26. 4,000 mg**

**27. E**

There are 1,000 milligrams in 1 gram. $500 \div 1,000 = 0.5$ g

**28. 27.25 cm**

**29. 22,620 g**

Convert all values to grams before attempting to add: 12 kg (1,000 g/kg) = 12,000 g; 10.5 kg (1,000 g/kg) = 10,500 g.

**30. A**

Multiply the number of milliliters of soda in a can by the number of cans: 355 ml × 6 = 2,130 ml. Convert to liters: 2,130 ml ÷ 1,000 = 2.13 l. Add the liters of soda and juice: 2.13 l + 2 l = 4.13 l.

# PRACTICE

## Directions

Each of the questions in this practice is a multiple-choice question with one correct answer unless otherwise indicated. Practice is not timed, but remember that, on the official exam, you will have approximately one and one-half minutes per question on average. Be on the lookout for alternative approaches that may save you time on some questions.

Note: Just as on the exam, the figures accompanying problems in this practice set are intended to provide information useful in solving the problem. The figures are drawn as accurately as possible unless the problem indicates that the figure is not drawn to scale. Figures can be assumed to lie in a plane unless the problem states otherwise. Lines shown as straight can be assumed to be straight, and the position of points can be assumed to be in the order shown. A right angle is denoted by the symbol ∟.

1. Eight paper slips are placed in a bag to be drawn as a science assignment. Each slip is labeled with the name of a different planet: Mercury, Venus, Earth, Mars, Jupiter, Saturn, Uranus, and Neptune. What is the probability of drawing at random a slip labeled with the name of a planet that does NOT start with the letter *M*?

   A. $\dfrac{1}{4}$

   B. $\dfrac{1}{3}$

   C. $\dfrac{3}{8}$

   D. $\dfrac{3}{4}$

   E. $\dfrac{5}{6}$

2. The user's manual for a stereo set includes a scale diagram in which 2 scaled inches represent 8 actual inches. If the speakers of the stereo set measure 6 inches tall in the diagram, how tall are they in reality?

   A. 1 foot 6 inches

   B. 1 foot 8 inches

   C. 1 foot 10 inches

   D. 2 feet

   E. 2 feet 2 inches

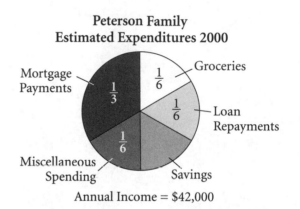

**Peterson Family
Estimated Expenditures 2000**

Annual Income = $42,000

3. The pie chart shown above represents the estimated expenditures of the Peterson family in 2000. How much did the Petersons manage to save that year?

   A. $5,000

   B. $6,000

   C. $7,000

   D. $8,000

   E. $9,000

4. If the area of the rectangle above is 15, what is its perimeter?

   A. 5

   B. 8

   C. 15

   D. 16

   E. 21

5. If $26 - y = 2x + 14 + y$, what is the value of $x + y$ ?

   A. 1

   B. 2

   C. 3

   D. 6

   E. 8

**Questions 6–7 refer to the following graph.**

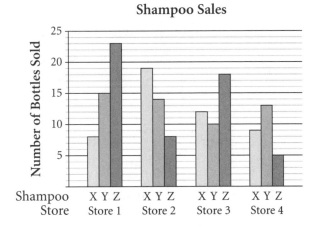

6. In how many of the stores studied were there at least twice as many bottles of shampoo X sold as there were of shampoo Z ?

   A. None

   B. One

   C. Two

   D. Three

   E. Four

7. What fraction of the total number of shampoo bottles sold at store 3 were bottles of shampoo Y ?

   A. $\dfrac{1}{4}$

   B. $\dfrac{1}{5}$

   C. $\dfrac{1}{6}$

   D. $\dfrac{1}{8}$

   E. $\dfrac{1}{10}$

8. What value times 0.15 is 525 ?

   A. 3.5

   B. 35

   C. 350

   D. 3,500

   E. 35,000

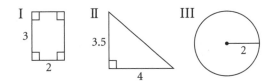

9. Which of the figures above has an area of 6 ?

   A. I only

   B. I and II

   C. II and III

   D. I and III

   E. I, II, and III

10. Which of the following, when divided into 137, leaves a remainder of 5 ?

    A. 12

    B. 10

    C. 9

    D. 8

    E. 4

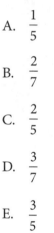

11. Which of the following is greater than 1.25?

    A. 125%

    B. $\dfrac{3}{2}$

    C. 0.125

    D. 12.5%

    E. $\dfrac{2}{3}$

12. A bus carries 15 sixth graders, 18 seventh graders, 12 eighth graders, and no other students. What fraction of the total number of students on the bus are seventh graders?

    A. $\dfrac{1}{5}$

    B. $\dfrac{2}{7}$

    C. $\dfrac{2}{5}$

    D. $\dfrac{3}{7}$

    E. $\dfrac{3}{5}$

13. To find 36 times 4, you could multiply what number by 12 ?

    A. 8

    B. 10

    C. 12

    D. 14

    E. 16

14. If $T$ is 40% of 900, then $T =$

    A. 300

    B. 320

    C. 360

    D. 380

    E. 400

15. What is the maximum number of points of intersection between a rectangle and a circle if both lie on a plane?

    A. 1

    B. 2

    C. 4

    D. 6

    E. 8

16. {15, 13, 6, 15, 8, 3, 24, 12, 5}

    What is the median of the above set?

    A. 6

    B. 8

    C. 12

    D. 13

    E. 15

**Questions 17–18 refer to the following graph.**

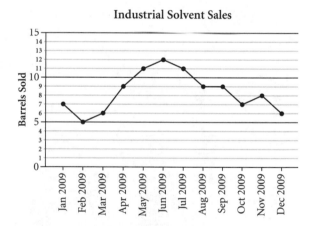

17. How many barrels of industrial solvent were sold in January 2009?

    A. 4

    B. 5

    C. 6

    D. 7

    E. 8

18. How many barrels of industrial solvent were sold in June and July of 2009 combined?

    A. 16
    B. 19
    C. 23
    D. 25
    E. 28

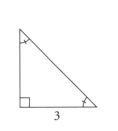

19. What is the area of the isosceles right triangle shown above?

    A. 3
    B. 3.5
    C. 4
    D. 4.5
    E. 6

20. If $J + 2 = \dfrac{K}{4}$, then $J =$

    A. $K - 2$
    B. $2K - 2$
    C. $\dfrac{K}{2} - 4$
    D. $\dfrac{K}{4} - 2$
    E. $4K - 4$

21. Of the following expressions, which is NOT equivalent to the others?

    A. $4 \times 48 \times 8$
    B. $4 \times 8 \times 48$
    C. $4^2 \times 12 \times 8$
    D. $4^2 \times 12 \times 2$
    E. $4^2 \times 3 \times 2$

22. A Ferris wheel has 12 cars that can seat up to 3 people each. If every car on the Ferris wheel is full except for 2 that contain 2 people and 1 that is empty, how many people are currently riding on the Ferris wheel?

    A. 30
    B. 31
    C. 32
    D. 36
    E. 40

23. If $(H)(J)(K) = J - (K \times H)$, then $(-3)(6)(2) =$

24. The four shapes below are made up of identical equilateral triangles. Which of the four shapes, if any, has the *least* perimeter?

    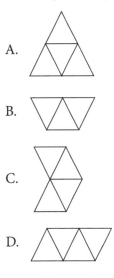

    E. All have the same perimeter.

25. Nine temperature readings are taken, one reading every four hours, with the first reading taken at noon. When will the final reading be taken?

    A. midnight
    B. 8:00 AM
    C. noon
    D. 4:00 PM
    E. 8:00 PM

26. Which of the figures below, if any, has a perimeter value in units that is the same as the value of its area in square units?

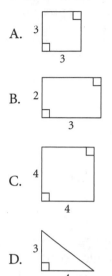

A.

B.

C.

D.

E. None has a perimeter equal to its area.

27. If the length, $x$, of a rectangle is doubled and its width, $y$, is divided by 3, then the area of the new rectangle is given by which formula?

A. $xy$

B. $2xy$

C. $\dfrac{2xy}{3}$

D. $3xy$

E. $6xy$

28. Apple pie is served only on every even-numbered day in February.

Ice cream is served only on days in February that are multiples of three.

If both statements above are true, and if there are 28 days in February, then it is valid to conclude that both apple pie and ice cream are served on how many days in February?

A. 2

B. 3

C. 4

D. 5

E. 6

29. What is the average (arithmetic mean) of $\dfrac{3}{5}$ and $\dfrac{9}{2}$ ?

A. $\dfrac{51}{10}$

B. $\dfrac{45}{10}$

C. $\dfrac{51}{20}$

D. $\dfrac{45}{20}$

E. $\dfrac{45}{40}$

30. Which of the following represents 89,213 written in scientific notation?

A. $8921.3 \times 10$

B. $892.13 \times 10^2$

C. $89.213 \times 10^3$

D. $8.9213 \times 10^4$

E. $0.89213 \times 10^5$

# ANSWERS AND EXPLANATIONS

## Practice

### 1.  D

The probability of an event is equal to the number of favorable outcomes divided by the number of possible outcomes. In this case, the number of slips labeled with a planet name that does *not* start with the letter *M* will be the number of favorable outcomes. As two of the eight planets have names starting with *M*, six do not. The number of favorable outcomes divided by the number of possible outcomes is $\frac{6}{8}$, which can be simplified to $\frac{3}{4}$, choice (D).

### 2.  D

This problem requires you to determine a scale factor and to apply that to a given measurement. Because 2 scaled inches on the diagram equal 8 inches in reality, a scale factor of $8 \div 2 = 4$ is being used. Since the speakers measure 6 inches in the diagram, multiply this by the scale factor to find their height in reality: $6 \times 4 = 24$. Because the answer choices are in feet and inches, convert 24 inches to feet by dividing 24 inches by 12 inches per foot to calculate that the speakers have an actual height of $24 \div 12 = 2$ feet, choice (D).

### 3.  C

The pie chart provided with this problem does not give the fraction of expenditure represented by savings, but it does give the fraction of expenditure represented by everything else. If $\frac{1}{3}$ is spent on mortgage payments, $\frac{1}{6}$ is spent on groceries, $\frac{1}{6}$ is spent on loan repayments, and $\frac{1}{6}$ represents miscellaneous spending, then these fractions can be subtracted from the whole to find the fraction saved:

$$1 - \frac{1}{3} - \frac{1}{6} - \frac{1}{6} - \frac{1}{6} = 1 - \frac{5}{6} = \frac{1}{6} \text{ saved}$$

Because the Petersons' annual income was $42,000 and $\frac{1}{6}$ of this was saved, $\$42,000 \div 6 = \$7,000$ in savings, choice (C).

### 4.  D

This question requires two steps, one working backward and one working forward. To find the perimeter of a polygon, you must know the length of each side. Here only one is marked. The opposite side is easy to determine because the figure is a rectangle; it is also 3. The other two sides will also be equal to each other but must be found using the other information given: the rectangle has an area of 15. This is where you must work backward. Because the area of a rectangle is determined as $A = lw$, you know that $15 = 3l$. Thus, $l = 5$. You now know that the rectangle has two sides of length 3 and two sides of length 5. To find the perimeter, add them together: $3 + 3 + 5 + 5 = 16$, choice (D).

### 5.  D

Begin by combining like terms:

$$26 - y = 2x + 14 + y$$
$$26 - 14 = 2x + y + y$$
$$12 = 2x + 2y$$

Now it is possible to divide both sides by the common factor of 2:

$$\frac{12}{2} = \frac{2x + 2y}{2}$$

$x + y = 6$, so choice (D) is correct.

### 6.  B

This question asks you to analyze the information in the graph to determine how many stores sold at least twice as many bottles of shampoo X as shampoo Z. Only Store 2 fits, with 19 bottles of shampoo X sold and only 8 of shampoo Z. Choice (B) is correct.

### 7.  A

To find bottles of shampoo Y as a fraction of the total number of shampoo bottles sold at Store 3, first find the total number of bottles sold and then find the number of bottles of shampoo Y sold. Store 3 sold 12 bottles of shampoo X, 10 bottles of shampoo Y, and 18 bottles of shampoo Z. Thus, the fraction is $\frac{10}{12 + 10 + 18} = \frac{10}{40} = \frac{1}{4}$. Choice (A) is correct.

**8.  D**

This question can be solved by creating an equation using $x$ to represent the unknown number of times that 0.15 is being multiplied:

$$525 = 0.15x$$

$$\frac{525}{0.15} = x$$

$$\frac{525 \times 100}{0.15 \times 100} = x$$

$$\frac{52,500}{15} = x$$

$$3,500 = x$$

Choice (D) is correct.

**9.  A**

This problem can most easily be solved by process of elimination. You may notice almost immediately that figure I has an area of 6, which allows you to eliminate choice (C). From there, go ahead to figure II, since II and III appear the same number of times in the remaining answer choices. Because figure II has an area of $\frac{1}{2} \times 3.5 \times 4 = 7$, it does not work, and choices (B) and (E) can be eliminated. To choose between (A) and (D), try figure III next. It has an area of $\pi(2^2) = 4\pi$, so it does not work, and choice (A) must be correct.

**10.  A**

If a number leaves a remainder of 5 when divided into 137, then two things must be true: the number must be greater than 5, and the number must divide evenly into (137 − 5), or 132. Only (A), 12, is greater than 5 and divides evenly into 132.

**11.  B**

To compare values easily, put them in the same form. To solve this problem, convert all values into either decimals or percentages. (B) is correct because $\frac{3}{2}$, or 1.5, is greater than 1.25. (A) is 1.25, (C) is 0.125, (D) is 0.125, and (E) is $0.\overline{66}$.

**12.  C**

This question asks you to identify the correct part-to-whole ratio from among the answer choices. In this

case, the fraction will have the number of seventh graders, 18, as the numerator and the total number of students on the bus, 15 + 18 + 12 = 45, as the denominator. Because $\frac{18}{45}$ is not an answer choice, it must be simplified:

$$\frac{18}{45} = \frac{18 \div 9}{45 \div 9} = \frac{2}{5}$$

Choice (C) is correct.

**13.  C**

This problem can be solved by translating the question into an algebraic equation, with $x$ as the number of times by which 12 must be multiplied:

$$36 \times 4 = 12x$$

$$\frac{36 \times 4}{12} = \frac{12x}{12}$$

$$3 \times 4 = x$$

$$12 = x$$

Choice (C) is correct.

**14.  C**

If $T$ is 40% of 900, then

$$T = 900 \times 40\%$$

$$T = 900 \times \frac{4}{10}$$

$$T = \frac{900 \times 4}{10}$$

$$T = 90 \times 4$$

$$T = 360$$

Choice (C) is correct.

**15.  E**

This question requires that you consider the different ways in which a rectangle and a circle lying on a plane could overlap and determine the maximum number of points of intersection. It might be helpful to sketch various possibilities. If the rectangle is placed so that one side is tangent to the circle, there will be one point of intersection. However, if the rectangle is placed so that each of the four corners overlaps the circumference of the circle, there will be eight points of intersection. It is impossible to sketch a scenario in which the figures share more than eight points of intersection, so choice (E) is correct.

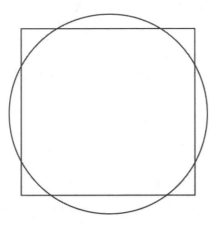

### 16. C

To find the median of a list of values, begin by ordering the values from least to greatest. Thus ordered, this list becomes {3, 5, 6, 8, 12, 13, 15, 15, 24}. Because there is an odd number of values in the list, the median is simply the middle value, which in this case is 12. Choice (C) is correct.

### 17. D

According to the graph, 7 barrels of solvent were sold in January 2009, choice (D).

### 18. C

Locate on the graph the number of barrels of solvent sold in June 2009, 12, and then locate the number of barrels sold in July 2009, 11. The combined number of barrels sold is 12 + 11 = 23 barrels. Choice (C) is correct.

### 19. D

This question asks you to find the area of a given triangle, so you will need the area formula for a triangle: $A = \dfrac{1}{2} \times$ base $\times$ height. Because this is a right isosceles triangle, we know that the height is equal to the base, which measures 3, because they are opposite the congruent angles. Now plug the measurements of the base and height into the area formula:

$$A = \frac{1}{2} \times 3 \times 3 = 1.5 \times 3 = 4.5$$

Choice (D) is correct.

### 20. D

Solve the equation:

$$J + 2 = \frac{K}{4}$$

$$J = \frac{K}{4} - 2$$

Choice (D) is correct.

### 21. E

To determine which answer choice is not equivalent to the rest, first simplify the choices by dividing each by their common factor of 4:

    A.  48 × 8

    B.  8 × 48

    C.  4 × 12 × 8, or 48 × 8

    D.  16 × 12 × 2 = 4 × 4 × 12 × 2 = 48 × 8

    E.  16 × 3 × 2 = 4 × 4 × 3 × 2 = 12 × 8

It is now clear that choice (E) is different.

### 22. B

The question states that each seat on the Ferris wheel can hold 3 people and that all but 3 of the 12 cars are full. Therefore, the 9 full cars containing 3 people each contain a total of 27 people. In addition, we are told that 1 car is empty and 2 cars contain 2 people each, adding 4 people to the 27 in the full cars for a total of 31 people on the Ferris wheel. Choice (B) is correct.

### 23. 12

This type of question involving symbols is a twist on a function problem, and boils down to substitution. Determine which numbers correspond to which letters and then plug them into the equation. Then, follow the order of operations and solve. In this case $H = -3$, $J = 6$, and $K = 2$. Plugging into the defining equation, you get 6 − [2 × (−3)] = 6 − (−6) = 6 + 6 = 12. Enter 12 in the box to receive credit for this question.

## 24. B

Because each figure is composed of identical equilateral triangles, we can call the length of any side of any triangle x. By counting the number of sides that form the perimeter of each figure, we can establish algebraic expressions for the perimeter of each figure.

    A.   has a perimeter of 6x.

    B.   has a perimeter of 5x.

    C.   has a perimeter of 6x.

    D.   has a perimeter of 6x.

Thus, choice (B) has the least perimeter.

## 25. E

The easiest way to solve this problem is to count in increments of four hours until the ninth reading, starting at 12:00 PM: 12:00 PM, 4:00 PM, 8:00 PM, 12:00 AM, 4:00 AM, 8:00 AM, 12:00 PM, 4:00 PM, 8:00 PM. Thus, the ninth reading will be taken at 8:00 PM. Choice (E) is correct.

## 26. C

Calculate the area and perimeter of each figure.

(A)  Area = 3 × 3 = 9 square units. Perimeter = 4 × 3 = 12 units. Eliminate.

(B)  Area = 2 × 3 = 6 square units. Perimeter = 2(2 + 3) = 10 units. Eliminate.

(C)  Area = 4 × 4 = 16 square units. Perimeter = 4 × 4 = 16 units. Correct.

(D)  Area = $\frac{1}{2}$ × 3 × 4 = 6 square units. Perimeter must be greater than 3 + 4 = 7 units. Therefore, perimeter cannot be equal to area for this figure. Eliminate.

## 27. C

When the length of a rectangle, x, is doubled, it becomes 2x. When its width, y, is divided by 3, it becomes $\frac{y}{3}$. The area formula for a rectangle can now be applied to these new dimensions:

$$A = \text{length} \times \text{width} = 2x \times \frac{y}{3} = \frac{2xy}{3}, \text{ choice (C)}.$$

## 28. C

By asking on how many days both apple pie and ice cream will be served in February, this question is asking how many days have numbers that satisfy both the first statement by being even and the second statement by being a multiple of three. To answer, simply count the number of dates in February that are even multiples of three, or multiples of 2 × 3 = 6: the 6th, the 12th, the 18th, and the 24th. Choice (C) is correct.

## 29. C

To find the average (arithmetic mean) of a set of values, divide the sum of the values by the number of values in the set. In this case, a common denominator must be found before $\frac{3}{5}$ and $\frac{9}{2}$ can be added; the lowest common denominator is 10:

$$\frac{3}{5} = \frac{6}{10} = \text{and} \frac{9}{2} = \frac{45}{10}$$

The sum is

$$\frac{6}{10} + \frac{45}{10} = \frac{51}{10}$$

The average is

$$\frac{\frac{51}{10}}{2} = \frac{51}{10} \times \frac{1}{2} = \frac{51}{20}$$

## 30. D

Scientific notation is correctly represented by a value with digits only in the ones place and to the right of the decimal multiplied by a power of 10. The exponent that 10 is raised to represents the number of places the decimal has been moved in order to leave a value with only one digit to the left of the decimal. Only choice (D) is in proper scientific notation, so no calculations need to be made.

# CHAPTER THREE

# Praxis Core Writing

## INTRODUCING PRAXIS CORE WRITING

The Praxis Core Writing test consists of two types of sections that test two very different kinds of writing skills. The first section tests your ability to read sentences, locating and correcting grammatical errors. This is followed by two essay sections, which will test your ability to write a clear, coherent essay in a limited amount of time.

Keep in mind that this test is not designed to discover the next Ernest Hemingway or Maya Angelou. Instead, this test assesses your ability to adhere to the basic rules of written English and to avoid common grammatical errors and traps.

Your approach to the Writing test should vary depending on the section. As with all other sections on the Praxis Core Writing test, strategic time management and understanding what the test maker is looking for are the keys to success.

### LEARNING OBJECTIVES

By the end of this chapter, you will be able to:

- Describe the structure and format of the Praxis Core Academic Skills for Teachers: Writing test
- Outline and employ the Kaplan Method for Praxis Writing
- Apply Praxis Writing strategies
- Refresh basic grammar and usage concepts and rules
- Outline and employ the Kaplan Method for Praxis Essay Writing
- Use the Praxis Core Writing practice test to assess your performance

# KNOW WHAT TO EXPECT

## Test Format

The key to success on any test is knowing what you can expect. The Praxis Core Writing test is no exception. Here's what you'll be up against on the test.

| Praxis Core Writing |
| --- |
| Format: Computer-delivered |
| Number of Questions: 40 multiple-choice (called "selected response" by the test maker); 2 essays |
| Time: 100 minutes (40 minutes for multiple-choice section; 30 minutes each for essays) |
| Essay Types: argumentative; source-based |
| Multiple-choice section may include pre-test questions that do not count toward your score |
| No penalty for incorrect answers |
| Scratch paper is available during the exam (it will be destroyed before you leave the testing center) |

As you can see, there are three sections to the Praxis Core Writing test, and they require different approaches. Your score report will have separate reports for your selected-response questions and your essays. However, keep in mind that the same rules of standard written English are applicable to both the multiple-choice questions and the essay components of the Writing test. We'll cover the grammar rules that are tested most frequently and give you the proven Kaplan strategies for each question type you'll see on your test.

# CORE WRITING: SELECTED-RESPONSE QUESTIONS

Ironically, the selected-response (multiple-choice) section of the Praxis Core Writing test does not require you to do any writing at all. You won't be tested on the names of grammatical terms. You won't need to identify nouns, pronouns, verbs, participles, or gerunds. Whereas a vague sense of how you diagrammed sentences back in the day may help a bit, it's not an essential skill on these questions.

What the selected-response Writing questions do test is your ability to recognize the elements of good writing, including basic grammar, sentence structure, agreement, and word choice.

As you prepare for the test, read everything—and we mean everything—with an eye toward sentence structure. Look for fragments in advertisements. Find run-on sentences in emails from your friends. Ferret out misplaced modifiers in the newspaper. Develop "proofreader's eyes" as you read, read, read your way to success.

As you hone your eyes and get ready to spot errors on the Praxis exam, be sure to fine-tune your ears as well. Develop a more critical ear that notes errors and awkward constructions when you hear them. Frequently, you will have to trust your ear to identify errors and avoid trap answers on test day.

# Introducing the Question Types

Because these question types may be new to you, you should begin by becoming familiar with the structure of the questions and the directions for each question type you will see on your test. Remember, you have only 40 minutes to answer 40 questions on the selected-response section of the Praxis Core Writing test. Getting familiar with the basics of each question type ahead of time will give you an edge when test day rolls around.

There are four main question types on the Core Writing exam: Usage, Sentence Correction, Revision in Context, and Research Skills. Within these four main categories, you may see some variation in the mode of delivery of the questions. The standard modes of delivery are shown below, but be prepared for some variation. Variations may include interactive questions that require some of the following:

- Selecting all of the answer choices that apply
- Constructing a short response in an entry box
- Entering more than one response in different places
- Checking off boxes (usually for all-that-apply questions)
- Selecting regions on a graph or other visual
- Choosing sentences in text
- Moving answer choices onto targets or into positions
- Choosing an answer from a drop-down menu

Each question type will be accompanied by clear directions for how to answer the question, so please read these carefully if you are not familiar with the question's mode of delivery. For additional practice and to build familiarity with the various modes of delivery, please refer to your online resources at **kaptest.com**.

### *Usage Questions*

Usage questions test a wide range of skills, including redundancy, singular versus plural nouns and verbs, pronoun reference, commas, verb tense, and capitalization. For these questions, you will always have four underlined portions of the sentence to choose from, as well as the option "No error." Your task is to choose which of the four underlined portions needs a revision, if any. You don't need to specify what the revision is, just the location of the error. If there is an error in the sentence, it will be in one of the four underlined portions.

The directions for Usage questions will look similar to this:

Directions: Each of the following sentence(s) will have four (4) underlined sections. After reading the sentence(s), decide which (if any) of the underlined portions contains an error of grammar, usage, punctuation, or capitalization. If there is an error, select the portion that has the error. Otherwise, select "No error." Each sentence contains at most one error.

Be sure to select an answer for each question.

Here's what a sample question might look like:

Even though he had to supervise a large staff, his salary was no greater
A.            B.                                                    C.

than a clerk. No error
D.                E.

The game you're playing with Usage questions is "Spot the Mistake!" You'll see a sentence like this one with words and phrases underlined. Look at each underlined part and decide which part is incorrect. Some sentences are correct as written.

The test makers put Usage questions on the Writing test to test your ability to catch words or phrases that are frequently used incorrectly in student essays. If you can spot these types of errors, the test makers assume that you can use appropriate words and phrases in your own writing.

In the example above, the correct answer is (D). The current wording makes it sound as though the size of the subject's salary is being compared to the size of a clerk; in fact, the subject's salary should be compared to the size of a clerk's *salary*.

Keep in mind that you only have 40 minutes to answer 40 questions and that there is no penalty for incorrect answers. That means you need to move quickly through the Usage questions to allow for the more time-consuming questions. Aim to answer between 2 and 3 questions per minute.

To improve your efficiency with these questions, practice moving quickly through the practice sets we've provided. Also, learn to trust your ear on your first read of a question; always choose an answer on your first read through. If nothing sounds wrong, choose (E) and move on. Make a note on your scratch paper of any questions you are unsure of; then use the review screen to return to them if you have time. Never leave a question unanswered on the Core Writing test.

### Sentence Correction Questions

Sentence Correction questions are similar to Usage questions, except there will be only one underlined portion for you to focus on. In this case, your task is to pick the best version of the underlined portion. Please note that the first answer will always be the same as the underlined portion in the question, so if there is an error, there is no need to consider the first choice.

The directions for Sentence Correction will look similar to this:

Directions: Each of the following sentences will have an underlined section and will be followed by 5 versions of that section. The first is a reprint of the original sentence. After reading each sentence, decide whether or not the sentence is in its best form as written or could benefit from one of the four (4) proposed adjustments.

For this type of question, choose the answer that best expresses the essence of the sentence through correct grammar, usage, punctuation, or capitalization. Be sure to maintain the meaning of the sentence.

Be sure to select an answer for each question.

Here's what a sample question might look like.

The experts from the Fish and Wildlife Department could not decide which one of eight possible nesting sites along the Platte River <u>will provide the best habitat</u> into which to release the crane.

A. will provide the best habitat
B. would be providing the better habitat
C. would provide the better habitat
D. would provide the best habitat
E. is providing the best habitat

In the question above, (D) is correct. A quick scan of the answer choices reveals that this question tests verb tense. The nonunderlined portion of the sentence speaks of a possibility and a decision about releasing the crane that has not yet been made, so the future tense *will provide*, which applies to a definite future action, is incorrect. Choice (A) is out. Likewise, the continuous present tense in (E) is out, because the nesting site is not doing anything for the crane right now. Given that the experts are speculating (rather than making a factual statement) about the possible nesting sites, you need to use the subjunctive form of *will*, which is *would*. More scanning reveals another split, this one between *best* and *better*. *Better/best* is a frequently tested idiom: use *better* to compare two things, *best* to compare more than two. There are eight possible nesting sites, so the experts need to find the *best* one. Eliminate (B) and (C). (D) is correct because it is the only answer choice that uses *would* and *best*. Quickly scanning your answer choices for differences such as these will help you identify what the question is testing and allow you to locate the correct answer efficiently.

Sentence Correction questions tend to take more time than Usage questions, and you should budget your time accordingly. Nonetheless, to perform well on the Writing section, you need to continue to move quickly and avoid getting stuck on any single question. Again, trust your ear and your instincts and press forward through the test. Getting one question wrong is not nearly as harmful as agonizing for five or six minutes on a question, regardless of whether you get it right. Always choose an answer on your first read through. If the sentence sounds good to begin with, choose (A) and move on. Don't waste time re-reading choice (A)—you already know what it says. As you move through the test, make a note on your scratch paper indicating the questions you are unsure of; then use the review screen to return to them if you have time.

You should spend no more than 1 to 1.5 minutes on each Sentence Correction question.

### Revision in Context Questions

For Revision in Context questions, the test makers will provide a short essay draft and ask you to choose the best version of a sentence or set of sentences considering the essay's context. They may also ask you to remove or insert sentences into certain paragraphs or adjust the sequence of the sentences in a given paragraph.

> <u>Directions</u>: This is an essay draft that requires some editing work. Choose the best versions of the sentences and/or paragraphs as examined in the questions. At times the passage cannot be improved using the answer choices, and in those circumstances you should indicate that it is correct as written. As you answer these questions, be sure to consider writing style; the author's tone and purpose; and standard English conventions of grammar, usage, punctuation, and capitalization.
>
> Be sure to select an answer for each question.

[The following is excerpted from a full-length essay.]

The oldest building still in use in California is the Mission at San Juan Capistrano, the seventh in the chain of California missions built by Spanish priests in the late eighteenth and early nineteenth centuries. The mission has gained fame as the <u>well-known summer residence</u> of the swallows of San Juan Capistrano.

    A.  NO CHANGE

    B.  seasonal residence for the summer

    C.  summer residence

    D.  residential summer home

    E.  famous summer mission home

The underlined selection may repeat something said elsewhere, so consider the underlined portion of the sentence in context before choosing an answer. This sentence already indicates that the mission gained fame, so the adjective "well-known" is unnecessary. Eliminate (A). Choice (B) unnecessarily uses the adjective "seasonal" along with "summer"; summer is a season, so you can eliminate (B). Choice (D) describes the home as "residential," but a home is, by definition, residential. Choice (E) is doubly redundant; "famous" and "mission" are both repetitive. Choice (C) is the only choice that eliminates all redundant language.

## Research Skills Questions

As the name suggests, Research Skills questions will test your basic understanding of acceptable research habits, including assessing the credibility of sources, recognizing different parts of a citation, recognizing different research strategies, and assessing the relevance of information to a research task.

    <u>Directions</u>: Consider proper research techniques while answering these questions.

    Be sure to select an answer for each question.

    A student is writing a paper about key people involved in the American Civil Rights Movement (1954-1968) and their contributions to the movement. Which of the following is the LEAST relevant to the paper?

    A.  During the Civil Rights Movement, Martin Luther King gave many inspirational speeches.

    B.  During the Civil Rights Movement, Rosa Parks chose to remain in her chosen seat on a city bus, which sparked a boycott of buses.

    C.  During the Civil Rights Movement, Malcolm X was featured in a New York City television broadcast (1959) during which he promoted the teachings of Islam.

    D.  During the Civil Rights Movement, the Supreme Court ruled in favor of Oliver Brown that segregation in schools was unconstitutional.

    E.  During the Civil Rights Movement, John F. Kennedy gave an address that urged Americans to embrace freedom (1963).

Choice (C) is correct, because its only relation to the Civil Rights movement is that it happened to coincide with the timing of the movement. Choice (C) does not mention anything for which the movement stood.

# HOW TO APPROACH PRAXIS WRITING

Earlier in this chapter, you learned about the importance of developing an eye for mistakes and trusting your ear to help you locate and fix potential errors. You then read about the various question types you'll encounter on your test. Now we're going to show you how to put your search-and-repair tactics to work on real Core Writing questions. Start with these three simple steps.

## THE KAPLAN THREE-STEP METHOD FOR USAGE AND SENTENCE CORRECTION

**STEP 1  Read the sentence, listening for a mistake**

**STEP 2  Identify the error**

**STEP 3  Check the answer choices**

This Method will serve you well for all types of Writing questions, although we'll show you how to refine it slightly to suit each question type.

# USAGE QUESTIONS

Usage is a great place for the Writing test to begin because you don't have to fix anything. You just have to point out what's wrong.

Try using Kaplan's Three-Step Method on this question. First, read the sentence, *listening* for a mistake. Note: In preparation for test day, you should get used to reading silently and listening to the sentence in your head.

> The <u>club members</u> are so busy <u>studying</u> for exams that attendance is
>    A.                              B.
> <u>rare</u> more <u>than 50 percent</u>. <u>No error</u>
>    C.            D.              E.

**Step 1. Read the sentence, listening for a mistake**

When you read the sentence, did you hear an error? If so, you're all set. You don't need to figure out how you would fix the error. You just need to click on the right choice and move on.

**Step 2. Identify the error**

If you didn't hear the mistake, read the sentence again. There's no problem with the phrase *club members*. *Studying* is OK here. How about *rare*? There's the clunker.

**Step 3. Check the answer choices**

The correct construction would be "rare*ly* more than 50 percent." This is a classic example of an adjective/adverb error. Choice (C) is correct.

Now let's see the Kaplan Method applied to a Sentence Correction question.

# SENTENCE CORRECTION QUESTIONS

Sentence Correction questions test the same skills as Usage questions. You'll still be using your eyes and ears to spot errors and oddities in sentences. Here's the difference: now you have to fix the mistakes you find. As you probably remember from earlier in this chapter, each Sentence Correction question has an underlined phrase. You need to decide whether the sentence is OK as is, in which case you should pick choice (A), or whether the underlined portion should be replaced by one of the answer choices.

Take a look again at the Kaplan Three-Step Method for Writing. You'll see that the wording is a little different so the Method works well for the Sentence Correction task.

> **STEP 1** **Read the sentence, listening for a mistake**
> **STEP 2** **Predict a correction**
> **STEP 3** **Select the answer choice that matches your prediction and eliminate clearly wrong answer choices**

Now apply the Three-Step Method to this Sentence Correction question.

Hoping to receive a promotion, <u>the letter he received instead informed Burt</u> that he had been fired.

- A. the letter he received instead informed Burt
- B. the letter having been received, instead informed Burt
- C. Burt instead received a letter informing him
- D. information from the received letter instead told Burt
- E. Burt, instead informed by the letter he received

**Step 1: Read the sentence, listening for a mistake**

Something sounds wrong. Burt hoped to receive the promotion, but this makes it sound as if the letter hoped to receive the promotion.

**Step 2. Predict a correction**

You should predict that *Burt* will be at the beginning of the correct answer choice.

**Step 3. Select the answer choice that matches your prediction and eliminate clearly wrong answer choices**

Choices (C) and (E) both put Burt at the beginning of the phrase, but choice (E) does not contain a main verb and creates a fragment instead of a complete sentence. Choice (C) is correct.

# REVISION IN CONTEXT QUESTIONS

Here is another variation of the Kaplan Method for Writing, this time well suited to answering Revision in Context questions:

> **STEP 1** **Read the passage and identify the issue**
>
> **STEP 2** **Eliminate answer choices that do not address the issue**
>
> **STEP 3** **Plug in the remaining answer choices and select the most correct, concise, and relevant one**

Now let's apply the Method to this Revision in Context question.

> I still remember the magic of walking home under the cold, brittle blue sky, watching the sun strike the glittering blanket laid down by that first snowfall. The world dripped with frosting, and everything was pure and silent. I breathed deeply, enjoying the sting of the icy air in my nostrils, and set off through the trees, listening to the muffled crunch of my footsteps and the chirps of the waking birds. Later, the cars and schoolchildren and mundane lives would turn the wonderland back into dingy slush; the hush would be interrupted by horns and shouts. <u>Indeed</u> for now, the sparkling, cloistered world was mine alone. I smiled, and for a moment, my mind was still.

A. Indeed

B. But

C. Consequently

D. In fact

E. After all

### Step 1: Read the passage and identify the issue

The underlined word is a continuation transition showing emphasis. It is incorrect as written because the sentence preceding it discusses what will happen to the surroundings (they will be dirty and noisy), while this sentence discusses what the world is like now (beautiful and quiet). A contrast transition would be more appropriate in this context. Eliminate choice (A).

### Step 2: Eliminate answer choices that do not address the issue

Eliminate (C), (D) and (E) because they are not contrast transitions.

### Step 3: Plug in the remaining answer choices and select the most correct, concise, and relevant one

Choice (B) is all that remains. Plugging it into the passage confirms that it is correct.

# RESEARCH SKILLS QUESTIONS

## Kaplan Method for Research Skills Questions

> **STEP 1** Read the question, looking for clues
> **STEP 2** Make a prediction
> **STEP 3** Evaluate the answer choices and select the choice that best fits your prediction

Research Skills questions test a different skill than the rest of the multiple-choice questions in the Writing test. While the other questions are testing grammar and mechanics, Research Skills questions focus on the information-gathering and sharing phase of the writing process. These questions will test a variety of concepts, including primary versus secondary sources, types of citations, and the relevance of information to the thesis. Let's take a look at Kaplan's Three-Step Method in action.

Dickens, Charles. *Great Expectations*. New York: Dodd, Mead, 1942. Print.

What type of citation is shown?

A. Interview
B. Magazine article
C. Website
D. Book
E. Encyclopedia

### Step 1: Read the question, looking for clues

This question provides a full citation, then asks what kind of citation it is. The key phrase is "type of citation," so we know that we need to predict a source medium (painting, interview, article, book, website, etc).

### Step 2: Make a prediction

For this example, we can predict that the source is a book because the citation includes the publisher and the date of publication. An italicized title is generally given to a longer work, such as a book. The citation also states that the medium was print. Note that websites and articles will also include the date of publication (often a specific day), and online sources often include the date of access as such content can change.

### Step 3: Evaluate the answer choices and select the choice that best fits your prediction

Choice (D) matches the prediction and is correct.

# CLASSIC ERRORS IN PRAXIS WRITING QUESTIONS

It may seem as though there are many things to think about during the selected-response (multiple-choice) portion of the Writing test, but many of the questions can be categorized according to a few common types of errors. Familiarizing yourself with the most common error types, shown in the following pages, will help you sharpen your focus and help you achieve test day success.

## Verb Tense Errors

As you know, the verb is the action part of the sentence. The verb's tense tells you when the action is taking place. You won't need to identify verb tenses by name on the test, but you will need to recognize the difference between correct and incorrect verb tenses.

> When David was in Holland, he was seeing many windmills.

You don't need to know the rules about proper use of the past tense to know that something's wrong here. Your ear should have told you that the verbs don't sound right. Try this instead:

> When David was in Holland, he saw many windmills.

That sounds better, and it's correct. Now let's look at a test-like question that has a verb tense error.

> <u>Unsatisfied</u> with the ending, the director <u>considering</u> <u>reshooting</u> <u>the entire</u>
>   A.                                                    B.         C.       D.
> film. <u>No error</u>
>        E.

Did this sentence make sense to you? If not, where did the confusion come in? We don't know when the director's action took place because *considering* isn't a complete verb. You could substitute *is considering* or *was considering* or even *considered*. Because choice (B) contains the error in this sentence, it's the answer.

## Subject-Verb Agreement Errors

Your grammar book tells you that the subject and the verb of a sentence must agree in number. Put simply, this means that a singular subject takes a singular verb and a plural subject takes a plural verb. Subject and verb also have to agree in person. This simply means that you need to use the right form of the verb depending on whether the subject is first person, second person, or third person.

You do this correctly a million times a day, and it's not as tricky as it sounds. Take a look at these sentences:

> The 4:05 train to Boston leave from the north platform.
>
> Henry's dog are brown with a white tail.
>
> The ballerinas practices for eight hours a day.
>
> You spends too much time thinking about subject-verb agreement.

Did you find the agreement errors? The sentences on the Core Writing test won't be quite this easy, but with a little practice, you'll be able to spot agreement errors in any sentence. You may have to learn to be on the lookout for the three classic subject-verb agreement traps. Let's take a look.

### Trap 1: Collective Nouns

A very common trap that the test makers use to try to trick you is collective nouns.

Words such as *group*, *audience*, or *committee* require a singular verb.

> The group has decided to plan a trip to a chocolate factory.
>
> The audience was moved to throw rotten vegetables at the mime.
>
> The committee votes to clean up the waterfront every year.

All of these sentences are correct. Now try the following out for size.

> That <u>particular</u> gang of pirates <u>were</u> often <u>referred to</u> as the <u>scourge of</u>
>       A.                  B.           C.                    D.
> the seven seas. <u>No error</u>
>                 E.

Even with advance warning, this one might have been tricky. The correct answer here is (B) because the subject is the collective singular noun "gang." Making the error harder to spot in this case was the prepositional phrase "of pirates," which was thrown in between the subject and verb just to confuse you. This brings us to Trap 2.

### Trap 2: Intervening Phrases

The test makers will often try to confuse the issue of subject-verb agreement by inserting an intervening phrase between the subject and verb. Try this one.

> Tax evasion, <u>a crime</u> that <u>has been documented</u> in many modern novels and
>            A.                  B.
> films, <u>remain</u> a relatively <u>uncommon offense</u>. <u>No error</u>
>      C.                 D.        E.

Did you pick choice (C)? You're right. The verb "remain" goes with "evasion," a singular word, which requires the verb form *remains*. Don't be fooled by the plural nouns "novels" and "films," which are part of the intervening phrase. Also, if you have trouble identifying the subject and verb, try ignoring all the extra adjectives, prepositional phrases, and subordinate clauses.

### Trap 3: Subject After Verb

Another way that the test makers try to confuse you is by placing the subject after the verb. Take a look at this example.

> <u>Although</u> nutritionists have <u>criticized pizza</u> for being too high in fat, there <u>is</u>
>     A.                          B.                         C.
> many people <u>who</u> continue to enjoy it. <u>No error</u>
>     D.                    E.

"People" is the subject of the verb "is," and it requires a plural subject: ... *there are many people* ... Choice (C) is correct.

## Pronoun Errors: Case and Number

You're sure to see at least a few questions on your Core Writing test that look at the use of pronouns. The key thing to remember about pronouns is that they must agree with their antecedents (the nouns they represent) in case and number.

### WHO IS *HE*? WHAT IS *IT*?

Every pronoun must have an antecedent. The antecedent is the noun that corresponds to the pronoun in the sentence. Look at this sentence: Beck is a great singer, and he is also a fine songwriter. "Beck" is the antecedent, and "he" is the pronoun.

**Case** refers to the form in which the word appears in the sentence. If the pronoun refers to the subject, it has a different case than if it refers to an object.

> Sally dances, and *she* also sings.
>
> Bob praised Sally, and he also applauded *her*.

These sentences are correct.

The **number** of a pronoun is just what it sounds like: singular or plural.

Give this question a try:

> A student <u>who</u> applies for a part-time job assisting Dr. Frankenstein <u>may get</u>
>     A.                                                                 B.
> more than <u>they</u> asked <u>for</u> in the bargain. <u>No error</u>
>          C.          D.               E.

Did you see the error here? The antecedent is "a student," and the pronoun is "they." To make the plural pronoun agree with its singular antecedent, you would have to use *he, she*, or even possibly *he or she*. Another option would be to repeat the noun: … *may get more than the student asked for* … .

Many people use *they* to refer to a single person of unknown gender. While this is a common practice that is generally acceptable in spoken English and informal writing, many disapprove of it in formal writing, and it is unacceptable on the Praxis exam. Watch out for *they* and *them* on test day!

## Pronoun Errors: Ambiguous Reference

Another common pronoun problem you'll find on the Core Writing test is ambiguous reference. As you just read, every pronoun must have a clear antecedent.

Give this question a try:

> To expand the newspaper's <u>coverage</u> of local politics, <u>they</u> transferred a
>                                    A.                                    B.
> <u>popular</u> columnist <u>to</u> the city desk. <u>No error</u>
>     C.            D.           E.

This one may have been easy because you knew what you were looking for. Choice (B), "they," is a pronoun without a clear antecedent. Who transferred the columnist? The sentence doesn't tell us. Choice (B) is correct.

Questions like this one can be tricky because they read smoothly, with no bumpy parts to jar your ear. Keep an eye out for ambiguous references in sentences that seem too good to be true.

## Idioms

The test makers also occasionally like to test whether students can recognize the proper use of idioms. This can be especially bad news for nonnative speakers of English because idioms are the hardest thing to learn in any foreign language. This is because idioms are simply word combinations that have become part of the language. They're correct, but there's no particular rhyme or reason to why they're correct. Most—although certainly not all—native speakers will know the proper idiom to use simply because their ears tell them what combination sounds correct.

Prepositions are the typically short words—such as *by*, *at*, *among*, and *before*—that link prepositional phrases to the rest of the sentence. Most preposition issues tested on the Praxis are idiomatic. This means that you'll be listening for word combinations that frequently go together. Use your ear to catch prepositions that just don't sound right.

Give the following question a try. Be sure to use the Kaplan Three-Step Method.

> Many people are <u>desensitized to</u> violence on TV shows, <u>but</u>
>          A.                       B.
> this does not mean that they are not sensitive <u>of</u> the real-life
>                                  C.
> violence around <u>them</u>. <u>No error</u>
>          D.     E.

There are two idiomatic uses of prepositions in this sentence. Did you spot them? "Desensitized to" and "sensitive of" are choices (A) and (C), respectively. "Sensitive of" simply isn't idiomatic—it should be *sensitive to*—and choice (C) is correct. If you're not a native speaker of English or you don't have a good ear for idioms, you'll need to immerse yourself in idioms as you study for the test.

## Comparison Errors

Another error that frequently shows up on the Core Writing test involves comparisons. This one can be a little sneaky because some of these sentences may sound OK to your ear. It's time to bring your brain into the picture!

When you compare two or more parts of speech, like nouns or verb phrases, the parts of speech must be in the same form. Take a look at this example:

The producer agreed that casting a drama series is harder than comedy.

If you heard this sentence, you'd probably understand what it means, although it's not crystal-clear. "Casting a drama series" is harder than … what exactly? The sentence would be clearer if it were written as follows:

The producer agreed that casting a drama series is harder than casting a comedy series.

Both parts of the comparison are in the same form, making the sentence easier to understand and grammatically correct.

See if you can spot the mistake in the next question.

Even though <u>he</u> is a Nobel Laureate, <u>Elie Wiesel's name</u> is still <u>less well-known</u>
A.              B.           C.
than <u>last year's</u> Heisman Trophy winner. <u>No error</u>
D.            E.

This is a bit subtle. Did you spot the faulty comparison? The sentence compares "Elie Wiesel's name" with the "Heisman Trophy winner." If we changed choice (B) to read simply *Elie Wiesel*, the comparison would be parallel and easier to understand.

## Adjective and Adverb Errors

You probably haven't thought about adjectives and adverbs since those junior high sentence diagrams. The good news is that you probably use adjectives and adverbs correctly all the time.

That painting is beautiful.

The artist painted it skillfully.

In the first sentence, "beautiful" is an adjective modifying "painting," a noun. In the second sentence, "skillfully" is an adverb modifying "painted," a verb form.

### KNOW YOUR MODIFIERS
An adjective modifies a noun or pronoun. An adverb modifies a verb, an adjective, or another adverb. Most but not all adverbs end in *-ly*.

Now take a look at how adjectives and adverbs might be tested in the Usage section.

<u>Since the onset</u> of <u>his</u> blindness, the artist <u>has sculpted</u> more <u>slow</u> than before. <u>No error</u>
A.     B.          C.      D.      E.

Choice (D) is correct. The adverb *slowly* is required to modify the verb "has sculpted."

## Double Negatives

In standard written English, the use of two negatives in a row can create ungrammatical or self-contradictory sentences. Just as in math, two negatives added together create a positive.

> I won't have none of that backtalk, young lady!

This sentence, if you cancel the negatives, translates as follows:

> I'll have that backtalk, young lady!

You'll find an occasional double negative question in the Usage section, although the sentences are a bit tougher than the one above. Give this one a try.

> The town hasn't <u>hardly any</u> money left in <u>its</u> budget <u>because of</u> the unexpected
>               A.                         B.         C.
>
> <u>costs</u> for snowplowing. <u>No error</u>
>  D.                      E.

The words "hasn't" and "hardly any" cancel each other out, making it sound as if the town doesn't have money problems. We can figure out from the rest of the sentence that the author's trying to tell us that the town does have money problems because of the unexpected costs. Changing choice (A), "hardly any," to *much* would eliminate one of the negatives, clearing up the meaning of the sentence.

## Sentence Fragments

Sentence fragments are incomplete sentences. To be complete, a sentence requires a main subject and a main verb. Some sentences are fragments because they lack the necessary elements to make logical sense or have an unnecessary connector like *that* or *because*.

Here are some fragments. How would you repair them?

> Stereo equipment on sale at the mall today!
>
> The busload of tourists that wandered curiously around the ancient ruins.
>
> Because Myrna likes the Adirondacks, frequently taking photos of them.

Did you get an empty feeling when you read these fragments? Watch for that feeling on test day, and you'll be able to spot the fragments.

Give this example a try, using the Kaplan Three-Step Method.

> Last of the world's leaders to do so, the prime minister admits that terrorist threats <u>credible enough to warrant</u> the imposition of stringent security measures.
>
> A. credible enough to warrant
> B. credible enough warrant
> C. are credible enough to warrant
> D. credible enough, warranting
> E. are credible enough to be warranted

That empty feeling sits right in the middle of the sentence. The subject of the part of the sentence beginning with "that" is "terrorist threats," but where's the verb? "Credible" is the adjective modifying "terrorist threats," so adding *are*, as choices (C) and (E) do, repairs the fragment. Choice (E), however, introduces a new problem with the phrase "to be warranted," which is confusing when read back into the sentence. Choice (C) clearly fixes the fragment and is correct.

## Run-On Sentences

A run-on sentence occurs when two complete sentences that should be separate are joined incorrectly. Here are some examples:

> Jane was the preeminent scientist in her class her experiments were discussed across campus.

> Jane was the preeminent scientist in her class, her experiments were discussed across campus.

You can tell that this is a run-on sentence because it sounds like it should be two separate sentences. There are four ways to fix a run-on sentence.

1.  **Use a period.**

    Jane was the preeminent scientist in her class. Her experiments were discussed across campus.

2.  **Use a comma with a coordinating conjunction (and, but, or, for, nor, yet, and so).**

    Jane was the preeminent scientist in her class, and her experiments were discussed across campus.

3.  **Use a subordinating conjunction, making one sentence dependent.**

    Because Jane was the preeminent scientist in her class, her experiments were discussed across campus.

4.  **Use a semicolon.**

    Jane was the preeminent scientist in her class; her experiments were discussed across campus.

Use the Kaplan Three-Step Method and the information you just learned to answer this question.

> Jonas Salk was born in East Harlem, New York, the developer of the polio vaccine.

A.  Jonas Salk was born in East Harlem, New York, the developer of the polio vaccine.

B.  Jonas Salk being the developer of the polio vaccine and was born in East Harlem, New York.

C.  Being the developer of the polio vaccine, Jonas Salk was born in East Harlem, New York.

D.  Jonas Salk was the developer of the polio vaccine, having been born in East Harlem, New York.

E.  Jonas Salk, who was born in East Harlem, New York, was the developer of the polio vaccine.

Because the entire sentence is underlined, you know that either it's correct or there's a better rewrite among the choices. What's wrong with the sentence? Well, it's clearly a run-on because there are two independent thoughts that aren't joined in any way. It's also a bit confusing because it sounds as if Salk was born the developer of the vaccine. (He probably had to grow up a bit and go to school for a while before he developed the vaccine.) Choice (E) fixes the problem by setting apart the facts about Salk's birthplace, thus clearing up the meaning and fixing the run-on problem.

## Coordination and Subordination Errors

Sometimes a sentence won't make sense because it contains clauses that aren't logically joined. There are two types of errors involving the improper joining of clauses in a sentence: coordination and subordination errors.

### DEFINITION ALERT

*Clauses* are groups of words that contain a subject and a verb. Dependent, or *subordinate*, clauses need to be linked to an independent clause by a conjunction, such as *because*, *although*, or *since*, in order for the sentence to express a complete thought.

Proper **coordination** expresses the logical relationship between two clauses. Misused conjunctions can bring about faulty coordination and make a sentence confusing or nonsensical.

Because he was very thirsty, he refused to drink the water.

This sentence doesn't make much sense (unless we're dealing with a very stubborn or confused person, but let's not overrationalize things too much). What would be a better conjunction?

Although he was very thirsty, he refused to drink the water.

This is better. We still don't know why he won't drink the water, but the conjunction *although* sets up the contrast between the two clauses so the sentence makes sense.

Problems with **subordination** occur when a group of words contains two or more subordinate clauses (also known as dependent clauses) but no independent clause.

Since the advent of inexpensive portable stereos, because there has been a boom in the manufacture of light, powerful headphones.

Connective words like *since, because, so that, if,* and *although* introduce subordinate clauses. As it stands, this sentence consists of two dependent clauses, with no independent clause. We can eliminate *because* in order to make this a grammatically correct sentence.

Since the advent of inexpensive portable stereos, there has been a boom in the manufacture of light, powerful headphones.

Try the following two questions, using the Kaplan Three-Step Method.

> New restaurants appeared on the <u>waterfront, however merchants</u> were finally able to convince diners of the area's safety.
>
> A. waterfront, however merchants
> B. waterfront; merchants
> C. waterfront, yet merchants
> D. waterfront, because merchants
> E. waterfront, although merchants

"However" is a conjunction that indicates contrast. This sentence is about cause and effect. Choice (D) is correct because the conjunction "because" shows the relationship between the appearance of the new restaurants and the merchants' ability to convince diners that the area was safe.

> Because Megan was unable to finish her tax forms before April 15, <u>so she filed</u> for an extension.
>
> A. so she filed
> B. but she was filing
> C. she filed
> D. and this led to her filing
> E. and she filed

This question tests subordination. The sentence contains two dependent clauses, each beginning with a linking word. Choice (C) eliminates the linking word and fixes the problem by creating an independent clause.

## Misplaced Modifier Errors

Modifiers are phrases that provide information about nouns and verbs in a sentence. A modifier must appear next to the word or words that it's modifying. Otherwise, things can get a bit confusing (not to mention ungrammatical).

> ### SPOT THE TROUBLE EARLY ON!
> Most misplaced modifier errors on the Praxis occur in sentences that begin with a modifying phrase. When a short phrase followed by a comma begins a sentence, make sure that what follows the comma is who or what the phrase is supposed to modify.

Take a look at this example.

> Dripping on his shirt, Harvey was so eager to eat his hamburger that he didn't notice the ketchup.

As the sentence is written, it sounds as if Harvey was dripping on his shirt, which isn't a very pleasant image. In fact, it's the ketchup that's dripping on his shirt.

As long as you can spot them, misplaced modifiers are easy to fix.

> Harvey was so eager to eat his hamburger that he didn't notice the ketchup dripping on his shirt.

This clears up the confusion and is a logical sentence.

Now let's look at a test-like question that involves a misplaced modifier.

> Flying for the first time, the roar of the jet engines intimidated the elderly man as the plane sped down the runway.

A. Flying for the first time, the roar of the jet engines intimidated the elderly man as the plane sped down the runway.

B. The roar of the jet engines intimidated the elderly man as the plane, flying for the first time, sped down the runway.

C. Flying for the first time, the elderly man was intimidated by the roar of the jet engines as the plane sped down the runway.

D. The plane sped down the runway as, flying for the first time, the roar of the jet engines intimidated the elderly man.

E. As the plane sped down the runway, flying for the first time, the elderly man was intimidated by the roar of the jet engines.

We need a choice that makes it clear that the elderly man, not the plane or the engines or the engines' roar, is flying for the first time. Choice (C) accomplishes this by placing the modifier "flying for the first time" next to "the elderly man." Note that choice (E) also places the two phrases next to each other, but the modifier is sandwiched between two phrases, making it unclear which phrase it is meant to modify. Choice (C) is correct.

## Parallelism Errors

Parallelism is very much like comparison, which we covered earlier. Essentially, whenever you list items, they must be in the same form.

Take a look at this sentence:

> On Saturday, Ingrid cleaned her apartment, bought her plane tickets for France, and was deciding to go out to dinner.

The first two verbs set us up to expect a parallel verb, but we get blindsided at the end with a nonparallel construction.

> On Saturday, Ingrid cleaned her apartment, bought her plane tickets for France, and decided to go out to dinner.

In this corrected sentence, "cleaned," "bought," and "decided" are all in the same form, so the parallel structure is correct.

Try the following question and see how you do.

Changing over from a military to a peacetime economy means producing tractors rather than tanks, radios rather than rifles, and <u>producing running shoes rather than combat boots</u>.

A. producing running shoes rather than combat boots

B. the production of running shoes rather than combat boots

C. running shoes rather than combat boots

D. replacing combat boots with running shoes

E. running shoes instead of combat boots

Choice (C) does the trick by maintaining the parallel structure of the sentence: "tractors rather than tanks, radios rather than rifles, and running shoes rather than combat boots."

# PRACTICE

## Praxis Writing

Now it's time to practice some writing questions. Make sure to use Kaplan's Three-Step Method when working through this quiz.

1. The first woman aviator <u>to cross</u> the English
   A.
   Channel, Harriet Quimby, <u>flown</u> <u>by mono-</u>
   B.          C.
   plane from Dover, England, to Hardelot,
   France, <u>in</u> 1912. <u>No error</u>
   D.          E.

2. The reproductive behavior of sea horses <u>is</u>
   <u>notable</u> <u>in respect of</u> the male, <u>who,</u> <u>instead of</u>
   A.          B.                    C.      D.
   the female, carries the fertilized eggs. <u>No error</u>
   E.

3. Early <u>experience</u> of racial discrimination
   A.
   <u>made</u> an <u>indelible</u> <u>impression for</u> the late
   B.       C.        D.
   Supreme Court Justice Thurgood Marshall.
   <u>No error</u>
   E.

4. More journalists <u>as</u> you would suspect are <u>se-</u>
   A.                                          
   <u>cretly</u> writing plays or novels, <u>which</u> they hope
   B.                              C.
   someday <u>to have published.</u> <u>No error</u>
   D.                     E.

5. <u>As long ago as</u> the twelfth century, before the
   A.
   division of alchemy into modern chemistry
   and a more metaphysical pursuit, French
   alchemists <u>have</u> perfected techniques <u>for</u>
   B.                           C.
   <u>refining</u> precious metals <u>from</u> other ores. <u>No</u>
   C.                    D.                E.
   error

6. Galileo begged Rome's indulgence for his <u>sup-</u>
   <u>port of</u> a Copernican system <u>in which</u> earth
   A.                          B.
   circled the sun <u>instead of</u> <u>occupied</u> a central
   C.          D.
   position in the universe. <u>No error</u>
   E.

7. Arthur Rubinstein was long ranked <u>among</u>
   A.
   the world's finest pianists, <u>although</u> he was
   B.
   sometimes known <u>as playing</u> several wrong
   C.
   notes <u>in a single</u> performance. <u>No error</u>
   D.                          E.

8. The new office complex is beautiful, but <u>nearly</u>
   A.
   two hundred longtime residents <u>were forced</u>
   B.
   to move when <u>they</u> <u>tore down</u> the old apart-
   C.      D.
   ment buildings. <u>No error</u>
   E.

9. Neither the singers <u>on stage</u> <u>or</u> the announcer
   A.      B.
   in the wings <u>could be heard</u> <u>over</u> the noise of
   C.          D.
   the crowd. <u>No error</u>
   E.

10. <u>Many of</u> the organic farms in the country <u>are</u>
    A.                                      B.
    based on rotating crops <u>so that</u> there is <u>hardly</u>
    C.                D.
    no soil erosion. <u>No error</u>
    E.

11. None of this injury <u>to life</u> and damage to
    A.
    property <u>wouldn't have</u> happened if the
    B.
    amateur pilot <u>had only</u> heeded the weather
    C.
    forecasts and <u>stayed</u> on the ground. <u>No error</u>
    D.                              E.

12. The doctor recommended that young athletes

    with a history of severe asthma take particular
    <u>A.</u>                        <u>B.</u>    C.

    care not to exercise alone. No error
          <u>D.</u>                   <u>E.</u>

13. <u>Amelia Earhart was born in Kansas the first
    person to fly from Hawaii to California.</u>

    A. Amelia Earhart was born in Kansas the
       first person to fly from Hawaii to Califor-
       nia.

    B. Amelia Earhart being the first person to
       fly from Hawaii to California and was
       born in Kansas.

    C. Being the first person to fly from Hawaii
       to California, Amelia Earhart was born in
       Kansas.

    D. Amelia Earhart was the first person to fly
       from Hawaii to California and was born
       in Kansas.

    E. Amelia Earhart, who was born in Kansas,
       was the first person to fly from Hawaii to
       California.

14. Beethoven bridged two musical eras; <u>his ear-
    lier works are essentially Classical, while his
    later ones are Romantic.</u>

    A. his earlier works are essentially Classical;
       his later ones, Romantic

    B. his earlier works are essentially Classical,
       nevertheless, his later ones are Romantic

    C. his earlier works being essentially Classi-
       cal; his later are Romantic

    D. his earlier works are Classical; likewise,
       his later ones are Romantic

    E. despite his earlier works' being essentially
       Classical; his later are more Romantic

15. Gaitskill, Mary. Interview with Charles Bock.
    *Mississippi Review*, vol. 27, no. 3, 1999, pp.
    129–150.

    What type of citation is shown?

    A. Interview

    B. Magazine article

    C. Encyclopedia

    D. Book

    E. Published interview

16. Goya, Francisco. *The Family of Charles IV*.
    1800, oil on canvas, Museo del Prado, Madrid.

    What type of citation is shown?

    A. Painting

    B. Photographic reproduction of a painting

    C. Book

    D. Article

    E. Sculpture

17. A student is writing a paper on the stock market.

    Which of the following would NOT be a primary source for this paper?

    A. An official daily report issued by a stock exchange

    B. A biography of George Soros, a securities trading strategist

    C. Emails between two investment bankers discussing the market

    D. A letter written from one stock exchange floor trader to another after the "Black Tuesday" stock market crash of 1929

    E. A photograph from a Wall Street stock exchange trading floor from last year

18. A student is writing a paper about the behavioral tendencies of domestic dogs.

    Which of the following would best serve as a primary source for this student?

    A. A blog in which dog lovers post photographs of their dogs in costumes

    B. An encyclopedia of the history and behavior of dog breeds worldwide

    C. A blog in which dog trainers share tips for training dogs

    D. An article written by an animal control agent about stray dogs in Chicago

    E. A magazine article that highlights the pros and cons of owning various breeds of dogs

# ANSWERS AND EXPLANATIONS

## Practice Questions

### 1. B

The use of the word "flown" isn't right. *Flown*, the past participle form of *fly*, can't be used as a main verb without a form of the verb *have*. What's needed here is the simple past form of *fly*, which is *flew*.

### 2. B

"In respect of" doesn't sound quite right. The phrase *with respect to* would be correct.

### 3. D

Does something make an "impression for" someone? No, it makes an *impression on* someone.

### 4. A

The correct comparative form is *more ... than*, not "more ... as."

### 5. B

This sentence describes an event that took place before another past event. The present perfect "have perfected" suggests that the improvement of these techniques is still going on. Instead, the sentence should use the simple past *perfected*.

### 6. D

"Instead of" takes a participle: "occupied" should be corrected to *occupying*.

### 7. C

The corrected sentence would read *known to play* . . . .

### 8. C

Who tore down the old buildings? Surely not the "longtime residents." The antecedent—some group such as *landlords* or *developers*—is missing.

### 9. B

"Neither" calls for *nor. Either* is used with *or*.

### 10. D

The phrase "hardly no" creates a double negative. If "hardly" were removed, the sentence would be correct.

### 11. B

To see the double negative more easily, remove the intervening words: "none of this ... wouldn't have happened." The correct phrase would be *would have*.

### 12. A

In this sentence, the plural noun "athletes" is modified by the prepositional phrase "with a history of severe asthma." But the athletes don't have a collective medical history; each athlete has his or her own. The sentence should read either *young athletes with histories of severe asthma* or *a young athlete with a history of severe asthma*. Because the prepositional phrase is the part of the sentence that is underlined, it must be changed.

### 13. E

The original sentence is a run-on. Choice (E) provides a fix by tucking the less important information about where Earhart was born into a subordinate clause. (D) also fixes the run-on, but awkwardly gives the two unrelated facts equal prominence.

### 14. A

The original sentence is correct. A semicolon is used to join two sentences with closely related ideas. (B) turns the sentence into a run-on because "nevertheless" is not a conjunction and cannot be used to join two ideas. (C) would be weak but correct if the semicolon were a comma. However, as written, it contains a fragment prior to the semicolon. (D) is incorrect because the conjunctive adverb "likewise" contradicts the implied contrast between the two musical eras. (E) begins with a connecting word ("despite") that turns the clause before the semicolon into a fragment.

### 15. E

This is a published interview. This is evidenced not only by the fact that the citation contains "Interview with Charles Bock," but also by the inclusion of the year of publication and the pages of the magazine in which the interview was published.

### 16. A

Choice (A) is correct: this is a citation for a painting. We can tell that (B) is incorrect because the citation does not include information about how or where it was published (the book edition, page number, or publisher). Choices (C) and (D) would also require information about the publisher, and choice (E) would highlight a medium other than "oil on canvas."

### 17. B

Choice (B) is correct, as a biography is a secondary source. The other sources listed are produced by people who were present during the event or activity being documented and are thus primary sources. (E) might have been tempting, but an artifact, recording, or other source of information, such as a photograph, from the time of an event can be a primary source.

### 18. C

Choice (C) is correct, as this document is created directly by experts in the field of dog behavior. Choice (A) is a primary source, but it is not on the topic of dogs' "behavioral tendencies." Choice (D) is also a primary source, but it focuses on stray dogs rather than "domestic dogs." Encyclopedia articles, choice (B), are often summaries of primary research by people other than the articles' authors and so are not primary sources. The magazine article in (E) could also be reporting on various experts' opinions rather than the author's observations.

# PRAXIS ESSAYS

Essay writing evokes an immediate reaction from nearly everyone, and prospective teachers are no exception. Generally speaking, you either love to write or you see it as a chore. Either way, the Praxis Core Writing test will require you to do a bit of it.

Keep in mind that even the strongest writers can have problems with the unique nature of the Praxis exam. You must respond directly to the topic, and you have to generate your essay in a short period of time. Overly ambitious or flamboyant essayists can run short on time or run too far afield from the topic at hand.

The test makers require you to perform a highly specialized type of writing. Creativity and improvisation are not the goals of a Praxis essay. Instead, an essay is defined as a short literary composition on a single subject, usually presenting the personal view of the author. That definition can take you a long way toward effective essay writing on the Praxis exam.

First, Praxis essays are meant to be *short*. For each essay, you have only 30 minutes to read and digest the essay prompt, compose the essay, and proof it for errors and clarity. That's not a lot of time. The test makers are looking for brief, clear essays.

Second, the Praxis essays are meant to be on a *single subject*. Although tangents, allusions, and digressions make for good fiction, they'll send you into dangerous territory on the Praxis exam. Be sure that whatever you include in your essays pertains to the subject at hand. Keep your essays on point. If a sentence or idea does not relate directly to the topic of your essay, it should be omitted.

Finally, the Praxis essays assess how well you respond *to the prompt provided*. One of the essays will ask you to express your views on a topic—you will need to express and support an opinion or argument. Remember, you will have to do more than simply express your views on this exam; you will be expected to provide illustrations, examples, and generalizations that support your view.

The other essay will ask you to evaluate two source texts and identify the main points of the issue as illustrated by the texts. A strong essay of this type addresses both texts with proper in-text citations. It does not take a stance on the issue provided but rather assesses the important points related to the topic.

The topics are selected such that any educated person should be able to draw from experience to answer the question. No specialized knowledge is required.

Keeping all three of the points above in mind as you pull your essay together will put you well on your way to success on the Praxis Core Writing test. Of course, the key to effective preparation is knowing what you're up against.

## Know What to Expect

You have only 30 minutes to write each essay, so effective time management is key. Be sure to complete each essay in the time allotted. Even a well-crafted essay that abruptly ends without a conclusion will lose valuable points.

Speaking of points, the essay section is scored differently than are the other sections of the Praxis exam. Instead of receiving a score based on the number of questions you answered correctly, your essay is scored "holistically" on a scale of 0 to 6. A score of 6 indicates "a high degree of competence in response to the assignment." A score of 4 or 5 also demonstrates competence, but to a lesser degree. A score of 3 or lower may show some competence but also demonstrates organizational flaws, poor mechanics, or other significant errors.

Your source text essay is graded by two human graders. The argument essay is graded by one human grader and one computer grading program. If your graders' scores differ by more than one point, a third reader will be brought in to decide where your mark should fall. The third reader will always be a human reader.

# HOW TO APPROACH THE PRAXIS ESSAYS

Even though you have only 30 minutes to complete each essay, you should take time to organize your thoughts before writing about a topic. You should also leave time to proof your essays after writing them.

Writing an essay for the Praxis exam is a two-stage process. First, you decide what you want to say about a topic. Second, you figure out how to say it. If your writing style isn't clear, your ideas won't come across no matter how brilliant they are. Good Praxis English is not only grammatical but also clear and concise. By using some basic principles, you'll be able to express your ideas clearly and effectively in your essays.

### Four Principles of Good Essay Writing

1.  **Your Control of Language Is Important**

    Writing that is grammatical, concise, direct, and persuasive displays the "superior control of language" that earns top scores. This involves using the same good grammar that is tested in the selected-response (multiple-choice) questions. It also involves good word choice or diction and sentence structure.

2.  **It's Better to Keep Things Simple**

    Perhaps the single most important thing to bear in mind when writing a Praxis essay is to keep everything simple. Because you are aiming to pass this test and get it out of your life, there is no reason to be overly wordy or complex as you write your essay. Simplicity is essential whether you are talking about word choice, sentence structure, or organization. Complicated sentences are more likely to contain errors. Complicated organization is more likely to wander off topic. Keep in mind that *simple* doesn't mean *simplistic*. A clear, straightforward approach can convey perceptive insights on a topic.

3.  **Minor Grammatical Flaws Won't Kill You**

    Small mistakes are bound to happen when working under the kind of pressures you face on this exam. So don't panic. Essay readers expect minor errors, even in the best essays. That doesn't mean you should include an error or two to keep them happy. It means you should be aware of the kinds of errors you tend to make. If you have trouble with parallelism, double-check how you listed groups of things. Knowing your strengths and weaknesses should help you proof your essay before completion.

4. **Keep Sight of Your Goal**

Remember, your goal isn't to become a prize-winning stylist. Write a solid essay and move on. Write well enough to address the topic and demonstrate that you can write. Remember, essay graders aren't looking for rhetorical flourishes. They're looking for effective expression. Express your ideas clearly and simply, and you'll be well on your way to success.

## THE KAPLAN FIVE-STEP METHOD FOR PRAXIS ESSAYS

**STEP 1  Digest the issue or source texts and the prompt**

**STEP 2  Select the points you will make**

**STEP 3  Organize**

**STEP 4  Write**

**STEP 5  Proofread**

By now, you should know what you're up against on the essay portion of the Praxis Core Writing test. You need to demonstrate that you can think quickly and organize an essay under time pressure. The essay you write is supposed to be logical in organization and clear and concise in its use of written English. Praxis essay writing is not about bells and whistles; it's about bread and butter. Nothing fancy—just answer the question in clear language.

The real challenge is to write an effective essay in a short time. With that goal in mind, we've developed a proven Five-Step Method that will help you make the most of your 30 minutes.

## Step 1. Digest the Issue or Source Texts and the Prompt (1–3 minutes)

- Read the prompt and get a sense of the scope of the issue
- Note any ambiguous terms that need defining
- Crystallize the issue

## Step 2. Select the Points You Will Make (4 minutes)

- Think of arguments for both sides of the issue and decide which side you will support
- Assess the specifics of the prompt
- Brainstorm about both source texts and select the elements of each that you plan to quote

## Step 3. Organize (2 minutes)

- Outline your essay
- Lead with your best arguments
- Think about how the essay will flow as a whole

## Step 4. Write (20 minutes)

- Be direct
- Use paragraph breaks to make your essay easy to read
- Make transitions, linking related ideas
- Finish strongly

### Step 5. Proofread (1–3 minutes)

- Save enough time for one final read through the entire essay
- Have a sense of the errors you are likely to make and seek to find and correct them

Now that we've quickly outlined the five steps to effective Praxis essay writing, it's time to see these steps in action.

## Applying the Kaplan Five-Step Method to the Argumentative Essay

Let's use the Kaplan Five-Step Method on a sample topic:

*The drawbacks to the use of nuclear power mean that it is not a long-term solution to the problem of meeting ever-increasing energy needs.*

### Step 1. Digest the Issue

It's simple enough. The person who wrote this believes that nuclear power is not a suitable replacement for other forms of energy.

### Step 2. Select the Points You Will Make

Your job, as stated in the directions, is to decide whether or not you agree and to explain your decision. Some would argue that the use of nuclear power is too dangerous, whereas others would say that we can't afford not to use it. So, which side do you take? Remember, this isn't about showing the admissions people what your deep-seated beliefs about the environment are—it's about showing that you can formulate an argument and write it down. Quickly think through the pros and cons of each side. Then choose the side for which you have the most relevant things to say. For this topic, that process might go something like this:

*Arguments for the use of nuclear power:*

- *Inexpensive compared to other forms of energy*
- *Fossil fuels will eventually be depleted*
- *Other sources, like solar power, still too problematic and expensive*

*Arguments against the use of nuclear power:*

- *Radioactive hyperproducts are deadly*
- *Safer alternatives like nuclear fusion may be viable in the future*
- *Other sources, like solar power, already in use*

Again, it doesn't matter which side you take. Let's say that in this case, you decide to argue against nuclear power. Remember, the question is asking you to argue *why* the cons of nuclear power outweigh the pros—the inadequacy of this power source is the end you're arguing toward, so don't list it as supporting evidence for your argument.

### Step 3. Organize

You've already begun to think out your arguments—that's why you picked the side you did in the first place. Now is the time to write them all out, including ones that weaken the opposing side.

*Nuclear power is not a viable alternative to other sources of energy because:*

- *Radioactive, spent fuel has leaked from storage sites (too dangerous)*
- *Reactor accidents can be catastrophic—Three Mile Island, Chernobyl, Fukushima (too dangerous)*

- More research into solar power will bring down its cost (weakens opposing argument)
- Solar-powered homes and cars running on biofuel already exist (alternatives proven viable)
- No serious effort to research other alternatives like nuclear fusion (better alternatives lie undiscovered)
- Energy companies don't spend money on alternatives; no vested interest (better alternatives lie undiscovered)

### Step 4. Write

Remember, open your essay with a general statement and then assert your position. From there, get down your main points. Your essay for this assignment might look like this one.

## SAMPLE ESSAY 1

At first glance, nuclear energy may seem to be the power source for the future. It's relatively inexpensive, it doesn't produce smoke, and its fuel supply is virtually inexhaustible. However, a close examination of the issue reveals that nuclear energy is more problematic and dangerous than other forms of energy production.

A main reason that nuclear energy is undesirable is the problem of radioactive waste storage. Highly toxic fuel left over from nuclear fission remains toxic for thousands of years, and the spills and leaks from existing storage sites are hazardous and costly to clean up. Even more appalling is the prospect of accidents at the reactor itself: incidents at the Three Mile Island, Chernobyl, and Fukushima power plants have proven that the consequences of a nuclear meltdown can be catastrophic and have consequences that are felt worldwide.

Environmental and health problems aside, the bottom line for the production of energy is profit. Nuclear power is a business just like any other, and the large companies that produce this country's electricity and gas claim they can't make alternatives like solar power affordable. Yet—largely because of incentives from the federal government—there exist today homes that are heated by solar power, and cars that are fueled by corn have already hit the streets. If the limited resources that have been devoted to energy alternatives have already produced working models, a more intensive effort is likely to make those alternatives less expensive and more reliable.

Options like solar power, hydroelectric power, and nuclear fusion are far better in the long run in terms of cost and safety. The only money required for these alternatives is for the materials required to harvest them: sunlight, water, and the power of the atom are free. They also don't produce any toxic by-products for which long-term storage—a hidden cost of nuclear power—must be found. Also, with the temporary exception of nuclear fusion, these sources of energy are already being harnessed today.

Whereas there are arguments to be made for both sides, it is clear that the drawbacks to the use of nuclear power are too great. If other alternatives are explored more seriously than they have been in the past, safer and less expensive sources of power will undoubtedly prove better alternatives.

### Step 5. Proofread

Take that last couple of minutes to catch any glaring errors. Be sure not to skimp on this step!

Tip: If you only have 30 seconds for this part, focus on your last paragraph to leave a good impression on your reader.

# HOLISTIC SCORING

The Core Writing essays are scored holistically. Holistic scoring uses a single letter or a number—on the Praxis, it's a number from 1 to 6—to provide an evaluation of an essay as a whole. A holistic score emphasizes the interrelation of different thinking and writing qualities in an essay (such as content, organization, and syntax) and tries to denote the unified effect that all of these elements combine to produce.

## Scoring Rubric for Argumentative Essay

### Score of 6

An essay with a score of 6 shows a high level of competence in responding to the assignment, though it may contain minor errors.

A level 6 essay:

- Has a clear thesis
- Is well organized and developed with strong connections between ideas
- Includes thoughtfully chosen reasons, examples, or details that support the main idea
- Demonstrates variety in sentence structure
- Demonstrates a command of the English language
- Contains few (if any) errors in grammar and usage

### Score of 5

An essay with a score of 5 shows clear competence in responding to the assignment, though it may contain minor errors.

A level 5 essay:

- Has a clear thesis
- Is organized and developed with connections between ideas
- Includes reasons, examples, or details that support the main idea
- Demonstrates some variety in sentence structure
- Demonstrates competence in the English language
- Contains few errors in grammar and usage

### Score of 4

An essay with a score of 4 shows competence in responding to the assignment.

A level 4 essay:

- Has a thesis
- Is organized and developed
- Includes some reasons, examples, or details that support the main idea
- Demonstrates some variety in sentence structure
- Demonstrates competence in the English language
- Is generally free of grammar/usage errors

### Score of 3

An essay with a score of 3 shows some competence in responding to the assignment, though it contains flaws.

A level 3 essay displays at least one of the following issues:

- Only weakly develops its thesis
- Needs more organization and development
- Includes reasons, examples, or details that are not adequate to support the main idea
- Contains several errors in grammar/usage

### Score of 2

An essay with a score of 2 is flawed.

A level 2 essay displays at least one of the following issues:

- Does not clearly define its thesis
- Lacks organization and development
- Fails to include enough reasons, examples, or details
- Commits several serious errors in language, grammar, usage, and/or mechanics

### Score of 1

An essay with a score of 1 is fundamentally deficient.

A level 1 essay:

- Has serious writing errors that detract from understanding the ideas; or
- is not coherent; or
- is almost completely lacking in development.

## Scoring Rubric for the Source Text Essay

### Score of 6

An essay with a score of 6 shows a high level of competence in responding to the assignment, though it may contain minor errors.

A level 6 essay:

- Explains well why the concerns are important with supportive examples, reasons, and details that tie the two sources together
- Includes information from both sources to explain the pertinent issues in the texts and cites the sources when paraphrasing or quoting
- Is well organized and developed with strong connections between ideas
- Demonstrates variety in sentence structure
- Demonstrates a command of the English language
- Contains few (if any) errors in grammar and usage

### Score of 5

An essay with a score of 5 shows clear competence in responding to the assignment, though it may contain minor errors.

A level 5 essay:

- Explains why the concerns are important with supportive examples, reasons, and details that tie the two sources together
- Includes information from both sources to explain the pertinent issues in the texts and cites the sources when paraphrasing or quoting
- Is organized and developed with connections between ideas
- Includes reasons, examples, or details that support the main idea
- Demonstrates some variety in sentence structure
- Demonstrates competence in the English language
- Contains few errors in grammar and usage

### Score of 4

An essay with a score of 4 shows competence in responding to the assignment.

A level 4 essay:

- Explains why the concerns are important with examples, reasons, and details that touch on both sources
- Includes information from both sources to explain the pertinent issues in the texts and cites the sources when paraphrasing or quoting
- Is organized and developed with connections between ideas
- Includes reasons, examples, or details that support the main idea
- Demonstrates some variety in sentence structure
- Demonstrates competence in the English language
- Is generally free of grammar/usage errors

### Score of 3

An essay with a score of 3 shows some competence in responding to the assignment, though it contains flaws.

A level 3 essay displays at least one of the following issues:

- Only weakly develops explanations of the importance of the concerns
- Works with only one source or does not adequately cover both sources
- Needs more organization and development
- Uses reasons, examples, or details that are not adequate to support the main idea
- Commits several errors in grammar/usage
- Fails to consistently cite the sources

### Score of 2

An essay with a score of 2 is flawed.

A level 2 essay displays at least one of the following issues:

- Does not demonstrate understanding of the importance of the concerns
- Works with only one source
- Lacks organization and development
- Fails to include enough reasons, examples, or details
- Commits several serious errors in language, grammar, usage, and/or mechanics
- Does not cite the sources even when paraphrasing or quoting

### Score of 1

An essay with a score of 1 is fundamentally deficient.

A level 1 essay:

- Has serious writing errors that detract from understanding the ideas; or
- Is not coherent; or
- is almost completely lacking in development.

## SOURCE TEXT ESSAY

Now it's your turn to use the Kaplan Method for Praxis Essays, this time on the Source Text essay. This essay is meant to assess your ability to establish the key points raised by both of the sources. Be sure to take notes from the sources as you read through them. Then write about the concerns that the two pieces raise, on your own scratch paper. On test day, you'll take your notes on your scratch paper, and will type your essay response on the computer. Don't worry: we've provided the framework for your planning stage below, and some sample essays follow so you can see how your work compares.

## Sample Prompt

**Directions:** In the following section, you will have 30 minutes to read two short passages on a topic and then plan and write an essay on that topic. The essay will be an informative essay based on the two sources that are provided.

Read the topic and sources carefully. You will probably find it best to spend a little time considering the topic and organizing your thoughts before you begin writing. DO NOT WRITE ON A TOPIC OTHER THAN THE ONE SPECIFIED. Essays on topics of your own choice will not be acceptable. In order for your test to be scored, your responses must be in English.

The essay questions are included in this test to give you an opportunity to demonstrate how well you can write. You should, therefore, take care to write clearly and effectively, using specific examples where appropriate. Remember that how well you write is much more important than how much you write, but to cover the topics adequately, you will probably need to write more than one paragraph.

**Assignment:**

Solar power is a clean energy source that individuals are using as an alternative to fossil fuels. The following sources discuss the impacts, both positive and negative, of switching to solar power. Read the two passages carefully and then write an essay in which you identify the most important concerns regarding the issue and explain why they are important. Your essay must draw on information from BOTH of the sources. In addition, you may draw on your own experiences, observations, or reading. Be sure to CITE the sources, whether you are paraphrasing or directly quoting.

**Passage 1: Solar Energy Council ("SEC"). The Topaz Solar Project and Beyond. New York: Fleming Press. 2015. Print.**

The largest solar farm in the world, known as Topaz, opened in late 2014. The plant, which cost $2.5 billion dollars to build, generates a whopping 550 megawatts of power. To put this number into perspective, this amount of power will be used to supply 160,000 homes. This switch from fossil fuels to solar power will save the environment exposure to approximately 377,000 tons of carbon dioxide emissions per year, which is equivalent to retiring 73,000 cars.

The benefits of constructing such a large-scale solar farm are not only environmental. There are also significant economic benefits. Over 400 construction jobs were added to the area during the construction phase, and $192 million in income was pumped into the local economy as a result. Economic benefits haven't stopped since the plant opened. Local energy suppliers are now able to enjoy $52 million in economic output.

Located in San Luis Obispo County in California, Topaz was built as part of California's Carrizo Plain. The plain is an area of native grassland northwest of Los Angeles. The land on which the plant sits was used as farmland in the past. Because of this, no new land disturbance was required in order to complete this large project. The land was no longer suitable for farming due to irrigation practices that had stripped the soil of its nutrients. The 4,700 private acres provided the perfect setting for a solar plant, meeting the developer's standards for low-impact development, which was a priority considering the site's proximity to the Carrizo Plain National Monument, a protected area that is home to native species and plants.

The plant's setup includes 460 panels mounted on steel support posts. The sunlight taken in by these panels is fed to power conversion stations. Each panel has its own conversion station. Made up of two inverters and a transformer each, the conversion stations are needed to make the power usable. The power is then sent to a substation that transforms it from 35.5 kilovolts to the standard 230 kilovolts. The Pacific Gas and Electric Company (PG&E) built a new switching station next to the solar farm. It is here that the power is looped into the grid that supplies neighboring areas.

Topaz will only remain the world's largest solar farm for a short period of time. The plant's owner, First Solar, is currently developing an even larger plant, also in California.

**Passage 2: Everly, Gwen. The Other Side of Solar. San Francisco: Goldstar. 2016. Print.**

With more and more large-scale solar farms being developed in the sunny southwestern United States, researchers and conservationists alike are beginning to notice surprising environmental effects. While solar energy is known for its positive environmental impacts, officials at the National Fish and Wildlife Forensics Laboratory have come to recognize one of its significant downsides: some species of birds that live in close proximity to large solar plants are dying off, including endangered birds.

A recent federal investigation recovered 233 birds that had been killed as a direct result of solar plants. Researchers believe that some of the affected birds have mistaken the large, reflective areas of the solar panels for bodies of water. This is a phenomenon referred to by scientists as "lake effect." The birds are drawn to what they assume to be water. They home in on the area and slam into the panels with great force. It is thought that the insects that birds eat fall victim to "lake effect" as well, leading the birds into the panels.

Researchers estimate that between 1,000 and 28,000 birds are killed each year as a result of harvesting solar energy. The number of birds affected by wind farming is much greater, ranging from 140,000 to 328,000 annually. Coal-fired electricity has the largest negative effect on birds, killing nearly 8 million a year. These numbers make solar farming seem like the best option. However, conservationists are quick to point out that the areas where solar is expected to boom between 2015 and 2020 are home to some of the rarest birds in the United States. This could put specific bird species at risk of extinction.

There exists a state mandate in California that 20 percent of all electricity sold must be renewable by the year 2017. This has been one driving force behind the rapid development of huge solar farms. The industry, which is expecting to boom as a result of this shift to renewable energy, is facing newly filed lawsuits by conservationist groups, citing the negative impact on wildlife. These lawsuits could prolong the approval process for the planned solar developments across the Southwest.

## Apply the Kaplan Method

### Step 1: Digest the issue or source texts and the prompt (3 minutes)

Topic of texts:

_____

_____

_____

_____

For what is the prompt asking?

_____

_____

### Step 2: Select the points you will make (3 minutes)

Main points from text 1:

_____

_____

Main points from text 2:

_____

_____

### Step 3: Organize (2 minutes)

Go back to Step 2 and star the points you want to put into your essay.

### Step 4: Write (20 minutes)

On test day, you'll compose your essay directly on the computer. However, the word processing software is basic, including only "cut," "paste" and "undo" commands; there are no spell- or grammar-check features. So, for the most realistic essay-writing practice, use a similarly basic word-processing software to type your practice essays.

_____

_____

### Step 5: Proofread (2 minutes)

Congratulations on writing your first Praxis essay! Please review your work against the essays below. Of course, your response will be a little different from these essays, but these will give you an idea of how the graders will score your essays.

### *High-Scoring Response*

*With the issue of global warming growing increasingly alarming, many individuals have turned away from fossil fuels to alternative power sources in an attempt to lessen the environmental damage caused by power generation. Despite the many benefits of cleaner energy production, however, its universal adoption is not without debate.*

*A recent example of the implementation of a large-scale clean energy project is the solar plant Topaz (southern California). The purpose of this project was to "save the environment exposure to approximately 377,000 tons of carbon dioxide emissions per year," which will greatly decrease the greenhouse gas levels in the atmosphere (Solar Energy Council "SEC" 2016). As a result of this decrease, the overall air quality will improve, and the depletion of the ozone layer will slow down. The SEC also tells us that the field on which Topaz stands was claimed for this purpose specifically because the field was already existing but was no longer fertile, and thus not useful as farmland. These facts presented in Passage 1 show that Topaz was meant to be an entirely positive environmental project, as it was constructed with the goal of creating clean energy without the need to clear-cut a forest, which is one of the main concerns with other solar plants.*

*Unfortunately, these positive effects of the construction of Topaz also come with negative effects, which are laid out by Everly in Passage 2. "The Other Side of Solar" describes a phenomenon that birds experience called the "lake effect," in which birds effectively misidentify the solar panels as bodies of water. This poses a problem when they attempt to land in the "water," as they instead crash into the solid glass surface, resulting in their demise. According to Everly, this is especially problematic in Southern California where Topaz is, because a number of endangered species of birds call that region home. The* author of Passage 2 does concede momentarily that "the number of birds affected by wind farming is much greater" and that "coal-fired electricity has the largest negative effect on birds," but this hardly dampens the author's argument against solar power, as the death of "between 1,000 and 28,000 birds" is hardly a negligible figure (Everly 2016).

Ultimately, the decision to use or scrap solar power as a means for clean energy is still up for debate. According to both sources, it would appear that solar power has the fewest negative impacts on the environment as compared to coal-fired or wind power. Solar power is not without its flaws, though, with negative effects ranging from using a field that could have other more beneficial uses to creating the "lake effect" that leads to a decrease in key bird populations.

### Medium-Scoring Response

Both of these passages talk about solar power. The author of Passage 1 is for solar power because it can power 160,000 homes, and will "save the environment exposure to approximately 377,000 tons of carbon dioxide emissions per year, which is the equivalent of retiring 73,000 cars" (SEC 2015). Also, building the Topaz plant put "$192 million" into the economy and it made lots of jobs when it was being built (SEC 2015). It also has "$52 million in economic output" (SEC 2015) which is really good for the economy because it pushes money into the area around Topaz.

The author of Passage 2 is against solar power because birds "slam into the panels with great force" (Everly 2016). There is also the issue of lawsuits from environmental groups because of the dead birds, so it's important that we not use solar power to avoid these lawsuits. Passage 2 makes a better argument, because it talks about other types of power and compares solar power to them based on the numbers of birds killed.

In conclusion, there are lots of things we need to think about when we consider whether or not we should use solar power. No solution is ever perfect, and we have to make trade-offs that lead to the best results possible in the real world.

### Low-Scoring Response

I think solar power is the best source of power because it usually hurts zero birds, which is not as many as coal-fired power or wind farming. Solar power also creates jobs for people, and makes money for people.

Honestly if people are so worried about birds then they should just use wave power, which doesn't hurt any animals and is the best power there is. It's a lot better than solar power.

# PRACTICE: ARGUMENTATIVE ESSAY

## Directions for the Written Assignment

This section of the test consists of a written assignment. You are asked to prepare a written response of about 300–600 words on the assigned topic. *The assignment can be found below.* You should use your time to plan, write, review, and edit what you have written for the assignment.

Read the assignment carefully before you begin to write. Think about how you will organize what you plan to write. Your response to the written assignment will be evaluated based on your demonstrated ability to:

- State or imply a clear position or thesis.
- Present a well-reasoned and -organized argument that connects ideas in a thoughtful and logical way.
- Use support and evidence to develop and bolster your ideas and account for the views of others.
- Display competent use of language through well-constructed sentences of varying lengths and structures.
- Express yourself without distractions caused by inattention to sentence and paragraph structure, choice and use of words, and mechanics (i.e., spelling, punctuation, and capitalization).

Your response will be evaluated based on your demonstrated ability to express and support opinions, not on the nature or content of the opinions expressed. The final version of the response should conform to the conventions of edited American English. This should be your original work, written in your own words, and not copied or paraphrased from some other work.

Be sure to write about the assigned topic and use multiple paragraphs. Please write legibly. You may not use any reference materials during the test. Remember to review what you have written and make any changes you think will improve your response.

# Written Assignment

With more violent acts occurring in our schools, there is a call for more obvious security measures, such as installing metal detectors, placing security guards in the hallway, banning backpacks, and requiring students to wear uniforms.

Do you believe these or other security measures are a good idea or bad idea?

Write an essay to support your position.

# Written Assignment Sample Response

The following is an example of a strong response to the written assignment.

I believe that some security measures in a school are important. If the idea of the security is actually to keep children safe while at school, it is a very good thing. If the measures have no safety value but infringe on the rights of the students, I would not be in favor of them. Let me explain my position with examples.

Security guards in the school, and even a local police precinct located in a school, can be very beneficial for all involved. In this way, students and police generally get to know each other on a more personal basis and can begin to trust and respect each other. If a police officer knew the students on a personal, informal basis, it might help him or her not to jump to conclusions based on a student's appearance or perceived behavior. It also might afford the students the opportunity to talk to the police when they thought trouble might be coming.

Since it is easy to hide a weapon in a backpack, another safeguard that might be helpful is not allowing students to carry backpacks to class. The backpacks can be kept in the lockers and only books carried to class. Schools might need to adjust the time allowed for changing between classes so students have the time to go to their lockers to exchange their books. This would be a minor modification and could mean a big difference in the safety of all the students.

On the other hand, I do not believe that all proposed changes would lead to greater student safety. For example, requiring students to wear uniforms would not have much impact on improving safety. Granted, in some schools, certain dress may have the appearance of gang clothing, but I think this is a limited argument. Dress, as long as it does not contain obscene material and sufficiently covers the student, is a matter of personal style. I do not believe it is the school's job to try to make everyone alike. Schools attempt to create individuals who can think critically and take a stand on an issue. By making everyone look alike, they tend to send the message that everyone should think alike. I do not believe that this is the job of school.

In summary, I believe that there are measures that can be taken to improve safety in schools. They should be well thought out and not unduly infringe on the rights of students in the school. In other words, the measures taken should have the sole purpose of improving safety of everyone in the school.

# PRAXIS: PRINCIPLES OF LEARNING AND TEACHING

# Introducing the Praxis Principles of Learning and Teaching (PLT) Tests

This section of the book is dedicated to the Principles of Learning and Teaching (PLT) tests. You should refer to the requirements for the state in which you plan on teaching to determine which of these tests you will need to take. See the table in the appendix of this book for more information.

## What is the PLT?

The Praxis PLT tests focus on the basic principles of learning and teaching that are essential for running a classroom. These principles are drawn from the theoretical foundations provided by key educational theorists and developmental psychologists.

Chapter 4 provides a review of the main names and theories that appear on the PLT tests. Although the PLT tests are divided up according to grade levels, the review here is designed to address universal concerns and theories relevant to learning and teaching. These same principles are tested in each of the four PLT tests (for Early Childhood and grades K–6, 5–9, and 7–12), as well as in the elementary education subject assessments covered in Chapter 5.

Consequently, Chapter 4 applies to you if you are required to take any of the following exams (test codes are included in parentheses after the test name):

- PLT: Early Childhood (5621), Grades K–6 (5622), Grades 5–9 (5623), or Grades 7–12 (5624)
- Elementary Education: Curriculum, Instruction, and Assessment (5017)
- Elementary Education: Content Knowledge (5018)

Please note that all four of the Praxis PLT tests reference the same PLT concepts and vary only slightly from each other. In this book, we have provided three sets of practice questions, one each for PLT: Grades K–6, PLT: Grades 5–9, and PLT: Grades 7–12. Because there is so much overlap, you may find it useful to practice with sets designed for grade levels other than the one for which you will test. Just keep in mind that each set will ask you to apply the common principles to the grade levels covered by the specific test. You can also find three full-length PLT practice tests—one for each of grades K–6, 5–9, and 7–12—in your online Study Plan.

If you are taking any of the PLT tests or the Elementary Education: Curriculum, Instruction, and Assessment test, begin by working through the review in Chapter 4. Then continue your preparation with the sample PLT practice questions and explanations and the full-length PLT tests in your online Study Plan. A set of practice questions for Elementary Education: Curriculum, Instruction, and Assessment can be found in Chapter 5, and a full-length practice test for that exam is in your Study Plan.

If you are taking the Elementary Education: Content Knowledge test, the review in Chapter 4 is less relevant, and your focus should shift to an overall review of the content on the test. If you are preparing for this test, skim the information in Chapter 4 and then move on to the preparation and practice for the Content Knowledge exam in Chapter 5.

## Taking the PLT

The four Praxis PLT tests share a similar format. Each is 2 hours long and consists of 70 multiple-choice questions and two case studies accompanied by four short essay questions. The test makers suggest spending approximately 1 minute on each multiple-choice question, leaving 50 minutes to read, evaluate, and answer the case study questions.

We agree with those timing guidelines. However, it's important to note that you need not take the sections of this test in order—in fact, Kaplan recommends against taking this test front to back.

Ideally, you should spend a little less than an hour on your first pass through the multiple-choice section. If you've spent enough time reviewing the content in this chapter, you'll have a framework to answer the majority of questions. But even the most prepared may find that a few questions on this test are outside their areas of expertise. Don't spend too much time when this happens; if you run into a stumper, "mark" the question using the computer interface, then move on.

Once you've wrapped up your case study answers, head back to the questions you marked earlier. Some of them might be easier to answer once you take a second look. Others may take a little longer. At this stage, you've done enough that you can afford to spend some extra time on the last few problems. Make sure to keep your eye on the clock, though. There is no wrong answer penalty on the PLT, so you should never leave a question blank. Use your last 2 minutes to randomly make choices for any unanswered questions.

Don't forget to go to your Study Plan for the PLT pre-test and the full-length PLT practice tests!

# CHAPTER FOUR

# Review of the Principles of Learning and Teaching (PLT) Test

## TEST STRUCTURE AND FORMAT

The following table shows you what to expect from the Principles of Learning and Teaching test.

| Praxis Principles of Learning and Teaching |
| --- |
| Format: Computer-delivered |
| Number of Questions: 70 multiple-choice (called "selected response" by the test maker); 4 constructed response<br>Time: 120 minutes |
| Test may include pre-test questions that do not count toward your score |
| No penalty for incorrect answers |
| Scratch paper is available during the exam (it will be destroyed before you leave the testing center) |
| Content covered:<br><br>Students as Learners: approximately 21 questions, 22.5 percent of the test<br><br>Instructional Process: approximately 21 questions, 22.5 percent of the test<br><br>Assessment: approximately 14 questions, 15 percent of the test<br><br>Professional Development, Leadership and Community: approximately 14 questions, 15 percent of the test<br><br>Analysis of Instructional Scenarios: approximately 4 constructed response questions, 25 percent of the test |

Multiple-choice (the test maker calls these "selected response") questions that test your understanding of the principles of learning and teaching make up 75 percent of the Praxis PLT test. The questions cover the following four content areas:

- Students as Learners
- Instructional Process
- Assessment
- Professional Development, Leadership, and Community

The other 25 percent of the test consists of four essay (the test maker calls these "constructed-response") questions for two case histories. These questions test your ability to apply your knowledge of the principles of learning and teaching to extended instructional scenarios.

The first four sections of this chapter cover the basics of the four content areas on the PLT. The final section in this chapter offers strategies for analyzing case histories and writing effective answers to constructed-response questions.

---

## LEARNING OBJECTIVES

By the end of this chapter, you will be able to:

- Describe the structure and format of the Praxis PLT test
- Outline the four major content areas covered on the PLT test
- Apply strategic analysis to evaluate and answer PLT case study questions
- Use the Praxis PLT practice test to assess your performance

---

# STUDENTS AS LEARNERS

## Human Development

The Praxis exam requires foundational knowledge in human development as it relates to learning. It is important to understand the stages of human development and how they are applied by various theorists. All children will meet developmental milestones at various times, so the ranges given by theorists are guidelines and not a hard standard for measurement.

Knowledge is acquired in stages, and mastery of one stage becomes the foundation for moving to the next stage. Since the methods with which children learn vary, it is imperative to be able to apply a broad range of educational theories to encompass a large variety of learning styles.

Skills acquisition is based on physical, emotional, and cognitive abilities. If a child has not met the minimum needs to acquire a new skill, there will be a delay until the child's abilities have caught up. This means that the developmental needs of a class will fall into a wide range of possibilities. It is important to understand what the possible ranges are for each class level and the techniques needed to meet those needs.

## Theories of Development

You must have knowledge of the basic theorists' views on developmental stages, ways of learning, social development, and moral and reasoning development to plan instruction. Following is a discussion of some of the most prominent theorists and their theories, which describe widely acknowledged stages of development.

### Piaget

Jean Piaget was a theorist who worked on the development of thinking. He observed infants and found that as they explored the objects in their environment, they gained knowledge of the world around them. Piaget called these skills **schemas**. When the infant used the schemas to observe a new object, Piaget called this **assimilation**, or interpreting an experience in terms of current ways of understanding. When the infant tried the old schema on a new object and molded it to fit the new object and be recategorized, Piaget called this **accommodation,** or a change in cognitive structures that produces a corresponding behavioral change.

Piaget developed four stages of cognitive development:

- **Sensorimotor Level:** Children from birth to age 2 base their thoughts primarily on their senses and motor abilities.

- **Preoperational Stage:** Children ages 2–7 think mainly in symbolic terms—manipulating symbols used in creative play in the absence of the actual objects involved.

- **Concrete Operational Stage:** Children ages 7–11 think in logical terms. They are not very abstract. At this stage, children need hands-on, concrete experiences to manipulate symbols logically. They must perform these operations within the context of concrete situations.

- **Formal Operational Stage:** Children ages 11–15 develop abstract and hypothetical thinking. They use logical operations in the abstract rather than the concrete. Children at this stage are capable of **metacognition**, or "thinking about thinking." Piaget noted that not all children move successfully to the formal operational stage.

Piaget believed in cognitive **constructivism**, which is the idea that students construct their own knowledge when they interact in social ways. Learning involves risk taking and mistakes, but over time, students develop greater moral and intellectual capacities.

Piaget, as well as Vygotsky and Dewey (see below), defined learning as the creation of meaning that occurs when an individual links new knowledge within the context of existing knowledge.

### Kohlberg

Lawrence Kohlberg expanded Piaget's work and presented six stages of **moral development**, based on **cognitive reasoning**. Everyone begins at Stage 1 and progresses through the stages in an unvarying and irreversible order. According to Kohlberg, few people reach Stages 5 and 6. Stages 1 and 2 in the **preconventional level** involve an "egocentric point of view" and a "concrete individualistic perspective." Children from ages 4 to 10 respond mainly to reward and punishment. Stages 3 and 4 of the **conventional level** involve the maintenance of positive relations and the rules of society. Children conform to the rules and wishes of society to preserve the social order. Stages 5 and 6 of the **postconventional level** involve reasoning from an abstract point of view and possessing ideals that take precedence over particular societal laws. Individuals act according to an enlightened conscience at this level.

### Montessori

Maria Montessori believed that childhood is divided into four stages: birth to age 2, ages 2–5, ages 5–6, and ages 7–12. Adolescence is divided into two levels: ages 12–15 and ages 16–18. Age ranges are approximate and refer to stages of the cognitive and emotional development common to most children. The process of learning is divided into three stages: (1) introduction to a concept by means of a lesson, something read in a book, or some other outside source; (2) processing the information and developing an understanding of the concept through work, experimentation, and creation; and (3) knowing the information or possessing an understanding of it, as demonstrated by the ability to pass a test with confidence, teach another, or express it with ease. Children learn directly from the environment and from other children more than from the teacher. The teacher prepares the environment and facilitates learning. The environment should nurture all **multiple intelligences** and **styles of learning**. Education of movement and of character comes before education of the mind. Children learn to take care of themselves, their environment, and each other and learn to speak politely, be considerate, and be helpful. Learning experiences provided for the children during their absorbent mind years are particularly designed to promote cognitive and emotional development.

### Dewey

John Dewey established the progressive education practice that fosters individuality, free activity, and learning through experience. **Cooperative learning** among peers; the individual needs of the students; and the introduction of art, music, dancing, etc. in education were all cornerstones of Dewey's educational approach. He believed that the school should prepare the child for active participation in the life of the community. He thought that education should break down, rather than reinforce, the gap between the experience of schooling and the needs of a truly participatory democracy. He felt that the school was primarily a social institution, and education was a social process and a process of living, not a preparation for future living. His *Pedagogic Creed*, published in 1897, explained his views on education and was a guide for teaching.

### Bruner

Jerome Bruner considered learning to be an active process in which learners construct new ideas or concepts based on their current and past knowledge. Within this **constructivist** theory, the learner selects and transforms information, constructs hypotheses, and makes decisions, relying on a cognitive structure to do so. This process allows students to go beyond the information given to them and encourages them to discover principles by themselves, or participate in **discovery learning**. Teachers and students should engage in an active dialogue. The curriculum should be organized in a spiral manner so that students continually build upon what they have already learned. This is known as **inquiry teaching**, in which the students are active partners in the search for knowledge.

### Vygotsky

Lev Semenovich Vygotsky's social development theory is based on the principle that social interaction plays a fundamental role in the development of cognition. Every function in the child's cultural development appears twice: first, on the social level, and second, on the individual level. The potential for cognitive development is limited to a certain time span called the **zone of proximal development**, in which full development depends on full social interaction either with teacher guidance or peer collaboration, as in **cooperative learning**. Cognitive development is limited to a certain range at any given age. The development of thought and language and their interrelationships led Vygotsky to explain consciousness as the end product of socialization. The learning of language begins with thought, undergoes changes, and turns into speech. Children's learning development is affected by their culture, including the culture of the family environment, in which they are enmeshed. The language used by the adults transmits to the child. Children's language serves as their primary tool of intellectual adaptation. Eventually, children can use their internal language to direct their own behavior in a process known as **self-regulation**.

Vygotsky also introduced an instructional technique called **scaffolding**, in which the teacher breaks a complex task into smaller tasks, models the desired learning strategy or task, provides support as students learn to do the task, and then gradually shifts responsibility to the students. In this manner, a teacher enables students to accomplish as much of a task as possible without adult assistance. The skills, in essence, are gradually transferred to the learner.

Teachers should know the above theorists' views on students' learning and have a general idea of the terms used in each theory and its proposed stages of development. Understanding each theory's implications for children and what, as a result, you will need to know and do in planning, assessment, motivation, and management will enhance your teaching.

# Diversity

You should have an understanding of the diversity of your students and the factors that may affect how they learn, including dialect, immigrant status, socioeconomic background, ethnicity, race, creed/religion, language, culture, gender, social styles, learning or thinking styles, scholastic abilities, challenges, and lifestyles. You will need to understand how the influences of students' culture, language, and experiences are related to the students' success in the classroom.

Regarding bilingual education, understand the differences between English immersion instruction, English as a second language instruction, transitional bilingual education, and two-way bilingual education.

- **English immersion instruction** is entirely in English. Teachers deliver lessons in simplified English so that students learn both English and academic subjects.

- **English as a second language instruction** may be the same as immersion but also may have some support for individuals using their native languages. These students may have a special class each day to work strictly on their English skills.

- **Transitional bilingual education instruction** is in the students' native language, but there is also instruction each day on developing English skills.

- **Two-way bilingual education instruction** is given in two languages to the students. The goal of this instruction is to have students become proficient in both languages. In this case, teachers team teach. This approach is sometimes called *dual-immersion* or *dual-language instruction*.

When working with students who are English language learners (ELLs), it is especially important to include collaborative (small-group) activities in class. Teachers should aim to include examples relevant to the students' cultural backgrounds, and visual representations of content should be included whenever possible.

### Learning Styles

Learning styles are different approaches or ways of learning. The four types of learning styles are **visual learning**, **auditory learning**, **tactile learning**, and **kinesthetic learning**.

- Visual learners learn through seeing. These students watch the teacher's body language and facial expressions to understand the content of the lessons. They learn best from visual displays, diagrams, illustrated books, overhead transparencies, videos, flip charts, and handouts. Visual learners take detailed notes to absorb information.

- Auditory learners learn through listening. Verbal lectures, class discussions, and listening to what others have to say is how they learn best. Written information may have less meaning for auditory learners unless it is read aloud. Auditory learners learn well by listening to a tape recorder or audio program on a computer.

- Tactile learners learn through touching. They have to actively explore the physical world around them. These tactile learning students learn best through a hands-on approach.
- Kinesthetic learners learn through moving and doing. These students find it difficult to sit still for long periods of time and need activity and exploration.

Another approach comes from David Kolb's theory of learning styles, which includes **concrete experiences** (being involved in a new experience), **reflective observation** (watching others or developing observations about their own experience), **abstract conceptualization** (creating theories to explain their observations), and **active experimentation** (using theories to solve problems and make decisions). Each of these learning styles requires teachers to offer different methods for students to learn the lessons.

The concrete experiencer learns well through activities such as field trips, lab work, or interactive computer programs. Writing in journals or learning logs is an effective means of helping reflective observers learn because it forces them to concentrate on the content of the lesson. Students who learn through abstract conceptualization will work well with lectures, papers, and text. Simulations, case studies, and active homework are the most helpful activities for students who are active experimenters.

### Multiple Intelligences

**Dr. Howard Gardner** developed the theory of **multiple intelligences** in 1983. Rather than accept the traditional and limited idea of intelligence, based on IQ testing of mathematics and reading skills, Dr. Gardner proposed eight areas of intelligence.

These eight multiple intelligences are as follows:

- **Verbal/linguistic intelligence or word smart:** These students demonstrate highly developed auditory skills and sensitivity to the meaning and order of words. They learn best by saying, hearing, and seeing words. Motivate them by talking with them, by providing them with books and recordings, and by giving them opportunities to use their writing abilities.
- **Logical-mathematical intelligence or number-reasoning smart:** These students demonstrate the ability to handle chains of reasoning and to recognize patterns and order. They are conceptual thinkers who explore relationships and patterns and like to experiment with things in an orderly and controlled manner. They typically compute arithmetic in their heads and reason out other problems. Provide them with time and concrete materials for their experiments such as science kits, games like chess, brainteasers, and a computer.
- **Visual/spatial intelligence or picture smart:** These students think in mental pictures and images. They have the ability to perceive the world accurately and to re-create or transform aspects of that world. These students learn visually. Teach these students with images, pictures, and color. Films, videos, diagrams, maps, and charts motivate them. Provide them with cameras, telescopes, 3-D building supplies, and art supplies.
- **Bodily-kinesthetic intelligence or body smart:** These students are athletically gifted and pick up knowledge through bodily sensations. They communicate by using gestures and body language. They like to act out their thoughts and are clever mimics. Their learning comes with touching and moving. Motivate them through role-play, dramatic improvisation, creative movement, and all kinds of physical activity. These students require hands-on activities for their learning opportunities.

- **Musical intelligence or music smart:** These students have sensitivity to pitch, melody, rhythm, and tones. They often sing, hum, or whistle melodies to themselves. They may play musical instruments or want to. They are also sensitive to nonverbal sounds that others overlook, such as chirping crickets or a singing bird. These students learn through rhythm and melody. They can memorize easily when they sing it out. They study effectively with music in the background. Motivate them with records, tapes, and musical instruments.

- **Interpersonal intelligence or people smart:** These students have the ability to understand people and relationships. They are "people people" who often become leaders in the classroom, on the playground, and around the neighborhood. These students know how to organize, communicate, mediate, and manipulate. They have many friends. Provide them with opportunities in peer group, school, and community activities that open learning doors for them.

- **Intrapersonal intelligence or self smart:** These students have the ability to assess their own emotional life as a means to understand themselves and others. They have a powerful sense of self and shy away from groups to work alone. Their inner life is rich and filled with dreams, intuition, feelings, and ideas. They write diaries. They learn best by themselves. Provide them with private space where they can work and spend time in quiet introspection. Respect their privacy and validate that it's all right to be independent.

- **Naturalist intelligence or nature smart:** These students have the ability to observe nature and discern patterns and trends. They recognize species of plants or animals in their environment. They learn the many characteristics of different birds. They are aware of changes in their local or global environment. They enjoy collecting and cataloging natural material. They learn best in the outdoors. Provide them with opportunities to explore the outdoors regularly and bring the outdoors indoors. Supply them with many books, visuals, and props related to the natural world. Have them create observation notebooks of natural phenomena. Have them draw or photograph natural objects. Provide them with binoculars, telescopes, or microscopes for their observational work.

According to Dr. Gardner, teachers should place equal attention on linguistic and logical-mathematical intelligence, along with incorporating strategies that include individuals who show gifts in the other intelligences. If teachers are trained to present their lessons in a wide variety of ways, using music, cooperative learning, art activities, role-play, multimedia, field trips, and inner reflection rather than lectures and worksheets, children will have an opportunity to learn in ways harmonious with their unique multiple intelligences.

By incorporating factors of the multiple intelligence theory into instruction, learning may be facilitated more effectively. Teachers will not have as much difficulty reaching students. Teachers do not have to teach all the lessons in all eight intelligences, but they should address multiple intelligences as appropriate for the lesson content.

### Differences Between Sexes

Boys and girls differ in their physical, emotional, and intellectual development. Numerous studies indicate several differences in the learning strategies typically adopted by these populations. It should be noted that not all of these behaviors will manifest in any given individual, and there is overlap between the groups. Girls tend to emphasize memorization. Boys learn more by elaboration strategies. Girls evaluate their own learning during the learning process. They use control strategies more often than boys. Boys may need more assistance in planning, organizing, and structuring their learning activities. Students who lack self-confidence in their ability to learn are often exposed to failure. Self-concept plays an important part in studying reading and mathematics. Girls perform well in reading activities but often lack self-confidence in mathematics. The opposite is true for boys.

Teachers must be aware of motivation and self-esteem differences among boys and girls and use appropriate teaching strategies in instruction. Classroom variables to consider when viewing gender differences are the grouping of the students, management of the class, the use of time on tasks, assessment standards, and expectations of the students.

## Cultural Expectations

By understanding the differences in thinking about other cultures that students have, the teacher is able to meet various student needs. Having a clear understanding of the students, their families, and their communities will help to provide meaningful instruction and help enhance your teaching methods and strategies.

Family expectations placed on a student—based on cultural influences such as tradition, religion, or hopes for future advancement—may differ from the expectations of the teacher. For example, a match between the cultural expectations for literacy and the teacher's expectations for literacy is vital in the successful acquisition of reading skills. Positive connections between life and culture at home and the school environment help to ensure the success of each student.

Having a diverse group of students means having students with numerous sets of expectations regarding teacher relationships and behaviors that most likely were set in their home countries, their former schools, or their families. Some students may expect more traditional teaching, and they may be offended or upset if their new teacher is more informal. These students may be used to a clear, ordered pattern of classroom activities. In certain cultures, students expect the teacher to be the only one to present knowledge. These students may be unfamiliar with working in groups and doing cooperative learning activities. They may have difficulty respecting other students' ideas, and they may be uncomfortable in classroom situations that disagree with their cultural understanding of how to learn.

In schools where migration is common, it is important to understand that such moves often affect students' learning, self-esteem, and behavior. Teachers must create an exceptional learning environment that enables all students to meet high academic standards and meets their other needs, such as health and nutrition. The needs of these students are often exacerbated as their families move around. In addition, many of these students lose quite a lot of schooling over the course of a year and can benefit from the careful guidance of their new teachers.

Accelerating the curriculum; using innovation in instruction; making positive use of time and other resources; and involving parents more centrally in planning, decision making, and instructional support roles will upgrade the effectiveness of the instruction and the academic achievement of migratory students. Teachers need to create lessons that use the previous knowledge of the students so that connections are made. Effective use of technology will help students learn in active ways. Teachers should try to create an accepting, comfortable climate in the classroom so that the students don't feel isolated.

Using appropriate topics for discussion and study in the classroom requires the teacher to know the cultural as well as personal sensitivity of the students and use discretion when presenting discussion topics. In a high-achieving classroom environment, teachers can have students explore ideas and issues by drawing on their own and other students' cultures, experiences, and knowledge. At-risk students need classroom environments that provide them with authentic tasks, many opportunities, and many ways to learn and succeed.

Teachers must remember that their own cultural values may not be the same as those of their students. Cultural values are formed from experiences in different social, historical, and economic environments. Cultural values are also formed with contact with other cultural groups.

Understanding age-appropriate knowledge and behavior, as well as working with the student culture at the school, will help teachers differentiate instruction for students. Knowing the family backgrounds, linguistic patterns and differences, cognitive patterns and differences, and social and emotional issues students bring with them to the classroom is also important for classroom instruction.

## Students with Special Needs

Areas of exceptionality in students' learning vary when the students are eligible for special education. Regular classroom teachers must know how to accommodate the diversity of learning abilities in the classroom when special education students are mainstreamed into the regular classroom. Special education students can have visual and perceptual difficulties, special physical or sensory challenges, learning disabilities, attention deficit disorder (ADD), attention deficit hyperactive disorder (ADHD), fetal alcohol syndrome, intellectual disability (ID), or giftedness.

Assuming responsibility for teaching each student in the classroom becomes challenging because of the increasing number of students with special needs. The task becomes determining which strategies will help these students succeed not only in the classroom but also in the environment in which they will live. Teachers must have an open mind, an understanding of what exceptionalities are, and a willingness to accept the challenge of teaching students who have them. Having an extensive repertoire of teaching methods and strategies and knowing that there is no one solution to meeting special education students' needs will allow you to be creative in developing new strategies to help your students succeed. Teachers should always try to use strategies that rely on the students' strengths.

## Legislative Influences

Teachers must know the legislation concerning students with exceptionalities and understand how to apply the legislation in the classroom. You may encounter questions about the following laws and provisions on the PLT test.

**The Americans with Disabilities Act (1990) (ADA)** established a clear and comprehensive prohibition of discrimination on the basis of disability. It provides a national mandate for clear, strong, consistent, and enforceable standards addressing discrimination against individuals with disabilities. It ensures that the federal government plays a central role in enforcing the standards established in this act. This act further invokes the sweep of congressional authority, including the power to enforce the 14th Amendment and to regulate commerce, to address major areas of discrimination faced by people with disabilities.

**The Individuals with Disabilities Education Act (IDEA)** became Public Law 105-17 in 1997 and ensures that children with disabilities and the families of such children have access to a free, appropriate public education. This act further provides incentives for whole-school approaches and prereferral interventions to reduce the need to label children as disabled to address their learning needs. It focuses resources on teaching and learning while reducing paperwork and requirements that do not assist in improving educational results. The federal government has a role in assisting state and local efforts to educate children with disabilities to improve results for such children and ensure equal protection of the law.

There are specific regulations related to students' rights and teachers' responsibilities within your own state and school district. Understand these laws as they relate to confidentiality and privacy, appropriate treatment of students, and procedures for reporting situations related to possible child abuse. Check local resources for specific regulations within your school and school district.

**The Individualized Education Plan (IEP)**, a provision of IDEA, describes the special education and related services specifically designed to meet the unique educational needs of special needs students. The IEP covers all deficit areas, related services, and needed accommodations in both general (regular and vocational) and special education. As a teacher, you will need to understand how IEPs are developed and used. The goals and short-term instructional objectives in the IEP must be stated in measurable, observable behaviors and fit the student's current level of functioning and probable growth rate. A sequence of skills must be indicated. A statement of related specific services, special education placement, and time and duration of services must be included. The language of the IEP must be written to be understandable to both parents/guardians and professionals. A consensus among parents/guardians, the students, and school personnel must be represented. The law requires an annual meeting to review progress and goals, but many states now use "benchmarks" as often as four times a year to let parents/guardians know the progress being made. If the goals need to be adjusted, parents/guardians must be called in for an IEP update meeting. A list of the individuals who are responsible for implementation of the IEP must be included.

Students with disabilities may also receive **504 accommodations**. Similar to IEPs, 504 plans may require that students receive needed accommodations to help ensure the chance for academic success. In contrast, students with IEPs receive specialized instruction and services.

IDEA requires a "least restrictive environment" to enable special education students to function effectively. The least restrictive environment provision stipulates that, when possible, students are not taught in separate settings but are taught along with their age peers. Specifics when considering the special education student for regular classroom activities must be stated in the IEP, indicating exactly what would be necessary to enable the student to receive satisfactory benefits in the regular environment with typical students. This may include receiving assistance in other areas of the school, away from the regular classroom.

## Motivation and Successful Learning

**Motivation** can be **intrinsic** (from within) or **extrinsic** (from without). Intrinsic motivation comes from self-determination—students are in control of their own destiny and can make choices. With intrinsic motivation, students themselves want to learn and do not need external incentives, such as stickers or candy. Motivation is what energizes, drives, and directs students' behaviors.

### Motivational Theories

**Skinner** and other behavior theorists suggest that teachers first identify the behavior they are trying to change, then reward positive behavior and provide consequences for negative behavior. This approach controls students' behaviors with immediate, extrinsic rewards. Critics charge that this approach works for short-term behavior changes but impairs learning and does not support long-term changes. To promote the development of intrinsic motivation in students, teachers can create celebrations of learning. Anything spontaneous that acknowledges students' accomplishments is more motivating over a longer period. Students are eager to learn when teachers provide a positive learning environment.

Using a mixture of teaching and learning methods, engaging emotions and natural curiosity, communicating high expectations, and showing students how to manage their own states of learning will spark intrinsic motivation. Teachers need to provide safe and optimal learning environments by ensuring the opportunity for intrinsic motivation as opposed to extrinsic motivation, which is often considered manipulative and believed to promote negative learning outcomes.

Using appropriate grouping in the classroom and correct curriculum and assessment systems, while limiting distractions, teachers can influence the motivation of students to learn. Teachers must consider students' learning strategies because these activate motivational issues.

The **humanistic** approach to motivation uses **Maslow's hierarchy of needs**. Maslow introduced the term *self-actualization* as one of these needs. The underlying assumption of self-actualization is that people are basically good and have within themselves all they need to develop their full potential to be worthwhile individuals. Maslow's hierarchy of five motivational needs consists of security, social, esteem, physiological, and self-actualization. Following Maslow's approach, teachers must make sure students are safe and secure in their environment—for example, not hungry or uncomfortable—because students cannot focus on the learning task in the classroom until the need for security is met.

The **cognitive** approach is based on the learning-goal theory, self-monitoring and reflective behaviors, and self-evaluation.

The **attribution theory** approach is centered on the social-cognitive needs of students. This theory allows students to accept ownership for their own performance or nonperformance. Attributions can influence cognition and behavior, such as emotional reactions to success and failure and expectations for future successes and failures.

Increased learning can take place if teachers provide **positive reinforcement** (or **operant conditioning**) for the responses students make. This often leads to students repeating successful learning responses. Teachers can promote better learning motivation if they capitalize on students' interests and communicate the belief that all students can learn. Teachers can develop appropriate strategies to focus students on learning rather than performance. Allow students to fail and model how to respond constructively.

# INSTRUCTIONAL PROCESS

## Choosing Objectives, Writing Objectives, and Modifying Objectives

As a teacher, you will need to know how to develop effective instructional objectives. Objectives should answer the question "What are students supposed to know or be able to do once the lesson is completed?" They should not describe what the teacher does during the lesson. They should not be overly specific, involved, or complicated. The objectives need to address behaviors and knowledge so that teachers can determine whether they are met. They must be observable, detectable, and measurable/assessable. Objectives must incorporate appropriate district, state, and national standards.

**Madeline Hunter** developed a **direct instruction** model for effective instruction. Her outline of a lesson consists of the objectives, standards of performance and expectations, anticipatory set or advance organizer, the teaching (input, modeling and demonstration, direction giving, and checking for understanding), guided practice and monitoring, closure, and independent practice. This model is generally referred to as the Madeline Hunter Method.

**David Ausubel** proposed an instructional technique called the **advance organizer**. Advance organizers are introduced before the learning begins and presented at a higher level of abstraction. They are selected on the basis of their suitability for explaining, integrating, and interrelating the material to be presented to the class. These are not overviews or summaries but rather act as bridges for the students between the new material they will learn and their previous knowledge. Making a semantic web with the students before the lesson or unit begins is an example of using an advance organizer.

You also will need to know how to use student-centered learning activities, such as collaborative learning, cooperative learning groups (CLGs), concept development, discovery learning, independent study, inquiry, interdisciplinary and integrated study, project-based learning, simulations, and units. When creating lessons and teaching strategies, involve some of the following concepts: creative thinking, concept mapping, higher-order thinking, induction, deductive reasoning, problem solving, and recall.

## Taxonomy of Objectives

Benjamin Bloom created a taxonomy or classification system for categorizing the level of abstraction of various skills and abilities that learners can develop once knowledge has been acquired. With the help of others, he established a hierarchy of educational objectives, which is often known as **Bloom's taxonomy**. They identified three domains, or types of learning of educational activities. The **cognitive domain** involves knowledge and development of intellectual attitudes and skills. The other domains are the **affective domain**, which deals with growth in feelings or emotional areas and attitudes, and the **psychomotor domain**, which deals with manual or physical skills. Teachers mainly use Bloom's taxonomy of educational objectives in the cognitive domain to write lesson plan objectives, to formulate questions, and to use methods and teaching strategies from the simplest to the most complex. If the lesson requires manual or physical skills, teachers use the psychomotor domain to plan.

### Bloom's Taxonomy of the Cognitive Domain

- **Knowledge:** Lowest level of learning outcomes; recall of specific facts and terms from the materials
- **Comprehension:** Ability to understand facts and principles and interpret the meaning of the material
- **Application:** Ability to use learned material concepts and principles in new and concrete situations
- **Analysis:** Ability to break down material into its component parts so that the organizational structure may be understood

- **Synthesis:** Ability to put parts together to create a new whole; uses creative behaviors to formulate new patterns and structure
- **Evaluation:** Ability to judge the value of the material for a given purpose; value judgments are based on either internal or external definite criteria

While the original version of Bloom's taxonomy is still often cited, some educators and educational researchers now refer to the revised version of Bloom's taxonomy, which emphasizes verbs instead of nouns: Remembering, Understanding, Applying, Analyzing, Evaluating, and Creating. Note that the placement of Evaluating and Creating (similar to Synthesis in the original version) have been switched.

## Planning to Teach the Lesson

You should use techniques for planning instruction that will meet curriculum goals, including the incorporation of learning theory, subject matter, curriculum development, and student development. Create effective bridges, such as advance organizers, between curriculum goals and students' experiences. Include **modeling** and use **guided** and **independent practice**. By using **transitions**, activating students' **previous knowledge**, encouraging exploration and **problem solving**, and building new skills, your lessons will be successful.

### Questions to Ask Yourself

1. **How will you group the students for instruction?** Be specific about why you have chosen the grouping and how it will help to achieve the desired objectives. Will you use small groups, whole groups, cooperative learning groups, or independent learning? Will you use **heterogeneous** or **homogeneous** groupings?

2. **What teaching method(s) will you use for the lesson?** Is this lesson teacher directed only? Is there a holistic question/activity? Do the methods incorporate the learning styles, learning modalities, and multiple intelligences of your students?

3. **Have you considered all the instructional strategies you could use?** Cooperative learning? Direct instruction? Discovery learning? Whole-group discussion? Independent study? Interdisciplinary instruction? Concept mapping? Inquiry method? Will any of these help to attain your educational goals?

4. **What specific activities have been planned?** What will the students do to meet the lesson's learning objectives? Do these activities incorporate learning styles, modalities, and multiple intelligences? Has sufficient time been allocated for the activities?

5. **What instructional and curricular materials are planned for use?** Include multimedia technology and websites. Curriculum materials include the textbooks, teacher guides, kits, models, visuals, and any other innovative means used to help deliver the curriculum. Resources to use in instructional planning may also include local experts, field trips, and library research.

6. **Will the accommodations for specific students be included in the lesson and meet the objectives?** Can you provide instructional support for students who are exceptional, are gifted, have ADD or ADHD, are intellectually disabled, are learning disabled, have visual or perceptual challenges, are hearing impaired, have physical or sensory challenges, or are second language learners?

7. **Is there a plan for evaluation and assessment given each student's learning style?** How will you know whether students met the objective? Is there a plan for follow-up of this lesson? Can you use the knowledge the students gained for future lessons?

## Adapting Instruction and Cultural and Linguistic Diversity

Teachers plan their teaching strategies and methods based on the needs of their students in the areas of cognition, physical activity, emotional growth, and social adjustment. You will need to know how to plan and implement **developmentally appropriate programs (DAPs)** based on knowledge of the individual development levels of the students.

Instruction should be amended or changed to meet the unique learning or social needs of students. All aspects of individual differences are considered in planning instruction. These include cultural diversity, exceptionalities, and students' developmental levels.

## Managing the Instructional Environment

Classroom management begins before students arrive in the fall. Communicate expectations clearly and with an understanding of your students. Effective verbal and nonverbal communication is a part of teaching. You need to have methods to stimulate discussion and responses in your classroom. Always consider the effect of cultural and gender differences on communication in your classroom. By using various instructional methods, you will enable more students to have the opportunity to participate in the learning environment. Having some general knowledge about the impact of limited English proficiency on students and parents/guardians and its implications for teachers in planning, teaching, assessing, motivating, managing, and communicating will allow you to better serve your students. Know how to use both verbal and nonverbal communication and understand the various questioning techniques.

Know the principles of effective classroom management and strategies to promote positive relationships, cooperation, and purposeful learning:

1. Establish daily procedures and routines.
2. Establish classroom rules, rewards, and consequences.
3. Give timely feedback.
4. Maintain accurate records.
5. Communicate with parents, guardians, and caregivers.
6. Use objective behavior descriptions.
7. Respond to student misbehavior.
8. Arrange the classroom physical environment.
9. Pace and structure the lessons.

## Classroom Management

Classroom management and management of student behavior are skills that teachers acquire and perfect over time. Effective classroom management skills are central to teaching and require consistency, courage, common sense, and fairness. Some very basic factors recommended for effective classroom management are (1) know what you want and what you don't want; (2) show and tell your students what you want; (3) when you get what you want, acknowledge it, but don't overly praise it as if the desired behavior was unexpected; and (4) when you get something else, act quickly and appropriately. By greeting each student at the door with a friendly greeting, you can handle many minor problems before they become public classroom confrontations.

For effective management, teachers should also do the following:

1. Maintain eye contact with the students.
2. Move around the room; being near the students can extinguish potential problems.
3. Establish a quiet signal, e.g., clapping hands, ringing a bell, or making a hand signal.
4. Let the students take ownership of their work.
5. Use age-appropriate humor, smiles, choices, and positive reinforcements.
6. Remember, learning is a social activity. When appropriate, allow students to talk during their work time. A totally quiet classroom is not always a good learning environment.

Know the basics of the these approaches to classroom management styles: authoritarian, laissez-faire, and authoritative. **Authoritarian** teachers establish rules and expect students to obey them. These teachers use reward and punishments that are administered for following and breaking rules, respectively. The motto of the authoritarian teacher is, "Do as I say because I say so."

The **laissez-faire** teacher establishes no rules, and students can do what they want. These teachers provide advice only when directly asked by a student. Their motto is "Do as I say because you like and respect my judgment."

The **authoritative** teacher provides rules and discusses the reasons for the rules with the students. These teachers teach the students how to meet the goals, reward the students for demonstrating self-control, and, as the students show more responsibility, reward them with more self-governance. This approach to classroom management leads to intrinsic motivation on the part of the students. These teachers have the motto "Do what I say because doing so will help you learn more." The authoritative style of teaching is considered most effective.

You will need to know the basics of conflict resolution and behavior modification and how they can be used in the classroom.

**Conflict resolution** is a constructive approach to interpersonal and intergroup conflicts that helps students with opposing positions work together to arrive at a mutually acceptable compromise. The main theme is active listening, by which each student can understand and summarize verbally the other's differences. Initially, teachers serve as facilitators and coaches and may use role-playing to model the mediation process to the students. Afterward, the teacher sets up an area in the classroom for students themselves to use for mediating their conflicts.

**Behavior modification** arose from Skinner's modern behavior modification techniques and Pavlov's classical conditioning techniques. Behavior modification is the application of the principles of conditioning and is used to promote desirable behaviors or to discourage undesirable behaviors. Behavior modification is used to change observable and measurable behaviors. All behavior is maintained, changed, or shaped by the consequences of that behavior. Students function more effectively under the right set of consequences or reinforcers that strengthen behavior and punishments that weaken behavior.

Steps a teacher can take to apply the behavior modification techniques are as follows: (1) identify the problem, (2) design a way to change the behavior, (3) identify an effective positive reinforcer and use it often when the behavior is positive, and (4) apply the reinforcer consistently to shape or change the behavior.

# ASSESSMENT

Teachers must know how to select and use culturally unbiased, informal, and formal assessment strategies to plan and individualize curriculum and teaching practices.

Knowing how to make **accommodations** for the various learning styles, the multiple intelligences, and the exceptionalities of your students will lead to them being successful in your classroom. This does not mean that you should lower your expectations of student learning, but it does mean students will learn and express their knowledge in different ways. The advantages for students of reasonable accommodations are more academic success, better motivation, and greater confidence. Some of the more common accommodations include having the student take an untimed test and providing a tape of your test. Other test-taking alternatives and modifications are used as well.

You should be able to provide **alternative** or **authentic assessment** options by which students originate a response to a task or question. Such responses could include demonstrations, exhibits, portfolios, oral presentations, or essays. You can then obtain information about the students' successes or failures on meaningful and significant tasks. Authentic assessments allow students to show what they can do.

A different kind of test, the paper-and-pencil objective test, is called **traditional assessment**. Traditional assessment is a means of securing information about what the students know in which the students select responses from a multiple-choice list, a true-or-false list, or a matching list. Assessment of students' learning will assist you in planning and in communicating with the students and with their parents/guardians.

**Standardized tests** are assessments that are administered and scored in exactly the same manner for all students. Traditional standardized tests are typically mass-produced and machine scored. They are designed to measure skills and knowledge that are to be taught to all students according to state standards provided to school districts. Standardized tests can be **norm referenced**, such that the performance results of the students who take the test are compared with the performance results of other students taking the test. Standardized tests that are **criterion referenced** compare students' knowledge and achievement in an academic area to the objectives of the curriculum established by state standards. Students are not compared to each other; instead, results show a student's level of mastery of particular content areas.

**Performance assessments** can also be standardized if they are administered and scored in the same way for all students. This is accomplished with systematic and direct observation of student performance or examples of student performance. These assessments are ranked according to pre-established performance criteria or guidelines that are listed on **rubrics**.

You will need to know how to communicate assessment results and integrate them for others as an active participant of the school team in the development and implementation of Individual Education Plan goals. As noted above, IEPs are made for specific students based on their individual abilities.

You will also need to know how to develop and use formative and summative program evaluations to ensure comprehensive quality of the total environment for children. **Formative assessment** is intended to aid learning by providing feedback about what has been learned so far and what remains to be learned. An example would be a quiz covering the material addressed by a particular lesson or homework assignment. Students and teachers can use this type of assessment as a diagnostic tool to identify and improve areas of weakness and as a means of practicing a skill.

**Summative assessment** is a measure of the students' achievement at the completion of a block of work. The students' learning is summarized at a specific point in time. Examples include an end-of-the-chapter test or a unit test.

**Informal assessments** are supplemental to the standardized testing formats and are used by teachers to optimally understand students' learning strengths and weaknesses. These assessments show the teacher the why and how of their students' learning. Such assessments include learning logs, journals, observations, checklists, teacher-made classroom tests, and anecdotal records of student work and behavior. Teachers use **holistic scoring**, in which each element of a student's work is used to assess the total quality of the student's work and receives one score. This is in contrast to **analytic scoring**, in which one score is given after separate grades are recorded for each element of the student's work based on whether the elements are correct or not; in this type of scoring, quality is not considered. Teachers can create detailed rubrics to use in holistic scoring of students' work. Students receive these rubrics beforehand so that they know the quality expectations for the work to be done.

# PROFESSIONAL DEVELOPMENT, LEADERSHIP, AND COMMUNITY

Dewey suggested that teachers understand the factors in their students' environments outside of school that may influence their lives and learning (family circumstances, community environment, health, and economics). You must be aware of ways to involve community personnel in the school setting. Develop ways to include parents and guardians in classroom lessons and treat them as partners in the educational process. Develop basic strategies for involving leaders in the community in the educational process. Remember that teachers and schools are a resource for the entire community.

You should have knowledge of professional literature and associations within your field of education. In addition, know the current views of specific professional associations and how they relate to best teaching practices in your area. Understand the purpose of the professional development requirements of your state and local agencies. Know what types of resources are available for professional development and learning in your field. Seek out opportunities to grow professionally.

You should know the value of reflection as it pertains to you in the teaching profession. Understand that being a **reflective practitioner** in your teaching practices is critical. Truly effective teachers are those who evaluate their teaching strategies at all times to become the most effective educators possible. Teachers must reflect on their methods and strategies continuously to ensure that they are reaching all students. Continually evaluating the effects of their choices and actions on students, parents, and other professionals in the learning community is part of the reflective process.

Effective teachers use reflective statements that include clear descriptions of the sources of information they have used to evaluate their teaching and students' learning. These teachers use methods of self-evaluation and problem-solving strategies to reflect on their practice and to make changes in their teaching, respectively. They also describe how they have used specific resources, such as readings and professional relationships with colleagues and others, to learn and grow as teachers.

You should also be aware of the support personnel available to assist you, your students, and their families. These include paraeducators, guidance counselors, special education teachers, IEP team members, therapists, teachers of the gifted and talented, and library media specialists.

# ANALYSIS OF INSTRUCTIONAL SCENARIOS

The PLT requires that you not only answer multiple-choice questions but also write your own short-answer responses to case histories of classroom scenarios. You will see two case histories on the day of your test, each with two associated questions. These four responses make up a total of 25 percent of your overall score, so it's important to be prepared. Also keep in mind that, on test day, you will type your responses directly on the computer, so for the most realistic practice you should type your practice responses directly into a basic word-processing program.

## Case Histories

The case histories are all approximately the same length, 800–850 words. They come in a variety of forms. Some are narrative, featuring a teacher's self-reflection and evaluation; others are document based, providing between three and five student responses, lesson plans, report cards, and/or other similar documents. Some focus on issues relating to one or more students; others are primarily concerned with the practices of a single teacher. Don't be overly concerned with these distinctions. Few case histories fall purely within a single category, and the strategy for success is the same for all of them.

Below is an example of a document-based, teacher-focused case history. Like all case histories, it begins with a brief scenario providing basic background information. The documents are clearly labeled.

### Scenario

Mr. Hallet is a ninth-grade English teacher beginning the second semester of his first year of teaching. His district encompasses mostly middle-class families on the outskirts of a major metropolis. However, about 15 percent of students in the district are from the poorer inner city and often face academic hardship. Mr. Hallet is successfully managing his three regular classes and one advanced class. He also has a remedial ELA class, which is giving him trouble. He has requested the guidance of his department head, Ms. Erdogan, in managing the situation. Ms. Erdogan has agreed to observe a class and is recording it on audio for reference.

### DOCUMENT 1

### Mr. Hallet's "connotation vs. denotation" lesson plan

*Objectives:* Students will:

1. Understand the difference between the denotation and connotation of words.
2. Be able to identify the tone of a piece of writing based on the connotation of the words chosen by the author.
3. Be able to alter the tone of a piece of writing by replacing words with synonyms that have different connotations.

*Assignments:*

> Students will receive a list of 10 words. In pairs, students should label 5 of them as "good" and 5 of them as "bad." Then, students should identify 5 pairs of words that have similar meanings.

> Students will receive a review of a restaurant. Individually, they will circle all the words with strong connotations and identify those words as having a positive or negative connotation.

> Students will rewrite the review. They will preserve the denotation of the review (e.g., whether the restaurant was hot or cold, whether the food was spicy or mild, whether the location was busy or quiet) but reverse the connotation (e.g., from "delicate" flavors to "bland" flavors, or from "lively" restaurant to a "noisy" restaurant).

*Assessments:*

> Students will have an opportunity to share their answers to the initial 10 words.

> Students will receive a grade out of 20 points for their writing.

## DOCUMENT 2

### Transcript of Mr. Hallet's class, 10:42 am

Mr. Hallet: What can I do for you, Darred, Mike?

Darred: We don't know what "sweltering" means.

Mike: Dude, who cares? I don't even get the point of this anyway.

Darred: Shut up, Mike. If I fail this class, my parents are gonna ground me!

Mr. Hallet: Well, think about the word. Have you heard it anywhere before?

Mike: Sounds like "shelter" or "sweater."

Mr. Hallet: Good! "Sweater" is exactly right, the word means "hot." And how does the word sound?

Darred: I dunno, if "sweltering" is like "sweating," then it's kinda gross or something?

Mr. Hallet: Exactly! It's an unpleasant word, very negative, that means "hot." Good guessing!

## DOCUMENT 3

### Transcript of Mr. Hallet's class, 11:04 am

(The class is very noisy. A few students mention things relating to the assignment. Most of the chatter is off-topic.)

Mr. Hallet (loudly): Students, this is quiet writing time.

(The conversations continue, albeit quieter.)

Mr. Hallet (walking up to a student): Rod, you're not writing anything.

Rod: I don't get what I'm supposed to do. How can I keep the writing the same *and* make it the opposite?

Mr. Hallet: You did very well on the worksheet—you know how to do this! Remember how "sweltering" meant hot and was bad, while "toasty" also meant hot but was good? (Mr. Hallet pauses. Rod nods.) Do you see anything here like that?

Rod: Tanya did most of that work. I didn't really get it. Like, is "truffle" a good or bad word?

Mr. Hallet: No, a truffle is a type of mushroom. It's not good or bad.

Mike (from across the room): See, I *told* you this assignment was dumb!

(The class laughs.)

Mr. Hallet: Mike! That attitude is inappropriate. Everyone, get back to your work. We'll talk about the assignment in more detail once we're done. For now, do your best.

(Several students make comments under their breath. Most stare at their papers; few go back to work.)

## DOCUMENT 4

### Conversation between Mr. Hallet and Ms. Erdogan, two days later

Mr. Hallet: . . . and in the end, I couldn't give a single assignment a score higher than a 10 out of 20.

Ms. Erdogan: What about Tanya's? She seemed surprisingly engaged, at least toward the beginning.

Mr. Hallet: I know. It was so disappointing. She wrote a completely original review. She made great use of negatively charged words, but she wasn't actually following instructions for the assignment—even though I went over the instructions *and* handed them out in writing. So 10 was the best I could give her under the circumstances.

Ms. Erdogan: And how did she take that grade?

Mr. Hallet: Poorly. I had to write her up; she skipped my class yesterday and today.

Ms. Erdogan: That's unfortunate.

Mr. Hallet: It's the worst possible outcome. I had her interest in learning, but then I lost it. But I'm not sure what I could have done differently.

Ms. Erdogan: Well, let's talk about it.

## Case History Questions

The questions associated with the case histories can test a variety of subjects. You will always have at least one question from the content category of "Students as Learners" and at least one from "Instructional Process." You may also see up to one question each on the topics of "Assessment" and "Professional Development, Leadership, and Community."

Although questions may differ in terms of subject matter, their formatting is formulaic. First, you will be provided with a summary of part of the case or a direction to review a particular section or document. Next, you will be asked to identify two specific things, such as two behaviors that are typical of an age group or two modifications to a failed activity. Finally, you will be instructed to justify your examples on the basis of various educational principles.

Make sure you read each question thoroughly. Generic or tangential explanations that do not directly address the assignment will not receive full credit, regardless of whether they are otherwise of high quality.

Below are the two questions that accompany the previous case history.

CR 1. Review Mr. Hallet's lesson plan in Document 1.

- Identify TWO shortcomings in Mr. Hallet's lesson plan.
- For EACH of those shortcomings, explain how addressing that flaw could have improved the effectiveness of Mr. Hallet's lesson. Base your response on principles of effective instructional strategies.

CR 2. Throughout the case history, Mr. Hallet's students display behaviors typical of students who struggle academically.

- Identify TWO such instances of the typical behavior of struggling students.
- For EACH example you identify, indicate what characteristic of the behavior is typical of the behavior of struggling students. Base your response on the principles of remedial education.

## Case History Answers

Short answers, technically known as constructed responses, don't have right or wrong answers in the same way that multiple-choice questions do. Instead, each response is assigned a score of 0, 1, or 2 by a team of professional educators. Multiple graders will review your answers, and their grading habits are in turn statistically reviewed by a computer to ensure consistency. If you're interested in precisely how these results are generated, ETS's official study material explains the inner workings of the process in detail. But for our purposes, it's enough to know that you don't have to worry about the "luck of the draw" assigning you a strict reviewer. Your writing will consistently and accurately receive the score that is merited.

As we've already explained, you can expect questions on a variety of educational themes. However, all responses are graded on the same basic rubric.

2   A 2 is the highest score possible. It represents an excellent and thoughtful answer—though not necessarily a perfect one, as the graders understand that you are working under time constraints! To earn a 2, you must produce a response that

- demonstrates clear and thorough understanding of pedagogy, methodology, and theory
- demonstrates clear and thorough understanding of the specifics of the case
- responds to all parts of the question
- supports its reasoning with evidence or examples, when required

1   A response that earns a 1 falls short. It still answers the question, but it fails to do so as accurately or as comprehensively as a response that earns a 2. Your response may earn a 1 if it

- demonstrates only basic understanding of pedagogy, methodology, and theory
- demonstrates only basic understanding of the specifics of the case
- does not fully respond to all parts of the question
- provides weak or insufficient evidence for its points, where required

**0** Finally, a response that earns a 0 makes one or more critical errors. It's likely that such an answer

- demonstrates little or no understanding of pedagogy, methodology, and theory
- demonstrates little or no understanding of the case
- does not respond to the question at all, including by giving an off-topic answer or one that attacks the basis of the question (e.g., when asked to modify a lesson, arguing that the lesson requires no modification)
- completely lacks requisite support or evidence

It's important to note what is *not* in these guidelines. For one, grammar and structure are not mentioned. ETS has gone out of its way to select multiple formats among the sample 2-scoring answers it provides. Single narrative paragraphs, pairs of unconnected paragraphs, and even bulleted lists can get a perfect score as long as they directly address the prompt and clearly display your knowledge.

Here are some effective responses to the two questions above. Each of these would earn a 2.

*Sample Response to CR 1:*

Mr. Hallet's plan doesn't scaffold effectively. He transitions too quickly from a very explicit and clear assignment in groups to a very challenging assignment that students must complete alone. An intermediate step could have helped Rod connect his success on the first assignment to the skills required on the second.

Mr. Hallet's objectives are very content focused. Mike repeatedly commented that the assignment was "stupid." If Mr. Hallet had included an objective related to applying the new concept, such as "Students will understand the effect word choice has on listeners and readers," and included things in the lesson designed to illustrate that concept, Mike and other students might have understood why they were studying the topic and thus been more engaged.

*Sample Response to CR 2:*

Mike and Darred reach for answers rather than admit they don't understand. Despite Mr. Hallet's praise, the connection they draw between "swelter" and "sweater" is pure coincidence. In a practice typical of many struggling students, Darred fired off several answers, more concerned with getting a positive response from the teacher than with actually understanding or learning.

Rod gives up on his assignment without asking for help. Remedial students are often resigned to academic failure, especially if they are struggling in multiple subjects. Also, many struggling students believe that teachers cannot be relied on or even trusted, and they may avoid asking questions on challenging assignments for that reason. Either or both of those common attitudes could explain Rod's silence.

# Case History Strategies

**Read the questions first.** Before you begin analyzing the case, take a look at the questions. Doing so can help focus your reading. If you look at the text first and then are surprised by an unusual question prompt, you may have to re-read part or even all of the case history looking for information you didn't think was relevant the first time through. If you know what you need, you can use that knowledge to go through the case history efficiently.

**Make a "map" of the case history.** It's important that you take notes, either by circling or underlining parts of your test booklet or jotting down the location of key details on your scratch paper. Your goal here is not to summarize or copy information—you can and should review pertinent details directly from the text itself. However, misplacing or forgetting about those details can cost you time. When you need that information, you want to be able to locate it instantly. We refer to these notes as "maps" because they are meant to help you find your way!

**Brainstorm.** Don't just write the first two ideas that come to your head. Spend a few minutes thinking of three or four possible responses. Then pick the two you are most comfortable with. Your final response will be much stronger this way. More importantly, you're less likely to find yourself halfway through composing an answer before realizing you can't justify your argument and need to start over from scratch.

**Refer to the case.** It may seem as though you can answer some case history questions, especially those related to pedagogical practice, in purely theoretical terms. However, such an answer would never score higher than a 1. The question will always ask you to relate your suggestions to the students or teachers in the case history in some way. Follow this instruction.

**Keep it simple.** Don't overcomplicate. One good piece of supporting evidence is sufficient to demonstrate deep understanding. However, one weak example can undercut your answer, even if you present it alongside other, more compelling points.

**Use one idea per paragraph.** As mentioned before, scores of 2 are awarded regardless of formatting. However, many lower-scoring answer samples take the form of a single paragraph that goes in depth about only one part of the prompt or that loses sight of the goal and meanders off-topic. You should write one paragraph for each of the two parts of your answer so you can more easily check your work and ensure that you've completed your task.

**Proofread.** Always double-check your work. Once you've written both responses to one case, re-read each question and answer. Make sure you've answered the question thoroughly and, though you aren't graded on grammar, make sure your work is at least intelligible.

# PRACTICE: PLT CONSTRUCTED-RESPONSE QUESTIONS

## PLT Case Histories

**Directions**: Each case history in this section is followed by two short-answer questions. Your responses to the questions will be evaluated with respect to professionally accepted principles and practices of learning and teaching. Be sure to answer all parts of the question.

## Constructed-Response Questions: Case History #1

### Case History #1: Early Childhood

### Scenario

Ms. Jackson is a second-grade teacher at the East Hill Elementary School, a well-run suburban school with a sizable low-income community. This is Ms. Jackson's first year of teaching. She meets regularly with her mentor, Ms. Evenson, to discuss her experiences as a new teacher.

### DOCUMENT 1

### Ms. Jackson's self-reflection notes

My college adviser described East Hill as a place where I could "make the mistakes of a beginning teacher and come out a better teacher on the other end." I'm starting to wonder what I'm doing here, though. For the most part, I've been focused on classroom management and on creating a structured and disciplined academic environment. In my classroom, no excuse is tolerated for behavior that disrupts others' learning or falls short on effort, and that goes for every student. But with all of my efforts to gain authority, I feel like I'm missing out on the mentoring role of teaching.

### DOCUMENT 2

### Excerpt from Ms. Evenson's observation of Ms. Jackson's class—November

During my observation, Ms. Jackson tried to conduct a reading group with the 8 slowest readers in the class, including a boy named William Baker. I was informed that last year's standardized test placed William at the lowest level in reading. He had been absent for 35 days last year and had spent a good number of his school days in the principal's office, many times missing the reading lessons in his first-grade classroom. When the 8 members of the reading group met, the rest of the class worked on workbook assignments at their desks.

Several times, I noticed that William would start an argument, and most of the children at their desks would snap to attention to watch the scene William was making. Ms. Jackson harshly censured William each time, telling him that his behavior was unacceptable and rude and sometimes loudly telling him to sit down and pay attention or she would call his parents. In one instance, when William openly defied her, Ms. Jackson directed William to sit in the time-out chair. When he refused, she sent him to the principal's office. Even in William's absence, the chemistry in the classroom seemed strained, with a lot of bickering among the children.

Ms. Jackson seems genuinely invested in helping her students progress. Whenever a child who was reading aloud hesitated with a word, Ms. Jackson pronounced the complete word two or three times, then had the child repeat what she had said. When Ms. Jackson asked the students to summarize the story they had read, most of the members of the small reading group were lost, and could not paraphrase the key events of the plot. Similarly, when she repeated a sentence from the story and asked students to tell her what the sentence meant, the children were hesitant to reply and often gave incorrect answers.

## DOCUMENT 3

### Excerpt from transcript of postobservation conversation between Ms. Jackson and Ms. Evenson

Ms. Evenson: I noticed that William Baker created quite a stir in your classroom today.

Ms. Jackson: That young man has really tested my resolve this year. How frustrating and embarrassing to be drawn into a battle of wills with a second grader!

Ms. Evenson: Can you expand on "battle of wills"? Beyond what I saw today, what kind of stuff is William doing in class?

Ms. Jackson: Throwing pencils and wadded paper at other students. Refusing to stay at his desk. Stepping out of line when we walk to lunch or to recess. Interrupting other students. You name it, really.

Ms. Evenson: That's got to be so frustrating. What strategies have you used for helping minimize the effect of William's disruptive behavior on others?

Ms. Jackson: I tell the others to ignore him—that their attention is only encouraging him. I've taken William out into the hall and told him to straighten up. Sometimes, I tell him right in the classroom that he needs to clean up his act—but nothing seems to embarrass him or get through to him. He just doesn't have any respect for others, and his little performances frequently derail the other students' progress in their workbook assignments.

1.  Ms. Jackson knows that the progress of the class in reading is being slowed down by external disturbances.

    - Identify TWO instructional strategies that she could use in teaching reading to the class to minimize the effect of distractions and improve progress.
    - Explain how EACH of the two strategies would improve the environment in her classroom and assist in her students' development as readers. Base your response on the principles of effective instructional strategies.

2.  There are a number of measures Ms. Jackson could take regarding William's conduct and behavior in the reading group.

    - Identify TWO teaching strategies or behavior management techniques she could use with William in particular.
    - Discuss how EACH strategy or technique would improve William's classroom behavior and make the classroom more conducive to his learning. Base your response on the principles and strategies of classroom management.

## Constructed-Response Questions: Case History #2

*Case History #2: Grades K–6*

*Scenario*

Ms. Carter is a fourth-grade teacher at the Hudson Elementary K–6 school. Approximately 430 of the 750 students at Hudson are ELL children. There are 10 languages represented in the school plus many dialects of each language. Ms. Carter, now in her second year of teaching, meets regularly with her mentor, Mr. Guo, to discuss problems and to share teaching and classroom management strategies.

### DOCUMENT 1

### Ms. Carter's journal notes

I'm worried that two of my special education students, Tuyet and Luis, are going to have trouble passing the upcoming state-administered reading test. I'm also slightly concerned that their behavior is making it harder for the other students to get ready for the test.

Tuyet is 10 years old and a first-generation immigrant from Vietnam. Her parents, whom I met at a beginning-of-the-school-year open house, seem open to a wide range of ideas when it comes to Tuyet's education. They're learning English themselves and are therefore keenly aware of the challenges Tuyet faces as a nonnative speaker in school.

Although Tuyet's English is limited, she can read at a third-grade level. However, she was recently diagnosed with ADHD. Although Tuyet is receiving medication, she has trouble concentrating and is extremely hyperactive.

Luis, on the other hand, doesn't speak any English and is not yet literate in Spanish, his native language. Until this year, he'd apparently had little in the way of formal schooling. He seems unhappy here at Hudson and often creates disruptions during my lessons.

### DOCUMENT 2

### Mr. Guo's notes following observation of Ms. Carter's class

Ms. Carter has 18 ELL students in her class of 35 fourth graders. These ELL students speak Arabic, Farsi, Spanish, Vietnamese, Lao, and Mandarin Chinese. Ms. Carter is bilingual, but her second language, Russian, is not spoken by any of the students in the class.

During my observation, non-English-speaking students spent some time individually with Ms. Carter or her paraprofessionals, and occasionally they left the classroom altogether to work with ELL teachers in the school's resource room. Now and then, one of the paraprofessionals chatted with several of the students in Spanish.

While Ms. Carter was speaking before the entire class, she shared some of her knowledge of Russian with curious students in the class. The students then took turns teaching her some phrases from their own languages. Ms. Carter asked them open-ended questions, praising them for their responses.

One student, however—a girl named Tuyet—had trouble staying on task, often failing to answer direct questions or playing private games instead of following along with the class's conversation. Ms. Carter, at one point, let one of her paraprofessionals take over primary instruction so that she could work with Tuyet one-on-one.

Another student, Luis, repeatedly got up from his seat and walked around the room, talking to himself and disturbing the rest of the class. The paraprofessional in Ms. Carter's room escorted him out, finally, and took him down to the ELL resource room where there was someone who spoke his language. The paraprofessional told me that this happens quite often for Luis.

After the observation, Ms. Carter and I agreed that it would be productive to schedule an IEP meeting with the parents of each child. Ms. Carter will recommend that Tuyet be allowed to take her reading test separately from the other students, but she is concerned that this special treatment might make the other children jealous. She isn't sure what changes are appropriate for Luis.

## DOCUMENT 3

### Excerpt from transcript of Luis's IEP meeting

Ms. Carter [through translator]: Luis's behavior is disruptive to some of the other children, but that's not what I'm really concerned about. I'm concerned that his acting out is a symptom of his need for an educational program better tailored to his specific challenges. And I'd love to listen to your thoughts about what those needs are and how I can help to meet them.

Luis's father [through translator]: Well, he shouldn't be misbehaving. I'll talk to him about that. On the other hand—if he can't understand what the teacher is saying, it makes sense that he would get bored, right?

Luis's mother [through translator]: Without disrespect—because I'm sure you're an excellent teacher—Luis has told us that he prefers to be in the ELL room with Ms. Martinez and Mr. Glass. He says that he learns more from those teachers than he does in your classroom—probably because he can't understand the words you use.

Ms. Carter [through translator]: I understand. But it's important for Luis to spend time with the other children at the school as well, including English-speaking students. And I need to work with him to make sure that he's ready for the state reading test.

Luis's mother [through translator]: The test—why is Luis taking it to begin with? What's the point of making him take a test he can't even read? Just let him spend his time in the ELL room. He learns a lot there.

3.   Ms. Carter's students have a wide range of special needs related, in some cases, to their relative inexperience with the English language.

   •   Identify TWO effective instructional strategies that Ms. Carter and the paraprofessionals, resource teachers, and administrators at Hudson Elementary are currently using in order to better meet the needs of the ELL students in Ms. Carter's class.

   •   For EACH strategy that you identify, describe how that strategy helps Ms. Carter's ELL students progress in their learning. Base your response on the principles of planning for students as diverse learners.

4.   Some of the ELL students in Ms. Carter's diverse classroom are not as engaged in the lessons as they should be.

   •   Identify TWO strategies Ms. Carter could use to improve student engagement and foster greater progress in the students' learning. Include one general strategy and one strategy that applies specifically to Luis and/or Tuyet.

- For EACH strategy you identify, describe how this strategy would help Ms. Carter improve the quality of her ELL students' English progress. Base your response on the principles of student motivation and learning theory and the principles of planning for students as diverse learners.

## Constructed-Response Questions: Case History #3

### Case History #3: Grades 5–9

### Scenario

Thomas Williams is a sixth-grade student in a relatively affluent suburban school district. His teachers describe him as quiet and shy; they comment that his work is inconsistent but is not a major cause for concern. He is heavily overweight and has been since childhood.

Ms. Ross is Thomas's third-period science teacher. It is Ms. Ross's second year, but she already has a reputation as a popular and exciting teacher. Her mentor, Mr. Perry, has just observed her teaching Thomas's class.

### DOCUMENT 1

### Ms. Ross's self-reflection—third-period science, Tuesday

Today's class went well. Most of the class was excited by the water cycle. The discussion of last year's blizzard was a great last-minute addition that let the students establish a personal connection to the weather. Carlos, Zhou, and Jenny all asked very insightful questions that let me reteach challenging parts of the lesson. I also tried to use my mentor's suggestions about handling off-topic questions, and I think I was able to turn Sasha's questions about acid rain into a teachable moment.

### DOCUMENT 2

### Excerpt from Ms. Ross's postobservation meeting with her mentor, Mr. Perry

Mr. Perry: And did your students meet all the learning objectives for your lesson?

Ms. Ross: Absolutely. When I asked review questions after the first 10 minutes of the lesson, the students answered quickly and accurately. And when I opened the floor for questions at the half-hour mark, the responses I got were surprisingly sophisticated and thoughtful. It's a good thing I knew enough about acid rain to answer them.

Mr. Perry: What about the quieter students? The reason I ask is that from the back of the room, I saw that Thomas gave incomplete answers to most of the study questions on his worksheet.

Ms. Ross: He did? Well, that's disappointing. He had several opportunities to ask if he was having trouble following the lesson.

Mr. Perry: Is it possible he just doesn't feel comfortable asking questions in front of his peers?

Ms. Ross: It could be. He has a few friends in class, but he isn't very popular and does get teased about his weight. I'll check with his guidance counselor to see what I can do for him.

**DOCUMENT 3**

**Thomas's answers to Ms. Ross's study questions:**

What are the steps of the water cycle? _____ → _____ → _____ → _____
→ _____ (Hint: the last step is the same as the first.)

*Thomas's answer:* Consation → Rain?? → Running water → _____ → Consation

How do plants play a role in the water cycle?

*Thomas's answer:* Roots in the ground are part of the water cycle.

Why is the water cycle important to the environment?

*Thomas's answer:* Acid rain can kill trees and fish.

**DOCUMENT 4**

**Guidance counselor's note to Ms. Ross**

Saw your message about Thomas. I've spoken to him several times recently about teasing from peers. According to Thomas, it's worse than it was in elementary school, but he "can put up with it." However, it wouldn't surprise me if he were trying to keep a low profile in class.

One other thing: He's made a few comments about teachers "playing favorites." He didn't specify how or why, but he may have gotten an impression that some teachers value other students' contributions more highly than his own.

**DOCUMENT 5**

**Excerpt from Ms. Ross's third-period science class, Thursday.**

*(The bell rings. Students are mostly in their seats, talking among themselves.)*

Ms. Ross: Hello, class!

*(The class replies "Hello, Ms. Ross!" Several conversations continue, while other students wait silently.)*

Ms. Ross: All right, settle down. Today, we're going to talk about different types of clouds and start work on your terrariums. But first, I wanted to talk about something important.

*(The class settles down. A few students still whisper.)*

Ms. Ross: In Tuesday's class, I got some really great questions. Carlos's questions about condensation were very helpful to let me know what parts of the lesson were hard to understand, and Sasha's question about acid rain was a great learning opportunity for all of us.

*(Sasha beams. Carlos laughs but is embarrassed.)*

Ms. Ross: So I want everyone to know that questions are very important to learning. Everyone should be okay asking questions about things you don't understand. It doesn't matter whether the person who asks is a boy or a girl, if they're good at science or having trouble, if they're a jock or overweight. This should be a safe environment. *(A student raises his hand.)* Arthur, do you have a question?

Arthur (*joking*): What if they're really *really* overweight like Tom Tub?

(*The class laughs. Thomas glares, then puts his head on his desk.*)

Ms. Ross (*angry*): Arthur, that's completely out of line. Go to the office. Now!

Arthur: But Carlos and Zhou call him that all the time. Why am I getting in trouble?

Ms. Ross: Don't argue with me, young man. Go to the office.

(*Ms. Ross starts her lecture. The class is subdued for the whole period, and Thomas doesn't pay any attention to the lesson at all.*)

5. Ms. Ross helped students take notes by having them complete a study sheet while she lectured. Review Thomas's notes on his study sheet in document 3.

   - Suggest TWO modifications to the study sheet activity that could have helped Thomas better understand Ms. Ross's lecture.
   - For EACH suggestion, explain how it would have helped Thomas produce more accurate and complete responses. Base your responses on the principles of planning instruction.

6. Ms. Ross's attempt to encourage a safe environment for students to participate in class was not successful, in part because she inadvertently singled Thomas out in front of his peers.

   - Propose TWO ways that Ms. Ross could make students like Thomas feel more comfortable participating in her classes.
   - For EACH of those methods, explain how they would encourage Thomas to participate more in classroom discussions. Base your responses on the principles of effective classroom management.

## Constructed-Response Questions: Case History #4

### Case History #4: Grades 7–12

### Scenario

Mr. Fayerwether is a math teacher in the only high school in a small suburb. Of the 24 students in his fourth-period Algebra II class, 21 are 10th-grade students. At the beginning of the second month of school, Mr. Fayerwether is collecting documents to prepare a self-evaluation, focusing in particular on the one freshman and two juniors in his class.

### DOCUMENT 1

### Mr. Fayerwether's first impression of the three students

**Johnny** is a bright, positive student one-on-one. However, as the only 9th grader in the class, he often seems uncomfortable interacting with students who are older than he is. On Johnny's first day, he was teased for his high-pitched voice; though the perpetrator was disciplined and the teasing has not recurred, I think the incident left a negative impression on him. Johnny has nevertheless proved to be one of the highest-performing students in the class despite his youth—he finishes most in-class assignments well before his classmates.

**Lucy** is a popular girl. She is comfortable speaking out in class, but makes as many off-topic jokes as she makes legitimate contributions. Math has consistently been a struggle for her. She failed Algebra I as a freshman and only passed her second time through with a C–. She is clearly a capable student, as demonstrated by her As in English and social studies and Bs in science. But it's hard to tell how dedicated she is to her math studies. She is determined to follow in the footsteps of her mother, a traveling art dealer, and has repeatedly made comments such as "I suck at Algebra, but who cares? I know what I want to do and don't need math to do it!"

**Karl** is struggling to recover after a car accident caused him to miss a significant part of his sophomore year. He has an aide to help him carry his belongings (as he is still on crutches) and, more importantly, to help him read; neurological damage makes it hard for him to focus his eyes on small text. Unfortunately, Karl often refuses to let his aide help him. His weekly quiz grades have been much lower than his B average from last year, and I am convinced that he would have done better if he had accepted assistance. Karl's parents are both very concerned with his recovery, academic and physical, but they do not live together and the information I get from them is sometimes contradictory. When I asked Karl about it, he told me his parents "are both full of it."

## DOCUMENT 2

### Lesson plan for class to be observed by Mr. Fayerwether's supervisor

Goals:

- Students will refresh knowledge of inequalities from earlier grades.
- Students will apply the tools for solving systems of equations to solve systems involving both equations and inequalities.
- Students will understand how real-world problems can translate to systems of equations and inequalities.

Students will work on a review sheet to start off the class. I offered Karl a large-print version of the review sheet, but he unsurprisingly refused. The small-group work that I used for this lesson last year was pure math. Lucy's grades in English suggest she is a verbal thinker, so I've replaced a few equations with word problems; I hope this will engage her. I have not made any modifications to the lesson for Johnny, as his performance suggests he does not need them.

## DOCUMENT 3

### Supervisor's notes on Mr. Fayerwether's class

Mr. Fayerwether begins by handing out a review sheet with symbols, terms, and images. He asks for an explanation of each term from a particular student. When students shout out an answer out of turn, Mr. Fayerwether politely but firmly tells them it's not their turn. Next, he lectures on applying concepts from the previous week's class. He pauses regularly to write equations, steps, and rules on the overhead projector. The class ends with a group-work activity. Each group of students is given 12 problems. Each student is instructed to do a third of the problems, then check his or her partners' work on the other problems.

**DOCUMENT 4**

**Mr. Fayerwether's postobservation self-evaluation**

Today's results were disappointing. My original plan had been to ask Lucy easy questions early in the review and to save the hard questions for high-performing students like Johnny. However, Lucy responded by making jokes about how I expected her to remember things from sixth grade. By the time I got an answer out of her, Johnny had already finished the entire review and stopped paying attention. Karl was one of several students who shouted out his answers, and he held a grudge; he refused to answer when it was actually his turn. And even Johnny stumbled when it was his turn to answer a question. He had finished and was no longer paying attention, and several students laughed out loud.

The second half didn't go much better. Karl was frustrated because he misread the problem numbers on his worksheet and ended up doing three of the same problems as his partners before his aide spotted the error. Lucy and her partners spent most of the period talking rather than doing math, and Johnny finished 10 of 12 problems before his partners were done with their 8. In retrospect, these were predictable outcomes given these students' recurring behavior, but I'm still frustrated.

7.  Mr. Fayerwether ends his self-evaluation by commenting that Johnny and Lucy's behavior during group work was part of a recurring pattern. Suppose that you are Mr. Fayerwether's supervisor.

    • For each of these two students, suggest ONE guiding question to ask Mr. Fayerwether about a specific aspect of that student's pattern of behavior.

    • For EACH question, explain how different answers would suggest different approaches for Mr. Fayerwether to improve his students' behavior. Base your answer on the principles of modifying instruction for diverse learners.

8.  Throughout the study, Karl refuses direct offers of assistance for coping with his disability.

    • Suggest TWO modifications Mr. Fayerwether could make to his teaching style that would indirectly help Karl.

    • For EACH modification, explain how it would aid Karl while still being indirect enough that he would not refuse. Base your answers on the principles of educating students with disabilities.

# ANSWERS AND EXPLANATIONS

## PLT Constructed-Response Questions

### Constructed-Response Questions: Case History #1

1. One strategy Ms. Jackson could use would be to teach reading using the phonetics approach and basal readers. The students in her class are attempting to learn in a volatile environment, and breaking down the reading lessons to form a narrow learning path will help her to gauge the success of individual students and the lessons better than if the class were trying to intake a broader curriculum. While Ms. Jackson intends to be helpful, interrupting a student who is struggling with a word, then supplying the complete pronunciation for the student, is actually ineffective: it further distracts from the learning environment and contributes to classroom outbursts. When Ms. Jackson pronounces the word to the student, the student may become embarrassed and others may laugh at the struggling student when they see the teacher intervene with such a harsh method of teaching the word. This frustration could further create an unpleasant learning environment, thereby undoing any progress made with the instructional strategies. An alternative approach such as the use of phonics would give students limited guidance when needed, while letting them find their way to the correct pronunciation.

   Ms. Jackson could also use writing as a strategy to enhance her students' focus and reading levels. Writing assignments based on reading passages that focus on correct spelling and grammar force the students to understand the individual words rather than attempting to decipher the meaning of an entire passage. If the students are busy working on these assignments, it is less likely that they will be so easily distracted by William's behavior.

2. Ms. Jackson should sit down and have a personal conversation with William in which she discusses his behaviors that must be changed. She can provide him with a list of positive and negative reinforcements that will come with certain types of behaviors. For instance, if he continues to disrupt the class, he will have to accept the consequences of that action. The list must be specific so that William's negative behavior will be shaped into a positive state. A contract designed by William and Ms. Jackson together to actually set goals not only for completed work but also for practiced behavior would also be useful. There should be an incentive for reaching these goals.

   In a parent/teacher conference with William's parents or guardians, Ms. Jackson can discuss the areas in which William shows strengths and her concerns about William's weaknesses in his performance in class. She needs to share with William's parents/guardians the positive growth and development William is making and how much more progress he can make. Ms. Jackson should find out in which room William completes his reading at home. For example: if William reads at the kitchen table, then is it free of distractions, such as physical objects on the table and other people in the room talking or eating? If William reads in his bedroom, is he supervised to make sure he remains on task? After asking about these rooms, Ms. Jackson can suggest how William's parents can help him succeed, such as having a clean area on the table where William can work, or having an older sibling also do work in William's room to make sure William remains on task. Ms. Jackson can share the reinforcement guidelines she is using to help with behavior modification in the classroom and ask the parents/guardians to do similar things at home so that William's behavior modification will be consistent. Finally, as a reward, William could be given time in the school library to select a book from his favorite genre. This would reward his good behavior and further encourage his reading skills.

## Constructed-Response Questions: Case History #2

**3.** Ms. Carter's class includes ELL students in an inclusion classroom. Hudson's administrators and staff are correct to consider ethnic diversity when placing non-English-speaking students new to this country in regular classrooms. In fact, the Individuals with Disabilities Education Act requires children with special needs to be placed in the "least restrictive environment" that is appropriate for their education. Immersion of ELL students in an English-speaking classroom fosters multiculturalism and can help ELL students learn English from their peers and from their teacher. Ms. Carter increases the benefits of immersion by including her ELL students in general discussions and by treating them as equal participants in the learning process. Also, she asks students open-ended questions without "correct" or "incorrect" answers and praises them for their responses. This technique is appropriate, for it provides the children with confidence to creatively use a new language.

Ms. Carter provides individual resources for students needing additional help. Special education students will learn effectively when placed in an environment that fosters diversity but also has resources catering to differentiating the instruction. In Ms. Carter's classroom, ELL students benefit from specialized, one-on-one attention during the regular classroom activities plus the additional support of a dedicated resource room where ELL resource teachers tailor instruction to the child's needs.

**4.** To ensure that non-English-speaking students do not feel different or left out, and thereby increase engagement, Ms. Carter could structure her lesson plan to include activities for the entire class that incorporate the ELL teachers and paraprofessionals to promote equality. She could, for instance, have a class discussion on culture using a concept web and have the students present their own definitions of culture and write them on the web. When all responses are written down, the students might see how different they all are and how different their responses were.

In working with Luis specifically, Ms. Carter might let him continue his successes in the ELL resource room because this seems to be a positive experience for him, but she needs to make sure he is included in the activities of his class. A home visit with a translator, in which Ms. Carter sits down with Luis and his parents, could be useful in identifying strategies for drawing Luis into the class's activities. When he learns some English, he may feel more comfortable being in a regular, English-speaking classroom full-time.

## Constructed-Response Questions: Case History #3

**5.** Ms. Ross could have included a word bank on her study sheet. This would make sure Thomas understood that the word was "condensation" and not "consation." It also makes it less likely that Thomas would mistake the side discussion on acid rain for a formal part of the lesson, because terms related to acid would not appear in the word bank.

Ms. Ross also could have given students a chance to compare notes in pairs. This would have given Thomas a chance to get missing pieces of answers from a peer. More importantly, it would let Ms. Ross circle the room and visually inspect student answers. This provides a more accurate assessment of the class's understanding than simply asking whether they have questions—she would know that Thomas (and possibly other students) needed assistance in understanding parts of the lesson.

6. Ms. Ross can make a safer environment for students by offering praise for behaviors other than asking questions. By singling out vocal students for praise, she may have worsened Thomas's impression that she is playing favorites in her classroom. If she had complimented Thomas for excellent work on a paper or homework assignment, her praise would let Thomas know that Ms. Ross did value his contributions, and would likely appreciate his questions and comments as well.

Ms. Ross could have gotten more value out of her praise to Carlos by eliciting from him that he was having trouble with the material, rather than pointing it out herself. Carlos might have been less embarrassed this way. But more importantly, Thomas would have seen a more popular student admit to having trouble with the material. This would let him know that many students found the material challenging, and there was nothing wrong with asking questions and admitting imperfect understanding.

**Constructed-Response Questions: Case History #4**

7. I would ask how Johnny behaves doing group work with other advanced students. If Johnny followed instructions and engaged with his advanced peers, then changes related to the difficulty of the assignment—such as giving Johnny a specific, challenging task when he works in a group—will alleviate the problem. However, if he works on his own and ignores even partners who can work at his level, Mr. Fayerwether might consider that the problem is one of socialization and is best addressed with the help of guidance.

I would ask whether Lucy was more productive during group activities that actually required conversation as part of the assignment. As Mr. Fayerwether pointed out, Lucy earns As in English. If she chats with her friends because she is primarily a verbal/auditory thinker, then giving her more opportunities to discuss problems will help her understand the mathematical concepts that are challenging her. If she won't talk about math problems even when instructed to, the root of her behavior probably lies elsewhere.

8. When reviewing answers on the test sheet, Mr. Fayerwether could put them on the overhead projector. This large image could be easier for students with visual difficulties to read—especially if he used assigned seating to ensure Karl was close to the front of the class. Additionally, Mr. Fayerwether should move several students to a new seating assignment in the room—and not just Karl's seat. By moving other students as well as Karl to different areas of the room, it removes the focus from Karl and instead explains the situation as an instructional change for the benefit of the entire class and not just a special-needs adjustment for Karl.

Mr. Fayerwether could further modify group activities in his class to include more conversation and collaborative work than was in the activity in this case. If he did so, Karl might be willing to ask his peers for the help he refuses from his aide.

# PRACTICE: PLT GRADES K–6

**Directions**: For selected-response questions 1–25, choose the response that best answers the question or completes the statement. Then follow the directions provided for constructed-reponse questions 1–2.

1. Ms. Sanchez, a sixth-grade teacher, wants to effectively manage and accommodate students from varying cultures while supporting their development of English language skills. Which of the following strategies would best support that goal?

    A. Instruct students not to speak their native language while completing classroom tasks.

    B. Set up daily cooperative learning activities with mixed groups of boys and girls.

    C. Allow students to communicate understanding through writing, drawing, or speaking.

    D. Support English language learners by correcting most errors in their speech so that they learn faster.

2. Ms. Lane, a second-grade teacher, notices that many of her pupils come to class with their homework incomplete. Ms. Lane plans an activity in which her students will fill out an after-school schedule, detailing tasks to be done at half-hour intervals from 3:30 until 9:00 PM each day of the school week. The activity described promotes which of the following capabilities in Ms. Lane's students?

    A. Awareness of consequences

    B. Risk-taking behavior

    C. Self-regulation

    D. Pro-social behavior

3. A kindergarten teacher is concerned with helping students make positive progress through the "initiative versus guilt" stage of development, as described by Erikson. Which of the following activities would most likely help students meet the goals associated with this stage of development?

    A. Students memorize a poem and recite it in front of the class.

    B. Students engage in independent play each day.

    C. Students watch a cartoon and discuss it together.

    D. Students play a supervised game together.

4. In Ms. Dickerson's sixth-grade French class, some students are successfully writing letters in French, while other students labor to write even a single sentence. Previous test results indicate these students have a similar level of French vocabulary knowledge. How could Ms. Dickerson use Vygotsky's zone of proximal development theory to help all students write paragraphs more successfully?

    A. The class could write a paragraph together, then write in small groups, then write individually.

    B. Students could write paragraphs in English, and then translate them into French.

    C. The teacher could show examples of well-written paragraphs in French for students to model.

    D. Students could write paragraphs in French about events occurring in their own lives.

5. Luz, a student in Mr. Lipnicki's classroom, typically completes in-class assignments very quickly. Her answers are usually correct and are well written. After she has finished her work, she often tries to strike up conversations with students who are still working on their own assignments. On occasion, she also loudly complains that the work in class is "boring."

   Which of the following would be an appropriate strategy for Mr. Lipnicki to use in light of Luz's pattern of disruptive behavior?

   A. Refer Luz to a school administrator for disciplinary measures.

   B. Create a reward structure in which students can win prizes like candy and toys for sitting quietly after all of their work is completed.

   C. Tell the other students in Luz's class that they are encouraging her misbehavior when they respond to the things she says and advise them to ignore her.

   D. Create appealing and intellectually challenging lesson-related "bonus activities" for students who finish work early.

6. In Mr. Hill's sixth-grade social studies class, students are asked to reflect on their learning over the past unit. They are provided with a reflection form that gives them the opportunity to describe in writing those learning activities that helped them and those that did not. Students are also asked to infer what this information reveals about their own learning styles and preferences.

   This strategy encourages the complex cognitive process of

   A. problem solving

   B. concept learning

   C. transfer

   D. metacognition

7. Ms. Ngo, a first-grade teacher, is teaching comparison word problems during math time in a classroom that includes several English language learners (ELLs). She uses several practices proven effective to help the ELLs, one of which is below.

   Choose the effective strategy.

   A. Exempt ELLs from word problems, having them focus instead on number comparisons.

   B. Have ELLs work on addition with pictures while the rest of the class does word problems.

   C. Have ELLs read the problems aloud to the class to make sure they understand the words.

   D. Make sure the comparison word problems incorporate multicultural references.

8. Mr. Ramirez is beginning a unit on the American Revolution with his sixth-grade social studies class. He first conducts a preassessment to determine students' understanding of the term "revolution" and its significance in the historical development of nations. With the results, Mr. Ramirez then plans instruction that begins just one step beyond the overall level of understanding of his students to ensure comprehension.

   The strategy described above most closely reflects an application of which of the following learning theories?

   A. B. F. Skinner's classical conditioning

   B. Lev Vygotsky's zone of proximal development

   C. Jerome Bruner's constructivist theory of learning

   D. Benjamin Bloom's taxonomy

9. Mr. Marsh's fifth-grade class is studying the wildlife of Australia. During one technology-aided class discussion, Mr. Marsh brings up an image of a platypus—a duck-billed, beaver-tailed, otter-footed monotreme—guarding several of its own eggs. He tells his students, "This venomous mammal is one of the oddest creatures on earth. What are some things about it that are strange?" Several students raise their hands. Mr. Marsh calls on a student named Olive, who answers: "It has fur."

Which of the following is the most constructive way for Mr. Marsh to respond to Olive's answer?

A. "You've never seen a mammal with fur before? Have you ever seen a dog or a cat?"

B. "Olive, why is it strange for an egg-laying, duck-billed creature to have fur?"

C. "No. Does someone else want to try?"

D. "Fur isn't really one of the strange features of the platypus, but that was a good guess, and I value your participation."

10. Which of the following approaches most effectively reinforces students' self-regulatory skills while assisting the teacher in communicating information about student progress to parents and other caregivers?

A. The teacher establishes a system in which students know that any test grade of F or A+ will result automatically in the teacher placing a phone call to the student's parents.

B. The teacher instructs students to regularly update their parents about their performance in school, as well as about upcoming projects and other major assignments.

C. Two times during each grading period, students write "progress letters" to their parents identifying recent successes and areas for future improvement.

D. The teacher requests that parents tether positive and negative incentives at home to students' academic performance and behavior in the classroom.

11. Which of the following lesson plan excerpts includes observable and measurable educational objectives?

A. By the end of the lesson, students will be able to describe the difference between a whole note and a half note and demonstrate the difference through rhythmic clapping.

B. By the end of the lesson, students will grasp the fundamentals of badminton and develop an appreciation of the importance of fair play and good ethics on the court.

C. By the end of the lesson, students will understand literary symbolism.

D. By the end of the lesson, students will be able to pass a multiple-choice test on the makeup of plant cells.

12. An earthquake occurs outside a small community. When students arrive at school the following day, they begin to ask their teacher all types of questions. Though the subject is not part of the lesson plan, the teacher uses this opportunity to teach the students about the causes of earthquakes.

What is the situation described above an example of?

A. Off-task behavior

B. Storytelling

C. Socratic questioning technique

D. Teachable moment

13. During oral presentations in his fifth-grade history class, Mr. Elliot noticed that many students were not listening to their classmates. Which technique could Mr. Elliot use that would be most likely to increase attentiveness for the presentations he has planned after the next unit?

    A. After the presentations, give a surprise quiz on what the presenters said.

    B. Sit in the front of the room to remind students that he is watching them.

    C. Create a new classroom rule that insists that students be polite to the speakers.

    D. Give students a graphic organizer to take notes during the subsequent presentations.

14. After several lessons in which Ms. Derringer taught her math class how to do long division using the method presented in their textbooks, some students in the class are struggling with similar problems. Which of these strategies would most likely help the students succeed in mastering this skill?

    A. Ms. Derringer could use data from newspaper articles to explain to students the importance of math skills like long division in many jobs.

    B. Ms. Derringer could find research-supported strategies from education research journals, model their use, and have students practice using these strategies.

    C. Ms. Derringer could obtain video clips of mathematicians demonstrating the steps of long division and have the whole class watch these clips.

    D. Ms. Derringer could obtain additional long division problems from websites designed for math teachers and use these questions as needed for extra practice.

15. Allowing "wait time" for student thinking, helping students reshape or sharpen verbal explanations, and establishing a noncritical classroom environment are all important aspects of

    A. written assessment

    B. instructional objective setting

    C. IEP development

    D. effective questioning

16. A school with a fine arts emphasis wishes to enroll students who have the potential to excel in musical studies. The admissions director plans to use a test to help identify students with strong musical potential. Which choice below serves as the best example of a test designed to measure what the student is capable of accomplishing musically?

    A. Ability test

    B. Achievement test

    C. Aptitude test

    D. Selected-response test

17. Ms. Le, an eighth-grade natural sciences teacher, instructs each student in her class to write a short essay explaining a biological process. When the students have handed in the essays, she breaks the class into pairs for "two stars and a wish" reviews. Each member of a pair reads the other's essay and awards a "star" to two sentences in the essay that are especially clear and interesting. Each student also expresses a "wish" to better understand some idea discussed in the peer's essay.

    Which of the following is the best rationale for peer assessment processes such as Ms. Le's?

    A. Peer assessments lessen the need for teacher-created feedback, giving teachers more time to focus on lesson planning.

    B. Peer assessments can help students think more deeply about their weaknesses as writers.

    C. Peer assessments can create opportunities for writers to receive and consider a variety of viewpoints and solutions.

    D. Peer assessments give students time to talk to one another, providing a break from listening to the teacher.

18. Which of the following scores would best indicate whether a student has developed the content knowledge and mastery deemed appropriate to the student's age?

    A. Stanine

    B. Raw score

    C. Grade-level equivalent

    D. Percentile rank

19. Which of the following types of scores results from statistically adjusting a raw score on a standardized test to account for discrepancies on different versions of the standardized test?

    A. Age-equivalent score

    B. Scaled score

    C. Percentile score

    D. Grade-equivalent score

20. Ms. Marylebone's fifth-grade class recently took the Idaho Test of Basic Skills, which is consistently administered to fifth graders. As she surveys the results of the reading exam, she notices that one of her students performed at the 24th percentile in reading. Which of the following inferences can Ms. Marylebone make from these results?

    A. Either Ms. Marylebone or the student's previous teacher did not teach reading in the most effective possible way.

    B. Ms. Marylebone's student did not perform as well on the assessment as would a typical fifth grader.

    C. Ms. Marylebone's student performed at a grade-appropriate level on the exam.

    D. Ms. Marylebone's student performed better than most fifth-grade students on the exam.

21. A number of teachers at a certain public school have noticed an increase in classroom distractions and honor code infractions, and they have concluded that these incidents are related to students' inappropriate dress choices. In addition, the teachers have become convinced that the wide disparity in the value of clothing worn by students is contributing to class divisions among students at the school. After informal discussion, and with the blessing of district administrators, these teachers have decided to advocate for the implementation of a district-wide school uniform program.

    Which of the following would be the most appropriate and productive next step for the teachers to take?

    A. Share their concerns and proposal with parents of the district's students and solicit and listen to the parents' ideas.

    B. Jointly sign a petition requesting that the school board institute a program mandating school uniforms.

    C. Begin to lead students by example by more carefully coordinating their own clothing choices.

    D. Notify parents by email that they may soon be required to purchase uniforms for students in the district.

22. Which support personnel would most likely be responsible for coordinating services for a child who felt unsafe at home?

    A. Guidance counselor

    B. Assistant principal

    C. IEP team leader

    D. Occupational therapist

23. Which of the following actions would best support a teacher seeking to deepen social studies content knowledge?

    A. Peruse the blog posts of teachers working on similar content.

    B. Read historical works set in the period during which the class's next unit takes place.

    C. Join a national organization of history teachers.

    D. Search for and watch video reenactments of historical events online.

24. A schoolteacher in a geographically isolated rural community wants to obtain a broad range of perspectives on lesson planning and classroom management problems on a daily basis. Which of the following professional resources would be most helpful for this purpose?

   A. A conference on behaviorist-oriented classroom management strategies

   B. Education-focused, news-aggregating web applications such as Google Reader

   C. A series of one-on-one meetings with a more experienced teacher of the same grade level at the same school

   D. Online educator forums and study groups

25. Mr. Quizar has just concluded a particularly trying day in his third-grade classroom. Throughout the afternoon, the behavior of a number of students was disruptive and provocative, and Mr. Quizar's own attempts to put the class back on track were met with frustration. Which of the following responses by Mr. Quizar would provide the best demonstration of reflective practice?

   A. Mr. Quizar gives two of his senior colleagues an account of the afternoon, including a description of his own teaching techniques, and asks for advice and guidance.

   B. Mr. Quizar contacts the parents of several of the students whose behavior was disruptive and urges them to take a more active disciplinary role in their children's lives.

   C. Mr. Quizar rearranges his classroom, removing two particularly popular "independent learning centers" that have been the subject of bickering among his students.

   D. Mr. Quizar begins crafting a plan for a lesson in which students will write letters apologizing for their disruptive actions and outlining how they will improve in the future.

# ANSWERS AND EXPLANATIONS

## Practice: PLT Grades K–6

**1. C**

Allowing ELL students to use nonverbal or verbal means of communicating helps the teacher assess their understanding. Therefore, (C) is the correct answer. Creating a classroom community is crucial to helping ELLs to learn, and prohibiting use of their native language (A) could lead to frustration or resentment. Daily use of mixed-gender groups (B) does not necessarily advance learning, and this strategy is not logically connected to Ms. Sanchez's goal of creating the best environment for English learners. Correcting most errors directly (D) will discourage students and interrupt the flow of the spoken word; the teacher could instead wait until the student is finished and restate the response with the correct language for the student to model in the future.

**2. C**

Choice (C) is the best option. By guiding her students to set up a schedule, Ms. Lane is promoting the self-regulation of students' after-school time. Ms. Lane is not instituting consequences as suggested by choice (A), and she is not addressing students' behavior with one another as in choice (D), since she is prompting students to think about how they spend their time once they have left school. The strategy presented in the question stem to encourage students to better structure their time is quite distinct from choice (B), which suggests that students take more risks and thus think less carefully about how they structure their time.

**3. B**

Choice (B) is the correct answer. Erikson's theory of initiative versus guilt states that children around kindergarten age need to learn by exploring the world and initiating their own activities without too much guidance or restrictions placed on them by adults. Independent play, as described in choice (B), allows a space for children to engage with one another and devise their own methods and solutions to problems. Choices (A) and (D) both suggest that adults will

be determining all of the children's actions and intervening frequently with overt guidelines. In choice (C), the children would have slightly more autonomy, but the activity has still been determined by an adult.

**4. A**

The zone of proximal development (ZPD) theory, when applied to education, is much like scaffolding, challenging students to accomplish with assistance what they may lack the skill and experience to accomplish independently. By writing paragraphs together before attempting to do so separately, struggling students can improve their French writing skills in stages with meaningful assistance; (A) is therefore the correct answer. Translating entire paragraphs into French (B) might, at this point, be extremely challenging for some of the students in this class; the activity therefore does not reflect the tenets of ZPD theory. Showing students well-written examples (C) could offer some benefits, but the activity does not require them to take on challenges with assistance. The personal essay-writing assignment in choice (D) also lacks ZPD theory's crucial element of taking on challenges on the edge of students' competence with assistance.

**5. D**

Luz seems to be struggling with her behavior in class, but she tends to do well on her assignments, suggesting that she can easily keep pace with the work. Her declaration that work is "boring" indicates that she may be a gifted student and that more challenging options for her, as described in choice (D), may be the solution. Enforcing punishments as in choices (A) and (C) is unlikely to serve Luz's best interests or get to the root of the issue, and choice (B) works on extrinsic motivation rather than building Luz's intrinsic motivation or addressing her desire for more challenging assignments.

**6. D**

Reflecting on how one learns best and why one might have gained more from different activities is a hallmark of metacognition (D). Metacognition, or "thinking about thinking," is distinct from problem solving (A), in which students are presented with an issue to resolve rather than asked to reflect; concept learning (B), in which students are guided to understand a new idea rather than to reflect on how and why they learned; and transfer (C), in which students use concepts from one area of study in another and make connections.

## 7.  D

English language learners (ELLs) can be expected to perform the same work as other students so long as they have sufficient scaffolding to understand the concepts on which they are working. This includes preteaching essential vocabulary and making connections to concepts with which ELLs are already familiar, as in choice (D). Multicultural references can help students understand concepts and feel more at home during the lesson. Allowing ELLs to skip the more complex work the class is doing (A) or work on addition (B) ensures that these students will fall farther behind the class in math without advancing in the development of their English language skills. Asking these students to read problems aloud (C) not only does not reveal whether the students understand what is being asked, as there may be no correlation between their pronunciation and comprehension, but also may make them feel uncomfortable if they encounter unfamiliar words.

## 8.  B

Vygotsky's zone of proximal development includes all tasks that a learner is unable to accomplish alone but can accomplish with assistance. By helping students as they work within their zones of proximal development, Vygotsky argued that teachers can facilitate student growth, enabling students to do more and more things independently. By beginning his instruction right at the point at which his students need help, Mr. Ramirez is focusing his instruction within his class's zone of proximal development, and (B) is correct. Classical conditioning is a behaviorist strategy in which a certain stimulus comes to be associated with a certain result. Mr. Ramirez is not using conditioning, so (A) is incorrect. Constructivism is a theory of learning under which the teacher acts as the facilitator of student-driven exploration and experiential learning. Nothing in the situation suggests that Mr. Ramirez is planning

to use student-directed learning, so (C) is incorrect. Finally, (D) is incorrect; Bloom's taxonomy is a system of educational objectives (broken into "domains") and is not obviously related to Mr. Ramirez's current lesson plan.

## 9.  B

To encourage student thinking and strengthen verbal skills, teachers need strategies for eliciting more articulate answers without finding fault. While it may be true that there is nothing inherently strange about an animal having fur, an egg-laying, billed, venomous animal with fur is rare indeed. Instead of focusing on the imperfection of Olive's response, Mr. Marsh's best move is to assume that she has something relevant and perceptive to offer and guide her toward a clearer expression of that insight. In choice (B), Mr. Marsh reflectively listens and uses positive language to encourage Olive to elaborate. (B) is the correct answer. Choice (A) might make Olive feel foolish and unlikely to respond again. A teacher's abrupt "no" to a student answer (C) likewise is not encouraging, nor is it correct in a situation that calls for an opinion about what the student defines as "strange." Choice (D) also invalidates the student's opinion and does not give her the opportunity to expand on her response.

## 10.  C

Correct choice (C) meets the two goals of promoting students' self-regulatory skills and keeping parents informed of student progress. The students write the letters to their parents, summarizing their own progress to date. Students could identify reasons for their successes and areas in which their own improvement is needed. It is probable that parents and students would discuss the letter and its implications for student progress. Choice (A) would give parents information on student progress only in rare situations. Additionally, the system described in (A) lacks any element of student self-evaluation, which is important in developing self-regulation. It is helpful for students to discuss projects and progress with parents, but choice (B) would not provide parents with definitive statements related to students' strengths, achievements, and areas for improvement. (B)'s vague instruction to "regularly update parents" also makes it likely that students will not really keep their parents informed about their progress. Choice (D) ties together student behavior and academic progress, and it may punish or reward students regardless of their level of effort, thus possibly serving as a disincentive for students to develop their self-regulatory skills.

## 11. A

Educational objectives are explicit statements that clearly express what students will be able to do at the conclusion of a lesson. Choice (A) requires students to describe and demonstrate knowledge of full and half notes. Because this objective includes tasks that the teacher can observe and thus use to clearly measure whether learning has taken place, (A) is the correct answer. While it is important for lessons to allow students to "grasp the fundamentals" and "develop an appreciation," as in choice (B), or "understand," as in choice (C), such goals can be difficult to observe and measure. Because neither (B) nor (C) includes any method of observing whether students have met those goals, both are incorrect. Finally, taking a multiple-choice test, choice (D), is one way of measuring educational objectives, but the ability to pass a test is not in and of itself an educational objective.

## 12. D

In this scenario, the teacher makes use of the opportunity to engage students in a topic made especially relevant by a real-world situation affecting students inside and outside of the classroom. This is a classic example of a teachable moment, choice (D). The teacher recognizes that, while this topic is not the planned lesson, it is still valuable learning for students, meaning it is not off-task (A). The students and teacher are reflecting on a true local event, rather than storytelling (B), and the teacher is not using the Socratic method (C), as the teacher is not leading the questioning and does not have a specific conclusion in mind for students to reach.

## 13. D

One highly effective strategy for holding students accountable for their learning is to require measurable and observable activities, such as using graphic organizers or taking notes during presentations. Therefore, choice (D) is correct. While administering a surprise quiz after the presentations (A) may indicate who was listening and who was not, this strategy is ineffective because it does not curtail the inattentiveness before it happens. Having the teacher watch students from the front of the room (B) will not guarantee their attention to the presenters and may be distracting. Classroom rules are essential, but in this case, adding a new rule (C) is not nearly as effective as providing students with a productive activity that requires their attention and directs it to the presentations.

## 14. B

By modeling proven strategies—of which educational journals are an excellent source—and then immediately giving students a chance to try those strategies themselves, Ms. Derringer would provide her struggling students with the best chance to improve their skills. (B) is the correct answer. The activity in (A) might help students see the importance of learning division, but it would not help them learn how to do long division; therefore, the activity is not logically connected to Ms. Derringer's immediate educational objective, making (A) wrong. (C) is also wide of the mark; while it might be helpful to have the steps of long division demonstrated, Ms. Derringer has likely gone through this process herself, and students must be given the opportunity to practice this skill rather than just observe it. (D) is incorrect as well. Merely drilling is not what is needed at this point; before drills can be useful, the students must understand what they are doing, how they should do it, and why.

## 15. D

Choice (D) is correct, as all strategies listed in the question stem correspond to laying the groundwork for effective questioning. Students must feel comfortable and supported as they work to express themselves. Verbal explanations by students are not present in written assessment (A). While establishing a noncritical classroom environment will support all students as they learn, allowing "wait time" does not apply to objective setting (B), as teachers engage in this activity separately. IEP development (C) is also an activity that adults will primarily work on in a distinct group, perhaps with the input of the individual student in question, and thus does not require the establishment of any particular type of classroom environment.

## 16. C

An aptitude test measures potential rather than achievement. Admissions exams—including selected-response tests like the SAT—are often measures of aptitude, since schools are interested in finding out what applicants are capable of accomplishing in the years ahead. (C) is the correct answer. Ability tests (A) and achievement tests (B) are not always designed to predict future achievement, so these choices are incorrect. A selected-response test (D) is a multiple-choice assessment. Such a test would not allow the applicant to demonstrate potential in the expressive arts, so it is not the correct answer here.

## 17. C

Choice (A), freeing up teacher time for lesson planning, does not express a rationale for incorporating peer assessments. Teachers should still provide feedback on student work, even when peer assessments are included. A focus on students' weaknesses, as in choice (B), is not the point of conducting peer assessments. Choice (C), especially when combined with teacher feedback, provides a strong benefit of peer assessment and is the correct answer. While students may enjoy talking to one another, choice (D) is not a strong reason to conduct peer assessments.

## 18. C

A grade-level equivalent score, choice (C), demonstrates the representative grade level at which a student is currently performing, so this is the correct answer. A student's stanine score (A) and percentile rank (D) both reveal how a student performs in relation to peers, while a raw score (B) shows how many of the items a student performed correctly on a given assessment.

## 19. B

A scaled score is a raw score that has been modified in some way to add consistency to results or to fit results to a certain format; (B) is therefore the correct answer. Age-equivalent scores (A) compare individual test takers' performance to performance averages for test takers of certain ages; an age-equivalent score of 9, for instance, means that the test taker did as well as a typical 9-year-old would have done on the same test. That is not what's happening here, so (A) is incorrect. Percentile scores (C) state which percentage of test takers performed below the test taker; a percentile score of 56, for instance, means that the test taker's score was better than that of 56 percent of test takers. There are no percentiles in the above description, so choice (C) is incorrect. Grade-equivalent (GE) scores (D) are very similar to age-equivalent scores, except that the scores refer to grades instead of ages; a GE score of 9 would mean that the student's performance matched that of a typical student entering high school. No grade equivalences are mentioned here, so (D) is wrong.

## 20. B

A percentile shows how well a student performed on an assessment compared to peers taking the same assessment. A student scoring in the 24th percentile has been outperformed by 76 percent of test takers, in line with choice (B). This is the opposite of choice (D), which suggests that the student outperformed most others, and also does not fit choice (C), that the student performed on par with others at the same grade level. Choice (A), that one of the student's teachers is at fault for the student's reading performance, cannot be determined from the information provided.

## 21. A

The issue of clothing choices is one that affects students, parents, and teachers. Because any change in the dress code will impact these families, choice (A) is the best response. Going straight to the school board with a petition (B) is likely to alienate people who were not given a chance to have a voice in the process. Leading "by example" (C) is not likely to change what students choose to wear for themselves. To notify parents with an email that sounds as if a decision has already been made without their feedback (D) may create confusion and resentment if they have not been aware of prior discussions.

## 22. A

A school guidance counselor has extensive training in responding to allegations or concerns about abuse or neglect in students' homes; (A) is the right answer. (B) is incorrect; while an assistant principal is someone with whom a teacher might share concerns about a student's welfare, it is the guidance counselor who, by training and job description, is primarily responsible for coordinating a response to those kinds of concerns. The IEP team leader's job is to tailor curricula and the school environment to the special needs of particular students; a person with this role would likely report abuse allegations to a counselor rather than coordinate the school's response, so (C) is incorrect. An occupational therapist is there to help students with special needs navigate and adapt to the challenges of the school environment, not to coordinate services for a student in an unsafe home environment; (D) is incorrect.

## 23. C

Choice (C) is correct, as a national organization of history teachers has a wide range of resources for both educators and their students on diverse topics. Choice (A) is not likely to result in new content knowledge, and choices (B) and (D), while entertaining, may not provide the deep or accurate content knowledge that best supports students' education.

## 24. D

Selective use of online educator forums and study groups as suggested in correct choice (D) would most effectively allow the teacher to consider a variety of perspectives on these educational issues. These forums would likely include educators and individuals with educational experiences from diverse backgrounds. Choice (A) focuses on one classroom management approach, rather than a variety of approaches, and it might not include lesson planning. The information available from news-aggregating web applications, as described in choice (B), might include topics that do not relate to the teacher's study goals, and the intended audience for the readings might be the general public rather than schoolteachers in particular. Developing a relationship with a more experienced educator, as suggested in choice (C), could be beneficial, but this one-to-one orientation in the school where the teacher is located would limit the perspective of these meetings to that of the mentor and school involved.

## 25. A

Two essential components of reflective practice are reviewing one's successes and areas for growth and seeking guidance about how to improve. Choice (A) demonstrates both of these as Mr. Quizar actively reflects on his actions and experiences and consults with more experienced mentors. Choice (B) places responsibility on students and their families rather than exploring what Mr. Quizar can do to improve his practice. Punitive measures, such as choice (C), are reactive rather than reflective, while choice (D) focuses on blaming students for their behaviors rather than actively seeking ways to avoid or refocus that behavior.

**Approximate time—25 minutes**

**Directions:** The case history below is followed by two short-answer questions. Your responses to the questions will be evaluated with respect to professionally accepted principles and practices in teaching and learning. Be sure to answer all parts of the question. Write your answers on the pages indicated in your answer sheet booklet.

### Scenario:

Naima is a student in Mr. Traister's fifth-grade class. While Naima gives indications of being highly capable—she participates in the school's Gifted and Talented program and routinely scores at or above the 95th percentile on standardized math and reading tests—she rarely participates in class discussions and frequently fails to submit required homework assignments. Recently, Mr. Traister has noticed that the quality of Naima's participation in certain collaborative classroom activities has declined sharply.

### DOCUMENT 1

### Excerpt from a conference between Mr. Traister and Naima's mother, Ms. McCarron

Mr Traister: On this recent math quiz, for instance, Naima left half of the questions unanswered and neglected to show her work as required.

Ms. McCarron: But these questions are too basic for her. I thought she was in the "high math" group. Is this what the high math group is doing? I used to play a computer game with her on a tablet that had problems like these.

Mr. Traister: If she's mastered the skill, she should be able to complete the quiz quickly and accurately. Notice that she missed a number of problems here.

Ms. McCarron: But I've seen her answer questions like these a million times! If she's not getting them right, it's because she's not paying attention.

Mr Traister: Even on open-ended, creative assignments, I have trouble getting Naima engaged. Here, for instance, is a sheet of drawing paper on which Naima was supposed to illustrate her essay about dinosaurs. She drew one tree in the corner and then stopped working on it. Her quizzes often come back to me covered in little pictures, so I know that she enjoys—and has a talent for—drawing. When we break into groups, Naima often won't participate in the work her group is doing until I goad her.

Ms. McCarron: Is it her job to teach the other children?

Mr Traister: The group work is about exploring new concepts collaboratively. It isn't about one student teaching the others.

Ms. McCarron: Well, I'll tell her to do a better job with her work in school. But I worry, Mr. Traister, that some of this work is not worth her time.

## DOCUMENT 2

### Excerpt from a transcript of a whole-class reading exercise in Mr. Traister's class

Billy: "'Thanks to this magic... potion, I will soon have...'"

Mr. Traister: Sound it out. The first syllable is—

Billy: ffff... ffrrr... *freckles*. "'Freckles, just like'"—

Mr. Traister: Nice job, but start again at the beginning of the sentence, Billy.

Billy: "'Thanks to this magic potion, I will soon have freckles just like my best... friend.'"

Mr. Traister: Great. Naima, please take over. Naima?

Naima: What page are we on?

Mr. Traister: Naima, I need you to follow along with us.

Naima: I read this book in first grade. It's dumb.

Andrew: You did not read it in first grade! Liar!

Mr. Traister: Andrew, that's inappropriate. Naima, we're on page 21. "'I will soon have freckles like my best friend.'" Please resume the reading.

## DOCUMENT 3

### Conversation between Mr. Traister and Ms. Benson, a Gifted and Talented resource teacher at the school

Mr. Traister: It's frustrating, because I know that Naima has the skills to be a real leader in our classroom.

Ms. Benson: She may have the skills, but we also need to make sure we give her the opportunities.

Mr. Traister: In small groups, I've asked her many times to use her abilities and her understanding to help the students who are struggling. I can't seem to cajole her into taking on that role.

Ms. Benson: She needs to get a chance to explore her own interests as well.

Mr. Traister: When the students were researching their book reports on biomes, she said that she had already read all of the books we were using, so I let her work with the librarian, Ms. Upshaw, to find some books she hadn't read. But when it came time for her to report back, she simply read undigested passages from a complicated book; she wasn't making any effort to paraphrase or synthesize.

Ms. Benson: It may be that she's shy, as well. I know that she enjoys our weekly GT small-group sessions in the resource room—but even there, she isn't particularly talkative.

Mr. Traister: I can see that. She doesn't seem to get along with the other kids in the class. At recess, for instance, I often find her sitting by herself reading a book, even though I've told her that recess time is for playing, not reading.

### Constructed-Response Questions

### Question 1

Mr. Traister's student Naima appears increasingly disengaged and unmotivated in the classroom.

• Identify TWO ways in which Naima's needs may currently be going unaddressed in Mr. Traister's classroom.

• For EACH of the needs you have identified, discuss a strategy that Mr. Traister could use to assist Naima. Base your response on the principles of teaching gifted and talented students.

### Question 2

Mr. Traister works at a school that employs a number of educational paraprofessionals.

• Identify TWO ways that Mr. Traister could collaborate with other professionals at the school to provide beneficial educational opportunities to Naima.

• For EACH of the collaborative relationships you identify, discuss how that relationship would improve the quality of the education offered to Naima. Base your response on the principles of collaboration with instructional partners in instructional planning.

# ANSWERS AND EXPLANATIONS

## Constructed-Response Questions

### Sample Response to Question 1

Naima appears to fall into the category of "gifted and talented (GT)," a flexible term that applies to highly capable students whose needs may not be addressed by the standard curriculum. GT students often already have accomplished the learning goals the teacher is setting for the class, or they are able to learn the content more quickly than other students and therefore become bored. GT students are not covered by the IDEA, so they are not guaranteed the right to accommodations to meet their special abilities. However, these students do have "special needs"; if these students' needs are not addressed, they may be denied an equal opportunity to learn. Given Naima's performance on standardized tests and her comments to Mr. Traister in class, it appears that she is not being challenged by his assignments. One partial solution would be for Mr. Traister to incorporate an element of choice into classroom assignments: students could opt to complete the standard assignment or do a more challenging and open-ended version. Mr. Traister could also "compact" Naima's curriculum, allowing her to skip lessons she does not need and use that time to work independently on intellectually challenging assignments.

On the other hand, it appears from Mr. Traister's comments to Ms. Benson and from Naima's own behavior in class that Naima also needs to be brought into the life of the classroom more. One solution would be to modify small-group instruction so that Naima can join other students without serving as a de facto teacher's aide. Assigning each group member a discrete role—reporter, connection finder, math solver— can bring each student into the group work without allowing any one student to take over or be unduly burdened.

### Sample Response to Question 2

Ms. Benson, the school's GT resource teacher, directs small-group GT sessions outside of the general classroom—but she is also a potentially valuable resource in helping Mr. Traister make decisions about his own classroom instruction. By consulting with Ms. Benson, Mr. Traister may gain insight about ideas for lesson plans that serve the needs of gifted students like Naima along with the others in the class.

The school librarian, Ms. Upshaw, is another paraprofessional whom Mr. Traister can bring into his instructional planning process. Ms. Upshaw should be able to identify reading materials that Naima would find challenging and interesting. By consulting with Ms. Upshaw, Mr. Traister may be able to craft compelling and challenging individualized assignments for students like Naima who have unusual needs.

# PRACTICE: PLT GRADES 5–9

**Directions:** For selected-response questions 1–25, choose the response that best answers the question or completes the statement. Then follow the directions provided for constructed-reponse questions 1–2.

1. Central Middle School is located in a metropolitan, middle-class suburb where families have similar incomes and cultural backgrounds. A fifth-grade class is studying government. The teacher uses videos, lectures, and worksheets to cover the material.

   One child in this class, Sarah, is an outgoing student who is well-liked by her peers. She is not doing well on this unit. She is doing well in her math and English classes, where the teacher uses hands-on activities to teach concepts.

   Which of the following is most likely a variable that is affecting how Sarah is learning and performing?

   A. Learning disability
   B. Self-confidence
   C. Learning style
   D. Maturity

2. A student has recovered from head trauma. However, the student's eyesight is permanently affected, resulting in the need for larger fonts on copies when available. The student also needs additional time to complete on-level assignments.

   Which type of documentation should be included in the student's records to ensure the student's needs are met?

   A. 504 plan
   B. IEP with modifications
   C. IEP without modifications
   D. Healthcare documentation signed by physician

3. A ninth-grade literature student with a learning disability in reading comprehension has been assigned the book *To Kill a Mockingbird*.

   Which of the following accommodations would be the LEAST beneficial in helping the student read the book successfully?

   A. Give the student extended time to complete the reading assignments.
   B. Place the student in the front of the class during independent, individual reading time.
   C. Allow the student to read along with an audio book.
   D. Have the student take turns reading aloud with a teacher or peer tutor.

4. Which of the following activities is LEAST characteristic of a constructivist learning approach?

   A. Students work in groups to compare contemporary music lyrics to the lines of a Shakespearean sonnet.
   B. Students write an essay, create a cartoon, or perform a skit demonstrating their understanding of unit content.
   C. Students watch the teacher quote a PowerPoint presentation about the atomic bomb and then write an essay summarizing key points of the presentation.
   D. Students identify an environmental problem, propose a solution, and share their results with the class.

5. Which of the following strategies could a math teacher use to increase students' intrinsic motivation most significantly?

    A. Allow students with a stronger understanding of math concepts to have fewer homework problems.

    B. Have students present examples of how math concepts in a unit apply to their own hobbies.

    C. Hold a pizza party for all students who earn an A on the semester exam.

    D. Allow students to complete assignments with a partner during class time.

6. Ms. Pridgeon's science lesson requires students to memorize details related to certain biology concepts; memorizing is a form of the cognitive process known as recall. In the same lesson, students will also analyze science data to reach conclusions.

    Which of the following terms most closely represents the thinking skill in which Ms. Pridgeon's students are engaged?

    A. Planning

    B. Problem solving

    C. Questioning

    D. Metacognition

7. In which of the following activities do students have an opportunity to demonstrate synthesis of new concepts?

    A. Using colored pencils, crayons, scissors, construction paper, and other craft tools, students collaboratively create vivid posters featuring and illustrating formulas such as $p = mV$ and $F = ma$.

    B. Students complete word-search worksheets including key terms from a unit on momentum, looking up each new word in a scientific dictionary.

    C. After students silently read a textbook chapter on momentum, work, and energy, the teacher explains the practical importance of each of these concepts in modern industry.

    D. Students drop balls of four different weights from a certain height, measure the height of each ball's bounce, and draw conclusions concerning the impact of weight on the height of a ball's bounce.

8. All of the following practices would most likely contribute to effective classroom management EXCEPT:

    A. posting behavior expectations in the classroom

    B. consistently using the same instructional strategy throughout the class period

    C. homogeneous grouping of students for reading groups

    D. heterogeneous grouping of students for a math activity

9. A teacher wants to use schema theory to help students learn most effectively. Which strategy would provide the teacher with the most information about students' schema related to a biology topic?

    A. Students complete an individual brainstorm activity related to the biology topic.

    B. Students write a 10-word main idea summary based on an article related to the biology topic.

    C. The teacher leads a whole-class discussion, comparing and contrasting a video and article discussing a similar biology topic.

    D. Students make predictions about the content of an article related to the biology topic based on the article's title and illustrations.

10. This week, the seventh graders at Chavez Middle School will be learning about Egyptian history, geography, and culture in their social studies classes. In their language arts classes, they will read and discuss *The Secret of the Pharaoh*, a contemporary young adult novel set in ancient Egypt. During their math classes, they will learn about Egyptian numerals as part of a broader lesson on nonstandard units of measurement.

Which of the following instructional processes is embodied in the lesson plans described above?

    A. Creating lesson plans that reflect the major contributions of a variety of educational theorists

    B. Creating practical opportunities for students to apply acquired knowledge outside of the classroom

    C. Accomodating differences in students' learning styles and creating a comfortable environment for English language learners

    D. Developing lesson plans within the framework of a thematic, interdisciplinary unit

11. Students go to the natural history museum for a lesson on fossils. While there, they see replicas of dinosaur skeletons and spend time on their own, examining tools used by archaeologists and paleontologists. At the end of the lesson, they participate in a simulated dinosaur dig in which they excavate bones and construct their own dinosaur skeleton.

Which is NOT an instructional model used during this field trip?

    A. Experiential

    B. Interactive

    C. Direct

    D. Independent

12. Which of the following teaching behaviors best exemplifies the assistive strategy of task and performance modeling?

   A. In her intermediate woodworking class, Ms. Hinton has students break into small groups, each of which will be responsible for creating a different part of a multi-hinged wooden toy.

   B. In his advanced biology class, Mr. Finch mixes chemicals in a beaker, causing them to fizz, and then asks students to describe the chemical process that produced the fizzing reaction.

   C. In her introductory French language class, Ms. Mignot greets students in French and encourages them to return the greeting.

   D. In her art studio class, Ms. Dawson projects photographs of a dog onto a screen and asks students to use their pencils to create sketches of the dog.

13. Which of the following techniques for equalizing student participation in whole-class discussions is most appropriate and constructive?

   A. The teacher provides a reward—such as a piece of candy or a drink—to the "top participant" in the discussion each week.

   B. The teacher spends part of each discussion period calling on students at random by drawing names out of a hat.

   C. The teacher deducts daily discussion points from "overparticipating" students who too frequently raise their hands.

   D. The teacher assigns additional homework to "underparticipating" students who too rarely raise their hands.

14. Mr. Jansch, a seventh-grade computer science teacher, gives his students untimed quizzes to complete at home every weekend. These quizzes include a mix of multiple-choice questions and open-ended mini-essay questions. They cover the material reviewed over the previous week but also include "engager" questions designed to get students thinking about the material that will be studied during the upcoming week. Mr. Jansch uses the quiz results to help shape his instruction for the upcoming week. All quizzes are graded on a pass/fail basis: provided that students complete each question to the best of their ability, they receive a passing mark for the assignment.

The weekly quizzes described above are examples of what kind of assessment?

   A. Formative assessment

   B. Summative assessment

   C. Diagnostic assessment

   D. Informal assessment

15. Results from a pre-test indicate that students are weak in multiplication skills. These same students have been previously identified as either kinesthetic or visual learners.

Which of the following instructional strategies would best suit the students' educational needs and learning strengths?

A. Demonstrate on the blackboard how to solve the multiplication problems, provide a hands-on activity, and follow up with a formative assessment.

B. Save multiplication for a later unit. Have the students draw graphic organizers reviewing previously studied addition concepts and follow up with a summative assessment.

C. Give a brief lecture on how to work multiplication problems and follow up with a formative assessment.

D. Provide a video on solving the problems, engage the students in a discussion related to the math concepts involved, and follow up with a summative assessment.

16. Ms. Meyer, a fifth-grade teacher at Nalpak Elementary, is concluding an educational unit on biomes. On the last day of the unit, each student gives a two-minute presentation on a different biome (alpine tundra, mountain forest, etc.). When the presentations are finished, Ms. Meyer announces that the class will have 10 minutes of silent thinking and writing time. During this quiet period, she requests that each student write down one thing he or she did well during his or her presentation, as well as one thing that he or she can improve on in future presentations.

The writing exercise described above is most likely to promote which of the following capabilities in Ms. Meyer's students?

A. Abstract reasoning

B. Physical manipulation

C. Self-regulation

D. Pro-social behavior

17. Ms. Petrie, an eighth-grade language arts teacher, is interested in using informal formative assessment methods to complement the formal diagnostic, summative, and formative assessments she is already using.

Which of the following is an example of the type of assessment Ms. Petrie is interested in adding to her class?

A. Interviews with students in which they evaluate their own work, discuss difficulties they encountered, and set expectations for coming weeks

B. Timed essay examinations in which students identify connections between events portrayed in the course texts and events in daily life

C. Collage projects that require students to demonstrate what they have learned about particular places and periods in world literary history

D. Multiple-choice tests given at the end of instructional units that determine how closely students read the course texts and how well they listened during class

18. A student received test results indicating that his level of reading comprehension was higher than that of 80 percent of students at his grade level.

What sort of test would provide this result?

A. Criterion-referenced assessment

B. Norm-referenced assessment

C. Standards-based assessment

D. Ipsative assessment

19. Which of the following describes an appropriate time and reason for a teacher to use a summative assessment?

    A. At the beginning of an educational unit, to assess preexisting knowledge of the material

    B. At the beginning of an educational unit, to encourage creative thinking about the material coming up

    C. In the middle of an educational unit, to aid in student comprehension of the material

    D. At the end of an educational unit, to judge how much students learned

20. Mr. Shinawatra is designing lesson plans for a unit on cell division. One of the ways in which he will ultimately assess his students' learning is by asking them, in a timed in-class assignment, to create a series of cartoon-like pictures depicting the various stages of mitosis, meiosis, and binary fission.

    Which of the following activities is best suited to helping Mr. Shinawatra achieve some of his instructional objectives for the unit on cell division described above?

    A. Showing students a short video that uses a blend of sophisticated microscopy and computer-generated imagery to illustrate mitosis

    B. Having an open discussion in which students share background knowledge and personal connections they have with the subject of cell division

    C. Conducting a thorough lecture, accompanied by a timeline, on the history of the study of binary fission

    D. Inviting pairs of students to engage in Lincoln-Douglas style debates on a variety of questions pertaining to mitosis, meiosis, and binary fission

21. Which of the following interactions between educators describes a collaborative relationship that is likely to provide the greatest educational benefit to students?

    A. To cut down on planning time, Mr. Small makes a habit of asking an experienced teacher on his team to email him the lesson plans she plans to use in the next day's classes.

    B. A school's technology teacher, Mr. Crumb, shares some entertainment sites students can visit as a reward when they finish their English writing assignment before their classmates.

    C. Mr. Grimm, an English teacher, stores up a secret trove of unique "five-star" lesson plans that he created, which he uses on days in which his class is visited by a school administrator.

    D. Before giving students their first research assignment, Ms. Wise invites the school's librarian to give a short presentation in which she introduces tools for library research.

22. Which of these strategies is most beneficial to a teacher in improving cross-cultural communication in the classroom?

    A. Maintaining universally applied rules about what kinds of communication are welcome in the classroom

    B. Communicating regularly with parents and treating them as collaborators in a program of instruction

    C. Grouping students homogeneously by culture and language to improve the clarity of intragroup communication

    D. Learning the basic grammar of every language spoken by a student in the class

23. Ms. Sanders has just been hired to teach science at the sixth- and seventh-grade levels for the upcoming school year. Ms. Sanders's new teaching position is in a public school in a state where she has never lived, and she is not familiar with the sixth- and seventh-grade science curriculum in this state.

Which of the following materials would be most useful in helping Ms. Sanders shape appropriate instructional units for this subject and grade level?

A. District pacing guide

B. Biology textbook from Ms. Sanders's undergraduate program

C. Biographies of famous scientists

D. Science books Ms. Sanders used in a sixth- and seventh-grade teaching position in a different state

24. Ms. Ramirez is developing a new unit related to genetics. She wants students to succeed in mastering the unit objectives she will be shaping.

Which approach should she follow to ensure that students have the most effective materials to help them achieve the unit objectives?

A. Identify the outcomes students should achieve; select textbook readings, Internet resources, and video clips that serve most effectively to help students achieve those goals.

B. Identify a variety of interesting and up-to-date materials related to genetics; find specific readings within these resources and create class activities based on those readings.

C. Share with students what she has learned about genetics; test students on the knowledge they obtained from her lectures.

D. Focus on the textbook's coverage of the genetics unit; allow students with different reading levels to work in groups to understand the readings most effectively.

25. Two teachers collaborate to develop a lesson on Japanese culture. Then, each teacher observes the other teacher as she teaches the lesson. The observing teacher identifies strengths and areas for improvement in the observed teacher's approach.

What educational goal is most directly served by the teachers' providing feedback on each other's teaching?

A. Reflective practice

B. 504 plan development

C. Formative assessment

D. Multiple intelligence theory

# ANSWERS AND EXPLANATIONS

## Practice: PLT Grades 5–9

**1. C**

Sarah's success in math and English shows that she is likely not affected by a learning disability. Likewise maturity and self-confidence do not factor into her educational abilities in a negative manner. Given her success with hands-on manipulatives, Sarah is most likely experiencing a learning style issue.

**2. A**

A 504 plan requires healthcare documentation and will then ensure the student has appropriate access to grade-level curriculum with medically necessary accommodations. Merely providing the healthcare documentation itself (D) will not ensure access to accommodations. Choice (A) is correct. Individualized Education Plans (IEPs), in choices (B) and (C), are for students with diagnosed cognitive learning disabilities. This student does not have a cognitive processing disorder; therefore, an IEP is not appropriate.

**3. B**

The student will benefit most from supplementary curricula, such as audio books, and curricular supports, including extended time and one-on-one help from a teacher or peer. Combined, these supports will provide appropriate access for this student. While priority seating can be a needed accommodation, it is not beneficial for individual reading time, making choice (B) the correct answer.

**4. C**

A constructivist learning approach is driven by student led inquiry. Summarizing a video or lecture would only entail low-level thinking and not implement the problem solving and reflection skills outlined in constructivism. Answer choice (C) is correct.

**5. B**

In order to boost intrinsic motivation, students need to be able to relate the curriculum to real-world situations. Given the developmental maturity at this age, real-world situations need to include things that directly affect the students. Incorporating their own hobbies into the examples, as in choice (B), will give the students buy-in to the curriculum to increase their intrinsic motivation.

**6. B**

Data analysis is a higher level of cognitive processing. It requires the students to synthesize information and determine how it applies to the question posed. This would be considered a form of problem solving.

**7. D**

A crucial step in the synthesis of new concepts is to have students demonstrate the application of the new skill set. In other words, the activity needs to go beyond recall skills, direct instruction, and replication. Students need to be able to analyze what the new skills mean and how they apply to a problem. Choice (D) is an appropriate activity for this purpose.

**8. C**

Effective classroom management involves utilizing a variety of teaching methods to promote differential instruction. This allows all students to have access to the curriculum in many ways so they can synthesize the information and apply new skills. Choice (C) promotes boredom in students, which leads to more classroom management issues. (C) is therefore correct.

**9. A**

Schema theory includes chunking information to help commit it to memory. A great activity to help students synthesize what they think will happen or want to learn is to brainstorm, as in choice (A). Brainstorming promotes the free flow of ideas to allow students to better process and commit new information to memory. Therefore, choice (A) is correct.

**10. D**

When thematic units of study from one subject can be implemented across multiple subjects, then teaching is considered thematic and interdisciplinary. This approach requires careful planning and, when more than one teacher is involved, thoughtful collaboration.

**11. C**

The students are utilizing many hands-on instructional methods on this field trip. Direct instruction relates to more traditional lecture methods. Since the students are not listening to lectures, but rather discovering instructional objectives on their own, choice (C) is correct.

**12. C**

Task and performance modeling is defined as the teacher demonstrating the desired skill to be learned. Ms. Mignot in choice (C) accomplishes this by modeling the language frame she desires of her students.

**13. B**

Ensuring that students find a reason to pay attention and be ready to participate in discussions is key to preventing a "monopolized" lesson in which a small group of students make most of the contributions. Random selection ensures a higher percentage of students will contribute and be engaged in the lesson.

**14. A**

Mr. Jansch is creating an assessment to help his students identify what areas they are strong in as well as areas of learning opportunities. This is the definition of a formative assessment, and choice (A) is correct.

**15. A**

Students with visual and kinesthetic learning styles require a varied teaching approach. Visual learners benefit from seeing notes, problems, data, and pictures to help them process the information. Kinesthetic learners require a hands-on approach to be able to interact physically with the curriculum. Therefore modeling and hands-on activities provide the strongest links for these learners. Choice (A) is correct.

**16. C**

Allowing students time to reflect on successes as well as develop a plan to work on improvement gives them more control over their education. This, in turn, teaches them to self-regulate through intrinsic motivation. This activity has a greater impact than simply telling students what their perceived strengths and weaknesses are.

**17. A**

An informal assessment does not generally have grading criteria, though it may have a rubric to follow. In addition, Ms. Petrie is already using formal assessments to assign class grades. The informal assessment described in choice (A) works as a supplement and, in this case, will allow the students to determine the strengths and weaknesses they see in their own work. This type of analysis and goal setting is important, but still considered informal.

**18. B**

Results that tell students where they rank in terms of other students at their grade/age level come from norm-referenced tests. The "higher than 80 percent" is referring to a percentile score, because the student scored better than 80 percent of the other students who took the test. Choice (B) is correct.

**19. D**

Summative assessments are appropriate for the final, or summary, portion of a unit. They belong at the end of the instructional unit. Choice (D) is correct.

**20. A**

Students are being asked to create visual aids to demonstrate the new information. To set them on the right path, Mr. Shinawatra needs to provide them with visual examples. Utilizing technology to provide the visuals creates a stronger impression than lectures, discussions, or debates. Choice (A) is correct.

**21. D**

It is important for educators to utilize all the resources available to them. To ensure that students are receiving the highest level of instruction, experts in other areas of the school play a crucial role. Using these professionals allows students to make cross-curricular connections that will assist them in success in multiple subject areas.

### 22. B

Garnering parent participation is a challenge for most educators. The first step in achieving this goal is to make sure parents know what is going on with their child. The means of communication needs to be adjusted based on the available methods of the parents. For example, the teacher should not rely solely on email for families who lack the technological resources to access it reasonably often.

### 23. A

Subject curricula will vary not only by state but also by district. State standards provide a foundation on which the district will build its pacing guide. District-developed resources should always be the first go-to resource for any new teacher. Choice (A) is correct.

### 24. A

As teachers prepare new lessons, professional best practices include using a variety of resources to develop the lesson. The foundation of developing any new unit is to determine the desired outcome: this includes learning objectives, standards, and skills to be mastered. From there, a diverse base of educational materials should be chosen, including readings and technology. Choice (A) is correct.

### 25. A

Anytime self-evaluation is involved, the teacher is participating in a form of reflective practice. By collaborating to develop, observe, and evaluate their teaching, these teachers are engaging in reflective practice. Choice (A) is correct.

**Approximate time—25 minutes**

**Directions:** The case history below is followed by two short-answer questions. Your responses to the questions will be evaluated with respect to professionally accepted principles and practices in teaching and learning. Be sure to answer all parts of the question. Write your answers on the pages indicated in your answer sheet booklet.

### *Scenario:*

Jenny Carmichael is an eighth-grade student in a heterogeneous urban classroom. It is the beginning of the year, and Mr. Koppel is getting to know his eighth-grade language arts class, which includes Jenny. Concerned about Jenny's responses to an introductory survey on the first day, Mr. Koppel is gathering documents to attempt to discern whether he needs to take any particular action regarding Jenny's education.

### DOCUMENT 1

**Jenny's answers to Mr. Koppel's introductory survey (including errors):**

What is your favorite subject in school, and why?

*I don't like any but I guess science is okay because sometimes we look at pretty animals and plants.*

What is your least favorite subject in school, and why?

*English. I don't get grammer and reading.*

What were three things you had fun doing as part of English class last year?

*I liked cutting up magazines to make a poem colage.*

*I liked when we found that the author messed up about how snakes are, so the detective was totally wrong when he said who did it.*

*I liked watching other people do sharades and act out parts of books. But I hated doing it myself.*

What was something that was very hard for you in last year's English class?

*I don't like long books because I can't remember who the characters are or what happened.*

### DOCUMENT 2

**Jenny's end-of-term evaluations from the final term of seventh grade:**

English: D+

Jenny has been struggling in this class from the beginning of the year, but her performance has declined this term. Her earlier difficulties seem to have discouraged her, and she has left her last few assignments incomplete.

Math: B

Jenny generally doesn't participate in class unless called upon. However, she completes most assignments and performs adequately on quizzes.

Physical Education: A

Jenny participates in all activities and passes all basic fitness requirements. She is sometimes hesitant to be involved in competitive games.

Science: B+

Jenny's performance has improved substantially this term. She still has trouble with reading assignments from the textbook, but her performance has improved noticeably since I've started providing her with visual organizers. This has also improved her motivation, and she has not missed a homework assignment this term.

Social Studies: B

This term, the majority of student grades were based on students' composing a report and presentation on a country of their choosing. Jenny's written report received only a C, but her presentation was excellent. In particular, she demonstrated a strong aptitude for making slides in the computer lab, even though she does not have a computer at home.

### DOCUMENT 3

**Note from Ms. Moran, Jenny's seventh-grade English teacher, to Mr. Koppel:**

I'm glad you're reaching out to me about Jenny. She's a good student, and she's occasionally shown glimmers of brilliance with regard to English. In particular, she wrote a very interesting story about horseback riding during a creative writing unit, even though she didn't seem to understand the importance of proofreading and revision.

Jenny's biggest challenge is with reading. She is very slow when we read aloud together in class; she also gets so focused on pronouncing individual words and sentences that she'll often be completely lost about what actually happened in the text she just read. I've tried to introduce her to metacognitive strategies such as making predictions while she's reading, organizing things in terms of cause and effect, and listening to her "internal voice" to see if it's talking to her or just reciting text. So far, they have been unsuccessful.

Finally, she left multiple assignments incomplete during the last term of the year, which nearly caused her to fail. I think the frustration is getting to her, and I'm hoping a fresh approach will make English accessible to her.

### DOCUMENT 4

**Note from Jenny's guidance counselor to Mr. Koppel**

According to my records, Jenny's parents are both blue-collar workers. Neither has a college degree, and her mother was a college dropout. Jenny's standardized test scores have been consistently low. She needed remedial literacy education in elementary school, and her reading level remains two grades below expectation.

She hasn't had any major disciplinary concerns. Past progress reports indicate that she has not always been thorough about completing assignments, but never to the point of failure. Meanwhile, teachers consistently describe her as well-behaved, if withdrawn.

### Constructed-Response Questions

#### Question 1

Ms. Moran mentioned that she attempted to introduce Jenny to metacognitive techniques to help her focus on reading. However, those techniques were unsuccessful.

• Suggest TWO reasons that the strategies Ms. Moran used might not have been effective for Jenny.

• For EACH of those reasons, propose an alternative that addresses that reason and is more likely to help Jenny understand challenging reading. Base your responses on the principles of modifying instruction for diverse learners.

#### Question 2

Throughout the case study, Jenny demonstrates indifference or frustration toward academics and toward language arts in particular.

• Briefly describe TWO activities that Mr. Koppel could plan to engage Jenny's interest.

• For EACH of those activities, explain how it could help Jenny become more involved in class material. Base your response on the principles of encouraging student motivation.

# ANSWERS AND EXPLANATIONS

## Constructed-Response Questions

### Sample Response to Question 1

Ms. Moran notes that Jenny is having serious reading comprehension problems. The strategies the teacher tried with Jenny in seventh grade would tend to promote comprehension, but they focused on written responses, while Jenny's past work and preferences indicate she is a strong visual learner. Instead of asking Jenny to think about the "voice in her head" as she reads, it might be more helpful for her to form a "picture in her head."

Another reason Ms. Moran's techniques might not have worked is that Jenny was told to try them while reading out loud. Jenny does not speak out in other classes and does not like to compete. Mr. Koppel might consider having students read aloud in small groups rather than in a whole class, "round robin" fashion, which is considered less effective—students such as Jenny who are not comfortable speaking in front of the class may develop anxiety during this activity, while other students may lose focus when it is not their turn to read aloud. Mr. Koppel should have Jenny focus on prereading metacognitive techniques, such as making predictions and looking at illustrations, tasks she can perform while she's not in the spotlight.

### Sample Response to Question 2

Mr. Koppel could pair Jenny up with a student with stronger verbal skills and have them collaborate on making a comic related to the week's reading. Jenny became involved in designing slides for her social studies class, and she would likely be engaged in designing visuals for a comic. Her classmate, with strong verbal skills, would likely be modeling to Jenny the strategies he uses when reading and writing, and this approach could encourage Jenny to use some of these same effective techniques.

Mr. Koppel could collaborate with the eighth-grade science teachers to do a joint unit. Jenny has demonstrated an interest in zoology and biological sciences—her survey response noted that she enjoyed a reading activity involving snakes, and she was very successful in her seventh-grade science class. Perhaps a "detective investigation," in which students find factual errors in the textbook, would be helpful. Such activities can remind students that authors are human and can make even challenging texts seem less intimidating.

## Practice: PLT Grades 7–12

**Directions** For selected-response questions 1-25, choose the response that best answers the question or completes the statement. Then follow the directions provided for constructed-reponse questions 1-2.

1. An English language arts teacher is concerned with helping his students make positive progress through the identity versus role confusion stage of development, as described by Erikson. Which of the following classroom activities would most likely help students meet the goals associated with this stage of development?

    A. Students memorize a series of lines spoken by Romeo or Juliet in Shakespeare's play and recite them in front of the class.

    B. Students choose among different responsibilities to create a modern version of a scene from *Romeo and Juliet*.

    C. Students research one character from *Romeo and Juliet* and explain that character's motivation.

    D. Students compare and contrast two film versions of *Romeo and Juliet* and discuss their findings with a partner.

2. Which approach to math instruction is best tailored to help the teacher engage a kinesthetic learner?

    A. The use of manipulatives such as blocks and geoboards to teach and reinforce mathematical concepts

    B. The use of colorful visual models and vivid animated displays to illustrate new mathematical concepts

    C. The use of engaging lectures and Socratic class discussions in which students summarize key information

    D. The use of complex logical problems to draw students into new math concepts and illustrate math's practical importance

3. Which of the following describes a challenge particular to English language learners in any classroom in which instruction is given primarily in English?

    A. Students have difficulty picking up on different uses of nonverbal cues in their new classrooms and their implied meanings related to expected student behavior.

    B. Students have trouble understanding the meaning of idioms and expressions, including the use of slang by teachers and students in the classroom.

    C. Students have less background knowledge of the subject matter and, as a result, are not familiar with concepts the teacher refers to when teaching new material.

    D. Students are accustomed to a didactic teaching approach and are not accustomed to the group work and student-centered approach used in their new classroom.

4. Vygotsky's scaffolding technique includes breaking a complex task into smaller tasks and modeling the desired learning strategy. What is the ultimate goal of this scaffolding process?

    A. Learners will be able to accomplish the task without assistance.

    B. Students will learn to monitor their own behaviors to increase attention to the task.

    C. Participants will be able to use a visual image of a scaffold to track learning progress.

    D. Students will use scaffolding to identify their own learning style preferences.

5. Which of the following is NOT an application of Skinner's behavioral theory?

   A. Group instruction is effective because students enjoy competing with their peers.

   B. Providing feedback as students work helps them more than providing feedback after a task is completed.

   C. Teachers must ensure that students have mastered necessary skills before going to the next level.

   D. Rewarding positive behaviors is more effective than punishing negative behaviors.

6. Before her 10th-grade biology class begins its unit on water ecology, Ms. Zehner asks students to write down everything they know about water issues in the Great Lakes. Then she asks them to spend time talking to other students and reading a relevant article in order to add items to and revise the list. For homework, she asks them to write a reflective essay in which they discuss what they have learned and how their conversations with peers impacted their understanding.

   What are Ms. Zehner's writing assignments, described above, well designed to foster?

   A. Creative thinking

   B. Deductive reasoning

   C. Metacognition

   D. Critical thinking

7. Troy is a student in Ms. Devine's eighth-grade class. Ms. Devine is concerned because Troy's performance has been repeatedly low, but his records show that he has above-average abilities. Ms. Devine wants to adjust her practice to better encourage Troy in her class. Which of the following would be most likely to support Troy?

   A. Pairing Troy with another student who also has low performance

   B. Reprimanding Troy whenever she notices he is off task

   C. Ensuring she is grading each piece of Troy's work

   D. Providing immediate feedback and chunking work

8. Which of the following purposes could iPad note-taking applications and "smart whiteboards" best achieve when used in the high school classroom?

   A. Enhancing communication

   B. Facilitating portfolio assessment

   C. Assisting with behavior management

   D. Serving as a counseling tool

9. Mr. Glee is preparing his eighth-grade class for their end-of-quarter essay. He plans to start by providing extensive support that he gradually removes until students are able to complete their task independently. Which of the following best describes Mr. Glee's instructional strategy?

   A. Effective questioning

   B. Peer tutoring

   C. Differentiating

   D. Scaffolding

10. Ms. Law is writing an objective for her English language arts class and wants to target an objective that focuses on the highest level of Bloom's taxonomy. Which of the following objectives best meets that goal?

    A. Students will be able to identify the proper use of an adverb in a given sentence.

    B. Students will be able to evaluate the use of rhetoric in a given essay.

    C. Students will be able to describe the use of similes and metaphors.

    D. Students will be able to demonstrate understanding of text structure through use of outlining and graphic organizers.

11. A flute player's adept physical manipulation of her instrument demonstrates skill within which of the following domains of learning?

    A. Affective

    B. Cognitive

    C. Psychomotor

    D. Synthesis

12. On an individual student's summative math assessment, the data analysis reveals the following:

| Topic | Correct/Total Number |
|---|---|
| Fractions | 8/10 |
| Algebraic Equations | 11/15 |
| Word Problems | 4/10 |

Which of the following would be an appropriate follow-up activity for the teacher to use, based on these assessment results?

    A. Allow the student to progress to the next unit.

    B. Give the student an additional quiz with six math problems to see whether the student can now answer them correctly.

    C. Have the student use a computer program that provides tutorial help with word problems.

    D. Work with the student individually to determine what aspects of word problems are causing the student difficulty.

13. A teacher identifies seven students in her class who need additional help in order to get up to grade level in mathematics. She identifies a different group of eight students who are significantly below grade level in reading. Finally, she identifies two groups of five students each who are performing well above grade level in math and reading, respectively. Each day, at recess, she pulls a different one of these four groups and takes them to the library, where students collaborate on teacher-directed math and reading challenges tailored to their ability levels.

Which of the following instructional grouping techniques is used above?

    A. Homogeneous grouping

    B. Heterogeneous grouping

    C. Dyad grouping

    D. Round robin grouping

14. At the end of their unit on the ecosystem, Ms. Sterling creates cooperative learning groups in her 11th-grade earth science class and gives the students an assignment to investigate ways they could make an ecological improvement in their school or community. After Ms. Sterling discusses several ways to gather information and shares a rubric that outlines her expectations for their final presentations, the learning groups work independently. The teacher guides the groups by asking the learners questions related to the information they have gathered, and she suggests additional resources they may wish to consult.

The teaching and learning strategy described above is an example of which learning concept?

    A. Vicarious learning

    B. Problem-based learning

    C. Mapping

    D. Direct instruction

15. After a test in an American literature class, Mr. Sullivan returns the written essays to his 11th-grade students and gives them a few minutes to look at his comments and corrections. He then tells the students to spend 10 minutes writing a reflection describing what they feel they did well on and what specific target they have for improvement on the next essay.

    The activity described above is most likely to promote which one of the following abilities in Mr. Sullivan's students?

    A. Abstract reasoning

    B. Classical conditioning

    C. Collaborative learning

    D. Self-regulatory skills

16. Mr. Leffingwell is creating a rubric that he will make available to students as they begin work on a new research and writing project. Each area of the rubric includes descriptions of "exemplary," "acceptable," and "unsatisfactory" work. He will use this rubric to give students targeted feedback on interim drafts of their papers and, later, to generate grades for the final drafts of the essays.

    Which of these descriptions of "acceptable" work in the area of "source selection" is most appropriate and useful?

    A. Selected sources are good but not great—could be improved.

    B. Selected sources are solid, but essay could be improved with more research and more rigorous selection process.

    C. Selected sources include a relevant library book, magazine article, and website.

    D. Selected sources are acceptable—work was neither exemplary nor unsatisfactory.

17. Ms. Trettin, a 12th-grade English teacher, decides to design a rubric for grading an expository composition that she assigns. Handing out the grading rubric with the instructions for the assignment at the onset is an effective scaffolding aid for her students because

    A. the rubric articulates the assignment prompts

    B. the rubric clarifies expectations

    C. the rubric sets a serious tone

    D. the rubric provides needed background information

18. Ms. Andrews noticed that the same students in her class were participating in class discussions repeatedly, while other students were unlikely to speak up. Which of the following would be most likely to encourage more students to participate and to allow all students to develop more thoughtful responses?

    A. Tracking the number of students who respond and how often they respond

    B. Partnering students during group work in a way that encourages peer tutoring

    C. Developing hand signals that allow students to indicate whether they are raising their hand to participate in the discussion or ask a logistical question, such as whether they may use the bathroom

    D. Extending the time that Ms. Andrews waits before calling on students

19. Which of the following is NOT an accurate depiction of analytical scoring?

    A. Analytical scoring provides separate scores for each targeted skill, thus making clear a student's areas of strength and weakness.

    B. With analytical scoring, a single skill deficit is less likely to dominate the teacher's assessment of student work.

    C. Analytical scoring improves grade reliability by requiring that the grader assign a number of scores to a single piece of work.

    D. Analytical scoring focuses on the total effect of student work, rather than the success of individual aspects of the work.

20. Mr. Heidel believes in keeping anecdotal notes on each of his seventh-grade students in a diary. He feels that anecdotal notes—a record of a student's accomplishments, learning progress, learning lapses, and behavior—are an excellent way to understand the whole child. However, he knows that when using his notes as an assessment tool, he must keep which of the following distinctions in mind?

    A. Student inner and outer life

    B. Knowledge and intelligence

    C. Questions and answers

    D. Observations and interpretations

21. To teach the causes of the Civil War, a history teacher paired up students and had them read an excerpt from the textbook together to learn the material. After reading the students' essays on the Civil War, the teacher realized that the students did not fully understand the causes of the war. The teacher retaught this material to his students and made a note in his lesson plans to emphasize this detail the following year and to try a different instructional strategy.

    Choose the answer below that best describes the teacher's actions.

    A. Analysis of and reflection on instruction

    B. Metacognition

    C. Effective use of learning styles

    D. Think-pair-share work

22. Which of the following would provide the greatest opportunity to involve the stakeholders in a high school?

    A. Invite community members to participate in the school's collection for a local food pantry.

    B. Hold a mock election in social studies classes to promote citizenship.

    C. Approve funding to take band, orchestra, and choral students to state competition.

    D. Sponsor both extracurricular activities and student membership in honor societies.

23. Ms. Benzi has noticed that one of her seventh-grade students has been coming to class with suspicious bruises on his face and arms. On two occasions several days apart, when she asked the student for an explanation, he said, "I fell down." Ms. Benzi does not believe that the boy's pattern of injuries is consistent with a fall. She lives in a state in which teachers are mandatory reporters to Child Protective Services in cases of "suspicion based on facts that could cause a reasonable person in a like position, drawing on his or her training and experience, to suspect child abuse or neglect."

Which of the following statements best describes Ms. Benzi's legal obligations?

A. She is permitted to make a report to Child Protective Services, provided that she has first alerted the student's parents to her suspicions.

B. She is permitted to make a report to Child Protective Services, provided that she has obtained the permission of a school administrator.

C. She is permitted to make a report to Child Protective Services or to school administrators, although she is not required to make such a report.

D. She is required to make a report to Child Protective Services even if she has been denied permission to do so by a school administrator.

24. It is partway through the semester, and Mr. Barrett, a new teacher at the school, asks Ms. Bruce for suggestions on how to improve his teaching practice. Ms. Bruce wants to recommend a practice that will specifically encourage reflection about his teaching practices. Which of the following would be the best recommendation?

A. Peer observation

B. Independent research

C. Subscription to an educational journal

D. Technology workshop

25. Ms. Bunch's eighth-grade history classroom has students with varying levels of background knowledge and literacy skills, thus challenging Ms. Bunch to slow down instruction and to provide substantial scaffolding support. In addition, her classroom includes several Spanish-speaking English language learners who, she feels, may not be receiving the individualized attention they require.

Which educational partner could most appropriately and effectively assist Ms. Bunch within her classroom on a daily basis?

A. ELL teacher

B. Bilingual-certified counselor

C. Media specialist

D. Language pathologist

# ANSWERS AND EXPLANATIONS

## Practice: PLT Grades 7–12

**1. B**

Choosing responsibilities is an activity that helps students assess the roles that best fit them as individuals. Therefore, the activity in (B) would help them meet the goals of the identity versus role confusion developmental stage. Choice (A), which focuses on memorization and recitation, may help students build confidence before a group but does not focus on self-identity. Choice (C) focuses on understanding a dramatic character rather than understanding oneself. Choice (D) develops the analytic skill of comparison and develops the understanding of genre, but it does not directly clarify identity or role issues.

**2. A**

Kinesthetic learners respond to movement and hands-on activities. The correct answer is (A), because the student is able to manipulate objects to learn math principles. Colorful visual models and displays (B) will attract visual learners. Lectures and discussions (C) meet the needs of students who respond to verbal activities. Choice (D) relies on abstract reasoning and providing intrinsic motivation for that reasoning, and it is not particularly suited to kinesthetic learners.

**3. B**

The English language is rich in idiomatic expressions that do not use literal word meanings. Because idioms can be misinterpreted easily even by students who have a good understanding of standard English, (B) is the correct answer. Nonverbal cues (A), such as when the teacher demonstrates a procedure or points to the object being named, are typically understood regardless of English fluency. The background knowledge and abilities of English language learners (C) can vary widely, but this challenge isn't "particular" to ELLs; assessing prior knowledge is an important step to teaching any and all students. Finally, didactic approaches to teaching (D) are neither universal among, nor unique to, ELLs. Some

students may not speak English at home and qualify as ELLs despite having spent their lives in American schools; meanwhile, students from some parts of Africa, Asia, or Europe may be native English speakers whose national education systems rely on didactic teaching. For these reasons, (D) is incorrect.

**4. A**

The final step of successful scaffolding occurs when targeted skills have been transferred directly to the learner, who then no longer needs support from others. Therefore, choice (A) is correct. Although monitoring one's own learning (B) is a valuable skill, it is not the ultimate goal of scaffolding. The term *scaffolding* is a metaphor for educators—educational supports, as in the construction of a building, are dismantled once the structure (learning) is complete—but it is not something that students need to visualize, so (C) is incorrect. Although scaffolding is particularly useful for meeting the needs of students with varied learning styles, it is not a tool for students to discover their own learning styles; (D) is not the correct choice.

**5. A**

Skinner's behavioral theories do not deal with competition, so (A) is the correct choice. Choices (B) and (D) deal with reinforcement, which is key to operant conditioning, a central part of Skinner's behavioral theory. Choice (C) relates to sequencing, a concept key to learning as understood through Skinner's theories.

**6. C**

Metacognition requires understanding one's own thought process, which is what Ms. Zehner's assignment is designed to do. Choice (C) is correct. Creative thinking (A) encourages students to look at situations from a new perspective. Deductive reasoning (B) involves logically combining multiple statements to come to a new conclusion. Critical thinking (D) involves analysis and evaluation of an issue.

**7. D**

Both providing immediate feedback and chunking Troy's work into smaller pieces, as in choice (D), would allow Troy to feel a greater sense of achievement and would be the most appropriate way to encourage Troy.

**8. A**

Choice (A) is the correct answer. Both note-taking applications and smart whiteboards are communication tools by definition. Furthermore, note taking is an activity that records information that is being communicated. Choices (B) and (D) involve assessment and counseling, respectively. While software applications for assessment and counseling are available, they are not specifically mentioned here. And finally, while behavior management (C) may be facilitated by electronic communication applications that hold students' attention, such management is incidental, not the primary focus of iPad note-taking apps and smart whiteboards.

**9. D**

In scaffolding (D), accommodations provided to the students are tapered off, as Mr. Glee is doing in this example. While questioning (A), peer tutoring (B), and differentiating (C) are all valuable practices, they are not being illustrated here.

**10. B**

Evaluating an essay focuses on level 6 of Bloom's taxonomy, so choice (B) is correct. Identification (A) is in level 1; description (C) is in level 2, involving comprehension; and demonstration (D) is an application of the concept, as in level 3.

**11. C**

The term "domains of learning" refers to the ways in which a person acquires knowledge. The psychomotor domain includes skills related to the physical manipulation of objects such as tennis rackets, woodworking tools, and musical instruments. A skilled flutist possesses excellent psychomotor skills, so (C) is the correct answer. The affective domain (A) encompasses attitudes and motivations; a person with high affective skill is able to empathize and get along with other people. The cognitive domain (B) includes skills such as problem solving and critically evaluating facts. Synthesis (D) is a subcategory of cognitive development that has to do with creatively combining information and ideas or finding new applications for ideas.

**12. D**

The assessment suggests that the student needs remedial help with word problems. Working individually with the student is an important first step toward identifying whether these test results are actually representative of the student's comprehension and, if so, what sort of remedial help would be most effective. (D) is therefore the correct answer. Choice (A) is incorrect; the summative assessment indicates that the student is having difficulties that, if left unaddressed, could impede progress in future instructional units. Choice (B)'s phrase "math problems" is too vague, and simply giving the student additional test problems is not likely to be helpful or revealing. Choice (C) is incorrect because it is not certain from one test that the student has difficulties, nor is it clear that this computer program would remedy such difficulties; the teacher must find out exactly what caused these discrepant test scores before proceeding.

**13. A**

Homogeneous grouping (A) is an instructional technique whereby students are grouped by a trait that they have in common. In the example above, students are grouped by their performance level in mathematics and reading. Heterogeneous grouping (B) is a technique whereby students are grouped in mixed levels. Dyad grouping (C) is strategic pairing. Round robin (D) is a strategy that can be implemented within groups but is not a technique by which teachers group students.

**14. B**

Ms. Sterling is engaging her class in problem-based learning because the students are directly collaborating to solve a real-world problem. Choice (B) is correct. In vicarious learning (A), students observe but do not engage directly in an activity.

Mapping (C) allows students to make connections between ideas. Direct instruction (D) is explicit, teacher-led learning.

**15. D**

Self-regulatory skills allow students to monitor and control their own behavior. By allowing the students to reflect on their performance and set a target for their next essay, Mr. Sullivan helps them gain insight into and practice with refining their behavior. Choice (D) is correct. Abstract reasoning (A) involves thinking that extends beyond concrete, tangible ideas into mental concepts. Classical conditioning (B) pairs one stimulus with another. Collaborative learning (C) involves students working together in a way that mutually benefits their learning processes.

**16. C**

The description in correct choice (C) is most useful for the student. This description makes clear to the student what sort of sources were to be included and confirms that they were selected appropriately. Choice (A)'s description—"good but not great"—is subjective and does not let the student know what was done well or what could be improved upon. Similarly, choices (B) and (D) do not provide specific examples related to the sources selected. Only (C) gives the student concrete examples.

**17. B**

A rubric clarifies the expectations for an assignment as it will be evaluated, and choice (B) is correct. While Ms. Trettin will likely want to include the prompts and background information for her students, as in (A) and (D), the rubric is not the space in which to do this. While Ms. Trettin may prefer a serious tone for her classroom (C), a rubric is an assessment tool and is not used for setting a tone.

**18. D**

Wait time (D) is a critical practice that stimulates more complex thinking and encourages more students to participate in the discussion. Choice (A) would give Ms. Andrews data on her students but would not stimulate additional participation. Choices (B) and (C) both illustrate commonly used teaching practices that are designed for other activities, not specifically for class discussions.

**19. D**

Analytical scoring measures a learner's proficiency by considering the essential elements of the key learning skills involved. Therefore, the correct choice is (D) because it describes holistic grading, which focuses on the effect of an entire work. With analytical scoring, the student's strengths and weaknesses are assessed for each targeted skill (A), making it less likely that only one skill becomes the focus of an assessment (B). Grade reliability is increased (C) because a variety of criteria are considered.

**20. D**

Observations are objective; they document what is visible. Interpretations are how Mr. Heidel might integrate and apply the information in his diary to draw conclusions about his students. Only observations are included in the anecdotal notes to ensure that the notes accurately capture student achievements. Interpretations are subjective and should be omitted from anecdotal notes. Choice (D) is correct.

**21. A**

Having the ability to reflect on one's own pedagogical practices is a key component of competent, effective teaching. With adequate reflection, teachers may assess whether learning objectives have been achieved, and they can change their strategies as needed. Therefore, choice (A) is correct. Metacognition, choice (B), refers to an awareness of one's own thinking processes; merely reflecting on an unsuccessful lesson plan and making changes is not necessarily a metacognitive practice. Learning styles (C) are different ways in which individual students most successfully learn. In this example, the teacher does not clearly incorporate attention to diverse learning styles in the design of his lesson. Although students were paired up, the activity the teacher originally used was not a think-pair-share (D). Think-pair-share is a strategy that requires students to briefly consider a question or problem individually, then turn and talk with a partner to discuss their thoughts, and finally share with the whole group.

## 22. A

The first option is the only one that involves stakeholders. Inviting members of the community to participate directly endows them with ownership in the work of the school. The other three options all limit involvement to members of the community within school walls.

## 23. D

Mandatory reporting is a law that requires a teacher or other caregiver to report suspected child abuse. Since the teacher suspects the bruising might be the result of abuse, (D) is the correct response. Parents are not to be alerted before a call to Child Protective Services (A), because it is the agency's job to determine whether abuse has occurred and, if so, who is responsible. The mandated reporter's legal responsibility supersedes the decision of any school official (B). Reporting under this law is not an option (C) but rather a legal requirement.

## 24. A

Peer observation allows teachers to share with each other and engage in a cycle of feedback and discussion about teaching practices. Of the options given, choice (A) would be most effective and is correct.

## 25. A

An ELL teacher would be best qualified to assist Ms. Bunch daily, so choice (A) is correct. A bilingual-certified counselor (B) would be effective at supporting bilingual students in their mental health and well-being. A media specialist (C) would assist the teacher in integrating information resources into her classroom. A language pathologist (D) would assess and provide intervention support for language and communication difficulties.

**Approximate time—25 minutes**

**Directions:** The case history below is followed by two short-answer questions. Your responses to the questions will be evaluated with respect to professionally accepted principles and practices in teaching and learning. Be sure to answer all parts of the question. Write your answers on the pages indicated in your answer sheet booklet.

**Scenario:**

Davis Budde is a popular member of his suburban school's football team. His teachers report that he is friendly and polite, but seldom puts effort into his academics. His grades are consistently low, but passing. He has several offers of athletic scholarships to notable universities.

Davis is in Ms. Kohl's senior elective class, Movies as Literature. Ms. Kohl is a second-year teacher. This is her first year teaching this elective. The class was taught the past 10 years by Ms. Adams, who recently retired. Ms. Kohl is planning the first unit of the class, based on the film *Citizen Kane*.

**Document 1**

**Lesson plan for Ms. Kohl's unit on *Citizen Kane*, Friday to Wednesday:**

Goals:

- Students will understand why *Citizen Kane* is considered by many critics to be the greatest film of all time.
- Students will understand the connection between the character Kane and the real-life William Randolph Hearst.
- Students will be able to identify basic cinematographic techniques by name and by appearance.

Activities:

- Students will read a short biography of Hearst for homework, then have an in-class discussion about what sort of legacy he left.
- Students will see short excerpts of films with examples of techniques like crosscut, ellipsis, and montage.
- Students will watch *Citizen Kane* for homework.
- Students will read critical reviews of *Kane*, both contemporary with the film and modern, and then write their own review in the style of a movie critic.

Assessment:

- Students will be graded on the quality of their reviews.
- Students will be given a quiz on the techniques used by the film, and on the similarities and differences between Kane and Hearst.

Planning note:

Several students have expressed concern that they would have to watch movies on their own time. I was disappointed to find that most of the class signed up to watch movies in class and expected to coast by. However, the student body is strong here, and I'm confident they will adjust to the challenges and learn to appreciate film as literature, even if it takes them more effort than they expected.

**Document 2**

**Email conversation between Davis and Ms. Kohl, Thursday evening:**

*Email 1*

Dear Ms. Kohl,

I got a D on my quiz. I don't understand what happened. It's very important that I get at least a C in your class so I can stay on the football team. I thought we would watch movies in class, that's why I chose the class.

Davis

*Email 2*

Davis,

This class used to have a reputation as an "easy A," but you are a senior and I don't think it's unreasonable to expect students in this class to work for their grades. I mentioned this at the beginning of class, so this should not come as a surprise. As for why you got a D, you got very few of the answers correct. In particular, I was disappointed to see that you got every question related to Kane and Hearst incorrect. I have to wonder whether you watched the movie at all.

Best,

Ms. Kohl

*Email 3*

Dear Ms. Kohl

I did watch the movie but it was very hard because of training. I watched most of it while I was on the treadmill. I guess I wasn't paying attention.

Davis.

**Document 3**

**Note from Davis's coach to Ms. Kohl:**

Hi Ms. Kohl,

Davis spoke to me about your Film in Literature class. I've emphasized to him the importance of doing well in his classes, but I'm concerned about the workload for your class. In addition to football practice, he is working with a tutor for his math grades three nights a week, which leaves him very little time for him to watch all the movies listed on your syllabus.

Davis's role on the football team is essential; I will work with him to get as much of his schoolwork done as possible, but any allowances you can make would be appreciated.

Coach Malory

**Document 4**

**Davis's weekly after-school and weekend schedule, as prepared by his coach**

Monday, Wednesday: 2:15–5:45, football practice; 6–7:30, travel home and dinner; 7:30–9:30, homework.

Tuesday, Thursday: 3:00–5:00, math tutoring; 5:15–6:15 gym; 6:30–7:00 dinner; 7:30–9:30, homework.

Friday: 5:00–7:00, football practice, team building; 7:00–10:00, free time.

Saturday: morning, run; afternoon, math tutoring; evening, free time.

Sunday: morning, church; afternoon, gym; evening, homework.

**Document 5**

**Ms. Kohl's self-evaluation for September**

This class has proven challenging. The students have strongly resisted the current structure of the class, and I get requests to watch films during school hours almost daily. It's important to me that class time be spent interacting and thinking; the last thing I want to do is have my students sit staring at a screen for an hour. But it's clear that as it stands, the "flipped classroom" model is not working—quiz grades and enthusiasm are low among almost all of my students.

### *Constructed-Response Questions*
### Question 1

Ms. Kohl attempted to change the structure of the Movies as Literature class, assigning the movies for homework and spending class time completing activities the teacher planned. Despite her interaction with the students each day, Ms. Kohl was not aware that Davis had little understanding of the movie until after he had failed his quiz.

- Suggest TWO ways that Ms. Kohl could alter her lesson plan to address this problem.

- For EACH of those alterations, explain how it would help students understand the film and enable Ms. Kohl to assess that understanding. Base your response on the principles of teaching in a flipped classroom.

### Question 2

Davis, like many other seniors in his school involved in extracurricular activities, has responsibilities that require a great deal of time.

- Suggest TWO strategies that Ms. Kohl could recommend to Davis to help him complete all of his assignments.

- For EACH strategy, explain how it would allow Davis to complete his homework in a meaningful way, while still fitting it into a busy schedule.

# ANSWERS AND EXPLANATIONS

### Constructed-Response Questions

### Sample Response to Question 1

Ms. Kohl could assign students tasks during viewing, intended to ensure the students' more active involvement when watching the films. She could prepare study guides for students to complete, related to the instructional objectives associated with the films. Ms. Kohl could then use class time to review student answers before moving on to further discussion of the film.

Ms. Kohl could arrange for students to view the film together. The logistics would depend on student availability and technology, but encouraging the students to watch the video in pairs or groups—even if they were sharing a streamed video feed or watching the video independently at home while chatting online—would encourage student interaction and collaboration. Ms. Kohl could allot some class time for the student groups to conduct a follow-up discussion in which they could share ideas and questions related to the movie.

### Sample Response to Question 2

Ms. Kohl could advise Davis to begin watching the movies early, and over a period of time, rather than all at one sitting. Any type of long reading, research, or video assignment can be overwhelming when taken all at once, but if Davis plans ahead, he can probably manage 20 minutes of a movie every day for a week. Davis could be responsible for completing an organizer or review sheet related to the film so as to demonstrate his progress throughout the week.

Ms. Kohl could arrange some sort of check-in system with Davis. Davis has previously emailed Ms. Kohl—he could be required to send two short emails every week, in which he could briefly describe his progress in watching the film and let her know when he was having trouble with assignments. This information would help Ms. Kohl gauge Davis's progress and plan supporting instructional activities as needed. It would also help her provide recommendations to Davis concerning how to prioritize his homework time effectively.

# PRAXIS ELEMENTARY EDUCATION

# CHAPTER FIVE

# Review of the Praxis Elementary Education Tests

## INTRODUCTION

This section of the book covers the most commonly administered Praxis Elementary Education tests. You should refer to the requirements for the state in which you plan to teach to determine which of these tests you will need to take. See the State Certification Information table in the appendix of this book for more information.

Chapter 5 applies to you if you are required to take any of the following exams (test codes are included in parentheses after the test name):

> Elementary Education: Content Knowledge (5018)
>
> Elementary Education: Curriculum, Instruction, and Assessment (5017)
>
> Elementary Education: Multiple Subjects (5001)

Most states require applicants to pass one or more of these tests for certification as an elementary school teacher. Note that Elementary Education: Content Knowledge (5018) emphasizes content-related information similar to what one might encounter in an English language arts, math, science, or social studies course. Elementary Education: Curriculum, Instruction, and Assessment (5017), on the other hand, focuses on pedagogical knowledge related to English language arts, math, science, and social studies. While content knowledge in these areas is helpful for the 5017 test, the questions will relate to teaching applications and teaching scenarios.

Elementary Education: Multiple Subjects (5001) covers material similar to that on Elementary Education: Content Knowledge (5018). The 4-hour 15-minute test consists of four separately timed subtests: Reading/Language Arts (5002), Mathematics (5003), Social Studies (5004), and Science (5005). Teacher candidates taking the 5001 exam should review Chapter 5 as well as all four chapters in Part IV of this book for subject-specific material in English language arts, mathematics, social studies, and science.

In this chapter, a brief summary of each test will be followed by a review of the subject areas covered on the test. The information in this chapter is current as of the time of publication. It is recommended that you supplement your review with information from the Praxis website (**ets.org/praxis**), as test names, codes, and content are subject to change.

By the end of this chapter, you will be able to:

- Describe the structure and format of the Praxis Elementary Education: Content Knowledge and Elementary Education: Curriculum, Instruction, and Assessment tests
- Outline the subject matter covered on these two tests
- Use the Praxis Content Knowledge and Curriculum, Instruction, and Assessment practice tests to assess your performance

# REVIEW OF THE ELEMENTARY EDUCATION: CONTENT KNOWLEDGE EXAM

If you are required to take the Elementary Education: Content Knowledge (5018) exam, the information in this section will provide you with a summary of the test followed by a review of the basic concepts, situations, and vocabulary that pertain to the core subject areas within the elementary education classroom. These core subjects consist of Reading/Language Arts, Mathematics, Science, and Social Studies. After reviewing this section, proceed to the Elementary Education: Content Knowledge full-length practice test that appears later in this chapter.

| Praxis Elementary Education: Content Knowledge |
| --- |
| Format: Computer-delivered |
| Number of Questions: 140 <br> Time: 150 minutes |
| Question Types: multiple-choice (called "selected response" by the test maker); numeric entry |
| On-screen scientific calculator available |
| Test may include pre-test questions that do not count toward your score |
| No penalty for incorrect answers |
| Scratch paper is available during the exam (it will be destroyed before you leave the testing center) |
| Content covered: <br><br> • Reading/Language Arts: approximately 49 questions, 35 percent of the test <br> • Mathematics: approximately 41 questions, 29 percent of the test <br> • Social Studies: approximately 25 questions, 18 percent of the test <br> • Science: approximately 25 questions, 18 percent of the test |

The Elementary Education: Content Knowledge test is designed to test the knowledge and skills necessary to teach in the elementary grades, with a focus on the major content areas. A scientific calculator is provided. For details on the calculator's functions and a tutorial, see **ets.org/praxis/test_day/policies/calculators**.

# Reading/Language Arts

The Reading/Language Arts section of the test covers the fundamentals of reading, writing, and communication skills.

You will need to understand the foundations of reading. Topics covered on the test include the foundations of reading development and literacy; the roles of phonological awareness and phonics; and the roles of fluency, vocabulary, and comprehension. You will need to be familiar with the basic elements of fiction, nonfiction, poetry, and drama for children, and you must understand the uses of simile, metaphor, and other figurative language. You should know how to use reading and language arts resource materials in the classroom.

You will also be tested on your knowledge of language in writing. To be successful, you will need to be familiar with the elements of grammar and usage. Know the various types of writing, including narrative and persuasive, and understand tone, purpose, and audience. Know the stages of writing development and the writing process. Understand sentence types and structure and be able to describe the organizational structures of a piece of writing.

Know the different aspects of communication skills, including speaking, listening, and viewing, and understand the role they play in language acquisition for English language learners.

### Reading Terms and Concepts

alphabetic principle

anecdotal record

background knowledge

compare and contrast

cloze procedure

comprehension

concept of print

concept web

conferencing

context clues

decodable text

decoding

detail

developmentally appropriate

during-reading

dyslexia

emergent literacy

expository text

fluency

graphic organizer

inference

informal reading inventory (IRI)

journals

language acquisition

language arts

linguistically diverse

literacy

miscue analysis

morphology

narrative text

onset

orthographic knowledge

phoneme

phonemic awareness

phonics

phonological awareness

phonology

portfolios

post-reading

predictable text

prereading

previous knowledge

print-rich environment

readability

reading strategies

retelling stories

rime

running record

scanning

semantic map

semantics

structural analysis

syllable

syntactic

theme

trade books

vocabulary development

word analysis

### Writing, Spelling, and Listening Terms and Concepts

brainstorming

clustering

complex sentence

compound-complex sentence

context

conventional

drafting

editing

etymology

graphophonemic knowledge

informative

inventive spelling

listening skills

narrative

opinion

oral language

orthographic knowledge

outlining

phonemes

phonetic

prefix

prephonetic

prewriting

primary source

publishing

punctuation

restructuring

revising

secondary source

simple sentence

spelling skills

structural analysis

suffix

syntax

transitional

webbing

writing conference

## Mathematics

You will be tested on your understanding of mathematical processes such as problem solving and representation; as such, you will need to:

Know the fundamental concepts of number sense and numeration systems, including prenumeration; basic number systems; and the four operations of addition, subtraction, multiplication, and division. Understand the basics of number theory. Know how to solve problems using multiple strategies and assess results. Understand the basics of numerical patterns.

Understand algebraic concepts. Be conversant with algebraic methods and representation. Understand the use of associative, commutative, and distributive properties in algebra. Understand inverse operations. Know the special properties of zero and one, understand equalities and inequalities, and know how to apply formulas. Be proficient in the analysis and manipulation of formulas, equations, and algebraic expressions.

Understand informal geometry and measurement, including figures, the coordinate plane, transformations, and different standards of measurement.

Know how to organize and interpret data. Understand basic statistics, probability, counting techniques, and the interpretation of graphs and charts.

### *Mathematics Terms and Concepts*

absolute value

addition and subtraction relationship

algorithm

arithmetic

associative property

attribute

base ten

basic math facts

calculator

classifying

commutative property

comparing

compose/decompose

composites

computation

computer

conservation of number

constructivist teaching

coordinate geometry

counting

decimals, fractions, percents

distributive property

equations

equivalence

estimation

expanded form

factors

geometric concepts

graphing

heuristic

informal geometry

logic

manipulatives

mathematics

measurement (time, money, length, volume, mass)

metric units

multiples

multiplication and division relationship

number concepts

number patterns

number theory

numeration systems

odd and even

operations

ordered sets

place value

Polya's problem-solving process

primes

probability

problem solving

ratio and proportion

rational counting

rational numbers

remainders

rounding

rubrics

sets

statistics

story problems

visual-spatial

whole numbers

# Social Studies

You will be expected to know regional and world geography and understand how humans change the environment and vice versa. Following is a list of the major requirements for success on this test.

Understand how to apply geography for different uses, such as to interpret the past or future. Be familiar with the ways in which people from different cultures relate to the environment and the people around them.

Know US history, from European exploration through the nation's founding and up to the present day. Understand the major changes and developments that occurred in the United States in the 20th century. Understand how historical events in the United States are related by cause and effect.

Have a basic understanding of world history, including the major contributions of ancient civilizations and the developments in world history from the 20th century through the present day. Be able to make cross-cultural comparisons.

Know the principles and structures of government, citizenship, and democracy and understand social studies processes and how to use social studies resource materials. Understand the fundamental terms and concepts of economics. Describe the effects of an economy on people, natural resources, and innovations. Explain the influence of the government on the economy and vice versa.

Apply inquiry principles to social studies using primary and secondary research material. Interpret data and information from many sources.

### *Social Studies Terms and Concepts*

assembly line

cause and effect

citizenship

colonization

comparison

concepts

contemporary society

cultural diversity

culture

democratic values

economics

federalism

geography

government

Great Depression

industrialization

inquiry

interrelationships

observation

political science

primary source vs. secondary source

research

revolution

society

space age

statistical data

supply and demand

westward expansion

# Science

You will be tested on your understanding of the structure and processes of the earth system. Know Earth history, including paleontology and the origin of Earth. Understand the relationship of Earth to the universe, including stars, planets, and galaxies. Understand the Earth's four spheres, their cycles, and their interactions: hydrosphere, geosphere, atmosphere, and biosphere.

Know the characteristics and function of living systems and understand how living things change over time. Understand reproduction, heredity, regulation, and behavior. Understand the interdependence of organisms and the diversity of life.

Understand basic physical science, including the properties and structure of matter, forces and motions, energy, and interactions between energy and matter. Identify and classify plant and animal organisms. Understand plant and human organ systems.

Be familiar with topics such as technololgy, personal health, science as a career, science as inquiry, and science processes. Understand the scientific method, data interpretation, and laboratory safety considerations.

### *Science Terms and Concepts*

analyze

atmosphere

biosphere

calculator

computer

concept

conceptualizing

conclusion

constructivism

control group

correlation

discovery learning

experiment

experimental design

experimental group
geosphere
hierarchical classification
higher-order thinking
hydrosphere
hypothesis
inquiry
interpretation
investigation
learning cycle
misconception
model
observation
rubric
scientific principle
scientific process
scientific skills
technology
variable

# PRACTICE: ELEMENTARY EDUCATION CONTENT KNOWLEDGE

## Reading and Language Arts

1. Which THREE of the following would be effective thesis statements for a persuasive essay?

   Select all that apply.

   A. The United States has no right to intervene in the internal affairs of other nations.

   B. Year-round schooling is an ill-conceived and simplistic solution to a complicated problem.

   C. Seventy-five percent of surveyed voters feel the president is doing an adequate job.

   D. Thoreau was right when he said, "The mass of men lead lives of quiet desperation."

   E. According to the latest numbers, many college graduates are choosing nontraditional career pathways.

2. Each of the 18 students in a class is required to make a 15-minute presentation on a given topic. The teacher has informed students that the use of effective nonverbal communication will make up a portion of the grade received on the presentation. Which of the following is the best example of effective nonverbal communication that a student should use during the presentation?

   A. Maintaining eye contact with the teacher

   B. Using no notes

   C. Standing still behind a podium

   D. Establishing eye contact throughout the presentation with all members of the audience

3. We will ponder your proposition and when we decide we will let you know. But should we accept it, I here and now make this condition that we will not be denied the privilege without molestation of visiting at any time the tombs of our ancestors, friends, and children. Every part of this soil is sacred in the estimation of my people. Every hillside, every valley, every plain and grove, has been hallowed by some sad or happy event in days long vanished. Even the rocks, which seem to be dumb and dead as they swelter in the sun along the silent shore, thrill with memories of stirring events connected with the lives of my people, and the very dust upon which you now stand responds more lovingly to their footsteps than yours, because it is rich with the blood of our ancestors, and our bare feet are conscious of the sympathetic touch. . . .

   From a speech given by Chief Seattle in 1854 as reprinted in the October 29, 1887, *Seattle Sunday Star*.

   Based on this passage, it is most reasonable to assume that the speaker believed which of the following?

   A. The government of the United States would honor the condition he set forth.

   B. The land of his people was sacred because of the ancestors who had lived and died there.

   C. The rights of Native Americans were unimportant to the government of the United States.

   D. Immigrants to the United States would come to see the land as sacred.

4. The sun sank rapidly; the silvery light had faded from the bare boughs and the watery twilight was settling in when Wilson at last walked down the hill, descending into cooler and cooler depths of grayish shadow. His nostril, long unused to it, was quick to detect the smell of wood smoke in the air, blended with the odor of moist spring earth and the saltiness that came up the river with the tide.

From *Alexander's Bridge* (1912)
by Willa Cather

The passage above contains characteristic elements of which of the following literary genres?

A. Fable

B. Autobiography

C. Folktale

D. Realistic fiction

**Questions 5–6 refer to the following excerpt:**

The stars were shining, and the leaves rustled in the woods ever so mournful; and I heard an owl, away off, who-whooing about somebody that was dead, and a whipporwill and a dog crying about somebody that was going to die; and the wind was trying to whisper something to me, and I couldn't make out what it was, and so it made the cold shivers run over me.

From *The Adventures of Huckleberry Finn* (1884) by Mark Twain

5. The style of writing employed in this passage can best be described as

A. standard English

B. formal English

C. jargon

D. dialect

6. The author uses imagery in this section to illustrate Huck's

A. fear and loneliness.

B. awareness of his environment.

C. loss of his father.

D. moral dilemma.

7. Words can have multiple meanings and be used as different parts of speech in different contexts. The word *appropriate*, for instance, has two meanings.

   1 *adj.* fitting; proper

   2 *v.* to claim or take for one's own, frequently without permission

Which of the following sentences uses *appropriate* as a verb, that is, the second definition in the list above?

A. Although he felt overdressed, his attire was appropriate for the cocktail party.

B. When learning a new language, it can be difficult to find the appropriate words to express one's thoughts.

C. The bank may appropriate the farm if the mortgage payments are not made on time.

D. Roughhousing is not appropriate in the workplace.

8.  In the phrase "parting brings such <u>sweet sorrow</u>," the underlined portion of the phrase is an example of

    A. a simile

    B. a personification

    C. a hyperbole

    D. an oxymoron

9.  Which of the following nonverbal responses from an audience member indicates attention and interest in a speaker?

    A. Crossed arms and crossed legs

    B. Leaning forward

    C. Gesturing to other audience members

    D. Leaning backward

10. Which of the following best describes the critical period in language development?

    A. If a child docs not learn to write by a certain age, he or she is likely to never acquire basic writing skills.

    B. If a child is not exposed to a second language by a certain age, he or she is likely to never fluently read or write a second language.

    C. If a child is not exposed to regular language use by a certain age, he or she is likely to never fully develop language capabilities.

    D. If a child does not learn phonetics by a certain age, he or she is likely to never acquire basic reading skills.

11. The act of preparing a response while listening to a speaker is referred to as

    A. forming a clarifying question

    B. rehearsing

    C. active listening

    D. restating information

12. A child can connect certain letters with sounds but has not yet grasped the concept that a number of letter-sound combinations make up most words. Which of the following types of errors would indicate this lack of understanding?

    A. Representing a word or a group of words by a single letter

    B. Misspelling words like *cat* or *grace* as *kat* or *grase*

    C. Making errors with exceptional spelling rules, such as "*i* before *e*, except after *c*"

    D. Spelling the word *dog* as *qxr*

13. A student has drafted a writing assignment and read it through one additional time, making revisions. She is now ready for which of the following stages of the writing process?

    A. Outlining

    B. Revising

    C. Proofreading

    D. Publishing

## Mathematics

14. Which of the following numbers is the greatest?

    A. 0.21

    B. 0.203

    C. 0.2042

    D. 0.2005

15. Tom is standing next to a fire hydrant. The hydrant casts a shadow that is 32 inches long. Tom casts a shadow that is 48 inches long. If the hydrant is 40 inches tall, how tall is Tom?

    A. 52 inches

    B. 60 inches

    C. 72 inches

    D. 84 inches

16. On a national reading test, 40 percent of the 540 students at Stevens Elementary School scored at or below their grade level. Which of the following computations can be used to determine the number of students who scored at or below their grade level on the test?

    A. $\dfrac{1}{40} \times 540$

    B. $\dfrac{2}{5} \times 540$

    C. $540 \div 0.40$

    D. $40 \times 540$

17. The owner of a hat shop buys hats at a cost of five for $17.50 and sells them for $4.00 each. How many hats must the owner sell in order to make a profit of $100?

    A. 50

    B. 100

    C. 150

    D. 200

18. All of the following are equivalent to dividing 420 by 21 EXCEPT:

    A. $(420 \div 3) \div 7$

    B. $420 \div (3 \times 7)$

    C. $(420 \div 3) + (420 \div 7)$

    D. $\dfrac{420}{3} \times \dfrac{1}{7}$

19. $7(8 + 5) = 7 \times 8 + 7 \times 5$

    The equation above demonstrates which of the following?

    A. The distributive property of multiplication over addition

    B. Additive inverse and additive identity

    C. The commutative property of multiplication

    D. The associative property of multiplication

20. Clinton bowled an average score of 180 over four games. If he bowled 156, 172, and 210 in his first three games, what did he bowl in the final game?

    A. 178

    B. 180

    C. 182

    D. 188

21.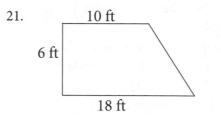

    What is the perimeter of the shape above?

    A. 34 ft

    B. 40 ft

    C. 44 ft

    D. 48 ft

22. Joyce baked 42 biscuits for her 12 guests. If 6 biscuits remain uneaten, what is the average number of biscuits that the guests ate?

    A. 2
    B. 3
    C. 4
    D. 6

23. What is the fifth term in the following series?

    6.5; 13.75; 21; 28.25; _____?

    A. 35.25
    B. 35.50
    C. 36.50
    D. 36.75

24. Marty has exactly 5 blue pens, 6 black pens, and 4 red pens in his knapsack. If he pulls out one pen at random from his knapsack, what is the probability that the pen is either red or black?

    A. $\frac{2}{3}$

    B. $\frac{3}{5}$

    C. $\frac{2}{5}$

    D. $\frac{1}{3}$

25. If each digit 5 is replaced with the digit 7, by how much will 258,546 be increased?

    A. 2,020
    B. 2,200
    C. 20,020
    D. 20,200

## Social Studies

26. Which of the following is considered a serious threat to the global environment?

    Select all that apply.

    A. Global warming
    B. Deforestation
    C. Plate tectonics
    D. Ozone layer depletion
    E. Atmospheric jet streams

27. The Agricultural Revolution has been called "the dawn of civilization" because

    A. it allowed hunter-gatherers to travel further from their homes in search of food
    B. it allowed for the development of agrarian societies and food surpluses
    C. it occurred soon after the founding of the first great civilizations
    D. it occurred concurrently with significant advances in astronomy and the arts

28. Which of the following terms is associated with the class structure of traditional Hindu society?

    A. Tao
    B. Caste
    C. Kabuki
    D. Zen

29. Which of the following was most responsible for the spread of Greek art, architecture, and thought throughout the ancient Mediterranean world?

    A. Hammurabi
    B. Genghis Khan
    C. Alexander the Great
    D. Herodotus

**Questions 30–31 refer to the following graph.**

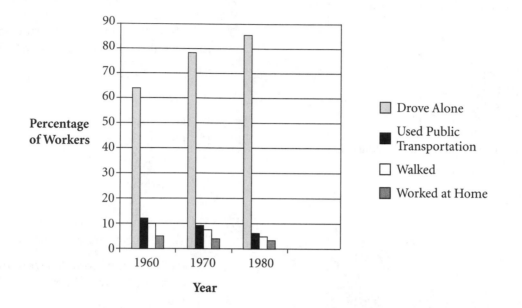

30. In the graph, the percentages of workers who used different modes of transportation to commute to work are shown. The number of workers accounted for in the 1960 Census was approximately 65,000,000. Of these workers, approximately how many walked to work?

   A. 7,800,000
   B. 6,500,000
   C. 5,200,000
   D. 3,250,000

31. Which of the following statements is best supported by data reported in the graph?

   A. The number of people who worked at home decreased between the years 1960 and 1980.

   B. Between 1960 and 1980, the percentage of the nation's population that used public transportation decreased.

   C. Urban sprawl is a primary factor in the increasing percentage of workers who drive to work.

   D. In 1970, more than 15% of the working population used public transportation or walked to get to work.

32. Which of the following correctly lists the first three positions in the order of presidential succession in the United States?

   A. President, vice president, attorney general

   B. President, attorney general, speaker of the House

   C. President, vice president, speaker of the House

   D. President, vice president, secretary of state

## Science

33. Which of the following depicts a chemical process?

   A. Helium is combined with neon.
   B. Iron forms rust.
   C. Water causes soil erosion.
   D. Ice melts.

34. Blood enters the right atrium of the heart from the

    A. aorta
    B. left ventricle
    C. pulmonary vein
    D. vena cava

35. Which of the following substances has the highest pH?

    A. Ammonia
    B. Battery acid
    C. Isopropyl alcohol
    D. Water

36.

| Type of bread | Temperature (°F) | Day 5 | Day 10 | Day 15 | Day 20 |
|---------------|------------------|-------|--------|--------|--------|
| White | 37 | $0 \text{ cm}^2$ | $0 \text{ cm}^2$ | $1 \text{ cm}^2$ | $4 \text{ cm}^2$ |
| White | 71 | $0 \text{ cm}^2$ | $2 \text{ cm}^2$ | $8 \text{ cm}^2$ | $18 \text{ cm}^2$ |
| Sourdough | 37 | $0 \text{ cm}^2$ | $0 \text{ cm}^2$ | $0 \text{ cm}^2$ | $1 \text{ cm}^2$ |
| Sourdough | 71 | $0 \text{ cm}^2$ | $0 \text{ cm}^2$ | $2 \text{ cm}^2$ | $7 \text{ cm}^2$ |

The chart shows the results of an experiment in which the growth of mold was measured, in terms of square centimeters of surface area covered, on different types of bread at different temperatures over a period of 20 days. It is most reasonable to predict that if the experiment were conducted for an additional five days, the amount of mold found on the sourdough loaf kept at 71°F would be

A. $7 \text{ cm}^2$
B. $8 \text{ cm}^2$
C. $16 \text{ cm}^2$
D. $40 \text{ cm}^2$

37. The major portion of an atom's mass consists of

    A. neutrons and protons.
    B. electrons and protons.
    C. electrons and neutrons.
    D. neutrons and positrons.

38. Over the course of 24 hours

    A. the earth rotates 360 degrees around the sun
    B. the moon rotates 360 degrees around the earth
    C. the earth rotates 360 degrees about its axis
    D. the moon rotates 360 degrees about its axis

39. Four specimens of three species of plants were exposed to different amounts of sunlight over a period of one week. At the end of the week, the number of new leaves on each plant was recorded.

| Hours of sunlight per day | New leaves on species A | New leaves on species B | New leaves on species C |
|---|---|---|---|
| 0 | 0 | 0 | 0 |
| 1 | 0 | 1 | 4 |
| 3 | 0 | 4 | 8 |
| 6 | 4 | 7 | 5 |

Which of the following conclusions is best supported by information in the table above?

A. Species A requires 6 hours of sunlight per day to produce new leaves.

B. No plants can grow without exposure to sunlight.

C. To optimize growth, species B should be exposed to more than 6 hours of sunlight per day.

D. To optimize growth, species C should be exposed to between 2 and 5 hours of sunlight per day.

# ANSWERS AND EXPLANATIONS

## Practice: Elementary Education Content Knowledge

### Reading and Language Arts

**1. A, B, D**

Carefully reading the question stem is essential to selecting the best answer here. A thesis statement puts forth the main point or argument of an essay. This question asks for you to find three sentences that are effective thesis statements. Choices (C) and (E) would be ineffective thesis statements for a persuasive essay because they do not clearly state an opinion or position that could be proved in the course of an essay. Choices (A), (B), and (D) state a clear opinion.

**2. D**

In a small-group setting such as this, establishing eye contact with several or all members of the audience is an effective way of maintaining the audience's focus on the presentation. Maintaining eye contact with only the teacher (A) will not encourage the other students to focus on the presentation. Although eye contact is important, it is not necessary to give a presentation of this length without the use of brief notes (B). In fact, it is usually a good idea for a speaker to have brief notes to refer to in order to convey all of the information planned for a presentation. Standing behind a podium (C) can provide a focal point for the audience, but hand gestures should be used as an additional method of nonverbal communication.

**3. B**

In this excerpt, the speaker clearly believes that Native Americans have a deep connection to the land. He states that "every part of this soil is sacred in the estimation of my people." One reason that the land is viewed as sacred is that "it is rich with the blood of our ancestors," an evocative image. Choice (B) is correct.

**4. D**

This passage appears to be telling a story about a character named Wilson. The story is told in the third person and appears to use the standard devices of realistic fiction (D). A fable, choice (A), is a fictitious story, usually involving animals, that attempts to illustrate a universal truth or moral. An autobiography, choice (B), is a biography in which the author is also the subject of the biography. Consequently, autobiographies are almost always written in the first person, and (B) can be eliminated. A folktale, choice (C), is a characteristically anonymous, timeless, and placeless tale that is or was once communicated orally.

**5. D**

The language Huckleberry Finn is using is a regional dialect, and choice (D) is correct. Because of grammatically incorrect phrases such as "rustled ... ever so mournful" and idiomatically odd phrasings such as "away off," you can conclude that Huck's use of English is neither standard nor formal, eliminating choices (A) and (B). Choice (C) may have been tempting, but jargon is terminology specific to an occupation or hobby.

**6. A**

The imagery in this selection about death helps to illustrate Huck's isolation and fear, so (A) is correct. The fact that Huck hears and sees these things certainly indicates that he is aware of his environment (B), but the author's purpose in including these details is not to illustrate that Huck perceives his surroundings but to show his state of mind. (C) may have been tempting if you recall the novel, because Huck does lose his father in the course of the narrative, but this selection has nothing to do with that event. (D) is out for the same reason: Huck does face a moral dilemma in the novel—but again, not in this particular selection.

**7. C**

Only choice (C) uses the word "appropriate" as a verb. In that sentence, the bank may appropriate, or take, the farm if mortgage payments are not made on time. In each of the other sentences, the word is used as an adjective, that is, to modify or describe a noun. In (A), "appropriate" describes someone's attire; in (B), it describes words; and in (D), it describes what roughhousing is not.

### 8. D

An oxymoron is a figure of speech in which two incongruous or contradictory terms are juxtaposed. In this case, "sweet" and "sorrow" are contradictory. Choice (D) is correct. A simile, choice (A), is a figure of speech that compares two unlike things using the word *like* or *as*. A personification, choice (B), refers to treating an inanimate or inhuman concept or thing as if it were human. Hyperbole, choice (C), refers to overstatement or exaggeration.

### 9. B

Visualizing each of the nonverbal responses can help you select the best answer. A listener who is leaning forward is likely interested in and focused on what a speaker has to say, so (B) is correct. The other choices indicate a lack of focus on the speaker. (A) describes a closed-off nonverbal response, suggesting the listener is not listening with an open mind. Gesturing to other audience members (C) suggests that the listener is distracted, engaged more with other audience members than with the speaker. (D) suggests a detachment from or boredom with the speaker.

### 10. C

The critical period is the time by which an individual must be exposed to language in order to fully develop language capabilities. Although it may be easier for young children to learn second languages than it is for adults, adults can learn to fluently use second languages (B). Choice (C) is most consistent with the idea of the critical period.

### 11. B

Mentally rehearsing responses or arguments is one roadblock to effective communication. Choice (B), rehearsing, is the term used to describe this type of ineffective communication. Choices (A), (C), and (D) all refer to active listening or techniques associated with active listening, which is generally viewed positively in that it leads to improved communication.

### 12. A

A child who makes the connection between letters and sounds but has not yet grasped that a number of letter-sound combinations make up most words would be likely to represent a word or group of words with a single letter, as in choice (A). (B) and (C) show mastery of the concept of a group of letters representing a word. These errors represent difficulty with higher-level spelling concepts. Lastly, (D) shows no correspondence to the sounds of the words and therefore does not match up with the example in the question.

### 13. C

The stages of the writing process appear occasionally on the Praxis exam. The stages proceed as follows: (1) prewriting, which involves brainstorming and outlining; (2) drafting, which involves writing an initial draft; (3) revising, which involves re-reading the draft for organization, logic, and grammar; and (4) proofreading, which involves a final read-through prior to publishing. In the example here, the writer has finished revising the document and is entering the proofreading stage, and choice (C) is correct.

### *Mathematics*

### 14. A

Choice (A) has a 1 in the second decimal place. All the other answer choices have a 0 in the second decimal place. This means that (A) is the greatest value and the correct answer. When comparing decimals, begin at the first place to the right of the decimal (the tenths place) and look for the largest number among the answer choices. If values are equal, move one place to the right and perform the same comparison. Once you find a larger value for a given decimal place, there is no need to continue to compare further decimal places to the right.

### 15. B

This is a proportion question. The relationship between the hydrant and the hydrant's shadow will be the same as the relationship between Tom and

Tom's shadow. So you could set up the following proportion:

$$\frac{\text{hydrant}}{\text{hydrant's shadow}} = \frac{\text{Tom}}{\text{Tom's shadow}}$$

$$\frac{40}{32} = \frac{x}{48}$$

Now it's time to cross multiply and solve. Keep in mind that you can use a calculator on this test.

$$32x = 40 \times 48$$
$$32x = 1920$$
$$x = \frac{1920}{32} = 60$$

Choice (B) is correct.

## 16. B

This question is nice in that you do not need to solve it. You simply need to determine the correct way to do so. You are told that 40% of the 540 students scored at or below grade level. Remember the formula part = percent × whole. You can write 40% as either 0.4 or $\frac{40}{100}$. For the purposes of this question, $\frac{40}{100}$ is what does the trick. In $\frac{40}{100} \times 540$, $\frac{40}{100}$ can be reduced to $\frac{2}{5}$, so you can rewrite the equation as $\frac{2}{5} \times 540$, choice (B).

## 17. D

To find the profit, subtract the cost from the revenue or money taken in. We know that the owner buys the hats at a cost of $17.50 for five hats and sells them for $4.00 each. So for every five hats sold, she takes in 5 × $4.00 = $20 and spends $17.50. That yields a profit of $20 − $17.50 = $2.50 for every five hats. To earn a profit of $100, she'd have to sell $\frac{100}{2.50}$ sets of five hats. That's 40 × 5 = 200 hats total, choice (D).

## 18. C

You are looking for the one choice that is *not* equivalent to dividing 420 by 21. You can work this out in your head or use your calculator. Just be careful; pay attention to the order of operations

(PEMDAS) and double-check your answers. (A), (B), and (D) all are equivalent to dividing 420 by 21, or 420 ÷ 21 = 20, so they can be eliminated. In (A), dividing 420 by 3 and then by 7 is the same as dividing 420 by 3 × 7 or 21. In (B), you do what's inside the parentheses first, so 420 is divided by (3 × 7) or 21. In (D), you begin by dividing 420 by 3 and then multiply that by $\frac{1}{7}$, which is the same as dividing by 7. Once again, you are dividing 420 by 3 and then dividing that by 7, which is the same as dividing 420 by 21. That leaves (C) as the correct answer since (420 ÷ 3) + (420 ÷ 7) = 140 + 60 = 200, which is not equal to 20.

## 19. A

The distributive property of multiplication over addition refers to the fact that if you have a value outside of a parentheses and you have two values added together inside the parentheses, you can multiply the outside term by each of the inside terms and then add the inside terms together. This is exactly what happens with 7(8 + 5) = 7 × 8 + 7 × 5. Choice (A) is correct.

## 20. C

Remember the average formula: $\frac{\text{sum}}{\text{number of terms}}$. If you apply this formula to the question, you know that $180 = \frac{156 + 172 + 210 + x}{4}$, where $x$ is the missing bowling score. Multiply both sides by 4 to simplify: $4 \times 180 = \frac{156 + 172 + 210 + x}{4} \times 4$. So 720 = 156 + 172 + 210 + $x$. Here's an excellent time to use your calculator: 720 = 538 + $x$. Subtract 538 from both sides to find that the missing score, $x$, must equal 182, choice (C).

## 21. C

If you think this question might take too much time, feel free to make a guess and return to it later if you have time at the end of the test. When faced with a strange shape like this one, think about ways to draw a line that will convert the shape into more familiar shapes. This figure is actually a rectangle and a right triangle. Here's how it looks:

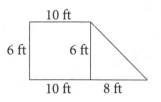

We're dealing with a 6 × 10 rectangle and a right triangle with legs of lengths 6 and 8. To find the third side of a right triangle, remember the Pythagorean theorem: $a^2 + b^2 = c^2$. In this case, $a = 6$ and $b = 8$:

$$6^2 + 8^2 = c^2$$
$$36 + 64 = c^2$$
$$100 = c^2$$
$$c = 10$$

So the third side of the right triangle has a length of 10. Now the figure looks like this:

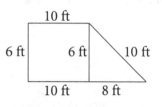

To find the perimeter, add up the lengths of the sides: 6 + 10 + 10 + 18 = 44 ft, choice (C).

## 22. B

If Joyce had 42 biscuits and 6 remained uneaten, that means that 42 − 6 = 36 biscuits were eaten. To find the average number of biscuits eaten, use the average formula:

$$\text{average} = \frac{\text{sum}}{\text{number of terms}} = \frac{36}{12} = 3, \text{ choice (B).}$$

## 23. B

To find the missing term in a series, you need to determine how each of the previous terms relates to the term that precedes it. Each of the terms in this series is 7.25 greater than the previous term. So the missing term will equal the last term plus 7.25: 28.25 + 7.25 = 35.50, choice (B).

## 24. A

The desired outcome is a red or black pen. The possible outcomes are a red, black, or blue pen. Use the probability formula to solve:

$$\text{probability} = \frac{\text{number desired}}{\text{number possible}} = \frac{\#red + \#black}{\#total}$$

$$= \frac{4 + 6}{5 + 6 + 4} = \frac{10}{15} = \frac{2}{3}$$

Choice (A) is correct.

## 25. D

To solve this question, begin by replacing the 5 digits with 7s. The new term is 278,746. The original term was 258,546. Subtract the original term from the new term to solve:

$$278,746 − 258,546 = 20,200$$

Choice (D) is correct.

### *Social Studies*

## 26. A, B, D

Global warming, deforestation, and ozone layer depletion are all considered serious threats to the global environment, making choices (A), (B), and (D) correct. Plate tectonics is the movement of the plates that make up the surface of earth. While plate tectonics (D) is linked to geological disturbances such as earthquakes and volcanoes, it is a natural phenomenon and not considered a serious threat to the global environment. Jet streams (E) are powerful winds far above earth's surface that affect weather but again are natural and not threats to the environment.

## 27. B

The Agricultural Revolution was the development of agricultural tools and techniques like the plow that enabled the creation of food surpluses that allowed for the division of labor, the development of trade, and the "dawn of civilization." (A) is the opposite of what happened with the Agricultural Revolution. Rather than searching further for food, because food production became reliable, humans were able to settle in one place. (C) is incorrect since the founding of the first great civilizations followed the Agricultural

Revolution, not the other way around. (D) is outside the scope of the Agricultural Revolution.

**28. B**

Traditional Hindu society is associated with a caste system in which individuals are born into somewhat rigid socioeconomic levels, or castes, that are associated with certain types of work. The highest caste is the brahmin, which is the caste of priests. Pariahs or "untouchables" are those beneath the lowest caste. Choice (B) is correct.

**29. C**

Alexander the Great is generally credited as one of the main reasons why elements of the Greek culture spread throughout the Mediterranean world. He was ruler of Macedonia in the 3rd and 4th centuries BCE, and his empire covered much of the Mediterranean world. Hammurabi (A) was a ruler of ancient Babylon who is credited with establishing a written code of law for that empire. Genghis Khan (B) was a Mongol emperor whose influence stretched across Asia and into the West. Herodotus (D) was a Greek historian who described much of the ancient Mediterranean world.

**30. B**

Based on the chart, approximately 10% of the workers in 1960 walked to work. Ten percent of 65,000,000 is 6,500,000, so choice (B) is correct. About 12%, or 7,800,000, of the workers in 1960 used public transportation (A). In that same year, about 5%, or 3,250,000, of the workers worked at home (D). Choice (C) is what you would get if you erroneously applied the 1970 percentage of workers who walked (about 8%) to the total number of workers in 1960.

**31. D**

Only (D) is directly supported by information in this graph. In 1970, about 9% of the workers used public transportation, and about 7% of the workers walked to work. Eliminate (A) because percentages, not total numbers, are reported in the graph. Although the percentage of people working at home decreased, the actual number of people working at home may have increased due to population increase over the 30-year span. Eliminate (B) because only the working population, not the general population, is represented in this graph. Eliminate (C) because although urban sprawl may have been responsible for the increase in the percentage of people driving to work, the graph does not provide information about why changes in transportation use occurred.

**32. C**

The correct order of presidential succession in the United States is president, vice president, and speaker of the House of Representatives. Choice (C) is correct.

*Science*

**33. B**

Iron forms rust when water (or an even better electrolyte) turns iron and oxygen into iron oxide ($Fe_2O_3$), a chemical process. Choice (B) is correct. Helium and neon (A) are both inert, so they do not react chemically. Water causing soil erosion (C) may or may not incur a chemical change, and melting ice (D) does not alter the chemistry of $H_2O$.

**34. D**

Blood enters the right atrium of the heart from the vena cava. Choice (D) is correct.

**35. A**

For a substance to have a high pH, it must be a base, or alkaline (a pH of 7 is neutral, like water; a pH of less than 7 is acidic; and a pH of greater than 7 is a base). Of the substances listed, only ammonia is a base, so choice (A) is correct.

**36. C**

The results shown in the chart suggest that mold grows at an increasingly rapid rate as the days progress. It would be unreasonable to predict that there would be little or no growth, as shown in (A) and (B), between days 20 and 25. Assuming that sourdough at 71°F realizes a growth rate in its third period of mold growth similar to that realized by white bread at 71°F (absolute increase of 10 $cm^2$, or a bit more than a doubling in size, from day 15 to day

20), it is unlikely that the surface area covered by the mold would increase almost six times over the course of five days, as represented by (D). An increase of 9 cm$^2$ between days 20 and 25 is the most reasonable projection that can be made based on the available data. So (C) is correct.

## 37. A

The major portion of an atom's mass consists of neutrons and protons, as in choice (A). Electrons, positrons, neutrinos, and other subatomic particles have negligible masses.

## 38. C

Over the course of 24 hours, earth rotates 360 degrees about its axis as in choice (C).

## 39. D

Only (D) is a valid conclusion. Since species C had the most new leaves at 3 hours of sunlight and demonstrated a drop-off by 6 hours of sunlight, the conclusion that optimal growth occurs for species C between 2 and 5 hours of sunlight is reasonable. Because the table does not record the number of new leaves produced with exposure to 4 or 5 hours of sunlight, (A) is invalid. (B) is too extreme—the experiment only included observations of four plant species. (C) is not supported by the data, since while the trend for species B is upward, no observations were made at more than 6 hours; growth of new leaves may drop off with more sunlight.

# REVIEW OF THE ELEMENTARY EDUCATION: CURRICULUM, INSTRUCTION, AND ASSESSMENT EXAM

If you are required to take the Elementary Education: Curriculum, Instruction, and Assessment (5017) exam, you will want to begin by reading Chapter 4, "Principles of Learning and Teaching," which covers many of the subjects that are on the 5017 test. Then, review the information from earlier in Chapter 5 concerning the Elementary Education Content Knowledge (5018) exam. Familiarity with content details related to English language arts, mathematics, science, and social studies will help you understand the scenarios and answer choices given in the 5017 test questions. Next, move on to the information in the section you are currently reading, which will provide you with a summary of the Elementary Education: Curriculum, Instruction, and Assessment test followed by additional review of the basic principles and processes that pertain to curriculum, instruction, and assessment of each subject area within the elementary education classroom. After reviewing Chapter 4 and these sections, proceed to the Curriculum, Instruction, and Assessment full-length practice test that appears later in this chapter.

| Elementary Education: Curriculum, Instruction, and Assessment |
|---|
| Format: Computer-delivered |
| Number of Questions: 120<br>Time: 130 minutes |
| Question Types: multiple-choice (called "selected-response" by the test maker) |
| Test may include pre-test questions that do not count toward your score |
| No penalty for incorrect answers |
| Scratch paper is available during the exam (it will be destroyed before you leave the testing center) |
| Content covered:<br><br>• Reading and Language Arts Curriculum, Instruction, and Assessment: approximately 37 questions, 31 percent of the test<br><br>• Mathematics Curriculum, Instruction, and Assessment: approximately 31 questions, 26 percent of the test<br><br>• Science Curriculum, Instruction, and Assessment: approximately 20 questions, 16 percent of the test<br><br>• Social Studies Curriculum, Instruction, and Assessment: approximately 17 questions, 14 percent of the test<br><br>• Art, Music, and Physical Education Curriculum, Instruction, and Assessment: approximately 15 questions, 13 percent of the test |

The Elementary Education: Curriculum, Instruction, and Assessment test is designed to test the knowledge and skills necessary for a teacher of the elementary grades with a focus on, unsurprisingly, curriculum, instruction, and assessment. The test consists of 120 multiple-choice questions that assess a prospective teacher's understanding of various principles and processes, including differentiation for a range of educational needs (e.g., special education, English language learners, and gifted). Most of the questions are posed in the context of the six most commonly taught subject areas in elementary school: reading and language arts, mathematics, science, social studies, arts, and physical education. Some questions will focus on general information about curriculum, instruction, and assessment. The test is aligned with the Common Core Standards for Language Arts and Mathematics and content standards for every subject area.

## Reading and Language Arts Curriculum, Instruction, and Assessment

The Reading and Language Arts section is the largest section on the test, making up 31 percent of the questions. You will need to be able to provide a balanced reading, writing, speaking, and listening program and recognize the importance of reading/language arts competence.

The reading process is an interaction among the reader, text, and context to construct meaning. You will need to recognize how reading competence emerges and be able to apply this knowledge in instructional contexts. Know the interrelationships between decoding and the comprehension processes. The competencies needed to develop proficiency in decoding text are phonological and phonemic awareness, application of the alphabetic principle, word analysis skills, phonics, syllabication, structural analysis/morphology, and use of semantic and syntactic clues. Know what role previous knowledge and developmental issues play in the emergence and extension of literacy.

Reading for various purposes requires the use of different reading strategies. Understand the factors that affect comprehension, reading fluency, word identification skills, and previous knowledge. Some strategies that help students understand written material are self-questioning, predicting, inferring, and summarizing. You should know how to include comprehension skills, such as comparing and contrasting, drawing conclusions, and finding the main idea, in your daily instruction.

Be able to recognize students' difficulties in their development of reading competence. Know how to use appropriate instructional methods and resources to help the students compensate for their difficulties. Certain reading disorders and difficulties that may arise are dyslexia, social-emotional issues, lack of previous educational experience, background knowledge, vocabulary knowledge, lack of phonemic and phonological awareness, and lack of reading fluency.

It is important to use a variety of children's literature in the classroom. Understand that using appropriate literature can promote students' social, emotional, intellectual, and literary development. Familiarity with major types of children's fiction and nonfiction literature, popular books, authors, and themes of children's literature will help in selecting books for students for purposes such as addressing individual student needs and interests, promoting independent reading, and encouraging the appreciation and critical evaluation of literature.

The three parts to reading instruction lessons are prereading, during-reading, and postreading instruction. Understand the importance of prereading activities like word recognition, context clues, and K-W-L charts. Know that during reading, students can work on vocabulary development, graphic organizers, and decoding skills. Postreading activities include journal writing, having reactions, rewriting information, and using comprehension and interpretation skills.

Be familiar with strategies for helping students transfer their oral language communication skills to writing. Prewriting, drafting, revising, editing, and publishing are all part of writing instruction.

Understand that students should have access to direct instruction and guided practice in the English writing conventions of grammar, capitalization, punctuation, and spelling. Know the various stages of spelling development: prephonetic, phonetic, transitional, and conventions. Know how to provide systematic instruction in common spelling patterns based on phonics skills already taught. Know how to provide opportunities for students to use and develop their understanding of English writing conventions in the context of meaningful written expression. Understand how to instruct students in properly researching and citing primary and secondary source materials.

Listening is an active cognitive process in which the listener constructs meaning from the content and intent of the speaker's message. Know how to guide students to improve their listening through instructional activities, such as directed listening/thinking and reading literature.

Know how to be clear when promoting students' awareness of the sounds (phonemes) of oral language to facilitate their understanding of the alphabetic principle and development of graphophonemic knowledge (letter-sound relationships). Some strategies to promote students' vocabulary development are retelling stories; creating semantic maps or concept maps; and using graphophonemic cues, structural analysis, etymology, and context clues to determine word meanings.

Understand the characteristics, uses, and limitations of various types of conventional reading assessment instruments and the rationales for selecting particular assessment instruments in given situations.

Understand how using multiple, ongoing assessments and knowledge of grade-level expectations to identify students' reading and language arts strengths assists in the development of specific reading and language arts skills. Know how to monitor student performance, plan appropriate reading and language arts instruction, and determine when a student may be in need of additional help (e.g., classroom intervention, individualized instruction, and help beyond the classroom). It is important to recognize when to use intervention before remediation becomes necessary. The instructional applications of diagnostic results are identifying students' reading strengths and selecting instructional methods and materials to respond to students' needs.

Know how to observe the stages of students' development and maintain appropriate records of these observations. Know how to analyze and assess student work using informal measures such as observation, informal reading inventories (IRI), running records, miscue analysis, the cloze procedure, anecdotal records, conferencing, oral reports, and portfolios.

Understand the basis for using the Frye Readability Index in assessing texts and other reading materials for suitability for student use. Know how to administer the basal reader assessment instruments, interpret the results, and plan instruction from the results. You should be able to plan and provide learning activities that build on students' stages of development (what they already know and what they are able to do at their stages of development).

Be able to adapt assessment materials for students with special needs, including gifted students. Know how to provide opportunities that use performance and authentic assessment as well as structured assessment situations.

## Mathematics Curriculum, Instruction, and Assessment

Mathematics is the second largest section on the test, making up 26 percent of the questions. You will need to understand mathematical communication and be able to use mathematical language and vocabulary, representations, and data to communicate information to students. Know that mathematical terms should be emphasized in the classroom to breed familiarity. Know how to describe and communicate quantitative information to students using symbolic, verbal, graphic, and concrete representations such as models, tables, graphs, diagrams, and drawings.

Know how to promote students' understanding of number and numeration by using such mathematical activities as measuring, ordering, comparing, and symbolizing. Be able to identify opportunities to integrate mathematical concepts into instruction in other content areas.

Learn how everyday situations can be used to aid students in their exploration of patterns, their understanding of the functional relationships shown in these patterns, their ability to represent patterns they have seen, and their ability to make predictions based on their observations. Also, learn to use mathematical operations and computations as an instructional technique.

Learn strategies that use nonstandard and standard units of measurement. Be able to instruct students on making conversions within a measurement system. Be able to instruct students in identifying one-, two-, and three-dimensional figures. Understand the relationships of measurement to perimeter, area, and volume. Apply geometry to the coordinate plane.

Know how to provide instruction that aids students in their ability to apply statistics and probability concepts; to collect, organize, and interpret data; to construct and interpret charts and graphs; to draw conclusions; and to make decisions in everyday statistical and probability situations. Explore the use of manipulatives and developmentally appropriate materials to enhance student learning.

Recognize the role of algebraic thinking and questioning in the mathematics curriculum. Know how to encourage the development of thinking and questioning skills in students by providing opportunities for them to discover and apply mathematical principles in a variety of contexts, including real-world applications. Be able to select appropriate strategies from a variety of approaches to problem solving such as acting out problems, making models, using manipulatives, guessing and checking, and working backward. Know how to guide students in the problem-solving process. Be able to develop students' ability to solve problems using a variety of strategies and techniques.

Know how to consider the developmental levels of students when implementing a mathematics instructional program. Understand how to assess previous mathematics knowledge, how to construct knowledge, how to model lessons, how to use informal reasoning, and how to use graphic organizers.

Know how to analyze students' work and correct misconceptions and errors. Understand the use of rubrics in assessment, when to remediate, and when to accelerate instruction. Know how to use the results of standardized tests as well as informal testing results.

## Science Curriculum, Instruction, and Assessment

The Science section makes up 16 percent of the questions on the test. You will need to understand learning cycles, constructivism, inquiry, and discovery learning. Know how to apply and encourage higher-order thinking skills in the sciences that will provide students with opportunities to develop these skills in meaningful contexts.

Understand basic science concepts and be able to apply these concepts to interpret and analyze phenomena in planning instruction. Understand the unifying concepts and processes in science, such as providing connections among the traditional scientific disciplines of systems, subsystems, models, and conservation.

Recognize procedures for systematically observing the natural and human-made world. Be able to instruct students in locating needed information, organizing science data, identifying similarities and differences, and arranging events and activities in appropriate sequential order to support a scientific investigation. Know the steps of the scientific method and be able to design instruction applying it.

Be familiar with the basic safety rules required in a scientific laboratory. You should know how to model the correct use of the equipment, technology, and instructional materials available in science laboratories.

Know how to provide students with meaningful and developmentally appropriate experiences to assist them in developing an understanding of experimental design. Setting up hypotheses; testing hypotheses using control and experimental groups; identifying variables; and recognizing changes, errors, and omissions in experiments are steps frequently required for experimentation.

Know how to analyze students' work. Understand how to recognize what a student does correctly, what misconceptions and errors are involved, and at what level of development concepts are being understood. Be able to use the results of rubrics, formal and informal testing, and remediation or enrichment. Explain what information can be gathered from various assessments, such as multiple-choice quizzes, open-ended essay tests, and portfolio assessments.

Know how to demonstrate to students an understanding of how the life, earth, space, and physical sciences relate to one another. Understand the interrelatedness of science to other curricular areas.

## Social Studies Curriculum, Instruction, and Assessment

The Social Studies section makes up 14 percent of the questions on the test. There are many components of the social studies curriculum. Some of the most important ones are scope and sequence, appropriate materials, technology, and learner objectives. Know how to provide developmentally appropriate experiences that will promote students' understanding of these concepts and skills. Be familiar with using inquiry-based instruction and assisting students in decision making, forecasting, planning, problem solving, comparing and contrasting, and organizing data. Know how to teach map and globe skills, the use of models, research skills, and appropriate use of technology.

Understand how to apply and encourage inquiry thinking skills in students who are evaluating decisions or who hold diverse views regarding a historical or contemporary issue.

The major characteristics of world civilizations, cultural groups, historical events, social structures, social organizations, and human behavior in society should be emphasized in each lesson. Know how to provide students with opportunities to gain an understanding of past societies and to recognize the connections between the past and the present. Be able to assist students in understanding the geography, government, and history of the United States and the world. Understand how to inform students about the major developments in the history of the United States, including the governmental system; the principles, ideals, rights, and responsibilities of citizenship; and the fundamental principles and concepts of economics. Be able to recognize the major developments in world history and foster students' understanding of those basic developments.

Know how to incorporate appropriate activities for students to explore the nature and significance of cultural diversity in historical and contemporary contexts, as well as how culture and cultural diversity have shaped the United States and other societies.

Know how to promote the development of appropriate concepts and skills in organizing data, problem solving, comparing and contrasting, model building, planning, forecasting, and decision making. Be able to adapt skills and methods to the developmental levels of students in formulating research questions; identifying primary and secondary sources to meet given needs; recognizing the uses of maps, observation, statistical data, and interviews; applying note-taking skills; and evaluating and organizing information gathered from source materials.

Understand how to create a social studies atmosphere in the classroom that encourages questions, promotes appreciation of and respect for human diversity, provides opportunities for students to explore and understand social interactions, and helps them recognize their own personal social responsibilities.

Know how the use of traditional and standardized testing results may assist in instruction. Be able to anticipate and identify common points of confusion in social studies such as factual errors, patterns of error, inaccuracies, and conceptual misconceptions. Select appropriate performance assessments and identify areas for cross-curricular study (such as integrating English language arts and social studies).

## Arts and Physical Education Curriculum, Instruction, and Assessment

The Arts and Physical Education section makes up 13 percent of the questions on the test. You will need to know the curriculum for art, including art history and its developments and movements. Review art design, including different products and mediums. You should be familiar with art techniques, with art as a form of visual communication, and with originality and imagination as they apply to art. Review art judgment and criticism theories.

Know components of music and key terms associated with music, such as melody and timbre. Review music appreciation and evaluation, including analyzing and describing music and musical performances. Be familiar with the basics of making music, including singing and using instruments, and notating music.

Be familiar with physical education concepts and principles, including proper exercise practices and general ideas for promoting physical fitness and an overall healthy lifestyle. Understand what qualities and skills are valued in games and sports. Note that elements of a health curriculum are included within Physical Education, as well as within Science, on the test.

Know a variety of instructional methods and strategies in the teaching of arts and physical education. Understand how to adjust instruction to meet the needs of diverse learners and take into account each student's physical, social, and emotional development. Know how to emphasize culturally diverse examples in teaching art and music. Know how to use materials and equipment, including musical instruments, art supplies, and physical education equipment, as well as software and the Internet.

As with the other content areas assessed in the 5018 test, keep in mind that the 5017 test emphasizes teaching applications for the art, music, and physical education principles tested. Nearly all test questions related to these areas will involve a classroom or teaching scenario.

# PRACTICE: CURRICULUM, INSTRUCTION, AND ASSESSMENT

## Reading and Language Arts

1. A third-grade teacher wishes to do an appropriate prereading activity that will encourage students to want to read the story. Which of the following prereading activities would be most likely to accomplish that?

   A. Telling the students about the author and the period in which the story was written

   B. Giving the students a list of literary devices they will find employed in the story

   C. Telling the children that there is a surprise ending and that they will be required to draw a picture showing that ending

   D. Telling the children the main plot of the story

2. A major distinction between the terms *phonics* and *phonemic awareness* is that

   A. phonemic awareness involves the activities done in student practice books (workbooks), but phonics does not

   B. phonics involves the written word, while phonemic awareness does not necessarily

   C. phonemic awareness includes reading, but phonics does not

   D. neither involves reading for meaning

3. Which of the following is an example showing Vygotsky's zone of proximal development?

   A. A child knows the short vowel sounds, so he is able to learn the long vowel sounds.

   B. A class "reads" the words under a picture as the teacher guides them while she points and says the word.

   C. Children read in groups based on their abilities.

   D. A teacher pairs students with other students of unlike ability and has them do their worksheets together.

4. My dog, Joey, likes to roam the hills. Every day, he walks with me to the bus, and then he heads out through the fields. One day, as he ran toward the hills, he saw a rabbit going toward a barn. Joey ran after the rabbit and into the barn.

   After having a child read the above paragraph, the teacher asks the child, "Where did the dog go?" In this case, the teacher is assessing the child's ability in

   A. phonics

   B. phonemic awareness

   C. fluency

   D. comprehension

5. If a child can spell and write his name at home but fails to do so in front of the teacher, he

   A. is displaying both spelling competence and performance

   B. has spelling competence but does not display spelling performance

   C. cannot actually spell

   D. is showing spelling performance but not competence

6.

| **Original Sentence:** |
| The girl was <u>cold</u>, so she put on her coat. |
| **Student Response:** |
| The girl was hot, so she put on a swimsuit. |

In the above exercise, the students were asked to rewrite the sentence replacing the underlined word with a synonym. The student's response indicates that she

A. has a good understanding of the concepts of synonyms and homophones

B. is confusing homophones with synonyms

C. has mastered the concepts of antonyms and synonyms

D. has not mastered the concept of synonym usage

7.

| *Tough Coughs as He Ploughs the Dough* |

In the title in the box above, the problem with a particular type of reading approach is demonstrated. Which approach?

A. Phonics-based approach

B. Whole language approach

C. Literature-based approach

D. Guided reading approach

8. When a person knows a part of a word because she has encountered the word before or has encountered words that are similar to it, this is called

A. partial recognition

B. decoding

C. cloze activity

D. using context

9. Students may be encouraged to write in reflection journals about their feelings toward a particular literary work and their perceptions of how the work applies to their belief system. Such journals address assessment primarily in which domain?

A. Cognitive

B. Social

C. Psychomotor

D. Affective

10. If a second-grade teacher has a student who, in early March, is still not reading, the teacher should

A. not be concerned, because eventually the student will catch up

B. consider sending the student for remediation so he can learn to read

C. assume the student is normal because most children do not read well until the third grade

D. decide that retention is the only option for the student

11. What is the first step a teacher should take in setting up guided reading?

A. Place the student in heterogeneous ability groups.

B. Give the students support when they are struggling with words.

C. Give the students a question to answer when they are reading the book.

D. Diagnose the students' reading levels.

12. What is a teacher's primary purpose for creating a bulletin board in the classroom?

    A. To provide a visually attractive learning environment

    B. To display the teacher's creativity so the students will be inspired to be creative as well

    C. To serve as a display for teacher-parent conferences

    D. To provide information that relates to the material being taught in the classroom

13. Placing students in reading groups based on their performance on formative assessments is called

    A. ability grouping

    B. homogeneous diversity

    C. heterogeneous tracking

    D. grade-level typing

14. When using peer revision to improve students' writing in the classroom, it is important that

    A. the rubric the students will be graded on be given out in advance

    B. only students who like each other be allowed to provide feedback on one another's work

    C. the teacher leave the classroom and stay out of the process

    D. peers revise individually, never in groups

## Mathematics

15. All of the students in an elementary teacher's classroom obtained stanine scores of 4 or 5 on math computation. The teacher can determine from these data that her students are

    A. performing at a mostly average level, with some just below average, in computation

    B. failing in computational abilities

    C. performing a little above average in computation

    D. performing at the fourth- and fifth-grade levels in computation

16. Students were given base ten blocks to demonstrate their understanding of numeration systems. The ones blocks are red. The tens blocks are green. The hundreds blocks are black. The table below shows how four students demonstrated the number 124.

    | Barbara | 4 red, 12 green |
    |---------|-----------------|
    | Carletta | 4 red, 2 green, 1 black |
    | Janice | 4 black, 2 green, 1 red |
    | Jeanne | 24 red, 1 black |

    Using a strict place value notation, which of the above students was correct?

    A. Barbara

    B. Carletta

    C. Janice

    D. Jeanne

17. While walking around the room, the teacher notices that Marquez has completed the following work:

| | |
|---|---|
| $\dfrac{1}{2} + \dfrac{2}{3} = \dfrac{3}{5}$ | $\dfrac{1}{2} + \dfrac{1}{2} = \dfrac{2}{4}$ |
| $\dfrac{3}{5} + \dfrac{2}{3} = \dfrac{5}{8}$ | $\dfrac{1}{2} + \dfrac{1}{6} = $ \_\_\_\_\_ |

If the error pattern continues, Marquez's answer to the next problem will be

A. $\dfrac{1}{3}$

B. $\dfrac{4}{5}$

C. $\dfrac{7}{14}$

D. $\dfrac{2}{8}$

18. When a teacher is drawing conclusions about a primary student's math ability based on standardized test results, the teacher should use caution because

A. very little research has been done on primary grade students

B. the population on which these tests are standardized is older children, not primary grade students

C. current standardized tests are invalid in the skills they test

D. children of this age change so rapidly that scores on a single test may not reflect a student's ability

19. Current best practices in mathematics instruction affirm which of the following?

A. Students should be encouraged to solve problems in any way that makes sense to them.

B. Students should learn appropriate algorithms and always show their work to display proficiency.

C. Mental math is not an important part of math class work.

D. Pencil-and-paper drills are the most important part of math class.

20. Which of the following are common methods of solving arithmetic problems?

Select all that apply.

A. Mental estimation

B. Using a calculator

C. Written calculation with paper and pencil

D. Conversion

21. A student adding 328 and 527 says the sum is 845. The most likely reason for this result is that the student

A. borrowed incorrectly

B. failed to regroup properly

C. used the wrong operation

D. does not know how to do subtraction

22. When students are working on word problems, what is the first step they should be encouraged to do?

    A. Figure out what information is being sought

    B. Determine a plan of action

    C. Write out an equation

    D. Figure out a similar problem

23. What does the word *algorithm* mean?

    A. Higher-level algebra

    B. A plan for solving a problem

    C. A geometric proportion

    D. Using a graphing calculator

24. In order to do mental math, students must have a mastery of

    A. basic facts and estimation

    B. the calculator

    C. pencil-and-paper drills only

    D. word problems

25. Based upon the Common Core State Standards, which of the following is NOT an appropriate time to introduce the algorithm for multidigit multiplication to students?

    A. After students understand place value

    B. After using skip counting to recognize multiplication as repeated addition

    C. After students have done multiplication with decimals

    D. After teaching students visual ways of multiplication, such as the area model

## Science

26. Which of the following best summarizes Glasser's control theory approach to classroom management, as it is applied to science instruction?

    A. Students are left on their own to figure out how they should behave in science class.

    B. Science students will follow the teacher's rules because the teacher is an authority figure.

    C. Students help decide what science topics within the curriculum to study, develop the classroom rules, and then accept ownership of the consequences.

    D. The teacher takes every opportunity to show students how their behavior and learning are relevant to the real world.

27. A teacher teaches a lesson on the properties of liquids and gases and then proposes an experiment using soap bubbles. As a class, a hypothesis is proposed. In groups, the experiment is carried out. The results obtained by Groups 1, 2, 3, and 4 confirm the hypothesis. The results from Group 5 do not. If the teacher's objective is for the students to be able to apply the scientific method, which of the following responses would be the LEAST helpful?

    A. Encouragement for the entire class to redo the experiment

    B. A recommendation that Group 5 discuss and compare their results and methods with those of another group

    C. An explanation by the teacher of what Group 5 did wrong

    D. A suggestion that the students reformulate a new hypothesis based on the data of Group 5 and do a new experiment to test it

28. A teacher in a fifth-grade classroom has children go out into the schoolyard and collect rocks. She then has the students sort the rocks according to igneous, sedimentary, and metamorphic. She is asking the students to classify the rocks according to

    A. type of mineral content
    B. how they were formed
    C. size and shape
    D. family and genus

**Questions 29–30 are based on the following scenario.**

A teacher constructs the following test question:

> Most people with type II diabetes have the disease because of a lifetime of abusing their pancreas. When a person digests food, the food is converted into "blood sugar" that the body then uses for energy. If the blood sugar level is too high, the pancreas secretes insulin to "vacuum up" the excess and store it in the fat cells for future use. If the pancreas is overused, it wears out and no longer works.
>
> The author describes diabetes as a disease that
>
> A. attacks people randomly
> B. is devastating to the person who has it
> C. is preventable
> D. is contagious
> E. should be treated

29. The teacher is asking the students to read the information and then

    A. make a judgment based on their comprehension
    B. evaluate the writing
    C. synthesize the information into a statement of fact, not opinion
    D. expound upon the information learned

30. The teacher wishes to use the information in the stimulus above in an integrated curriculum. Which of the following activities would NOT suggest true integration?

    A. Reading a memoir about the author's grandmother with diabetes who loved eating chocolate
    B. Graphing the sugar content of various foods
    C. Having the students write a report on the disease of diabetes and its treatment
    D. Creating a reading center containing many books on hospitals and hospital workers

## Social Studies

31. A social studies teacher gives his students a broad subject with a list of terms used to discuss the subject. From this list, students are to learn the basic ideas and then determine a topic they wish to further investigate. This list is thus being used as

    A. an outline
    B. a scaffold
    C. an objective
    D. a goal

32. A social studies teacher is teaching a unit on the three branches of the federal government. Which of the following topics will NOT be a major component of this unit?

    A. The offices and duties of the executive branch
    B. The various types of judges, from district court judges to Supreme Court justices
    C. The legislative duties of Congress
    D. The role of state governors

33. A social studies teacher introduces a unit on democracy by discussing the concept of self-governance. She then allows the students to determine how they would like to have the unit taught, how to organize the material, and what activities they feel would be useful for achieving the objectives of the unit. By doing so, she is

   A. planning for integration across the curriculum

   B. assessing the students' previous knowledge of the subject

   C. teaching the students to brainstorm

   D. invoking metacognition

34. Which of the following would be the most appropriately written instructional objective?

   A. The students will understand the events leading to the start of World War I.

   B. The students will learn the US state capitals.

   C. The students will explain three key outcomes of the Geneva Conventions.

   D. The students will enjoy explaining different economic systems.

35. The National Curriculum Standards for Social Studies are centered around 10 themes. The third theme is "People, Places, and Environments." Which of the following questions for upper elementary students addresses this theme?

   A. What are the two main sources of water in the Sahara?

   B. How does the climate of the Sahara Desert affect the animal husbandry practices of nomads?

   C. Why do people live in the Sahara Desert?

   D. When did the earliest people start living in the Sahara Desert?

## Arts and Physical Education

36. When an elementary child tries to throw a softball using a chest pass similar to the one she had learned to throw a basketball, she is following Piaget's concept of

   A. egocentrism

   B. reversibility

   C. assimilation

   D. cognitive balance

37. Elementary students produce many works of art during their elementary school years. Which of the following is the LEAST important ability or understanding for them to develop at this age?

   A. The ability to use various art materials in a safe and effective manner

   B. An understanding of multiple processes that can be used in creating works of art

   C. The ability to represent objects and the human form with a high degree of accuracy

   D. An understanding of how the world and their imagination can be used to trigger artistic interest within themselves

38. Howard Gardner believes that students have various intelligences. A student who has good map-making skills and can draw representationally probably has strong

   A. verbal-linguistic intelligence

   B. interpersonal intelligence

   C. bodily-kinesthetic intelligence

   D. spatial intelligence

39. An elementary music teacher has an objective that the students be able to distinguish among the sounds of various musical instruments. What activity would allow her to assess whether that objective is being met?

    A. Have the students learn about various instruments from around the world.

    B. Have the students draw pictures of the various instruments and write the sound each makes below the instrument.

    C. Have the students choose an instrument and play it along with the other students in a group jam session.

    D. Play a recording of an instrument making music and have students write down the name of the instrument.

40. A teacher wants to do an interdisciplinary activity in which the concept of decimals she is teaching in math is used in a P.E. class. Which of the following activities would be most appropriate to meet that goal?

    A. Comparing the students' times for running the 100-yard dash

    B. Keeping score for a basketball game

    C. Counting the jumping jacks each person can do in 1 minute

    D. Setting up relay teams to run against one another

# ANSWERS AND EXPLANATIONS

## Practice: Curriculum, Instruction, and Assessment

### *Reading and Language Arts*

**1. C**

Whereas giving the students background information (A) is a good thing, it will not necessarily invoke a desire to read the story. Recognizing literary devices (i.e., flashbacks) and understanding their usage (B) will help the students gain depth of understanding, but again, this introduction would not create anticipation of the story. (C) is the correct answer because it works as an anticipatory set and notifies the students that they will be held accountable for the content by having to produce a product at the end. Telling the students the plot (D) may actually cause some students to decide *not* to read the story because they already know what is going to happen.

**2. B**

The activities done in workbooks (A) involve both phonics and phonemic awareness. (B) is the correct answer because phonemic awareness is being conscious of the various sounds within a word, whereas phonics involves the relationship between the sounds and letter symbols; one can have phonemic awareness in spoken language as well as in written language, but phonics always involves the written word. (C) is the opposite: phonics does involve reading, while phonemic awareness does not have to involve the written word. While (D) is true, it does not provide a distinction between the two terms.

**3. B**

Choice (A) shows transfer, not Vygotsky's ZPD. (B) is correct because Vygotsky's ZPD refers to the idea that children with proper scaffolding can experience doing skills at a level above their understanding. Group reading in homogeneous ability groups (C) does not involve Vygotsky's ZPD. Pairing students in heterogeneous ability couples (D) does not involve Vygotsky's ZPD.

**4. D**

Phonics (A) refers to the relationship between sounds and symbols. Phonemic awareness (B) refers to a person's consciousness of sounds within words. Fluency (C) refers to a person's ability to read text accurately and fluidly. (D) is the correct answer because comprehension refers to a person's ability to understand meaning.

**5. B**

*Competence* means having the ability to do a task; *performance* means being able to perform a task in public or in a testing situation. (B) is the correct answer because the child has the ability (competence) but is not able to show performance. (A) is incorrect because the child does not demonstrate performance. The child can spell (competence), making (C) incorrect. (D) is the opposite of the correct answer.

**6. D**

Synonyms are words with similar meaning (e.g., *help/assist*), and homophones are words with the same sound but different meanings (e.g., *their/there*). The student does not have a good understanding of synonyms because she replaced *cold* with the antonym *hot*. Eliminate (A). The student is not confusing homophones with synonyms as in choice (B); instead, she is confusing synonyms (similar meaning) with antonyms (opposites). Choice (C) is incorrect because the student has not mastered either of the concepts but instead is confusing the two. (D) is the correct answer.

**7. A**

Choice (A) is the correct answer because the various sounds made by the *ough* (i.e., *uff* in *tough*, *off* in *cough*, *ow* in *plough*, and *oh* in *dough*) are exceptions to the decoding rules of phonics. (B), (C), and (D) are approaches that do not involve sounding out words.

**8. A**

The correct answer is (A) because the person has some knowledge of the word and can thus recognize it enough to possibly use it. Decoding (B) is sounding out the various phonemes in the word. A cloze activity (C) is a fill-in-the-blank activity. While a person may use context to figure out the meaning of a word (D), this strategy is not described here.

**9. D**

The cognitive domain (A) is about thinking. The social domain (B) is about interaction between people. The psychomotor domain (C) is about the physical. Choice (D) is correct because the affective domain is about a person's feelings and emotions.

**10. B**

Most children are reading by the end of second grade, so this student's competence is cause for concern. Eliminate (A) and (C). However, retention (D) should be an option to consider only after all other options have been exhausted. (B) is the correct answer.

**11. D**

While a teacher will need to place students in groups, the guided reading process involves using homogeneous ability groups, so (A) is incorrect. While giving students support (B) is a part of the process, it is not the first step. Giving students a question to answer (C) is an anticipatory step but not the first step in the guided reading process. Choice (D) is correct because the first step in the guided reading process is to determine the students' reading levels so books at the proper levels can be chosen.

**12. D**

(A), (B), and (C) would all be good uses of a bulletin board, but none of them are the primary use. Choice (D) is correct because a bulletin board should first and foremost serve as reinforcement for material being taught in the classroom.

**13. A**

Choice (A) is correct because grouping students by performance is the definition of ability grouping. *Homogeneous* means "same" and *diversity* means "different," so (B) is a nonsense term. *Heterogeneous* means "different" and *tracking* means "to place children on a track and keep them there," so (C) is likewise a nonsense term. Grade-level typing (D)

refers to placing children by chronological age, not by ability.

**14. A**

Students need guidelines when doing peer grading, so (A) is correct. Teaching students to be fair in grading products, even if they do not like each other, is an important part of the process, so (B) is out. The teacher should not actually do the grading, but the teacher should definitely stay present and guide students in their work; eliminate (C). Peer grading in groups is an excellent way for students to discuss products objectively, so (D) is incorrect.

*Mathematics*

**15. A**

A stanine of 5 is average, and 4 is slightly below average, so choice (A) is correct. Stanines are norm references, so they do not tell the teacher whether the students are failing or passing, as in choice (B). The teacher knows only that in comparison to the other students who took the test, her students scored average to just below average. Because 5 is average and 4 is below average, (C) is not correct. Stanines do not indicate grade level abilities, making (D) incorrect.

**16. B**

(B) is the correct answer because Carletta's 4 ones, 2 tens, and 1 hundred map to the digits' place values. Barbara's manipulatives (A) represent 4 ones and 12 tens; this adds up to 124 but does not indicate place value notation. Jeanne's manipulatives (D) represent 24 ones and 1 hundred; these values also sum to 124, but her choice of blocks does not indicate place value notation. Janice's manipulatives (C) represent 4 hundreds, 2 tens, and 1 red for a total of 421.

**17. D**

The student is adding the numerators and then adding the denominators. Following this pattern, his next answer will be (D).

**18. D**

Much research has been done on primary children, so (A) is incorrect. Choice (B) is out because tests are standardized against the populations who take them; thus, tests for primary grade students would be standardized and normed based on children in these grades. Standardized tests today are considered more valid than ever because measures have been taken over the years to increase and test validity. Choice (C) is incorrect. Children at this age do in fact change rapidly and may test very differently on one day than on another, so (D) is the correct choice.

### 19. A

(A) is the correct answer. Because knowledge is growing at such a rapid rate, a teacher's goal is to instruct students how to figure out how to solve a problem. Showing work and using the standard way of reaching an answer, as in choice (B), are no longer considered best practices; students should be encouraged to discover answers in ways they understand. Mental math (C) is an important part of the work done in math class because mental math is a part of everyday life. Pencil-and-paper drills (D) are still used but are definitely no longer considered the most important part of math class.

### 20. A, B, C

Choices (A), (B), and (C) represent the three most common methods of doing arithmetic. Conversion (D) is not a method of doing arithmetic.

### 21. B

Borrowing (A) is not necessary when doing addition. The student did much of the addition correctly but did fail to carry the 1 to the tens column after adding 8 and 7 to get 15, so (B) is correct. (*Regrouping* is an updated term for *carrying*.) The student used the correct operation, so (C) is not right, and subtraction (D) was not needed in this problem.

### 22. A

Students must first figure out what they are seeking before they can proceed, so (A) is the first step. Choice (B) is the second step. Writing out an equation (C) may be a part of solving the problem, or it may not, but either way it is definitely not the first step. Figuring out a similar problem (D) may help the student to understand the math, but it is not the first step in working this new problem.

### 23. B

Choice (B) supplies the correct definition of the term. Whereas higher-level algebra may involve use of algorithms, the term *algorithm* does not mean "higher-level algebra." Solving geometric proportions (C) may involve using algorithms, but the proportions are not algorithms. One may use a graphing calculator (D) to do algorithms, but again, a calculator is not the algorithm itself.

### 24. A

Mental math requires a knowledge base of facts and the ability to estimate, so (A) is correct. One does mental math without using a calculator (B). Pencil-and-paper drills (C) will not necessarily build the knowledge base students need to do mental math. Students can do mental math without having complete mastery of word problems, so (D) is incorrect.

### 25. C

Students must understand place value (A) in order to understand multidigit multiplication. Teachers should precede teaching of the algorithm by introducing multiplication in a number of ways, such as with manipulatives, skip counting (B), and area models (D), that connect prior knowledge of addition and single-digit multiplication to multidigit multiplication. However, students do not learn multiplication of decimals until they have mastered multidigit multiplication of whole numbers, making (C) correct.

### *Science*

### 26. C

Glasser's control theory is about students having control of their learning environment, so choice (C) is correct. (A), (B), and (D) describe behaviors that are not included in the theory.

### 27. C

Choices (A) and (D) would have the students apply the scientific method and get more practice performing the experiment. If the students in Group 5 did something wrong the first time, they may discover their error as they try the experiment again. Choice (B) also involves use of the scientific method and will promote deeper understanding of the science topic.

(C) is the correct answer because telling the students what they did wrong will not be as beneficial as having them try the experiment again or discuss their findings with one another.

**28. B**

The minerals contained in a rock (A) and the size and shape of a rock (C) do not determine this set of classifications. Family and genus (D) are classifications used with animals, not rocks. (B) is the correct answer because these classifications are based on how the rock was formed.

**29. A**

Choice (A) is correct because the question asks the student to make a judgment. More than one answer could be correct, based on the information in the stimulus. No evaluation of the writing (B) is called for, nor is the student asked to synthesize the material or to state a fact (C). The student is also not asked to expound on (give further explanation of) the information, so (D) is incorrect.

**30. D**

(A), (B), and (C) all describe activities that would integrate other subjects into the science topic of diabetes. (D) is the correct answer: while the subject of the proposed reading center is tangentially related to the topic, having these books available would not integrate subjects.

### Social Studies

**31. B**

A scaffold (B) provides support for students as they seek to do their own learning, and this is the approach described here. An outline (A) includes the major components with their subordinate parts organized to show the relationships. An objective (C) is the behavioral outcome of a lesson. A goal (D) is the global plan for the lesson.

**32. D**

(A), (B), and (C) all represent major components of this unit on the federal government (executive, judicial, and legislative branches). State governors

(D) do not have a constitutional connection to the branches of the federal government.

**33. D**

The teacher's strategy is for a unit within social studies and does not necessarily address integration, making (A) incorrect. Assessing previous knowledge (B) is not happening in this activity, at least not on a large scale. This is not a brainstorming activity, so (C) is out. (D) is the correct answer because in teaching the students about democracy, the teacher is having them participate in democracy; this is metacognition.

**34. C**

Instructional objectives must include measurable outcomes; understanding (A), learning (B), and enjoying (D) are not measurable. (C) is correct because one can measure whether students can identify three key outcomes of the Geneva Conventions and score the quality of their responses using a rubric.

**35. B**

(A) and (D) ask general recall questions about details concerning the Sahara Desert. (C) asks students to speculate about why people live in the region. (B) is correct because it connects how the cultural and economic practices of the Sahara's nomadic peoples are affected by the climate of the region, thus connecting all three parts of the theme: the people, the place, and the environment.

### Arts and Physical Education

**36. C**

Egocentrism (A) refers to the belief that the world centers around oneself. Reversibility (B) is the understanding of the relationship between two things and the reverse of that relationship (i.e., the box is under the bed; the bed is over the box). Cognitive balance (D) means one's view of the world agrees with one's belief system. Choice (C) is correct because in Piaget's model, assimilation is the process of invoking old skills and using them to attempt a new activity.

## 37. C

(A), (B), and (D) are all important goals of an elementary art program. (C) is the correct answer because development of a child's ability to draw accurate representations is not necessary.

## 38. D

Verbal-linguistic intelligence (A) involves a person's ability to communicate orally and with written language. Interpersonal intelligence (B) involves a person's ability to interact with others and be cognizant of another's body language and feelings. Bodily-kinesthetic intelligence (C) involves a person's ability to use the body skillfully and move easily in response to a stimulus. Choice (D), spatial intelligence, is correct because drawing and map making both involve a person's understanding of where an object is in its space and in relationship to other objects in that space.

## 39. D

Learning facts about various instruments (A) will not assess whether students can identify and distinguish the sounds of instruments. Writing a word representing a sound (B) will not assess whether the student can make the distinction when listening. Doing a group jam session will not enable the students to show they can distinguish among different instruments' sounds. (D) is the correct answer because the teacher is asking the students to identify the sound when listening to it, thereby demonstrating their ability to meet, or not meet, the objective.

## 40. A

(A) is the correct answer because times for the 100-yard dash are scored to the tenths, hundredths, and sometimes even thousandths places. Basketball scores involve whole numbers, not decimals, so eliminate (B). Counting repetitions also involves whole numbers, not decimals, so (C) is out. Setting up teams does not involve the use of decimals; (D) is incorrect.

# PRAXIS SUBJECT ASSESSMENTS

# Introducing the Subject Overviews and Question Banks

In addition to the reviews and full-length practice tests for the PLT and Elementary Education tests in this book, this section provides you with additional preparation for certain Praxis Subject Assessments. This additional preparation comes in the form of brief overviews of key English, science, social studies, and mathematics tests followed by question banks testing content knowledge related to these fields.

If you are required to take any of the tests discussed in this section, these overviews and question banks provide helpful preparatory materials.

Be aware that the question banks that follow are most appropriate for the Praxis Subject Assessments. The question banks provide a thorough review of a wide range of content, but they are not designed to resemble any single test. Rather, they test a broad cross-section of each subject area through a series of multiple-choice questions and explanations.

If you are required to take an essay-based exam in one of the subject areas covered in this section, be sure to practice your essay-writing skills in addition to reviewing the content that appears in the question banks. In that regard, the essay-writing component of the Praxis Core Writing test is useful in preparing for these tests as well.

In addition, it is recommended that you supplement your review with information from the Praxis website (**ets.org/praxis**), as test names, codes, and content are subject to change.

Good luck!

# CHAPTER SIX

# Science

In this chapter, we will cover several key science Subject Assessments. We will begin with a brief summary of the major science subject tests, outlining the content covered on each. The chapter concludes with four question banks you can use to brush up on your content knowledge and test-taking skills in biology, earth sciences, chemistry, and physics. Depending on the test you are preparing for, you may need to refer to some or all of these question banks.

## PRAXIS SCIENCE SUBJECT ASSESSMENTS

This chapter applies to you if you are taking one of the following tests:

### General Science Tests

- General Science: Content Knowledge (5435)
- Middle School Science (5440)

### Biology Test

- Biology: Content Knowledge (5235)

### Chemistry Test

- Chemistry: Content Knowledge (5245)

### Physics Test

- Physics: Content Knowledge (5265)

### Earth and Space Sciences Test

- Earth and Space Sciences: Content Knowledge (5571)

# GENERAL SCIENCE TESTS

Several Praxis Subject Assessments focus on general science. These tests pull questions from a wide range of science content areas. Consequently, much of the material covered in the four question banks at the end of this chapter applies to the general science subject tests.

## General Science: Content Knowledge (5435)

Test Format: 135 selected-response (multiple-choice) questions

Test Length: 150 minutes

Content covered:

- Scientific Methodology, Techniques, and History: 15 questions, 11 percent of the test
- Physical Sciences: 51 questions, 38 percent of the test
- Life Sciences: 27 questions, 20 percent of the test
- Earth Sciences: 27 questions, 20 percent of the test
- Science, Technology, and Society: 15 questions, 11 percent of the test

This test assesses knowledge of the broad range of science concepts covered in all four question banks at the end of this chapter. Note that the question banks contain questions with four answer choices, whereas the actual test has questions with five answer choices. Otherwise, working through the questions should give you a good sense of how general science content is tested on this exam.

## Middle School Science (5440)

Test Format: 125 selected-response (multiple-choice) questions

Time: 150 minutes

Content covered:

- Scientific Inquiry, Methodology, Techniques, and History: 15 questions, 12 percent of the test
- Basic Principles of Matter and Energy: 15 questions, 12 percent of the test
- Physical Sciences: 28 questions, 22 percent of the test
- Life Sciences: 30 questions, 24 percent of the test
- Earth and Space Sciences: 22 questions, 18 percent of the test
- Science, Technology, and Society: 15 questions, 12 percent of the test

This test covers the broad range of science concepts covered in all three question banks at the end of this chapter. Note that the question banks contain questions with four answer choices, whereas the actual test has questions with five answer choices. Otherwise, working through the questions should give you a good sense of how general science content is tested on this exam.

# BIOLOGY TEST

The test described in this section focuses on biology and life sciences. If you are required to take this test, be sure to work through the Biology question bank at the end of this chapter.

## Biology: Content Knowledge (5235)

Test Format: 150 selected-response (multiple-choice) questions

Test Length: 150 minutes

Content Covered:

- History and Nature of Science: 21 questions, 14 percent of the test
- Molecular and Cellular Biology: 30 questions, 20 percent of the test
- Genetics and Evolution: 30 questions, 20 percent of the test
- Diversity of Life; Organismal Biology: 30 questions, 20 percent of the test
- Ecology: Organisms and Environments: 24 questions, 16 percent of the test
- Science, Technology, and Social Perspectives: 15 questions, 10 percent of the test

# CHEMISTRY TEST

The test described in this section covers many of the key concepts addressed in the Chemistry question bank at the end of this chapter. If you are required to take this test, be sure to work through those questions.

## Chemistry: Content Knowledge (5245)

Test Format: 125 selected-response (multiple-choice) questions

Test Length: 150 minutes

Content Covered:

- Basic Principles of Matter and Energy; Thermodynamics: 17 questions, 14 percent of the test
- Atomic and Nuclear Structure: 15 questions, 12 percent of the test
- Nomenclature; Chemical Composition; Bonding and Structure: 19 questions, 15 percent of the test
- Chemical Reactions; Periodicity: 25 questions, 20 percent of the test
- Solutions and Solubility; Acid/Base Chemistry: 19 questions, 15 percent of the test
- Scientific Inquiry and Social Perspectives of Science: 15 questions, 12 percent of the test
- Scientific Procedures and Techniques: 15 questions, 12 percent of the test

# PHYSICS TEST

The test described in this section covers a wide range of physics content and concepts. If you are required to take this test, be sure to work through the Physics question bank at the end of this chapter.

## Physics: Content Knowledge (5265)

Test Format: 125 selected-response (multiple-choice) questions

Test Length: 150 minutes

Content Covered:

- Mechanics: 40 questions, 32 percent of the test
- Electricity and Magnetism: 24 questions, 19 percent of the test
- Optics and Waves: 16 questions, 13 percent of the test
- Heat and Thermodynamics: 15 questions, 12 percent of the test
- Modern Physics: Atomic and Nuclear Structure: 15 questions, 12 percent of the test
- Scientific Inquiry, Processes, and Social Perspectives: 15 questions, 12 percent of the test

# EARTH AND SPACE SCIENCES TEST

The test described in this section covers a wide range of content from both earth and space sciences. If you are required to take this test, be sure to work through the Earth and Space question bank at the end of this chapter.

## Earth and Space Sciences: Content Knowledge (5571)

Test Format: 125 selected-response questions

Test Length: 150 minutes

Content Covered:

- Basic Principles and Processes: 15 questions, 12 percent of the test
- Tectonics and Internal Earth Processes: 21 questions, 17 percent of the test
- Earth Materials and Surface Processes: 29 questions, 23 percent of the test
- History of the Earth and Its Life Forms: 17 questions, 14 percent of the test
- Earth's Atmosphere and Hydrosphere: 24 questions, 19 percent of the test
- Astronomy: 19 questions, 15 percent of the test

# SCIENCE QUESTION BANK

## Biology

1. The columns in the chart below (A, B, C, and D) represent four different chemical compounds. The rows represent elements that could be found in these compounds. An X indicates the presence of a particular element. Which compound could be a carbohydrate?

| Elements | Compound | | | |
|---|---|---|---|---|
| | A | B | C | D |
| Calcium | X | | | |
| Carbon | | X | | X |
| Sodium | | | | |
| Hydrogen | X | X | | X |
| Magnesium | | | X | |
| Nitrogen | | | X | X |
| Oxygen | | X | X | |

    A. A

    B. B

    C. C

    D. D

2. Which element is found in all proteins but not in all carbohydrates and lipids?

    A. Carbon

    B. Nitrogen

    C. Oxygen

    D. Hydrogen

3. Which list of molecules is arranged in order of increasing molecular size?

    A. Oxygen, starch, glucose, sucrose

    B. Sucrose, oxygen, starch, glucose

    C. Oxygen, glucose, sucrose, starch

    D. Starch, glucose, sucrose, oxygen

4. In general, plants and animals are similar in that they both

    A. change light energy into the chemical bond energy of carbohydrates

    B. use atmospheric oxygen to release the chemical bond energy of carbohydrates

    C. are able to trap light energy in the building of carbohydrates

    D. require a source of carbon dioxide to build up carbohydrates

5. Twenty-five plants were placed in each of four closed containers. All environmental conditions, such as amount of water and light, were held constant for three days. At the beginning of the investigation, the quantity of $CO_2$ in each closed container was 250 $cm^3$. The data table shows the amount of $CO_2$ remaining in each container at the end of the three days.

| Container | Temperature (C°) | $CO_2$ ($cm^3$) |
|---|---|---|
| 1 | 25 | 60 |
| 2 | 30 | 40 |
| 3 | 15 | 150 |
| 4 | 20 | 100 |

The independent variable in this investigation was the

    A. temperature.

    B. light.

    C. number of days.

    D. amount of $CO_2$ in each container at the end of the investigation.

**Questions 6–7**

For questions 6–7, choose the term from the list below that best applies to the situation described.

A. parasitism
B. commensalism
C. mutualism
D. competition

6. Plants with nitrogen-fixing bacteria in root nodules of legumes grow faster and larger than plants without them. The bacteria obtain their nourishment from the plant.

7. Two species of algae-eating turtles are introduced to the same pond. One increases in number, whereas the other decreases in number.

8. Geographers discover tundra at the equator. Which of the following must be true?

A. The tundra is located at a high altitude.
B. The temperatures must be similar to those of a rain forest.
C. Most of the land at the equator is comprised of tundra.
D. None of the above, as the finding is not possible.

9. In mitosis, distribution of one copy of each chromosome to each of the resulting cells virtually guarantees

A. reduction of the chromosome number to half of the original chromosome number.
B. formation of daughter cells with identical DNA sequences.
C. cell growth.
D. maximum cell size.

10. The molecule pictured below could be found in all the following places EXCEPT

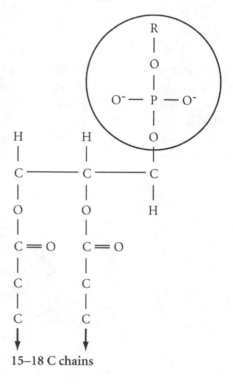

15–18 C chains

A. the nuclear membrane.
B. cell walls in fungi.
C. Golgi vesicles.
D. secretory vesicles.

11. A major difference between ectotherms and endotherms is that

A. as ambient temperature rises, ectotherms maintain nearly constant body temperature.
B. endotherms receive most of their body heat from their surroundings.
C. endotherms derive body heat from metabolic reactions and use energy derived from metabolic reactions to cool their bodies.
D. ectotherms maintain their body at lower temperatures than endotherms, therefore being described as "cold-blooded."

12. Which of the following must be true regarding a sex-linked recessive disorder that is 100 percent lethal in infancy?

   A. Females are unable to carry the recessive allele.

   B. The disease will cause death in both males and females.

   C. Male children of male carriers will also be carriers.

   D. The condition will cause death only in males.

13. In the earthworm and the grasshopper, the gizzard is an organ that increases the surface area of food for faster chemical digestion. In humans, this increase in digestible surface area is accomplished by

   A. the large intestine.

   B. the small intestine.

   C. the esophagus.

   D. teeth.

**Questions 14–15**

For questions 14–15, choose the term from the list below that best applies to the situation described.

   A. alveoli

   B. trachea

   C. nasal cavity

   D. diaphragm

14. The exchange of oxygen and carbon dioxide takes place through thin membrane walls.

15. Muscular tissue contracts to permit air to enter the lungs.

# Earth and Space Science

1. The salinity of the ocean has remained relatively constant over billions of years, even though salt-bearing minerals continue to dissolve into it through erosion processes. Which of the following processes would be most likely to contribute to the maintenance of a stable oceanic salinity?

   A. Evaporation of seawater in the open ocean

   B. Suboceanic volcanic events melting minerals deposited on the ocean floor

   C. Evaporation of "trapped" bodies of water in former inlets from the sea

   D. Coastal residue deposited by ocean currents

2. Which of the following samples would be best suited to carbon dating?

   A. Hominid skull, approximately 500,000 BCE

   B. Preserved fish skeleton fossil

   C. Living redwood tree, sample taken 3 inches from perimeter

   D. Felled redwood tree, sample taken from core

**Questions 3–4**

The city of Atlanta experiences an unusually high number of localized, intense thunderstorms that cannot be explained through classic environmental weather patterns.

3. Which of the following facts, if true, would best begin to explain the unusual number of small thunderstorms in Atlanta?

   A. Automobile exhaust in the city creates a dense, low-hanging cloud of smog.

   B. The air temperature in metropolitan Atlanta is 5–8 degrees hotter than that of the surrounding regions.

   C. The number of trees in Atlanta is significantly less than that in most other major US cities.

   D. Greenhouse gas emissions within the city of Atlanta are higher by several factors of magnitude than those of the surrounding regions.

4. Which of the following mechanisms would best explain the formation of these localized thunderstorms?

   A. Smog released in the city increases the saturation of the air, leading to an increased release of moisture.

   B. Greenhouse gases above the city of Atlanta warm the surrounding air, causing it to rise and release moisture.

   C. Warmer air from the city rises, creating a vacuum that cold air fills, creating wind. The rising warm air cools and releases moisture.

   D. The lack of trees in the city results in a higher concentration of carbon dioxide, which warms the upper atmosphere to a sufficient degree to release precipitation.

5. The flow of a large aquifer in Texas was determined by scientists to be exhibiting a slow northward flow between the years 1977 and 1997. Which of the following is the most likely explanation for this phenomenon?

   A. Water use is higher on the northern side of the aquifer than on the southern side.

   B. Inflow into the aquifer from the Gulf of Mexico has gradually pushed the body of water northward.

   C. Isostatic forces leading to a depression in the northern half of the land draw the bulk of the aquifer's water northward through simple gravity.

   D. Hotter temperatures inland cause the aquifer to evaporate at a faster rate on its northern side.

6. Rocks categorized as vesicular are characterized by tiny holes formed by gas bubbles. They are extremely porous, and some types have the unusual property of floating on water. What general type of rock would vesicular rocks be categorized as?

   A. Metamorphic

   B. Igneous

   C. Sedimentary

   D. Both metamorphic and igneous

7. Jet streams can reach speeds up to 300 miles per hour and are thousands of kilometers long. The position and strength of the jet stream generally is dependent upon temperature contrasts between different latitudes of the earth. When will jet streams tend to be the strongest?

   A. Summer

   B. Fall

   C. Winter

   D. Spring

8. Which of the following statements is NOT true of the ozone layer?

   A. The hole in the ozone layer allows ultraviolet light to pass through, significantly increasing the magnitude of global warming.

   B. Chlorofluorocarbons, the primary source of artificial ozone breakdown, remain in the atmosphere long after their initial release.

   C. The degradation of ozone molecules is necessary to achieve the ultraviolet-shielding effect of the ozone layer.

   D. Ozone breakdown is primarily caused by the chain reaction initiated by chlorine molecules.

9. Which of the following is NOT true regarding the solar system's planetary orbits?

   A. Planetary orbits can be modeled using laws formulated by Johannes Kepler.

   B. The outermost planet has the greatest eccentricity of orbit.

   C. The line joining a planet to the sun sweeps out equal areas in equal times as the planet travels around its orbit.

   D. One focus of any planetary ellipse in the solar system is always the sun.

10. Which of the following methods would be most appropriate and accurate for the dating of a dinosaur fossil?

    A. Carbon-14 dating

    B. Radioisotope dating of the fossil

    C. Radioisotope dating of surrounding rocks

    D. Age determination through the law of superposition

11. Which of the following features of the earth contains the greatest total amount of carbon dioxide by mass?

    A. Liquid oceans

    B. Polar caps

    C. The atmosphere

    D. Rain forests

12. Water's solid state is slightly less dense than its liquid state. Which of the following results would likely occur if this were not true?

    I. The earth's oceans would consist of a sheet of ice with a very thin liquid surface.

    II. The overall surface albedo of the earth would decrease.

    III. The overall size of the polar caps would decrease.

    IV. The boiling point of water would be significantly lower, leading to increased oceanic evaporation.

    A. I only

    B. I and II only

    C. II, III, and IV only

    D. III only

13. Which of the following exhibit tidal pull?

    I. Oceans

    II. Lakes

    III. Land masses

    IV. Streams

    A. I only

    B. I and II only

    C. I and III only

    D. I, II, III, and IV

14. During the crescent phase of the moon, the dim face of the rest of the moon can often be made out in addition to the brightly lit crescent portion. This phenomenon, called earthshine, is particularly common in spring months. Why is this most likely the case?

    A. The regular progression of the moon's phases ensures that the crescent phase occurs most often during spring months.

    B. The surface albedo of the earth during spring months is higher because of greater cloud cover.

    C. During spring, the earth's tilt is at a perpendicular angle to the sun, ensuring maximum reflectivity.

    D. The greater size of both polar ice caps during the spring leads to greater reflectivity.

15. Which of the following statements regarding the sun is false?

    A. The sun is constantly losing mass.

    B. Sunspots are higher in temperature than the surrounding areas of brightness.

    C. Energy release in the sun is accomplished through the fusion of hydrogen to helium atoms.

    D. Neutrinos released by the sun are nearly impossible to detect without sophisticated observational equipment.

# Chemistry

Note: when you take the Praxis Chemistry: Content Knowledge Test, you will have a Help screen available with a periodic table, necessary physical constants and some SI unit conversions. Have those resources handy before you begin this practice set.

1. A 100 g substance is known to contain 32 percent $SO_4$ by weight. Approximately how many grams of lead are required to completely convert all available $SO_4$ to $PbSO_4$?

    A. 34.5 g
    B. 69.0 g
    C. 103.5 g
    D. 169.0 g

2. The sun's core consists primarily of $^1H$ and $^4He$, as well as various other trace elements and isotopes. Which of the following statements is NOT true regarding the fusion reaction that occurs within the core?

    A. Electrons are released as a product of the fusion reaction.
    B. The mass of the products is less than the mass of the reactants in the balanced fusion equation.
    C. Six photons are emitted as a product of the fusion reaction.
    D. Four hydrogen atoms combine to form a single helium atom.

3. Lead is a critical element of most automotive batteries. These are the reactions at the negative and positive terminals of a typical battery:

    1. $Pb(s) \rightarrow PbSO_4 + 2e^-$
    2. $PbO_2(s) + SO_4^{2-} + 4H^+ + 2e^- \rightarrow PbSO_4(s) + 2H_2O$

Is the first reaction at the anode or the cathode, and does it represent oxidation or reduction?

    A. Anode, oxidation
    B. Anode, reduction
    C. Cathode, oxidation
    D. Cathode, reduction

4. A chemist performs an experiment involving the solubility between two calcium solutions.

    What will be the molar solubility of calcium fluoride ($K_{sp} = 3.9 \times 10^{-11}$) in a solution containing 0.01 M $Ca(NO_3)_2$?

    A. $3.1 \times 10^{-10}$
    B. $3.1 \times 10^{-5}$
    C. $9.8 \times 10^{-5}$
    D. $9.8 \times 10^{-10}$

5. What is the principal reason for adding acid to water in a laboratory setting, rather than adding water to acid?

    A. Adding water to acid would result in a very concentrated water-acid reaction, potentially releasing a great deal of heat and boiling the acid.
    B. Adding water to acid can skew the calculations associated with the reaction because it is simpler to titrate acid.
    C. Adding acid to water concentrates the acid within the surrounding water, preventing it from spreading too quickly and creating a runaway reaction.
    D. Adding acid to water allows the chemist to observe any resultant color changes more accurately than would be possible by adding water to acid.

6. Potassium bromide is a common anticonvulsant used in veterinary medicine. The frequently used upper guidelines for administration of the anticonvulsant recommend a 2.5-mg/mL dosage. What is the molality of a solution of KBr in which 1 liter of the full-strength medicine is diluted with an additional liter of water?

   A. 0.0084 m
   B. 0.0105 m
   C. 0.0210 m
   D. 0.058 m

7. A liter of sand is added to a liter of small rocks, yielding a final total volume of 1.8 liters. Which of these additions is most analogous to this situation?

   A. 75 mL $H_2O$ (g) + 75 mL EtOH (l)
   B. 40 mL $H_2O$ (l) + 40 mL $CH_4$ (l)
   C. 50 mL $H_2O$ (l) + 50 mL $CH_3(CH_2)_4CH_3$ (l)
   D. 60 mL $H_2O$ (l) + 60 mL EtOH (l)

8. What are the likely electronic and molecular geometric properties, respectively, of $XeF_2$?

   A. Trigonal bipyramidal, linear
   B. Linear, bent
   C. Trigonal bipyramidal, bent
   D. Bent, linear

9. Given the reaction $4NH_3 + 3O_2 \rightarrow 2N_2 + 6H_2O$ and bond enthalpies NH = 389 kJ/mol, OO = 498 kJ/mol, and NN = 941 kJ/mol, which of the following is the enthalpy of the OH bond?

   A. 67 kJ/mol
   B. 253 kJ/mol
   C. 462 kJ/mol
   D. 986 kJ/mol

10. Which of the following will act as a Lewis acid but not a Bronsted-Lowry acid?

    I. $AlCl_3$
    II. $H_2PO_4$
    III. BF
    IV. NO

    A. I only
    B. IV only
    C. I and III only
    D. II and III only

11. Which of the following is NOT true of geometric isomers?

    A. They are a subclass of diastereomers.
    B. They are mirror images around a double bond.
    C. They are not superimposable.
    D. Two geometric isomers have the same molecular formula.

12. The rate for a given reaction is dependent upon the concentrations of two compounds, A and B. Given the table below, what is the order of the reaction with respect to A and B?

| [A] | [B] | Reaction rate (mmol/L$^*$se) |
|-----|-----|------------------------------|
| 0.2 | 0.2 | 10 |
| 0.4 | 0.2 | 20 |
| 0.6 | 0.6 | 270 |

    A. 1, 1
    B. 1, 2
    C. 2, 2
    D. 1, 3

13. Which of the following is the primary function of ultraviolet spectroscopy?

   A. UV spectroscopy determines the conjugation level in a substance through selective reflection of UV rays based on bond strength.

   B. UV spectroscopy is used to determine the chemical composition of a substance through varying levels of atomic UV absorption.

   C. UV spectroscopy is used to determine conjugation level in a substance by increasing electrons to a higher energy level.

   D. UV spectroscopy is useful for determining the half-life of a substance by ionizing atoms within a given compound.

14. A reaction's spontaneity is temperature-dependent for which of the following sets of enthalpy and entropy changes?

   I.   $\Delta S = 83.0 J/K \cdot mol$; $\Delta H = -2.10 \times 10^4$ J/mol
   II.  $\Delta S = 83.0 J/K \cdot mol$; $\Delta H = 2.10 \times 10^4$ J/mol
   III. $\Delta S = -83.0 J/K \cdot mol$; $\Delta H = -2.10 \times 10^4$ J/mol
   IV.  $\Delta S = -83.0 J/K \cdot mol$; $\Delta H = 2.10 \times 10^4$ J/mol

   A. I and II only
   B. I and IV only
   C. II and III only
   D. II and IV only

15. Which substance will, when 20 mL is added to a beaker containing 50 mL of pure water at room temperature, result in the highest electric conductivity of the resulting solution?

   A. HCl
   B. HBr
   C. HI
   D. HF

## Physics

1. Scientists attempt to measure a possible new force by examining the force of two neutral particles separated by a small distance in the absence of any other known force. Based on the experimental data collected (see table below), what can we conclude about the relationship between the force in question and the distance between the objects?

| Distance between objects A and B ($10^{-13}$ m) | Measured Force on B ($\times 10^{-9}$ J) |
|---|---|
| 1.13 ± 0.02 | 3.41 ± 0.005 |
| 2.74 ± 0.02 | 0.583 ± 0.003 |
| 5.32 ± 0.03 | 0.156 ± 0.002 |
| 6.78 ± 0.04 | 0.094 ± 0.002 |
| 10.66 ± 0.05 | 0.038 ± 0.001 |

   A. They are inversely related.
   B. They are directly related.
   C. The force is inversely related to the square of the distance.
   D. No relationship can be determined from the data.

2. When electrons are in an excited state, they can fall to a lower energy state by emitting a photon with the difference in energy between the two states. This can happen spontaneously or through stimulated emission by a passing photon of the requisite energy. In a standard HeNe laser, the stimulated emission of photons is used to produce a coherent beam of light. Which of the following statements best explains why the stimulated emission of photons, instead of spontaneous emission, is necessary in the laser?

A. Stimulated emission produces photons of higher energy than those produced by spontaneous emission.

B. Stimulated emission produces photons that travel in the same direction as the photon that induces their emission.

C. Stimulated emission produces photons with longer wavelengths than those produced by spontaneous emissions.

D. Either spontaneous or stimulated emission alone would be sufficient to produce laser light.

3. The position of a particle as a function of time is given by this equation:

$$x(t) = x^3 - 4x^2 + 3$$

Starting from $t = 0$, where would the particle have both a positive velocity and acceleration?

A. $t > 0$

B. $0 < t < 1.33$

C. $t > 1.33$

D. $t > 3$

4. An object at rest with the shape of an equilateral triangle is subject to three external forces, as shown in the diagram. If the object does not exhibit translational motion, what must $F$ and $\theta$ be, respectively?

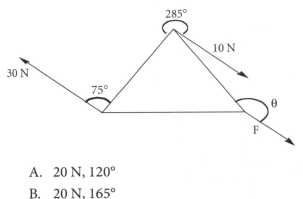

A. 20 N, 120°

B. 20 N, 165°

C. 10 N, 120°

D. 10 N, 165°

5. Two cylinders, one a hollow copper pipe and the other a solid plastic tube, are placed on an inclined ramp and released from the same height. Assuming both cylinders roll without slipping, what can we say about the resulting motion?

A. Both reach the bottom of the ramp at the same time.

B. The copper pipe reaches the bottom of the ramp first.

C. The plastic tube reaches the bottom of the ramp first.

D. It cannot be determined from the information given which cylinder will reach the bottom of the ramp first.

6. Two identical rockets of length 20 m (as measured on earth) are in outer space. If rocket A is at rest and rocket B passes by at a speed of 0.5c, what is the length of rocket B as measured by the astronauts in rocket A?

   A. 17.3 m

   B. 20 m

   C. 23.1 m

   D. 28.3 m

7. If the earth's orbit around the sun has a radius of $1.5 \times 10^{11}$ m and a period of 1 year, approximately what is the period of Mars's orbit if it has a radius of $2.3 \times 10^{11}$ m?

   A. 0.55 years

   B. 1 year

   C. 1.5 years

   D. 1.9 years

8. If oxygen has a molecular weight of 32 g/mol and hydrogen has a molecular weight of 2 g/mol, what is the ratio of the rms speed of an oxygen atom to a hydrogen atom if both are at 300 K?

   A. 1:1

   B. 1:2

   C. 1:4

   D. 1:16

9. A turbine in a steam power plant has an efficiency that is 80 percent of the ideal Carnot engine efficiency. The turbine works by condensing water vapor at 520°C into water at 100°C. How much energy does the turbine require in order to produce 50 MJ of usable energy?

   A. 94 MJ

   B. 118 MJ

   C. 212 MJ

   D. 6,250 MJ

10. Suppose a wire of length 2.0 m is conducting a current of 5.0 A toward the top of the page and through a 30 Gauss ($1 \text{ T} = 10^4$ G) uniform magnetic field directed into the page (see diagram below). What are the magnitude and direction of the magnetic force on the wire?

    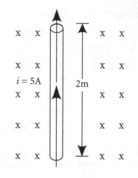

    A. 300 N toward the left

    B. 300 N into the page

    C. 0.03 N toward the right

    D. 0.03 N toward the left

11. The plates of a capacitor are originally separated by a vacuum. If a dielectric $K > 1$ is introduced between the plates of the capacitor, and the capacitor is allowed to charge up, which of the following statements is/are true?

    I. The capacitance of the capacitor will increase.

    II. The voltage across the capacitor plates will increase.

    III. The charge stored on the capacitor will increase.

    A. I only

    B. I and II

    C. II and III

    D. I and III

12. A hydrogen atom is in its first excited state ($n = 2$). How many associated angular momentum states does the atom have?

    A. Two states, corresponding to one vertical and one horizontal

    B. Three states, corresponding to the orientation in space of the angular momentum

    C. Three states, corresponding to the three possible spin states

    D. Four states, corresponding to $n^2$

13. An 8 kg bowling ball rolls down a hill (height = 10 m) and collides elastically with an identical bowling ball at rest. If the moment of inertia for a spherical object is $\frac{2}{5}Mr^2$ and the diameter of the bowling ball is 20 cm, what is the speed of the second bowling ball after the collision?

    A. 5.8 m/s

    B. 6.9 m/s

    C. 11.8 m/s

    D. 14 m/s

14. The cornea in a human eye acts like a lens, focusing the incoming light on the retina. The retina lies approximately 1.8 cm behind the iris. What can we say about the human eye?

    A. It acts like a convergent lens with an inverted image on the retina.

    B. It acts like a convergent lens with an upright image on the retina.

    C. It acts like a divergent lens with an inverted image on the retina.

    D. It acts like a divergent lens with an upright image on the retina.

15. An airplane wing is constructed so as to minimize turbulent flow over the wing and ensure that the air flowing over the top surface of the wing travels a greater distance in a given amount of time than the air flowing over the bottom wing surface. Why does such a design generate a lift force when air flows over the top and bottom wing surfaces?

    A. The velocity of the air on the top surface is greater than the velocity of the air on the bottom surface.

    B. The velocity of the air on the top surface is less than the velocity of the air on the bottom surface.

    C. The density of the air on the top surface is less than the density of the air on the bottom surface.

    D. The density of the air on the top surface is greater than the density of the air on the bottom surface.

# ANSWERS AND EXPLANATIONS

## Science Question Bank

### Biology

**1.  B**

The word *carbohydrate* literally means "carbon and water." All carbohydrates therefore contain only carbon, C, and water, $H_2O$.

**2.  B**

Carbohydrates and lipids contain only carbon, hydrogen, and oxygen. Carbohydrates contain these three elements in the ratio of 1 carbon to 1 water ($CH_2O$), whereas lipids contain much less oxygen relative to the other two elements. Proteins contain carbon, hydrogen, and oxygen but also contain nitrogen in a chemical group called an amino group.

**3.  C**

Glucose, sucrose, and starch are all carbohydrates that contain the element oxygen. Therefore, oxygen is the smallest of the four choices. Of the three carbohydrates listed, glucose is a monosaccharide, sucrose is a disaccharide, and starch is a polysaccharide. As the names indicate, disaccharides are made up of two monosaccharides, and polysaccharides are made up of many monosaccharides.

**4.  B**

Plants are unique and vitally important to life on our planet because they have the ability to capture light energy and build high-energy macromolecules from atmospheric carbon dioxide. Animals must eat to receive their high-energy macromolecules. But both plants and animals need to break down the macromolecules to use their energy for cell functions. This process is called cellular respiration and requires atmospheric oxygen.

**5.  A**

The amount of light, the number of days, and the initial levels of $CO_2$ were constant for all plants. The amount of $CO_2$ at the end of the investigation was the dependent variable. The experimenter varied the temperature for each plant across the four containers of plants.

**6.  C**

The terms listed in the key refer to various ways in which organisms interact with one another. The first three terms fall into the category of symbiosis, which means two organisms existing in a continually intimate way. In each of the relationships, at least one of the organisms benefits. In parasitism, the benefit comes to the detriment of the other organism. In commensalism, the benefit comes with negligible effect to the other organism. In mutualism, both organisms benefit from the relationship.

**7.  D**

*Competition* refers to two organisms vying for the same resources. The statements indicate that the turtles are in competition with one another. One of the species is using the existing resources in abundance and therefore increasing in number. The other species is left with fewer resources and is not reproducing at an adequate rate.

**8.  A**

A distinguishing characteristic of tundra is an average monthly temperature near 10°C. Near the equator, such temperatures occur at high altitudes. Remember that there are glaciers in the Andes located on the equator.

**9.  B**

The term *mitosis* is often used interchangeably with *cell division*. Technically, mitosis is the process of chromosomal replication that results in two daughter nuclei with identical DNA sequences. Because of this process, all of the cells in your body contain the same DNA, even though you started out as one cell. Sexually reproducing organisms undergo another cellular replication that happens in sex cells. This process is called meiosis.

## 10. B

The molecule pictured is a phospholipid found in all membranes that make up cells and their organelles. Because secretory and Golgi vesicles derive from the membranes of organelles, they too are made of phospholipids. The only structure listed that is not made of lipid, but rather of the amino sugar chitin, is the chitinous cell wall of fungi.

## 11. C

The major difference between endo- and ectotherms comes not from the temperature at which either type of organism maintains its body but rather from the source of body heat that each type of organism uses. Ectotherms derive most of their body heat from the surrounding environment—surrounding temperature is termed the *ambient temperature*. However, endotherms can use metabolic reactions to generate body heat or cool themselves off, keeping their body temperature fairly constant.

## 12. D

Recall that a sex-linked (or X-linked) allele is carried on the X-chromosome and can be passed from fathers to daughters only and from mothers to both sons and daughters. An early-acting lethal disease will kill all males in infancy because males can never carry a pair of sex-linked alleles (they have only one X chromosome). Because of this, there will be no males of reproductive age to pass along the allele to daughters, so only female carriers, who will pass the allele to 50 percent of their sons and daughters, can pass on the disease. A female can never be homozygous because she could never have received an allele from her father (males don't survive past infancy with the disease).

## 13. D

Teeth are responsible for the mechanical breakdown of food, just like the gizzard in some organisms. Mechanical digestion begins in the mouth, where food is chopped into bits by the teeth so that enzymes in the stomach and small intestine can work more quickly and effectively.

## 14. A

The alveoli are the location for the exchange of oxygen and carbon dioxide at the lungs. It is here, in these grape-like clusters, that gas exchange takes place between the lungs and the blood through thin membranes.

## 15. D

The diaphragm is a muscular band of tissue that contracts to permit air to enter the lungs. As the diaphragm contracts, the pressure in the chest cavity decreases, and air rushes in through the nose or mouth. As the diaphragm relaxes, pressure in the chest cavity returns to normal, and air is pushed out.

### *Earth and Space Science*

## 1. C

This question requires critical thinking both in understanding the information given in the question and in analyzing the answers. If minerals continue to dissolve in the ocean, yet its salinity and its volume remain relatively constant, there must be a process that removes minerals as well. Evaporation (A) would not work because the minerals would be left in the ocean as the water evaporated. Likewise, (B) and (D) provide less-than-convincing mechanisms. If, however, "pieces" of ocean are trapped and evaporate completely, leaving dried beds (such as the salt plains in the Western United States), the overall mineral content of the oceans - and hence, their salinity - will remain constant.

## 2. D

The key to answering this question is to remember that carbon dating is only useful for dating relatively recent samples that do in fact contain carbon from the atmosphere. The first two answer choices, being fossils, will not contain significant amounts of carbon. Furthermore, remember that oceanic creatures and those that feed primarily upon them are unreliable for carbon dating because of carbon variations in the ocean. Given the two remaining answer choices, remember that trees grow by adding layers to the outside. Therefore, the most accurate determination of a tree's age will come from its core, and the answer is (D).

**3. B**

Thunderstorms are created when warm air rises, cools, and releases precipitation because of its reduced capacity to hold moisture. Therefore, the fact that Atlanta is significantly warmer than the surrounding regions means that cool air pushes the warmer air up, which in turn cools and causes precipitation.

**4. C**

This is a "gimme" question if the mechanism has been predicted in the last question. The other answers can also be eliminated as mechanisms that might contribute to overall global warming or environmental effects but would not cause the localized effects observed in Atlanta.

**5. A**

Aquifers generally display movement based on the direction that water is draining. In heavily populated areas or areas that use a particular aquifer heavily, the water is being drained through the extensive use of wells. Therefore, a general northward flow of a large aquifer usually indicates that water is being drawn from above the northern portion of that aquifer. Answer choices such as (D) can be eliminated easily, as evaporation is not a significant factor for a subterranean aquifer.

**6. B**

It is not necessary to be familiar with the type of rock mentioned in the question to answer the question. Consider that gas bubbles would occur in areas of high heat. Thus, the correct answer can be quickly deduced to be igneous. Moreover, the pressures associated with metamorphic rock would surely not allow for a rock of low enough density to float on water.

**7. C**

Again, this is a question for which it is important to ask what is being tested. The information about jet streams serves only to set up the fact that they are strongest when temperature contrasts between different latitudes are the most pronounced. This is

the case when a given hemisphere is tilted away from the sun - i.e. during that hemisphere's winter season. In winter, the more extreme latitudes will receive far less sunlight than more central latitudes (compare New York to Miami in winter versus summer). The question is ultimately less about meteorology and more about earth-sun systems.

**8. A**

This question can be answered either by recognizing a statement that is incorrect or by getting rid of everything you know to be true, whichever is more efficient. Choice (A) articulates the common misconception that the ozone layer contributes to global warming, when in fact the two are not related.

**9. B**

Elimination is likely the fastest way to answer this question. The last two answer choices are an expansion on the first; they are paraphrases of Kepler's first two laws. Specific knowledge about Mercury might also help to narrow the answer choice down to (B), as Mercury has the most eccentric orbit of any of the planets.

**10. C**

For the reasons described in the previous dating question, (A) is out immediately. Whereas the law of superposition might be useful for determining a general age, it will not be as accurate as radioactive dating. Radioactive dating of the rocks surrounding the fossil will be more accurate than dating of the fossil itself because the fossil's composition has not been stable for long enough that radioactive isotopes can be used with confidence.

**11. A**

The oceans are the largest reservoir of carbon dioxide on earth, containing many, many times more carbon dioxide than the atmosphere.

**12. A**

The critical aspect of water is that liquid water is denser than solid water, allowing ice to float to the top of oceans. If this were not the case, ice would settle to the bottom, and eventually, only a thin upper layer of water would be warmed sufficiently to be liquid. If ice did sink, surface albedo would increase from the increase in ice, and the polar caps would increase in size commensurately. The difference between the states will not affect the overall boiling point of the water. When encountering a tough answer choice to evaluate, remember to think about overall trends. The trend associated with a heavier solid state would be an ice planet, which is the opposite of what would happen with a lower boiling point.

### 13. D

In fact, everything exhibits tidal pull, which is caused by the difference in the moon's and sun's gravities on one side of the earth as opposed to the other. In smaller masses, the difference is less pronounced, and so in anything less massive than oceans, such as lakes, or with less liquid than oceans (such as rock), the difference is barely noticeable. Lake Michigan, for example, has a tide of approximately half an inch to an inch and a half daily.

### 14. B

The dim outline of the moon can be inferred to be caused not directly by the sun itself, but rather by the reflection of light from the earth off the moon and back again to earth. This reflection will be greatest when the amount of light reflected off the earth is the greatest. Whereas all answer choices but (A) discuss reflectivity, only (B) offers a mechanism that does not contradict fact.

### 15. B

This question can be attacked by elimination, although it may be quicker to look for an answer that clearly jumps out as false. Sunspots are in fact darker because of their lower temperature. It is important to remember that the area just around sunspots is particularly bright and hot, far hotter than the normal surface of the sun. This might lead some to be confused and think that the entire sunspot is higher in temperature, but in fact, just the outer rim of the sunspot is higher in temperature.

## Chemistry

### 1. B

If the 100 g substance contains 32 percent $SO_4$, then there are 32 g of the compound to react with the lead. Calculate the molar weight of $SO_4$ as 96, which means that there is one-third mol in the substance. Lead will react with it in a 1:1 ratio, which means that a third of a mol of lead is required. A quick check on the periodic table and division by 3 will result in a mass of lead of 69.0 g.

### 2. A

Electrons are in fact required for the fusion reaction, which makes sense because the hydrogen is being converted into helium. In fact, the core of the sun is so hot that any electrons around atoms are stripped away. The remaining three answers are all properties of the standard fusion reaction.

### 3. A

Don't be thrown off by the long equation; this can be made very simple. Because the first reaction is releasing electrons, it is by definition an oxidation. Further, the anode always contains the oxidation half-reaction, so the answer must be (A). Note that (A) and (D) are the only meaningful answers; the others can be eliminated even without reading the equation.

### 4. B

This problem requires a bit more calculation than the ones before. The key to solving this problem is to recognize that it is a common ion problem. Because the solution already contains a large number of calcium ions, the amount of calcium added will be small enough to be neglected in calculations. The equation should be set up like this:

$$3.9 \times 10^{-11} = [Ca^{2+}][F^-]^2 = (x + 0.010)(2x)^2$$
$$3.9 \times 10^{-11} = (0.010)(2x)^2$$
$$x^2 = \frac{3.9 \times 10^{-11}}{4(0.010)} = 9.8 \times 10^{-10}$$
$$x = 3.1 \times 10^{-5} \text{ M}$$

**5. A**

This is a standard laboratory safety question. Acid is always added to water so as to dilute the acid as it reacts. If water were added to acid, the concentration of acid around the water would result in a possibly violent reaction. Recall that the combination of water and acid is exothermic, and the acid might spill outside the vial as it boils.

**6. B**

If 1 L of the full dose is used in 2 L of water, 2,500 mg, or 2.5 g, will be present in the solution. The mols must be calculated next. Because KBr has a molar weight of 119 g/mol, 0.0210 mols are present. Dividing by the 2 kg of water yields the molality: 0.0105 m.

**7. D**

Recall that certain substances, when mixed together, will "fall between the cracks" much as sand does through rocks. If the substances are immiscible liquids, this will not happen. Therefore, answers (B) and (C) can be eliminated, as mixing water with a hydrocarbon will not yield a high level of miscibility. Answers (A) and (D) are identical except for states; water is a gas in (A) and so cannot be miscible with the liquid EtOH.

**8. A**

The best way to answer this question is to draw a quick Lewis diagram, consulting the periodic table to ensure accuracy. Xenon will have three empty spaces containing three lone pair electron groups in addition to the two fluorines that it binds. To determine the electronic geometry, the three lone pair groups must be taken into account in addition to the fluorines. Having five groups around the central xenon will result in trigonal bipyramidal geometry. The two fluorine atoms are all that need be considered along with the xenon atom in the molecular geometry; they will oppose each other and will not bend because of the presence of the three equatorial lone pair groups, resulting in a linear geometry.

**9. C**

This problem can be solved by calculating the bond energies on each side of the equation, but such a time-consuming process should drive you to search for a quicker way. The bond enthalpy of OH should be greater than that of NH, as oxygen is more electronegative than is hydrogen. Everything below the bond energy of NH can be eliminated, getting rid of (A) and (B). The enthalpy of OH will also be lower than the strong oxygen double bond, so everything above that enthalpy can be eliminated. (C) is all that remains. Always be on the lookout for a conceptual way to answer a tough question.

**10. C**

Remember that Lewis acids act as electron acceptors. A Lewis acid can be a Bronsted-Lowry acid as well, but it must have hydrogen ions to donate. Both I and III are frequently used Lewis acids, neither of which has a proton to donate. Notice that IV is not an acid at all, whereas II is a Bronsted-Lowry acid. As a side note, make sure you are familiar with diprotic acids such as $H_2PO_4$; many questions will test your ability to recognize that these compounds can contribute two hydrogen ions.

**11. B**

Geometric isomers are a subclass of stereoisomers, with all the accompanying implications, knocking out (A), (C), and (D). Whereas geometric isomers do deal with double bonds, stereoisomers are not mirror images, and neither, consequently, can geometric isomers be mirror images.

**12. B**

The easiest place to start is with compound A, because B's concentration is held constant in the first two rows of data. Because the rate of the reaction doubles when the concentration of A does, the order with respect to A must be linear, or 1. B is a little trickier. Look at the last two rows of the table. Because an increase in A from 0.4 to 0.6 M should increase the reaction rate from 20 to 30 by virtue of the order we just calculated, any further increase in reaction rate must be caused by B. Therefore, as B increases threefold in concentration from 0.2 to 0.6 M, the reaction rate increases from 30 to 270, by a factor of 9. Be careful not to jump to the conclusion that the order of the reaction with respect to B is 3, though; we are taking an exponent rather than multiplying. 3 squared gives us 9, meaning that the order of the reaction with respect to B must be 2.

## 13. C

UV spectroscopy is primarily used to determine conjugation within a substance, and it does this by absorbing the rays and increasing electrons to a higher level.

## 14. C

The Gibbs free energy equation will be helpful here. It is $\Delta G = \Delta H - T\Delta S$, and can show whether a reaction will be spontaneous or not. A reaction is spontaneous when $\Delta G$ is negative and nonspontaneous when $\Delta G$ is positive. You need to determine which of the Roman numeral situations depend on the value of $T$ to determine whether $\Delta G$ is negative or positive. $T$ is the temperature in Kelvin, so it will always be positive. Analyze the four Roman numerals using the signs of the elements involved:

I. $\Delta G = (-) - T(+)$. A negative minus a positive. $\Delta G$ will always be negative.

II. $\Delta G = (+) - T(+)$. A positive minus a positive. $\Delta G$'s sign will depend on $T$.

III. $\Delta G = (-) - T(-)$. A negative minus a negative. $\Delta G$'s sign will depend on $T$.

IV. $\Delta G = (+) - T(-)$. A positive minus a negative. $\Delta G$ will always be positive.

Thus, the sign of $\Delta G$ in II and III depends on the value of $T$—the reaction's spontaneity is temperature-dependent only when changes in both enthalpy and entropy are either positive or negative. The correct answer is (C).

## 15. C

This question is essentially asking in a complicated way for the strongest acid. The highest electric conductivity will result from the solution that has the highest degree of ionization. Because each of these compounds consists of a halide and hydrogen ion, high dissociation will by definition be equivalent to high acidity. The less electronegative the atom holding the hydrogen, the more easily the hydrogen ion will escape into the surrounding solution. Iodine, being the largest halide, will be least able to hold on to the hydrogen ion. This acid, incidentally, is rarely seen in laboratory use because of its high cost.

## Physics

## 1. C

This problem can be Backsolved by testing the answer choices. First, eliminate (B) since the force gets smaller as the distance gets larger. Second, use the formula $F = \dfrac{x}{r}$, with $x$ representing an unknown constant, and plug in the pairs of force and distance from the chart. If $x$ is a constant for all pairs, then we have an inverse relationship. Since $x$ is NOT constant, eliminate (A). Try $F = \dfrac{x}{r^2}$, which gives an approximate value of $x = 4.34$ for all pairs. This result shows that (C) is the correct response.

## 2. B

Stimulated emission is necessary because it produces identical photons with the same energy, direction, and wavelength as the original photon. The result is a coherent beam of light.

We can eliminate (A) and (C) because stimulated and spontaneous emission both produce photons with the same energy and wavelength. (D) is incorrect because without the stimulated emission, the photons produced would have every possible direction, and thus no coherent beam would be created.

## 3. D

The first derivative of the equation yields the velocity: $v(t) = 3x^2 - 8x$. The second derivative gives us acceleration: $a(t) = 6x - 8$.

The equations do not need to be solved exactly—try some possible numbers based on the answer choices. At $t = 0.5$, both equations are negative—eliminate (A). At $t = 1$, both equations are negative—eliminate (B). At $t = 2$, the velocity is negative—eliminate (C).

## 4. B

It is not necessary to break the forces down into their $x - y$ components. Start by finding the angles based upon the fact that an equilateral triangle has 60° angles at each corner. From this, we get the fact that the 30 N force is antiparallel to the 10 N force. So we need a force of 20 N parallel to the 10 N force: eliminate (C) and (D). The correct $\theta$ that makes $F$ parallel to the 10 N force is 165°.

**5. C**

When rolling down the ramp, the objects will gain rotational kinetic energy $\left(E = \frac{1}{2}I\Omega^2\right)$ as well as translational kinetic energy $\left(E = \frac{1}{mv^2}\right)$. The gravitational potential energy is converted into both forms of kinetic energy, and the object with less rotational energy will thereby have a greater translational energy and a higher translational velocity, thus reaching the bottom first. The solid plastic tube will have more mass closer to its center, which equates to a smaller moment of inertia, $I$. So the plastic tube has less rotational energy and greater translational energy, and it reaches the bottom first.

**6. A**

According to special relativity, an observer in a stationary inertial frame will measure the length of a moving frame to be *shorter* by a factor of $\frac{1}{\gamma} = \gamma\left(1 - \frac{v^2}{c^2}\right)$. From this, we can eliminate (B), (C), and (D) since they are longer than the rest length. We could also do the actual calculation to prove (A) is correct:

$$L\gamma = 20\sqrt{1 - \frac{v^2}{c^2}} = 20\sqrt{1 - 0.5^2} = 20\sqrt{0.75} = 17.3 \text{ m}$$

**7. D**

Use Kepler's third law: the square of the period of any planet is proportional to the cube of the radius of its orbit. So $\frac{T_E^2}{r_E^3} = \frac{T_M^2}{r_M^3}$, where $T$ is the period.

Plugging in the numbers from the problem gives us

$$T_M^2 = \frac{1 \cdot \left(2.3 \cdot 10^{11}\right)^3}{\left(1.5 \cdot 10^{11}\right)^3} \approx 3.6. \text{ Therefore, } T_M \approx 1.9$$

years.

**8. C**

The kinetic theory of gases states that $\frac{1}{2}mv^2 = \frac{3}{2}kT$. Since the gases are at the same temperature, they must have the same kinetic energy per atom:

$$\frac{1}{2}m_Hv_H^2 = \frac{1}{2}m_Ov_O^2$$

Which leads to $\frac{v_O}{v_H} = \sqrt{\frac{m_H}{m_O}} = \sqrt{\frac{2}{32}} = \frac{1}{4}$.

**9. B**

Start with the efficiency of a Carnot engine: $\frac{(T_H - T_C)}{T_H}$ and remember to use temperature in Kelvin (K = °C + 273):

$$\frac{(793 - 373)}{793} = 0.53$$

The turbine then has an efficiency of 0.8 × 0.53 = 0.424. So to create 50 MJ of usable energy, the turbine will require $\frac{50}{0.424} = 118$ MJ of energy; (B) is the correct answer.

**10. D**

The magnetic force on a wire is given by $F = il \times B$. The direction is given by the right-hand rule. Since the current is perpendicular to the magnetic field, the magnitude of the force is given by $ilB = (5 \text{ A})(2 \text{ m})(3 \times 10^{-3} \text{ T}) = 0.03$ N. The right-hand rule gives the direction: to the left.

**11. D**

The purpose of a dielectric is to increase the capacitance of a capacitor, so the correct answer must include statement I—eliminate (C). But the voltage across a capacitor depends only upon the circuit it is in, so the voltage will not change—eliminate (B). Finally, recall that capacitance is defined as the ratio of charge to voltage, so increasing capacitance without changing the voltage must mean an increase in the charge—the correct answer is (D).

## 12. B

In general, for the primary quantum number $n$, there are $l = 0, 1, (n - 1)$ orbital quantum numbers. For each $l$, there are $m_l = 0, \pm 1, \pm 2, \pm l$ magnetic quantum numbers. For $n = 2$, we have $l = 1$ and $m_l = 0, \pm 1$. The orbital angular momentum states, given by $m_l$, represent the three possible orientations of the angular momentum with respect to the $z$-axis: up, down, and zero. (B) is correct.

## 13. C

This problem involves energy conservation to calculate the velocity of the first ball at the bottom of the ramp and then momentum conservation during the collision.

Using $mgh = \dfrac{1}{2}mv^2 + \dfrac{1}{2}I\Omega^2$ with $I = \dfrac{2}{5}Mr^2$ and

$\Omega = \dfrac{v}{r}$ yields $mgh = \dfrac{1}{2}mv^2 + \dfrac{1}{5}mv^2$ and

$$v = \sqrt{\left(\frac{10}{7}\right)gh} = \sqrt{\left(\frac{10}{7}\right)(9.8)(10\,m)} = 11.8\frac{m}{s}$$

This is the speed of the first ball at the bottom of the ramp. But since the second ball is identical to the first and the collision is elastic, you should recognize that the result of the collision will be to transfer all of the linear velocity to the second ball. Thus, the correct answer is (C).

## 14. A

Only converging lenses produce real images, a process necessary for the human eye. We can therefore eliminate (C) and (D). And since the eye focuses on the object, we think of the diagram in which the object is placed at the focal length, resulting in an inverted image. Choice (A) is correct.

## 15. A

The information in the question allows us to conclude that the air on the top of the wing must travel at a higher velocity than the air below. The density of air will not change on either surface, so we can eliminate (C) and (D). Remember that the faster a fluid moves, the less pressure it offers. Combine this information with the fact that we want less pressure on top of the wing, and you see that (A) is the correct answer.

# CHAPTER SEVEN

# English Language Arts

In this chapter, we will cover several key English language arts Subject Assessments. We will begin with a brief summary of the major English language arts tests, outlining the content covered on each. The chapter concludes with a question bank that will allow you to brush up on your content knowledge and test-taking skills in English language arts.

## PRAXIS ENGLISH LANGUAGE ARTS SUBJECT ASSESSMENTS

This chapter applies to you if you are taking one of the following tests:

- English Language Arts: Content Knowledge (5038)
- English Language Arts: Content and Analysis (5039)

Several Praxis Subject Assessments target English language arts. These tests pull questions from a wide range of English content areas, with a special emphasis on literature, English language, composition, and rhetoric as well as the best practices for teaching each. Consequently, much of the material covered in the English Language Arts question bank at the end of this chapter applies to the English subject tests. Be advised that the question bank focuses primarily on content knowledge, making only some reference to pedagogy. Nonetheless, the content covered provides a solid review of this broad and varied subject.

### English Language Arts: Content Knowledge (5038)

Test Format: 130 selected-response (multiple-choice) questions

Test Length: 150 minutes

Content covered:

- Reading: 49 questions, 38 percent of the test
- Language Use and Vocabulary: 33 questions, 25 percent of the test
- Writing, Speaking, and Listening: 48 questions, 37 percent of the test

This test covers the knowledge and skills a beginning secondary school English language arts teacher needs to master. As identified in the list above, three broad categories are tested. Reading questions assess your knowledge of comprehending and teaching both literature and nonfiction texts. For instance, you may be asked to identify an author/work, classify a piece by literary genre, determine the central idea or argument of a provided passage, recognize the evidence or writing devices an author uses to make a point, or identify an effective reading comprehension strategy. Next, Language Use and Vocabulary questions assess your ability to use conventional written English and determine word meanings, as well as how to teach these skills to students. For instance, you may be asked to identify a grammar error, explain the structure of a sentence, or assess strategies for effectively teaching students vocabulary. Finally, Writing, Speaking, and Listening questions assess your knowledge of effective techniques for written and oral communication, as well as your understanding of how to best teach these strategies to students. For instance, you may be asked to identify strategies for writing for varying purposes, explain effective speaking strategies, recognize proper research methods, or identify effective teaching and assessment methods for writing and speaking.

Working through the question bank that follows should give you a good sense of how English language arts content is tested on this exam. In preparation for this test, it is also advisable to review the Praxis Core Writing chapter and the Principles of Learning and Teaching chapter. Both chapters contain topics—such as writing/grammar rules and pedagogy—that are applicable to teaching English language arts and that are assessed on these Subject Assessments.

## English Language Arts: Content and Analysis (5039)

Test Format: 130 selected-response (multiple-choice) questions, 2 constructed-response (essay) questions

Test Length: 180 minutes (150 minutes for selected-response section, 30 minutes for constructed-response section)

Content covered:

- Reading: 48 selected-response questions and 1 constructed-response question, 40 percent of the test
- Language Use and Vocabulary: 33 selected-response questions, 19 percent of the test
- Writing, Speaking, and Listening: 49 selected-response questions and 1 constructed-response question, 41 percent of the test

The selected-response portion of this test assesses the same three question categories as does the English Language Arts: Content Knowledge test above. The primary difference is the addition of two constructed-response questions, which together account for 25 percent of your total score and will measure your ability to analyze literature and rhetorical features. One constructed-response question is associated with the Reading portion of the test; it will ask you to analyze a short literature passage, perhaps by explaining its central idea and rhetorical devices. The other constructed-response question, associated with the Writing, Speaking, and Listening portion of the test, will ask you to analyze the development of an argument in a provided essay.

# ENGLISH QUESTION BANK

## Praxis English

1. Proverbs are hard to define, but one could do worse than the pithy definition offered by an 18th-century British statesman, Lord John Russell. A proverb, Russell is said to have remarked at breakfast, is "one man's wit and all men's wisdom." Proverbs have been identified in all the world's spoken languages, and—unlike Lord Russell's adage—they are almost always anonymous. Interestingly, similar sayings seem to have developed independently in many parts of the world. For example, the English saying "A bird in the hand is worth two in the bush" has counterparts in Romania, Spain, and Iceland.

   Which of the following best expresses the author's attitude toward Lord Russell's definition of a proverb?

   A. Dismissive
   B. Skeptical
   C. Favorable
   D. Exuberant

2. Arthur Miller's play *Death of a Salesman* has been called a "tragedy of the common man" because it

   A. depicts an important person's fall from grace
   B. fits Aristotle's formal definition of tragedy
   C. gives an ordinary salesperson's life weight and meaning
   D. is written in a poetic and serious style

3. Which outline correctly organizes and categorizes information pertaining to the work of William Shakespeare?

   A. **I. Plays**
      a) Tragedies
      1) *King Lear...*
      b) Histories
      1) *Richard III...*
      c) Comedies
      1) *Twelfth Night...*
      **II. Poems**

   B. **I. Plays**
      a) Tragedies
      1) *Hamlet...*
      b) Poems
      1) *My Mistress' Eyes...*
      c) Comedies
      1) *All's Well That Ends Well...*
      **II. Histories**

   C. **I. Plays**
      a) Tragedies
      1) Comedies
      b) Histories
      1) *Henry V*
      c) Poems
      1) *Not Marble nor the Gilded Monuments...*
      **II. The Tempest**

   D. **I. Plays**
      a) Tragedies
      1) *Hamlet...*
      b) Histories
      1) *King Lear...*
      c) Comedies
      1) *Titus Andronicus...*
      **II. Poems**

4. Which of the following is an example of the "slippery slope" fallacy?

A. "Of course you oppose divorce; you're a priest."

B. "I admit I cheated on the test—but half the class did, too."

C. "God must exist, because the Bible says so, and the Bible was written by God."

D. "If you allow the government to censor the Internet today, it will be banning books tomorrow."

**Questions 5–6** are based on the following excerpt from Mary Shelley's *Frankenstein*.

As the night advanced, a fierce wind arose from the woods and quickly dispersed the clouds that had loitered in the heavens; the blast tore along like a mighty avalanche
(5) and produced a kind of insanity in my spirits that burst all bounds of reason and reflection. I lighted the dry branch of a tree and danced with fury around the devoted cottage, my eyes still fixed on the western
(10) horizon, the edge of which the moon nearly touched. A part of its orb was at length hid, and I waved my brand; it sank, and with a loud scream I fired the straw, and heath, and bushes, which I had collected. The wind
(15) fanned the fire, and the cottage was quickly enveloped by the flames, which clung to it and licked it with their forked and destroying tongues. . . .
And now, with the world before me,
(20) whither should I bend my steps? I resolved to fly far from the scene of my misfortunes; but to me, hated and despised, every country must be equally horrible. At length the thought of you crossed my mind. I
(25) learned from your papers that you were my father, my creator; and to whom could I apply with more fitness than to him who had given me life? . . . Unfeeling, heartless creator! You had endowed me
(30) with perceptions and passions and then cast me abroad an object for the scorn and horror of mankind.

5. The narrator of this passage is

A. Victor

B. Elizabeth

C. the monster

D. the author

6. "A part of its orb was at length hid, and I waved my brand; it sank, and with a loud scream I fired the straw, and heath, and bushes, which I had collected."

Which of the following is a correct restatement of the above?

A. "When my branding iron sank, I screamed and shot at the bushes."

B. "When the moon set, I screamed and burned the cottage."

C. "When I could not find the orb, I screamed and kicked at the straw and the bushes."

D. "I waited until the sun set, and then I screamed and set fire to the forest."

7. A Marxist interpretation of *Waiting for Godot* would probably focus on

A. the poverty and despair of its working-class characters

B. the use of archetypes in the portrayals of the characters

C. the power imbalances in the relationships of the characters

D. the reliance of the two main characters on the eventual arrival of a "savior"

8. "The meeting will be catered by Anita's Deli. Justin and yourself will be responsible for making sure the room is in order."

What is the error in the sentences above?

A. The clauses should be joined by a comma, not a period

B. "Deli" should be "deli'"

C. "yourself" should be "you"

D. "will be responsible" should be "were responsible"

**Questions 9–11** are based on the following analysis of one of Willa Cather's (1873–1947) novels.

*Sapphira and the Slave Girl* was the last novel of Willa Cather's illustrious literary career. Begun in the late summer of 1937 and finally completed in 1941, it is often regarded

(5)  by critics as one of her most personal works. Although the story takes place in 1856, well before her own birth, she drew heavily on both vivid childhood memories and tales handed down by older relatives to describe

(10)  life in rural northern Virginia in the middle of the 19th century. She even went on an extended journey to the area to give the story a further ring of authenticity.

Of all of Cather's many novels, *Sapphira*

(15)  *and the Slave Girl* is the one most concerned with providing an overall picture of day-to-day life in a specific era. A number of the novel's characters, it would seem, are included in the story only because they are

(20)  representative of the types of people to be found in 19th-century rural Virginia; indeed, a few of them play no part whatsoever in the unfolding of the plot. For instance, we are introduced to a poor white woman, Mandy

(25)  Ringer, who is portrayed as intelligent and content, despite the fact that she has no formal education and must toil constantly in the fields. And we meet Dr. Clevenger, a country doctor who, with his patrician

(30)  manners, evokes a strong image of the pre-Civil War South.

The title, however, accurately suggests that the novel is mainly about slavery. Cather's attitude toward this institution may best

(35)  be summed up as somewhat ambiguous.

Although *Sapphira and the Slave Girl* was certainly not meant to be a political tract, the novel is sometimes considered to be a denunciation of bygone days. Nothing could

(40)  be further from the truth. In spite of her willingness to acknowledge that particular aspects of the past were far from ideal, Willa Cather was, if anything, a bit of a romantic. Especially in the final years of her life, an

(45)  increasing note of anger about the emptiness of the present crept into her writings. Earlier generations, she concluded, had been the real heroes, the real creators of all that was good in America.

9.  In the discussion of Willa Cather's *Sapphira and the Slave Girl*, the author refers to the book primarily as a

    A.  sweeping epic of the old South

    B.  story based on personal material

    C.  political treatise on slavery

    D.  scathing condemnation of 1930s America

10.  In paragraph 2, Mandy Ringer and Dr. Clevenger are mentioned in order to emphasize which point about *Sapphira and the Slave Girl*?

    A.  A number of the characters in the novel are based on people Cather knew in her childhood.

    B.  Cather took four years to complete the novel because she carefully researched her characters.

    C.  One of Cather's purposes in writing the novel was to paint a full portrait of life in rural Virginia in the years before the Civil War.

    D.  The characters in the novel are portrayed in a positive light since Cather was a great admirer of the old South.

11. In context, "a bit of a romantic" (line 43) suggests that Willa Cather

    A. favored the past over the present

    B. disliked writing about life in the 1930s

    C. denounced certain aspects of 19th-century life

    D. exaggerated the evils of earlier generations

12. In English, you can tell whether a word is being used as a noun or a verb based on its placement in a sentence relative to other words. In the Slovak language, there are no placement rules; usage is determined by word endings. This is an example of a difference in

    A. syntax

    B. semantics

    C. morphology

    D. phonemes

13. The works of Charles Dickens, Harriet Beecher Stowe, and Upton Sinclair

    A. examined 19th-century cultural values

    B. broke with the literary traditions of the past

    C. argued against the mistreatment of the working class

    D. awakened readers to social wrongs

14. The writing style used by Salman Rushdie and Gabriel Garcia Márquez is most often referred to as

    A. stream of consciousness

    B. magical realism

    C. socialist realism

    D. minimalism

15. It is essential that we reject the proposed changes to the company's insurance plan. The changes that were made to the company's retirement plan have had negative consequences for many of us.

    Which type of logical fallacy is demonstrated by this argument?

    A. Slippery slope

    B. Red herring

    C. Straw man

    D. Circular reasoning

**Questions 16–17** are based on the following excerpt from Christopher Marlowe's "The Passionate Shepherd to His Love."

> Come live with me and be my love,
> And we will all the pleasures prove
> That hills and valleys, dale and field,
> And all the craggy mountains yield.
> There will we sit upon the rocks
> And see the shepherds feed their flocks,
> By shallow rivers, to whose falls
> Melodious birds sing madrigals. ...
> A gown made of the finest wool
> Which from our pretty lambs we pull,
> Fair linèd slippers for the cold,
> With buckles of the purest gold. ...
> The shepherd swains shall dance and sing
> For thy delight each May-morning:
> If these delights thy mind may move,
> Then live with me and be my love.

16. Which of the following is the most accurate classification of the poem?

    A. Ballad

    B. Ode

    C. Pastoral

    D. Dramatic monologue

17. Which of the following poetic devices are used in the first stanza of the poem?

    Select all that apply.

    A. Alliteration
    B. Iambic pentameter
    C. Simile
    D. Personification
    E. Caesura

18. A teacher requires each of the students in her class to make a 10-minute speech on a given topic. The teacher has informed students that a portion of their grade will be based on their use of nonverbal communication. Which of the following is the best example of a form of nonverbal communication that a student should use during his or her speech?

    A. Using a constant rhythm
    B. Varying tone and pitch
    C. Speaking without referring to notes
    D. Maintaining eye contact with the teacher

19. Which of the following are key components of brainstorming?

    Select all that apply.

    A. Organizing ideas
    B. Generating questions to be researched
    C. Listing examples associated with a given topic
    D. Evaluating information
    E. Writing citations

20. Which of the following works of literature was originally written in Modern English?

    A. *The Decameron*
    B. *Sir Gawain and the Green Knight*
    C. *War and Peace*
    D. *Paradise Lost*

**Questions 21–22** are based on the following excerpt from a 19th-century American writer recalling his boyhood in a small town along the Mississippi River.

My father was a justice of the peace, and I supposed he possessed the power of life and death over all men and could hang anybody that offended him. This was distinction
(5) enough for me as a general thing; but the desire to be a steamboatman kept intruding, nevertheless. I first wanted to be a cabin boy, so that I could come out with a white apron on and shake a tablecloth over the side, where all
(10) my old comrades could see me. Later I thought I would rather be the deck hand who stood on the end of the stage plank with a coil of rope in his hand, because he was particularly conspicuous. …
(15) Boy after boy managed to get on the river. Four sons of the chief merchant, and two sons of the county judge became pilots, the grandest position of all. But some of us could not get on the river—at least our parents
(20) would not let us.

So by and by I ran away. I said I would never come home again till I was a pilot and could return in glory. But somehow I could not manage it. I went meekly aboard a few of
(25) the boats that lay packed together like sardines at the long St. Louis wharf, and very humbly inquired for the pilots, but got only a cold shoulder and short words from mates and clerks. I had to make the best of this sort
(30) of treatment for the time being, but I had comforting daydreams of a future when I should be a great and honored pilot, with plenty of money, and could kill some of these mates and clerks and pay for them.

21. As used in line 4, the word "distinction" most nearly means

    A. difference
    B. prestige
    C. desperation
    D. clarity

22. In the last paragraph, the author reflects on

  A. his new ambition to become either a mate or a clerk

  B. the wisdom of seeking a job in which advancement would be easier

  C. the impossibility of returning home and asking his parents' pardon

  D. his determination to keep striving for success in a glorious career

**Questions 23–24** are based on the following excerpt from Booker T. Washington's *Up From Slavery: An Autobiography*.

From the very beginning, at Tuskegee, I was determined to have the students do not only the agricultural and domestic work, but to have them erect their own
(5) buildings. My plan was to have them, while performing this service, taught the latest and best methods of labour, so that the school would not only get the benefit of their efforts, but the students themselves
(10) would be taught to see not only utility in labour, but beauty and dignity; would be taught, in fact, how to lift labour up from mere drudgery and toil, and would learn to love work for its own sake. . . .
(15) I told those who doubted the wisdom of the plan that I knew that our first buildings would not be so comfortable or so complete in their finish as buildings erected by the experienced hands of outside workmen, but
(20) that in the teaching of civilization, self-help, and self-reliance, the erection of the buildings by the students themselves would more than compensate for any lack of comfort or fine finish. . . . Mistakes I knew would be made,
(25) but these mistakes would teach us valuable lessons for the future.
During the now nineteen years' existence of the Tuskegee school, the plan of having the buildings erected by student labour has
(30) been adhered to. In this time forty buildings, counting small and large, have been built, and all except four are almost wholly the

product of student labour. As an additional result, hundreds of men are now scattered
(35) throughout the South who received their knowledge of mechanics while being taught how to erect these buildings. Skill and knowledge are now handed down from one set of students to another in this
(40) way.

23. Which of the following quotations from the passage provides evidence that directly supports the central argument of the passage?

  A. "From the very beginning, at Tuskegee, I was determined to have the students do not only the agricultural and domestic work, but to have them erect their own buildings."

  B. "I told those who doubted the wisdom of the plan that I knew that our first buildings would not be so comfortable or so complete in their finish as buildings erected by the experienced hands of outside workmen. . . ."

  C. "During the now nineteen years' existence of the Tuskegee school, the plan of having the buildings erected by student labour has been adhered to."

  D. "As an additional result, hundreds of men are now scattered throughout the South who received their knowledge of mechanics while being taught how to erect these buildings."

24. Which of the following authors expressed direct disagreement with Booker T. Washington's views on education for African Americans?

  A. Toni Morrison

  B. Frederick Douglass

  C. W. E. B. DuBois

  D. Ishmael Reed

Questions 25–27 are based on the following excerpt from Carl Sandburg's "Chicago."

> Hog Butcher for the World,
> Tool Maker, Stacker of Wheat,
> Player with Railroads and the Nation's
> Freight Handler;
> (5)  Stormy, husky, brawling,
> City of the Big Shoulders:
>
> They tell me you are wicked and I believe
> them, for I have seen your painted women
> under the gas lamps luring the farm boys.
> (10) And they tell me you are crooked and
> I answer: Yes, it is true I have seen the
> gunman kill and go free to kill again.
> And they tell me you are brutal and my
> reply is: On the faces of women and children
> (15) I have seen the marks of wanton hunger....
> Under the smoke, dust all over his mouth,
> laughing with white teeth,
> Under the terrible burden of destiny
> laughing as a young man laughs,
> (20) Laughing even as an ignorant fighter
> laughs who has never lost a battle,
> Bragging and laughing that under his wrist
> is the pulse, and under his ribs the heart of
> the people,
> (25)    Laughing!
> Laughing the stormy, husky, brawling
> laughter of Youth, half-naked, sweating,
> proud to be Hog Butcher, Tool Maker,
> Stacker of Wheat, Player with Railroads and
> (30) Freight Handler to the Nation.

25. Which of the following most accurately identifies the form of this poem?

    A. Blank verse

    B. Ode

    C. Narrative

    D. Free verse

26. The line "They tell me you are wicked and I believe them, for I have seen your painted women under the gas lamps luring the farm boys" is an example of which of the following?

    A. Apostrophe

    B. Irony

    C. Hyperbole

    D. Metonymy

27. This poem was most likely influenced by which of the following?

    A. Industrialization

    B. Increased immigration

    C. Westward expansion

    D. World War II patriotism

Everything was in confusion in the Oblonskys' house. The wife had discovered that the husband was carrying on an intrigue with a French girl, who had been (5) a governess in their family, and she had announced to her husband that she could not go on living in the same house with him.... The wife did not leave her own room; the husband had not been at home (10) for three days. The children ran wild all over the house; the English governess quarreled with the housekeeper, and wrote to a friend asking her to look out for a new situation for her; the man-cook had walked off the (15) day before just at dinner-time; the kitchen-maid, and the coachman had given warning.

Three days after the quarrel, Prince Stepan Arkadyevitch Oblonsky—Stiva, as he was called in the fashionable world—woke (20) up at his usual hour, that is, at eight o'clock in the morning, not in his wife's bedroom, but on the leather-covered sofa in his study. He turned over his stout, well-cared-for person on the springy sofa, as though (25) he would sink into a long sleep again....

28. This excerpt is most likely from the novel's

    A. exposition
    B. rising action
    C. climax
    D. denouement

29. Which of the following authors are generally recognized as part of the Irish Renaissance?

    Select all that apply.

    A. William B. Yeats
    B. Lady Gregory
    C. James Joyce
    D. John M. Synge
    E. Victor Hugo

30. The poetry of Walt Whitman is significant in the development of American literature primarily because Whitman

    A. used the epic form to tell distinctly American tales
    B. developed his own poetic form and style instead of adhering to traditional poetic forms
    C. commemorated in verse the lives of public leaders such as Abraham Lincoln
    D. was heavily influenced by Emerson's call for a new national poet

31. Most of the children requested chocolate, but Timmy asked for vanilla ice cream.

    The sentence above can best be classified as

    A. complex
    B. compound
    C. compound-complex
    D. simple

32. Populations in different regions of the United States use varying words to refer to submarine sandwiches, such as *hoagie*, *hero*, or *grinder*.

    The words listed above are examples of which of the following?

    A. Aphorisms
    B. Colloquialisms
    C. A creole language
    D. A pidgin language

33. Place a mark in the column next to each scenario that most accurately identifies the appropriate reference material to be used to complete the task.

    For each scenario, select one reference material.

| Scenario | An Atlas | An Index | A Style Guide | A Website Ending in *.gov* |
|---|---|---|---|---|
| A student wants to determine whether a book discusses a certain author. | | | | |
| A student wants official data from the Census Bureau to include in a research paper. | | | | |
| A student is uncertain about how to format citations in a term paper. | | | | |
| A student wants to understand a state's geographic position in relation to other states. | | | | |

# ANSWERS AND EXPLANATIONS

## English Question Bank

**1. C**

The simple fact that the author cites Russell's definition is a clue that she considers it a good one. She also writes, "but one could do worse than...," indirectly showing her approval. In other words, she is saying that worse definitions than this one exist. This matches choice (C). (A) and (B) are the opposite—the writer is not dismissive or skeptical. And (D) is extreme: the writer seems positive, but *exuberant* implies high spirits that aren't consistent with the paragraph's tone.

**2. C**

Miller described his play as a "tragedy of the common man" because it gave the dramatic weight and importance once reserved for kings and warriors to a small and seemingly insignificant salesperson; this matches choice (C). In (A), the definition of classical tragedy, the mention of an "important person" contradicts the "common man" of the question stem. (B) can be eliminated along with (A): classical tragedy was *never* about the "common man," so Miller's play must be something different. (D) may be tempting. The play is certainly serious, but it is not written in a poetic style. Also, style independent of the subject matter is not what defines a tragedy.

**3. A**

Outlines can be thought of as nested boxes—sets and subsets. Read carefully to make sure you understand which item is a subset of which category. To eliminate incorrect answer choices, focus on the largest categories first to see whether there are any errors at this surface level. This can save you a great deal of reading time. In this example, the two broadest categories, labeled I and II, should be *plays* and *poems*. Everything Shakespeare wrote fits into these two general categories. Therefore, (B) and (C) can be eliminated right away without having to look any deeper. (D) is incorrect because *King Lear*, a tragedy, is listed as a history and *Titus Andronicus*, also a tragedy, is listed as a comedy.

**4. D**

Each answer choice is an example of a different kind of logical fallacy. You can use the imagery in the term "slippery slope" to help remember the fallacy. It is a fallacy of believing that one action will lead to taking things to extremes (or taking one step and sliding all the way down the hill). (D) is an example of this. (A) commits an ad hominem fallacy, assigning an opinion to people based on their role or title. (B) is an example of appeal to common practice or getting on the bandwagon—other people do it, so it must be acceptable. (C) is an example of begging the question—using the matter under question as the answer to the question.

**5. C**

Clues in the passage that can alert you to the answer include "you were my father, my creator" (lines 25–26) and "then cast me abroad an object for the scorn and horror of mankind" (lines 30–32). Central to the plot of *Frankenstein* is the fact that the main character creates life—a monster—so clearly this is the monster speaking, choice (C).

**6. B**

This question may seem daunting if you have trouble deciphering older texts. However, the question is actually easier than it might at first seem. You do not need to read each choice carefully. If you go back to the passage, you will find that there are enough context clues in the sentences surrounding the quoted text (lines 11–14) to help you quickly eliminate some wrong answer choices. The "orb" described here is the moon, which is referred to in the sentence before the quoted text. Thus, you can eliminate (A) and (D) right away. The burning cottage is referenced just after the cited text ("the cottage was quickly enveloped by the flames" in lines 15–16), which will help you choose (B).

**7. C**

If you do not know much about Marxist theory or Samuel Beckett's work, you may feel hopeless in tackling this question, but you shouldn't. What is the major theme of Marxism, in terms of literary theory? It is that all relationships are power relationships, based on economic class standing. This points to either (A) or (C). Of the two, (C) is more closely aligned with Marxist ideas. (A) mentions class, but not class conflict. (B) would correspond to Jungian or mythical analysis more than Marxist theory. (D) may seem tempting if you remember the plot of Godot. However, this choice is more about a philosophical/existential interpretation of the play and has nothing to do with Marxist theory.

**8.  C**

A reflexive pronoun such as "yourself" may only be used when the subject and the object of the sentence are the same person (e.g., "You left yourself no other option"). In all other cases, "you" should be used. Therefore, (C) is correct. Joining the sentences with a comma, (A), would create a run-on sentence. (B) is incorrect because proper nouns should be capitalized, and "Anita's Deli" is a proper noun. (D) is incorrect because it would create a shift in verb tense within the sentence.

**9.  B**

Paragraph 1 holds the answer. It tells us that *Sapphira* is one of Cather's most personal works and draws heavily on her childhood memories. The correct answer is thus (B). Regarding (A), nothing in the text suggests that *Sapphira* is a sweeping epic. If anything, it's the opposite—a very personal novel. (C) can't be right, because the first sentence in paragraph 4 states that *Sapphira* is "not meant to be a political tract." Also in paragraph 4, the author tells us Cather was dissatisfied with the present, but a "scathing condemnation" of the present is extreme, so (D) is incorrect.

**10.  C**

Go back to paragraph 2 and see what's going on. The keywords "for instance" indicate that the two people are mentioned as examples of characters "included in the story only because they are representative of the types of people to be found in 19th-century rural Virginia" (lines 19–21). Other answer choices might agree with points the author makes elsewhere in the passage, but this question asks specifically about certain details in paragraph 2. (A) and (B) are discussed in paragraph 1, while (D) is an overstatement of the content in paragraph 4.

**11.  A**

The last paragraph refers to Cather as "a bit of a romantic" who cherished what she perceived as the heroism of the past over the emptiness of the present, choice (A). With regard to (B), nothing suggests Cather disliked writing about the 1930s. As for (C), Cather did dislike certain aspects of mid-19th-century life, but that's the opposite of romanticizing those times. And Cather didn't exaggerate the evils of the past, as in (D); if anything, she underestimated them.

**12.  A**

This question draws on your knowledge to recognize the terms in the answer choices. The correct answer is (A), syntax, which relates to the grammatical structure of a language. (B) relates to the meanings of individual words. (C) deals with the structure and formation of words, including such things as derivation and inflection. (D) refers to the smallest building blocks of languages—individual sounds.

**13.  D**

In a comparison question like this, any answer choice that does not apply to *all* of the things being compared can immediately be eliminated. (A) can be eliminated because Upton Sinclair was a 20th-century author. (B) can be eliminated because it does not apply to *any* of the works. (C) can be eliminated because Harriet Beecher Stowe was concerned with the issue of slavery, not the working class. (D) is the only choice general enough to apply to all three authors.

**14.  B**

You do not need to be familiar with *both* of these authors to get the correct answer. The question states that they share a writing style, so any answer that is correct for one should be correct for the other. Knowledge of either Márquez or Rushdie should point toward the phrase *magical realism*, and this is choice (B). (A) applies more to early 20th-century authors such as James Joyce. (C) refers to artists of the Stalinist era in communist countries, whose work was garishly realistic, touting progress in science and technology and the virtues of happy working-class people. (D) can be eliminated by anyone who has held a book written by either author, as there is nothing minimalist about their writing—quite the contrary!

## 15. B

A "red herring" involves the introduction of an irrelevant issue to an argument. The issue of the effects of the changes made to the company's retirement plan is irrelevant to the issue of the proposed changes to the company's insurance plan. The correct answer is (B). A "slippery slope" argument, (A), involves reasoning that because of an initial event, a second, more extreme event must inevitably follow. The "straw man" fallacy, (C), involves distorting a position taken in an argument. Circular reasoning, (D), involves using the conclusion of an argument as evidence to prove the validity of the argument.

## 16. C

A pastoral poem is characterized by a simplicity of thought and action in a rural, rustic setting. The shepherd's desire to please his love with the beauty of this rural setting categorizes this as a pastoral poem, choice (C). A ballad, (A), refers to a narrative poem that was originally sung. This is a lyric poem. An ode, (B), would typically deal with a more serious or elevated topic than this poem does. A dramatic monologue, (D), is also a narrative poem.

## 17. A

Alliteration is found in stanza 1 in the phrase "we will all the pleasures prove," with multiple consonant sounds repeated. This makes (A) correct, but we must test the other answer choices as well. (B) can be eliminated because iambic pentameter requires 10 beats per measure. The first line of this poem has eight beats. No similes are present in the first stanza of the poem, so eliminate choice (C). Nor is personification used in the first stanza, so eliminate (D). Finally, the first stanza lacks any caesuras, rhythmic pauses often found in the middle of a line, so (E) is incorrect.

## 18. B

To maintain the audience's interest and to emphasize certain points, speakers should vary their tone and pitch. Therefore, (B) is the correct answer. Speakers should also vary the rhythm of their speech, as an audience may find a constant rhythm, (A), to be dull. Choice (C) is incorrect because it is usually a good idea for a speaker to have brief notes to refer to in order to convey all of the information planned for a presentation. Maintaining eye contact with only the teacher, (D), is incorrect because the speaker should establish eye contact with several or all members of the audience as an effective way of maintaining the audience's focus on the presentation.

## 19. B, C

Brainstorming and freewriting are steps taken at the very beginning of the writing process. In this step, the goal is to generate as many ideas or questions related to a given topic as possible. Therefore, (B) and (C) are correct. During brainstorming and freewriting, it is important to focus only on generating ideas, not on evaluating or organizing those ideas. These steps come later in the writing process, so (A) and (D) are incorrect. Likewise, while it would be possible to brainstorm potential source materials, formal citations, (E), would not be prepared until much later in the writing process.

## 20. D

Although you might not know the exact dates of the publication of Milton's *Paradise Lost* (1667) and the beginning of Modern English (1500s), you can get to the answer through elimination. (A) can be eliminated because *The Decameron* was written in Italian in the 1300s. (B) is an Arthurian tale written in Old English. You should be able to identify Leo Tolstoy as the author of *War and Peace* (C); it was originally written in Russian.

## 21. B

*Distinction* has several meanings, as reflected in the answer choices. The key to its use here is context. In the previous sentence, the author discusses his naive ideas of his father's great power. Choice (B), "prestige," suggesting high status and honor, fits this context; choices (A) and (D) don't. (C), "desperation," is not a meaning of *distinction* at all.

## 22. D

The last paragraph discusses the author's failed attempts to become a pilot and his daydreams about someday still becoming one, so (D) is correct. Mates and clerks are mentioned as ignoring the author, but he never considers becoming either a mate or a clerk (A), looking for some other job (B), or asking his parents' forgiveness (C).

## 23. D

The central argument of this passage is that having the students construct the buildings at the Tuskegee school would benefit the students by teaching them "civilization, self-help, and self-reliance" (lines 20–21). Only (D) provides a direct example of how students were benefited by constructing the buildings. Many of the students went on to learn a trade in mechanics through their work on the buildings. Choice (A) provides only the idea that the students would construct the buildings, omitting the reasoning for this practice (its impact on the students) that constitutes Washington's argument. Choice (B) describes only a negative result of Washington's plan rather than the passage's central argument. Choice (C), like (A), merely asserts that the plan was carried out rather than giving evidence of its results.

## 24. C

During the early 1900s, W. E. B. DuBois argued against Booker T. Washington's strategies for improving the lives of African Americans, so (C) is correct. In *The Souls of Black Folk*, DuBois argued that Washington's methods focused on economic advancement at the expense of social equality. After the Civil War, Frederick Douglass (B) had made efforts to create opportunities for former slaves to learn technical trades. Douglass's efforts greatly influenced Washington. Toni Morrison (A) and Ishmael Reed (D) are contemporary African American authors.

## 25. D

A free verse poem has no formal pattern or structure of rhythm or rhyme. Since these qualities characterize the poem excerpt, (D) is correct. A blank verse poem (A) is not rhymed, but it is written in iambic pentameter. (*Paradise Lost* is an example of blank verse.) An ode (B) is typically a much more formal poem. Although this poem praises Chicago, it is more accurate to describe the poem as free verse than as an ode. A narrative poem (C) tells a story with identified characters and action.

## 26. A

The "you" in this line is Chicago itself. This is a form of apostrophe, an address to a person or thing that is incapable of answering. Sandburg gives the city human qualities, such as wickedness. Therefore, (A) is correct. None of the other devices appear in these lines. There is no irony in Sandburg's observation here. Hyperbole is extreme exaggeration. Metonymy replaces a person or thing with a word closely associated with that person or thing. For example, "no news from the White House" indicates that the president has not released a statement.

## 27. A

This poem was written during the early 1900s, a time when Midwestern cities such as Chicago, Kansas City, and St. Louis experienced increased industrialization and population growth. Descriptions such as "Hog Butcher, Tool Maker, Stacker of Wheat, Player with Railroads and the Nation's Freight Handler" indicate that industrialization of Chicago influenced this poem, so choice (A) is correct. Although immigrants (B) may have settled in Chicago, the poem's subject is the impact of industry. A poem from the mid-1800s that expressed the experience of living on the frontier would be more likely to have been influenced by westward expansion (C). Sandburg wrote and published this poem before World War II (D).

## 28. A

The exposition of a work of fiction (A) provides important background information about characters, setting, and other story elements. In this excerpt, the various members of the Oblonsky household are introduced generally, and Stiva is introduced in particular, so (A) is correct. While conflict is introduced in this excerpt, the conflict is not developing during this passage, so choice (B), rising action, is not correct. Similarly, climax (C), the highest point of the conflict, and denouement (D), the resolution of the conflict, are not found in this excerpt.

### 29. A, B, C, D

The Irish Renaissance spans the late 19th and early 20th centuries. During this period, many Irish writers revived Irish folklore and legends in their works. William B. Yeats, who wrote the poems "The Second Coming" and "Sailing to Byzantium," was generally thought of as the leader of the Irish Renaissance. Lady Gregory is best known for her recordings of folklore and her work in establishing the Abbey Theatre. James Joyce, famous for his stream-of-consciousness prose in *Ulysses*, was also an Irish writer during this period. John M. Synge wrote plays, such as *The Playboy of the Western World*, that were performed at the Abbey Theatre. Victor Hugo (E), however, was a French writer of the Romantic movement. Therefore, choices (A) through (D) are correct.

### 30. B

The poems in Whitman's collection *Leaves of Grass* make a sharp departure from traditional metered poetic forms. In the introduction to this work, Whitman writes that "the expression of the American poet is to be transcendent and new." Whitman popularized free verse, and his work influenced later poets such as Wallace Stevens and Allen Ginsberg. Therefore, (B) is correct. Whitman did not use the epic form (A). Although Whitman did write of Lincoln's

death in "O Captain! My Captain!" (C), this is not his most significant contribution to the development of American literature. Similarly, Whitman was deeply influenced by Emerson (D), but this influence is not his key contribution to the development of American literature.

### 31. B

This sentence is formed by two independent clauses, so it is a compound sentence (B). A simple sentence (D) has a single independent clause and no dependent clauses. A complex sentence (A) contains an independent clause and at least one dependent clause. A compound-complex sentence (C) is most complicated, containing more than one independent clause and at least one dependent clause.

### 32. B

Locally used, informal words can be referred to as colloquialisms, so (B) is correct. An aphorism (A) is a short statement of truth, similar to a proverb or adage. A creole (C) is a language derived from the combination of two other languages. A pidgin (D) is less formal than a creole, being a simplified method of communication between groups with different parent languages.

### 33.

A student should consult a book's index to determine whether any given topic is included in a book. Official data can be reliably obtained from a *.gov* website. For instructions about how to format references and citations, a student should consult the style manual for the particular style being used. Finally, an atlas would include a variety of maps that display a state's relative location.

# CHAPTER EIGHT

# Mathematics

In this section, we will cover the format and content outline of the Mathematics: Content Knowledge test. The chapter includes a question bank of relevant questions. The practice questions here are all in multiple-choice format with one correct answer, although other question types will appear on the exam. See the following description of test format for more details. You can find additional details about the Mathematics: Content Knowledge test from the menu provided at **www.ets.org/praxis/ prepare/materials/5161**, along with additional practice tests and materials. The content provided in this chapter is not intended to provide complete or exhaustive preparation for the test, but it will help you assess your strengths and weaknesses and provide guidance for additional study.

## PRAXIS MATHEMATICS SUBJECT ASSESSMENT

This chapter applies to you if you are taking the following test:

- Mathematics: Content Knowledge (5161)

### Mathematics: Content Knowledge (5161)

Test Format: Computer-delivered; 60 questions, including multiple-choice with one correct answer, multiple-choice with one or more correct answers, numeric entry, text completion, drag-and-drop, and other possible question types.

Test Length: 150 minutes

- Number theory, algebra, functions, and calculus: 41 questions, 68 percent of the test
- Geometry, statistics, probability, and discrete math: 19 questions, 32 percent of the test

An on-screen graphing calculator is provided. For more information and a tutorial on the graphing calculator, see **www.ets.org/praxis/test_day/policies/calculators**.

This test is designed to assess your mathematical knowledge and ability if you are interested in teaching mathematics at a secondary school level. The typical test taker has completed a bachelor's degree in math or in a math-related field. The mathematical content covered conforms to the curriculum, evaluation, and professional standards of the National Council of Teachers of Mathematics, the Common Core standards, and the standards of other relevant organizations. This test focuses on problem solving, communication, reasoning, and making mathematical connections. The question bank that follows tests many of the concepts that might appear on the test.

Note: The question bank that follows is not designed to be a simulation of a Praxis Subject Assessment. Rather, it is a study aid that will acquaint you with many of the concepts tested on the Mathematics: Content Knowledge (5161) test.

# MATHEMATICS QUESTION BANK

1. Provide a complete solution set for the equation $x^3 + 25 = 33$.

   A. $\left\{ 2, 1 + i\sqrt{3}, 1 - i\sqrt{3} \right\}$

   B. $\left\{ 2, -1 + i\sqrt{3}, -1 - i\sqrt{3} \right\}$

   C. $\left\{ -2, 1 + 2i\sqrt{3}, 1 - 2i\sqrt{3} \right\}$

   D. $\left\{ -2, 2 + 2\sqrt{3}, 2 - 2\sqrt{3} \right\}$

2. Identify the inflection point(s) of the curve $f(x) = x^3 - 12x^2 + 21x + 4$.

   A. $(4, -40)$

   B. $(0, 4)$

   C. $(1, 0), (7, 0)$

   D. $(1, 14), (7, -94)$

3. If the function $f(x) = \dfrac{1}{\left( 1 - \left| \sin x \right| \right)}$ is graphed for all $x$ such that $-2\pi < x < 2\pi$, how many asymptotes are there?

   A. 2

   B. 3

   C. 4

   D. 6

4. What is the sum of the coefficients for the expansion of $(x + y)^8$ ?

   A. 10

   B. 254

   C. 256

   D. 264

5. Find the first term, $a_1$, of a geometric sequence where the common ratio is $\dfrac{1}{3}$ and the sum of the first six terms is 10,920.

   A. 4,860

   B. 6,075

   C. 7,290

   D. 8,505

6. What is the equation of an ellipse centered at $(6, -4)$ with a major axis of 18 that is parallel to the $y$-axis and a minor axis of 14 that is parallel to the $x$-axis?

   A. $\dfrac{(y + 4)^2}{81} + \dfrac{(x - 6)^2}{49} = 1$

   B. $\dfrac{(y - 4)^2}{81} + \dfrac{(x + 6)^2}{49} = 1$

   C. $\dfrac{(y + 4)^2}{324} + \dfrac{(x - 6)^2}{196} = 1$

   D. $\dfrac{(y - 4)^2}{324} + \dfrac{(x + 6)^2}{196} = 1$

7. What is the approximate area under the curve of $f(x) = \dfrac{1}{x}$ from $x = 1$ to $x = 10$ ?

   A. 2.30

   B. 2.93

   C. 3.17

   D. 3.44

8. Suppose that $f(x) = e^{2x}$ and $g(x) = 2x^2 - 7x + 6$. If $g(f(x)) = 0$, what is the solution set?

   A. $\{1.5, 2\}$

   B. $\left\{ \dfrac{\ln 1.5}{2}, \dfrac{-\ln 2}{2} \right\}$

   C. $\left\{ \dfrac{\ln 1.5}{2}, \dfrac{\ln 2}{2} \right\}$

   D. $\{\ln 1.5, \ln 2\}$

9. Which of the following is NOT a continuous function where $\mathbb{R}$ is mapped into $\mathbb{R}$?

   A. $f(x) = x^2$
   B. $f(x) = \sin(e^x)$
   C. $f(x) = e^{\cos x}$
   D. $f(x) = \sec(x)$

10. Find the inverse of the following matrix:

$$Z = \begin{vmatrix} 4 & 2 \\ 5 & 3 \end{vmatrix}$$

   A. $\begin{vmatrix} 3 & -2 \\ -5 & 4 \end{vmatrix}$

   B. $\begin{vmatrix} \dfrac{3}{2} & -1 \\ \dfrac{-5}{2} & 2 \end{vmatrix}$

   C. $\begin{vmatrix} \dfrac{1}{4} & \dfrac{1}{2} \\ \dfrac{1}{5} & \dfrac{1}{3} \end{vmatrix}$

   D. $\begin{vmatrix} -4 & -2 \\ -5 & -3 \end{vmatrix}$

11. A coin is flipped nine times. What is the probability that heads will be flipped at least three times?

   A. $\dfrac{23}{256}$

   B. $\dfrac{123}{512}$

   C. $\dfrac{389}{512}$

   D. $\dfrac{233}{256}$

12. If a cube with edges of 12 is divided into 27 smaller cubes of equal size and each of the smaller cubes contains a sphere whose volume occupies the maximum possible space, what is the total surface area of the spheres?

   A. $288\pi$
   B. $384\pi$
   C. $432\pi$
   D. $648\pi$

13. Find $\dfrac{d}{dx} \dfrac{x \ln x}{\sin(\ln x)}$.

   A. $\dfrac{\left(\sin(\ln x)\right)\left(1 + (\ln x)\right) - x(\ln x)\left(\cos(\ln x)\right)}{\sin^2(\ln x)}$

   B. $\dfrac{\left(\sin(\ln x)\right)\left(1 + (\ln x)\right) - (\ln x)\left(\cos(\ln x)\right)}{\sin^2(\ln x)}$

   C. $\dfrac{\left(\dfrac{1}{x}\right)}{\cos(\ln x)}$

   D. $\dfrac{1 + \ln x}{\cos(\ln x)}$

14. Consider the function $f(x) = e^{2x}$. If the area under the curve between $x = 1$ and $x = 3$ is rotated around the $x$-axis, what will be the volume of the solid?

   A. $\dfrac{\pi e^4}{4}\left(e^8 - 1\right)$

   B. $\dfrac{\pi e^2}{3}\left(e^4 - 1\right)$

   C. $\pi e^2\left(e^4 - 1\right)$

   D. $\dfrac{4\pi}{3}\left(e^{18} - e^6\right)$

15. Find the inverse of the function

$f(x) = \ln \cos(3x - 2) + 3$ for $\dfrac{2}{3} \le x < \dfrac{2}{3} + \dfrac{\pi}{6}$.

A. $f^{-1}(x) = \dfrac{\arccos\left(e^{x-3}\right) + 2}{3}$

B. $f^{-1}(x) = \dfrac{\left(e^{x}\right) - \arccos 3 + 2}{3}$

C. $f^{-1}(x) = \dfrac{\arccos\left(e^{3x-2}\right)}{3}$

D. $f^{-1}(x) = \arccos\left(e^{2x-3}\right) + 1$

16. If $\log_{16}(x) + \log_4(2x) = 5$, what is the value of $x$?

A. 16
B. 32
C. 64
D. 128

17. $\int \cot(x)\,dx =$

A. $\tan x \sec x + C$
B. $\ln|\sin x| + C$
C. $-\csc(\ln(x)) + C$
D. $\ln|\csc x| + C$

18. The three vertices of a triangle are on the circumference of a circle, and two of the vertices of the triangle are the endpoints of a diameter of the circle. If the area of the circle is $36\pi$ and the measure of one of the interior angles of the triangle is 34 degrees, what is the approximate area of the triangle?

A. 26.6
B. 33.4
C. 38.9
D. 56.5

19. Working alone, Sam, Fred, Ernest, and Jacqueline each take 24, 20, 16, and 15 hours, respectively, to paint a house. All four start working together on the same house-painting job, but Ernest quits after 2 hours. If Sam, Fred, and Jacqueline finish the job, how many hours does it take the group to paint the house?

A. $\dfrac{20}{7}$

B. $\dfrac{22}{7}$

C. $\dfrac{67}{19}$

D. $\dfrac{105}{19}$

20. What is the equation of the line that goes through the point (20, 3) and is perpendicular to the line with the equation $y = -\dfrac{1}{4}x + 8$?

A. $y = 4x - 77$

B. $y = \dfrac{1}{4}x - 2$

C. $y = 2x - 37$

D. $y = \dfrac{1}{2}x - 2$

21. A student draws marbles from a bag containing 6 blue marbles, 5 red marbles, and 10 green marbles. If the marbles are selected without replacement, what is the smallest number of marbles that the student must draw to have at least a 50% chance of having drawn a blue marble?

A. 2
B. 5
C. 9
D. 10

22. The function $f(x) = x^3 - \dfrac{1}{2}x^2 - 2x + 2$ has local maxima and local minima at what points?

A. $\left(\dfrac{2}{3}, \dfrac{20}{27}\right), \left(1, \dfrac{1}{2}\right)$

B. $\left(\dfrac{2}{3}, \dfrac{20}{27}\right), \left(-1, \dfrac{5}{2}\right)$

C. $\left(-\dfrac{2}{3}, \dfrac{76}{27}\right), \left(1, \dfrac{1}{2}\right)$

D. $\left(-\dfrac{2}{3}, \dfrac{20}{27}\right), \left(-1, \dfrac{5}{2}\right)$

23. Solve the following equation for all values of $x$ in the interval $[0, 2\pi]$.

$$\sin^2 x + \dfrac{1}{2}\sin x = \dfrac{1}{2}$$

A. $\dfrac{\pi}{6}, \dfrac{5\pi}{6}, \dfrac{3\pi}{2}$

B. $\dfrac{\pi}{4}, \dfrac{\pi}{2}, \dfrac{11\pi}{6}$

C. $\dfrac{\pi}{6}, \dfrac{\pi}{2}, \dfrac{5\pi}{6}$

D. $\dfrac{\pi}{4}, \dfrac{3\pi}{4}, \dfrac{11\pi}{6}$

24. $\displaystyle\lim_{n \to \infty}\left(1 + \dfrac{1}{n}\right)^n$

A. $\dfrac{3}{2}$

B. $\sqrt{5}$

C. $e$

D. $3$

25. A rectangular prism has dimensions of $10 \times 5 \times 10$. If the longest diagonal between two points in the prism is used as the radius of a sphere, what is the surface area of the sphere?

A. $675\pi$

B. $900\pi$

C. $3{,}375\pi$

D. $4{,}500\pi$

# ANSWERS AND EXPLANATIONS

## Mathematics Question Bank

### 1.  B

Strategy: Step-by-Step

$x^3 + 25 = 33$

$x^3 - 8 = 0$

$(x - 2)(x^2 + 2x + 4) = 0$

Therefore, one root is 2.

Use the quadratic formula on the second factor:

$$\frac{-2 + \sqrt{4 - 16}}{2}, \frac{-2 - \sqrt{4 - 16}}{2}$$

$$\frac{-2 + 2\sqrt{-3}}{2}, \frac{-2 - 2\sqrt{-3}}{2}$$

$$2, -1 + i\sqrt{3}, -1 - i\sqrt{3}$$

### 2.  A

Strategy: Step-by-Step

To determine the inflection point(s), if any exist, the second derivative test must be applied. Set the second derivative equal to zero to find values of $x$. These values will be the points where the curve changes from facing up to facing down or vice versa.

If $f(x) = x^3 - 12x^2 + 21x + 4$,

then $f'(x) = 3x^2 - 24x + 21$.

If $f'(x) = 3x^2 - 24x + 21$, then $f''(x) = 6x - 24$.

If $6x - 24 = 0$, $x = 4$

At $x = 4$, $f(x) = -40$. The point of inflection is $(4, -40)$.

### 3.  C

Strategy: Picking Numbers

The function will be undefined at any value of $x$ where $|\sin x| = 1$. Over the interval $[-2\pi, 2\pi]$, there are four values of $x$ where the sine of $x$ will be either 1 or −1. These values are $\dfrac{-3\pi}{2}, \dfrac{-\pi}{2}, \dfrac{\pi}{2}$, and $\dfrac{3\pi}{2}$.

### 4.  C

Strategy: Cut the Jargon

The sum of the coefficients in any standard binomial expansion $(x + y)^n$ is $2^n$. Here, $n = 8$. The sum of the coefficients is $2^8 = 256$.

### 5.  C

Strategy: Backsolving

Although the formula for the sum of a finite geometric ratio can be used, it is easier in this case to pick an answer and test the choices. Try choice (B) first.

$6{,}075 + 2{,}025 + 675 + 225 + 75 + 25 = 9{,}100$.

Too small: try the next largest.

$7{,}290 + 2{,}430 + 810 + 270 + 90 + 30 = 10{,}920$.

Correct.

### 6.  A

Strategy: Cut the Jargon

Put the ellipse into its standard form, distinguishing between the major and minor axes.

### 7.  A

Strategy: Cut the Jargon

The area under the curve will be the integral of the function over the interval $[1, 10]$.

$$\int \frac{1}{x}\, dx = \ln x \,\Big|_{1}^{10}$$

$\ln(10) \approx 2.30$

$\ln(1) = 0$

$2.30 - 0 = 2.30$

**8. C**

Strategy: Step-by-Step

Substitute one function into the other:

$2(e^{2x})^2 - 7(e^{2x}) + 6 = 0$

$2e^{4x} - 7e^{2x} + 6 = 0$

$(2e^{2x} - 3)(e^{2x} - 2) = 0$

Therefore, $e^{2x} = 1.5$ or $e^{2x} = 2$.

$2x = \ln 1.5$, or $2x = \ln 2$

$x = \dfrac{\ln 1.5}{2}$, or $x = \dfrac{\ln 2}{2}$

**9. D**

Strategy: Cut the Jargon

For a function to be continuously mapped from a domain to a range, all members of the domain must have a corresponding value in the range. Because $\sec(x)$ is undefined at $\dfrac{\pi}{2}$ as well as other values, it cannot be continuous.

**10. B**

Strategy: Step-by-Step or Backsolving

The inverse of a matrix is done as follows:

$$\begin{vmatrix} a & b \\ c & d \end{vmatrix} = \dfrac{1}{\text{determinant}} \times \begin{vmatrix} d & -b \\ -c & a \end{vmatrix}$$

The determinant of the 2-by-2 matrix $= ad - bc$. The determinant of the matrix in this question is $(4)(3) - (2)(5) = 2$.

Rearranging and multiplying by the determinant, you get the correct answer.

You could also multiply the answer choices by the given matrix and determine which product gives the identity matrix.

**11. D**

Strategy: Step-by-Step

If a coin is flipped nine times, the number of different possible sequences of heads and tails is $2^9 = 512$.

Flipping at least three heads encompasses the possibility of flipping three, four, five, six, seven, eight, and nine heads. It is easier in this case to calculate the probability of this not happening and then subtract that probability from 1.

$${}_9C_2 \begin{pmatrix} 9 \\ 2 \end{pmatrix} = \dfrac{9!}{2!7!} = 36$$

$${}_9C_1 \begin{pmatrix} 9 \\ 1 \end{pmatrix} = \dfrac{9!}{1!8!} = 9$$

$${}_9C_0 \begin{pmatrix} 9 \\ 0 \end{pmatrix} = \dfrac{9!}{0!9!} = 1$$

The probability of failure is

$$\dfrac{36}{512} + \dfrac{9}{512} + \dfrac{1}{512} = \dfrac{36 + 9 + 1}{512} = \dfrac{46}{512} = \dfrac{23}{256}.$$

Therefore, $Pr(H > 3) = 1 - \dfrac{23}{256} = \dfrac{233}{256}.$

**12. C**

Strategy: Step-by-Step

Because the cube is divided into 27 smaller cubes, the change in the dimensions will be the cube root of $\dfrac{1}{27}$ (the scale factor), or $\dfrac{1}{3}$.

Because each cube will have edges of $12 \times \dfrac{1}{3} = 4$, the radius of the largest sphere that can fit in the smaller cubes is 2. The formula for the surface area of a sphere is $4\pi r^2$; $4\pi(2)^2 = 16\pi$. Because there are 27 cubes, $27 \times 16\pi = 432\pi$.

## 13. B

Strategy: Step-by-Step

The quotient rule for finding a derivative is as follows:

$$\frac{d}{dx}\left(\frac{u}{v}\right)=\frac{v\frac{du}{dx}-u\frac{dv}{dx}}{v^2}$$

To find the derivative of $\frac{x\ln x}{\sin(\ln x)}$, in addition to the quotient rule, you will need the product rule and the chain rule.

Use the quotient rule, the product rule, and the chain rule:

$$\frac{d}{dx}\frac{x\ln x}{\sin(\ln x)}$$

$$=\frac{\sin(\ln x)\left[x\left(\frac{1}{x}\right)+(\ln x)(1)\right]-(x\ln x)\left[\cos(\ln x)\left(\frac{1}{x}\right)\right]}{\left[\sin(\ln x)\right]^2}$$

$$=\frac{\sin(\ln x)(1+\ln x)-(\ln x)(\cos(\ln x))}{\left[\sin(\ln x)\right]^2}$$

$$=\frac{\sin(\ln x)(1+\ln x)-(\ln x)(\cos(\ln x))}{\sin^2(\ln x)}$$

## 14. A

Strategy: Step-by-Step

For each value of x such that $1\le x\le3$, $f(x)$ is the distance from the curve to the x-axis, so for each value of x such that $1\le x\le3$, $f(x)$ is the radius of one circle. Because the formula for the area of a circle is $\pi r^2$, a differential volume element is $\pi[f(x_k)]^2(\Delta x)_k$. The volume is

$$\int_1^3\pi\left(e^{2x}\right)^2dx=\int_1^3\pi e^{4x}dx=\frac{\pi e^{4x}}{4}\bigg|_1^3$$

$$\frac{\pi e^{12}-\pi e^4}{4}=\frac{\pi e^4\left(e^8-1\right)}{4}$$

## 15. A

Strategy: Step-by-Step

To solve for the inverse function, simply solve the original equation for the variable x, which pertains to the domain, in terms of $f(x)$, which pertains to the range. If the function f is defined by $f(x)=$ an expression involving x, it is convenient to replace $f(x)$ with y so that we have $y=$ an expression involving x. Then we can solve the equation $y=$ an expression involving x for x in terms of y. The last step is to replace y with x and x with y to describe the inverse function.

Start with the equation $f(x)=\ln\cos(3x-2)+3$. Here, the expression involving x described above is $\ln\cos(3x-2)+3$. Now replace $f(x)$ with y. Then $y=\ln\cos(3x-2)+3$. Now solve for x in terms of y.

$$y=\ln\cos(3x-2)+3$$
$$y-3=\ln\cos(3x-2)$$
$$e^{y-3}=\cos(3x-2)$$
$$\arccos(e^{y-3})=3x-2$$
$$\arccos(e^{y-3})+2=3x$$
$$\frac{\arccos(e^{y-3})+2}{3}=x$$

Thus, $x=\frac{\arccos(e^{y-3})+2}{3}$. This equation tells us, for an appropriately chosen value of y in the range, what value of x in the domain gets mapped to that value of y. To describe the inverse function, replace y with x and replace x with y. Then write $f^{-1}(x)$. So here, replacing y with x and x with y, we have the following:

$$y=\frac{\arccos(e^{x-3})+2}{3}$$

Then $f^{-1}(x)=\frac{\arccos(e^{x-3})+2}{3}$.

## 16. C

Strategy: Backsolving

Plugging in (B) as the middle answer choice, $\log_{16}(32) + \log_4(64) = 1.25 + 3 = 4.25$. Incorrect.

Plugging in (C): $\log_{16}(64) + \log_4(128) = 1.5 + 3.5 = 5$. Correct.

To solve this question algebraically, use the identity $\log_a c = (\log_a b)(\log_b c)$.

Here $\log_{16} x = \log_{16} 4 \log_4 x = \frac{1}{2}\log_4 x$.

So $\log_{16} x + \log_4 2x = 5$ becomes $\frac{1}{2}\log_4 x + \log_4 2x = 5$.

Solve this equation for $x$.

$$\log_4 x^{\frac{1}{2}} + \log_4 2x = 5$$

$$\log_4 \left(x^{\frac{1}{2}}\right)(2x) = 5$$

$$\log_4 \left(2x^{\frac{3}{2}}\right) = 5$$

$$2x^{\frac{3}{2}} = 4^5$$

$$2x^{\frac{3}{2}} = \left(2^2\right)^5$$

$$2x^{\frac{3}{2}} = 2^{10}$$

$$x^{\frac{3}{2}} = 2^9$$

$$x^{\frac{1}{2}} = \left(2^9\right)^{\frac{1}{3}} = 2^3$$

$$x = 8^2$$

$$x = 64$$

## 17. B

Strategy: Step-by-Step

By knowing that the cotangent function is equivalent to the cosine divided by the sine, the problem can be rewritten as $\int \frac{\cos x}{\sin x}\, dx$. Now let's use the rule that $\int \frac{1}{u}\frac{du}{dx} = \ln|u| + C$. With $u = \sin x$, we have

$\frac{du}{dx} = \cos x$, and then $\int \frac{\cos x}{\sin x}\, dx = \ln|\sin x| + C$.

Thus, $\int \cot x \, dx = \ln|\sin x| + C$.

## 18. B

Strategy: Step-by-Step

The area of a circle with a radius $r$ is $\pi r^2$. The area of this circle is $36\pi$, so here $\pi r^2 = 36\pi$, $r^2 = 36$, and $r = 6$. (Since radii are never negative, we cannot have $r = -6$.) The diameter of a circle is always twice the radius, so the diameter of the circle is $2(6) = 12$. Thus, one side of the triangle has a length of 12. Since one side of the triangle is a diameter of the circle, the measure of the interior angle of the triangle that is opposite the diameter must be 90 degrees. The area of any triangle is $\frac{1}{2}$ times base times height. The area of a right triangle is $\frac{1}{2} \times \text{leg}_1 \times \text{leg}_2$ because one leg can be considered the base and the other leg can be considered the height. The length of one leg of this right triangle is $12 \sin 34°$, and the length of the other leg of this right triangle is $12 \cos 34°$. So the area of this right triangle is

$$\frac{1}{2} \times (12 \sin 34°)(12 \cos 34°)$$

$$= 72(\sin 34°)(\cos 34°) \approx 33.4.$$

**19. D**

Strategy: Step-by-Step

Since all four people work on the same job, their cumulative rate, in houses per hour, is computed as follows:

$$\text{Rate} = \frac{1}{24} + \frac{1}{20} + \frac{1}{16} + \frac{1}{15}$$

$$= \frac{10}{240} + \frac{12}{240} + \frac{15}{240} + \frac{16}{240}$$

$$= \frac{53}{240}$$

The amount of work that all four complete in 2 hours:

$$\frac{53}{240} \times 2 = \frac{53}{120}.$$

There will be $\frac{67}{120}$ of the job remaining. After Ernest quits, the new rate, in jobs per hour, will be this:

$$\frac{1}{24} + \frac{1}{20} + \frac{1}{15} = \frac{38}{240} = \frac{19}{120}$$

$$\frac{19}{120} \times \text{time remaining} = \frac{67}{120}$$

$$\text{time remaining} = \frac{67}{19}$$

The total number of hours the group spends to paint the house is $2 + \frac{67}{19} = \frac{105}{19}$.

**20. A**

Strategy: Cut the Jargon

If a line $Z$ is not parallel to the $x$-axis or the $y$-axis, then the slope of a line that is perpendicular to line $Z$ is the negative reciprocal of the slope of line $Z$. The given line has a slope of $\frac{-1}{4}$, so a perpendicular line will have a slope of 4. The only answer choice that is the equation of a line with a slope of 4 is choice (A), $y = 4x - 77$.

**21. A**

Strategy: Step-by-Step

Because we are looking for when the probability of having drawn a blue marble climbs above 50%, it is easier to calculate the cumulative probability of when not drawing a blue marble hits 50% or below.

First draw: $\frac{15}{21}$ (the number of marbles that are not blue divided by the total)

The probablity that when one marble is selected, that marble is not blue is $\frac{5}{7}$.

This is greater than $\frac{1}{2}$, so keep going.

Second draw: $\frac{14}{20} = \frac{7}{10}$

The probability that when two marbles are selected, no marble is blue is $\frac{5}{7} \times \frac{7}{10} = \frac{1}{2}$.

At least two marbles are needed to drive the cumulative probability of drawing a blue marble to 50% or above.

**22. C**

Strategy: Step-by-Step

The maxima and minima are determined by setting the first derivative equal to zero.

$$f(x) = x^3 - \frac{1}{2}x^2 - 2x + 2$$

$$f'(x) = 3x^2 - x - 2 = 0$$

$$(3x + 2)(x - 1) = 0$$

When the product of a group of numbers is 0, at least one of the numbers must be 0. If $(3x + 2)(x - 1) = 0$, then $3x + 2 = 0$ or $x - 1 = 0$. If $3x + 2 = 0$, then $3x = -2$, and $x = \frac{-2}{3}$. If $x - 1 = 0$, then $x = 1$.

The x-values where $f'(x) = 0$ are $x = \dfrac{-2}{3}$ and $x = 1$.

Now let's find the local maxima and local minima.

Again, $f'(x) = (3x + 2)(x - 1)$. Let's consider $x = \dfrac{-2}{3}$. If $x < \dfrac{-2}{3}$, then $f'(x) > 0$. If $x > \dfrac{-2}{3}$, then $f'(x) < 0$. Thus, this is the x-coordinate of a local maximum.

Let's consider $x = 1$. If $x < 1$, then $f'(x) < 0$. If $x > 1$, then $f'(x) > 0$. So 1 is the x-coordinate of a local minimum.

Now let's find the y-coordinates of the local maximum and the local minimum.

For the local maximum, substitute $x = \dfrac{-2}{3}$ into $y = x^3 - \dfrac{1}{2}x^2 - 2x + 2$. Then, the y-coordinate of the local maximum is

$$y = \left(\dfrac{-2}{3}\right)^3 - \dfrac{1}{2}\left(\dfrac{-2}{3}\right)^2 - 2\left(\dfrac{-2}{3}\right) + 2$$

$$y = \left(\dfrac{-8}{27}\right) - \dfrac{1}{2}\left(\dfrac{4}{9}\right) + \dfrac{4}{3} + 2$$

$$y = \dfrac{-8}{27} - \dfrac{2}{9} + \dfrac{4}{3} + 2$$

$$y = \dfrac{-8}{27} - \dfrac{6}{27} + \dfrac{36}{27} + \dfrac{54}{27}$$

$$y = \dfrac{-8 - 6 + 36 + 54}{27} = \dfrac{76}{27}$$

There is a local maximum at $\left(\dfrac{-2}{3}, \dfrac{76}{27}\right)$.

For the local minimum, substitute 1 for $x$ into $y = x^3 - \dfrac{1}{2}x^2 - 2x + 2$. Then, the y-coordinate of the local minimum is

$$y = (1)^3 - \dfrac{1}{2}(1)^2 - 2(1) + 2$$

$$y = 1 - \dfrac{1}{2} - 2 + 2 = \dfrac{1}{2}$$

There is a local minimum at $\left(1, \dfrac{1}{2}\right)$.

## 23. A

Strategy: Step-by-Step

$$\sin^2 x + \dfrac{1}{2}\sin x = \dfrac{1}{2}$$

$$\sin^2 x + \dfrac{1}{2}\sin x - \dfrac{1}{2} = 0$$

$$(\sin x + 1)\left(\sin x - \dfrac{1}{2}\right) = 0$$

$$\sin x = -1 \text{ or } \sin x = \dfrac{1}{2}$$

In the interval $[0, 2\pi]$, $\sin \dfrac{3\pi}{2} = -1$, $\sin \dfrac{\pi}{6} = \dfrac{1}{2}$, and $\sin \dfrac{5\pi}{6} = \dfrac{1}{2}$. So all the possible values of $x$ are $\dfrac{\pi}{6}$, $\dfrac{3\pi}{2}$, and $\dfrac{5\pi}{6}$.

## 24. C

Strategy: Cut the Jargon

This is one of the definitions of $e$.

## 25. B

Strategy: Step-by-Step

In a rectangular prism with dimensions 10 × 5 × 10, calculating the longest diagonal will require using the Pythagorean theorem twice. Let's suppose that 10 and 5 are the length and width of the rectangular base. Let's say that the diagonal of this rectangular base is $d$. Then

$$d^2 = 10^2 + 5^2$$

$$d^2 = 100 + 25$$

$$d^2 = 125$$

$$d = \sqrt{125}$$

We could rewrite $\sqrt{125}$. However, we are going to use the Pythagorean theorem a second time, in the process squaring $\sqrt{125}$, so working with $\sqrt{125}$ is fine.

Let's say that the longest diagonal, which is the space diagonal, has a length of $g$ ($g$ could be thought to be the first letter of the word *greatest*, since we are working with the greatest diagonal). Then with the diagonal of the base being $\sqrt{125}$, and the height of the rectangular prism being 10, we have

$$g^2 = \left(\sqrt{125}\right)^2 + 10^2$$

$$g^2 = 125 + 100$$

$$g^2 = 225 = \left(\pm 15\right)^2$$

$$g = 15$$

(Since lengths cannot be negative, we cannot have $g = -15$.)

The length of the longest diagonal is the radius of the sphere. The surface area of a sphere with a radius $r$ is $4\pi r^2$. The radius of this sphere is 15. So the surface area of this sphere is $4\pi(15^2) = 4\pi(225) = 900\pi$.

# CHAPTER NINE

# Social Studies

In this chapter, we will cover several key social studies Subject Assessments. A brief summary of some of the relevant tests, which outlines the content covered on each, is followed by a question bank of social studies questions that will help you refresh your knowledge of the relevant topic areas and hone your test-taking skills.

## PRAXIS SOCIAL STUDIES SUBJECT ASSESSMENTS

This section applies to you if you are taking one of the following tests:

- Social Studies: Content Knowledge (5081)
- Social Studies: Content and Interpretation (5086)

### Social Studies: Content Knowledge (5081)

Test Format: 130 selected-response (multiple-choice) questions

Test Duration: 120 minutes

Content Covered:

- US History: 26 questions, 20 percent of the test
- World History: 26 questions, 20 percent of the test
- Government/Civics/Political Science: 26 questions, 20 percent of the test
- Geography: 19 questions, 15 percent of the test
- Economics: 19 questions, 15 percent of the test
- Behavioral Sciences: 14 questions, 10 percent of the test

This test is designed to assess your knowledge if you are interested in teaching social studies at a secondary school level. The test draws from a wide range of social science content areas with special emphasis on US history; world history; and government, civics, and political science. The question bank that follows includes questions from each of the content areas listed above and is a useful study aid in preparation for this test.

# Social Studies: Content and Interpretation (5086)

Test Format: 90 selected-response (multiple-choice) questions, 3 constructed-response questions (short-answer essays)

Test Duration: 120 minutes

Content Covered:

- US History: 18 questions, 15 percent of the test
- World History: 18 questions, 15 percent of the test
- Government/Civics: 18 questions, 15 percent of the test
- Economics: 13 questions, 11 percent of the test
- Geography: 13 questions, 11 percent of the test
- Behavioral Sciences: 10 questions, 8 percent of the test
- Short Content Essays: 3 essays, 25 percent of the test

The Social Studies: Content and Interpretation test is designed to test the knowledge and skills necessary to teach social studies at a secondary school. Test takers answer 90 multiple-choice questions covering the social science fields listed above and the relationships between them. Some questions may involve the interpretation of charts, graphs, diagrams, tables, and such primary sources as cartoons and photographs. The three short-answer essay questions are interdisciplinary and may require you to interpret, draw inferences from, and contextualize various types of materials such as primary sources, maps, or charts.

Although the question bank that follows does not contain sample essay questions, the content areas covered are consistent with the topics you may encounter in the essay portion of this test. To prepare for this test, therefore, it is worthwhile not only to use this question bank but also to review the basic writing skills discussed in the chapter on the Core Writing test.

# SOCIAL STUDIES QUESTION BANK

1. A drop in interest rates will most likely lead to which of the following pairs of trends?

   A. Increased debt, increased home ownership

   B. Decreased debt, decreased home ownership

   C. Increased debt, decreased home ownership

   D. Decreased debt, increased home ownership

2. The purpose of the Dawes Act passed by the US Congress in 1887 was to encourage Native Americans to

   A. live on reservations

   B. adopt European Americans' style of dress, culture, and religion

   C. cease their efforts to retake the Great Plains region

   D. abandon tribal ways and have privately owned land

3. A researcher studying the motives behind the dropping of the atomic bomb on Japan in World War II would find which of the following types of resources most useful?

   A. Novels

   B. Primary sources

   C. Encyclopedias

   D. Scientific handbooks

4. The partition in Pakistan in 1947 resulted most directly from which of the following circumstances?

   A. Oppression of Muslims in India by the presiding British government

   B. Laws depriving Hindus of the right to vote

   C. Demands of Muslim nationalists in India for an independent state

   D. Conditions placed by the British government on Indian independence

5. The Code of Hammurabi and the Justinian Code of the Byzantine Empire were similar in that they both

   A. were some of the earliest expressions of basic democratic rights

   B. provided a consistent rule of law

   C. became blueprints for religious doctrine

   D. dictated very strict guidelines for trade

6. Which of the following features was developed most fully during the American colonial period?

   A. Universal suffrage

   B. Representative assemblies

   C. An independent court system

   D. Separation between church and state

**Questions 7–8**

"To the Honorable Senate and House of Representatives in Congress Assembled: We the undersigned, citizens of the United States, but deprived of some of the privileges and immunities of citizens, among which is the right to vote, beg leave to submit the following Resolution: …"

—Susan B. Anthony and
Elizabeth Cady Stanton

7. The statement is an example of a citizen's constitutional right to

   A. seek election to public office

   B. assemble peacefully

   C. exercise the right to vote

   D. petition for a redress of grievances

8. The strongest support for the cause of women's rights in the 1800s came mostly from those tied to

   A. social Darwinist thinking

   B. the abolitionist movement

   C. the settlement house movement

   D. civil service reform

9. The parliamentary system's primary disadvantage in comparison to a bipartisan system of legislative organization is

   A. infrequent elections

   B. greater difficulty building governing coalitions

   C. less accountability of officials to public demands

   D. less representation by elected officials

10. The outcome of the Opium War showed that in the 19th century,

    A. the Chinese army was the most highly disciplined army in the world

    B. the Chinese people could be successful in eliminating foreign influence

    C. the Chinese government was no longer strong enough to resist Western demands for trading rights

    D. the Chinese government preferred to continue the opium trade

11.

| Line | Scientific Theory | Relevance | Time Period |
|------|-------------------|-----------|-------------|
| 1 | Theory of Relativity | Theoretical basis for use of atomic energy | 20th century |
| 2 | Theory of Universal Gravitation | Perspective that made possible the calculation of the speed of falling objects and movement of planets | 17th century |
| 3 | Heliocentric Theory | Church-supported view that sun was center of universe | 18th century |
| 4 | Evolutionary Theory | Idea that species arise and develop through natural selection | 19th century |

Which row *incorrectly* matches the scientific theory with its significance and time period?

A. Line 1

B. Line 2

C. Line 3

D. Line 4

12. The US Federal Reserve most directly influences the American economy through

    A. periodic fiscal forecasts

    B. alterations in marginal tax brackets

    C. recommendations for long-term interest rates

    D. influence on the American monetary supply

13. The tropical rain forests of the world are threatened by all of the following EXCEPT:

    A. government policies that encourage road building

    B. those who want to take advantage of the mineral-rich soil

    C. loggers interested in selling wood products

    D. landless peasants seeking economic opportunity

15. The situation shown in the map threatened the US policy of

    A. intervention

    B. containment

    C. neutrality

    D. collective security

16. Which of the following is an accurate description of environmental conditions in the savanna biome?

    A. High rainfall and exceptionally cold temperatures

    B. Extensive grassland and moderate rainfall

    C. Desert-like and sparse vegetation

    D. Heavily forested and very low rainfall

14. The most frequently proposed solution to the problem shown in the cartoon is to

    A. establish poll taxes

    B. use public funds to pay for political campaigns

    C. eliminate primaries from the election system

    D. have candidates finance their own campaigns

17. The work of John Maynard Keynes most influenced fiscal policies under which leader?

    A. George III

    B. Vladimir Lenin

    C. Lyndon Johnson

    D. Andrew Jackson

18.  A major effect of the decline of the Roman Empire was that Western Europe

A.  came under the control of Muslim rulers

B.  returned to a republican form of government

C.  entered a period of disorder and chaos

D.  was absorbed by the Byzantine Empire

**World Energy Use in the 1980s**

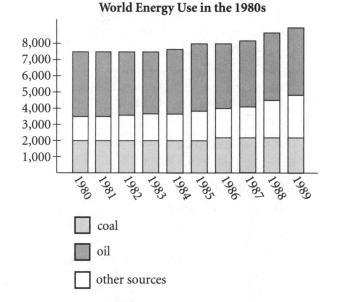

coal

oil

other sources

19.  Which statement is accurate according to the graph above?

A.  Energy use has declined in the 1980s.

B.  Nuclear energy has become the most common energy source.

C.  Coal has become a less important energy source.

D.  Oil is the energy source on which the world most depends.

20.  Statement A: Each person must be able to voice his or her concerns on all issues that involve this new nation and bear responsibility for the decisions made.

Statement B: The power of this new nation must rest in a strong, stable group that makes important decisions with the approval, but not the participation, of all.

Statement C: There must be several governments within one nation to ensure adequate voice and responsibility for all.

Statement D: Individuals must not allow their freedoms to be swallowed by an all-powerful government.

Which statement best represents the ideas of the Bill of Rights?

A.  Statement A

B.  Statement B

C.  Statement C

D.  Statement D

21.  Camillo di Cavour, Giuseppe Mazzini, and Otto von Bismarck are similar in that they

A.  strengthened the power of the Catholic Church

B.  appealed to nationalistic sentiment

C.  adopted communist philosophy

D.  led nations that faced economic depression

22. The Magna Carta and the Glorious Revolution contributed to the development of

    A. imperialism

    B. absolute monarchy

    C. civil rights

    D. parliamentary democracy

23. Which of the following statements about presidential power over foreign policy is correct?

    A. It decreased due to the Louisiana Purchase.

    B. It has decreased during Republican administrations.

    C. It increased due to the passing of the Gulf of Tonkin Resolution.

    D. It increased due to the ratification of the Treaty of Versailles.

24. Which of the following is true, based on Kohlberg's theories of moral development?

    A. Students will be more likely to follow rules and procedures they played a role in creating.

    B. In order to follow the principles Kohlberg expressed in the stages of postconventional moral reasoning, teachers must apply consequences consistently for all students in all circumstances.

    C. How students react to a moral dilemma is independent of their current stage of moral development.

    D. Postconventional individuals believe laws should be regarded as rigid edicts.

25. The gross national product is a

    A. means of calculating the next year's national debt

    B. basic estimate of the value of the nation's natural resources

    C. method of calculating the profits of the nation's largest corporations

    D. barometer of the nation's economic growth

26. President Franklin Roosevelt's New Deal programs and policies were successful according to most supporters because they

    A. prohibited speculation in corporate stocks and bonds

    B. set a precedent for future balanced budgets

    C. accelerated the government's move away from laissez-faire policics

    D. increased employment by creating a larger bureaucratic government structure

27. A graph shows that output per worker hour has increased from 50 in the base period of 1975 to 65 by 1985. A labor union in 1985 could best use this statistic to support

    A. an expansion of its apprenticeship program

    B. a drive for a shorter workweek

    C. a campaign against sex discrimination

    D. an increase in membership dues

28. All of the following helped to limit the power of the English monarchy except the

    A. Act of Supremacy
    B. Magna Carta
    C. Glorious Revolution
    D. Petition of Right

29. The issuance of King James II's Charter of Liberties and Privileges allowed New York

    A. to limit slavery
    B. to exercise limited self-government
    C. to gain representation in the House of Commons
    D. to trade freely with Dutch and French merchants

30. The construction of the Erie Canal did all of the following EXCEPT:

    A. deny the British the fruits of trade in western North America
    B. dramatically lower the cost of shipping goods from Albany to New York City
    C. open up the Ohio Valley to trade
    D. ensure that New York City would be the most important port on the East Coast

# ANSWERS AND EXPLANATIONS

## Social Studies Question Bank

**1. A**

This is an economics question that relies on somewhat abstract principles. If interest rates drop, more capital is made available for lending, and so debt goes up as more people take out loans. Home ownership goes up because the payments on the homes go down and mortgages are easier to obtain. Putting the situation into a real-world scenario is helpful: think about what behavior a lower interest rate on a credit card incentivizes or what friends give as their reason for finally buying a house. Abstract questions can almost always be made more tangible and relevant to current events.

**2. D**

In 1887, Congress passed this act to "Americanize" the Native Americans by cultivating the desire to own property and to farm. The act broke up the reservations and distributed some of the reservation land to each adult head of a family. The actual result of this act was the seizure of most reservation land for white settlers.

**3. B**

Primary sources would be the best resource of the four listed because they offer the best chance of learning about decision makers' motivations. Novels (historical ones) are fictionalized accounts of events. Encyclopedias can be useful as an initial research tool, but they do not go into enough depth to address the questions a researcher would have. Scientific handbooks might provide insight into the mechanics and working of a bomb, but they are unlikely to illuminate people's motivations for using it.

**4. C**

Overall, trends are more important than the event itself. Which answer choices simply don't make sense? You might have eliminated (D) very quickly. Why would the British demand a Muslim state as a condition of Indian independence? Likewise, why would laws discriminating against Hindus trigger Muslim nationalism? Scratch (B). Between (A) and (C), choice (C) is a more direct and in fact inevitable cause of Pakistani independence. Once again, previous knowledge will help to answer the question; any student familiar with the situation surrounding Pakistani independence will get this question in very short order. However, even a passing knowledge of the situation in that area in the 1940s is sufficient to answer the question accurately.

**5. B**

This is one of those questions that compares (not contrasts) two items. Sometimes it is enough to know about just one of the items to answer the question. Both codes established a consistent rule of law throughout these empires. Quickly eliminate (A) because these sets of laws are too ancient to be democratic. Choices (C) and (D) might have been tempting, but note how specific they are. A characteristic both sets of laws share is more likely to be general.

**6. B**

Representative assemblies such as the Virginia House of Burgesses and other colonial assemblies were important precursors to America's independent representative assemblies, such as Congress. Universal suffrage was not developed at all in the colonial period. Enslaved people, women, and in many cases men without property were not allowed to vote. Church and state were not separated in the colonies, and there wasn't an independent court system.

**7. D**

Choice (C) is intended to confuse you. The authors of the document use the right to vote as an example of a right women lack. However, the document itself is an attempt to have grievances redressed, which is any citizen's constitutional right. (D) is the correct answer.

## 8. B

This is another women's rights question. Most of the people involved in the women's rights movement in the 1800s were involved in abolitionist campaigns. They sought the freedom of enslaved persons as well as women. Many male abolitionists supported women's rights. (C) and (D) were Progressive Era reforms in the final years of the 1800s and early 1900s. Choice (A), social Darwinism, is the belief that unrestrained competition will ensure that only the economically and socially strongest individuals and businesses will thrive.

## 9. B

Governments in parliamentary systems are sometimes weak because of the need to build party coalitions to rule. If parties withdraw their support from a governing coalition, the government in power can collapse or be ineffective. The motivation to build coalitions in a parliamentary system is usually strong, but coalitions can be difficult to achieve at times.

## 10. C

The Chinese government was defeated in the Opium War with Western nations. The Chinese government wanted to eliminate the opium trade and Western trading influence. Instead, these nations gained full access to the Chinese market. The war demonstrated the weakness of the Chinese armed forces as well.

## 11. C

Line 3 is inaccurate because the Catholic Church did not support the view that the sun was the center of the universe; rather, the Church believed that Earth was the center of the universe. (It is now recognized that the sun is the center of the solar system, rather than the center of the universe.) Also, the time period is inaccurate. Copernicus (1473–1543) is credited with advocating the heliocentric theory, and Galileo (1564–1642) helped to prove this theory. The other three lines are correct.

## 12. D

This question requires knowing that taxation (B) is exclusively the province of Congress, whereas (A) and (C) would lack fiscal clout. You may have predicted

something close to (D) before looking at the answer choices, and making a prediction is the best way to attack this question. If you looked at the answer choices first, you might have been tempted by (C) because the news often mentions interest rates in conjunction with discussions of "the Fed."

## 13. B

(B) is the correct answer because rain forests are not known for their mineral-rich soil. In fact, farmers have discovered that the land is rather infertile. Farmers who encroach on rain forests often work a plot of land for only a few years before needing to move on to another plot of land, because they have used up the soil's nutrients.

## 14. B

(D) may be tempting, especially if you have seen high-profile candidates finance their own campaigns and claim that they are thus free of special interest influences. However, the use of public funds and calls to use public funding are much more common solutions. Campaign reform laws around the country have begun to implement programs that use limited public funds to pay for campaigns.

## 15. C

The date on the map indicates that it represents World War I, and knowledge of this war is very helpful in answering this question. The United States tried to stay neutral during the initial years of the war but eventually entered in 1917. The *Lusitania* was a British liner that was sunk off the coast of Ireland by a German U-boat in 1915. Many American lives were lost, and the attack on a ship carrying civilian passengers prompted an outcry in the United States, preparing public sentiment for an eventual declaration of war.

## 16. B

If you have watched nature documentaries, the word *savanna* may evoke images of Africa or lions. If so, you may know immediately that (B) accurately represents the savanna. Even if you don't, you can eliminate (A) and (D) because they include environmental conditions that do not make sense: cold temperatures and high rainfall or heavy forestation with little rainfall simply do not go together. Therefore, even without knowledge of this particular biome, you can narrow the answer down to a 50/50 choice.

### 17. C

Knowing when Keynes lived (1883–1946) would be helpful in eliminating (A) and (D). Lenin and Johnson are the only two 20th-century figures in the answer choices. You may have eliminated (B) because Keynes is associated with capitalism, not communism. Keynes was a British economist who proposed that high unemployment, being a result of insufficient consumer spending, could be relieved by government-sponsored programs such as the Great Society programs that President Johnson initiated. Keynes also advocated deficit spending by governments to stimulate economic activity, which was a hallmark of the Johnson years.

### 18. C

After the fall of centralized authority in Rome, Europe entered the Middle Ages, a feudal period in which local lords had authority over the people on their land. Europe was not taken over by Muslim rulers or the Byzantines, nor were European governments republics.

### 19. D

According to the graph, oil, which is represented by the solid dark shading, accounts for the majority of energy used in the world. Other sources have increased their percentages of the total but have not equaled oil. Overall energy use has increased, not declined as in (A). Nuclear energy and natural gas would fall under "other sources," which all together supply less energy than does oil. Usage of coal has remained steady over the period shown.

### 20. D

The Bill of Rights was created because many people feared that the new national government created by the Constitution would be too powerful, leading to an usurpation of the rights of individuals. The Bill of Rights is essentially a set of protections against our government. Statement D expresses this idea.

### 21. B

You may not remember all of these leaders, but if you know about just one, you may be able to answer the question correctly. All three were nationalist leaders who wanted to unite their countries. Cavour and Mazzini were 19th-century Italian leaders, whereas Bismarck was a 19th-century German leader.

### 22. D

The Magna Carta was a document that nobles forced King John to sign in 1215, establishing the foundation for a parliament, and the Glorious Revolution saw the overthrow of James II by William III and Mary II, who accepted the 1689 Bill of Rights. In both cases, power was shifted away from the king, and (D) is correct. Choice (B) contradicts this, whereas (C) doesn't fit the time periods associated with these two events.

### 23. C

The Gulf of Tonkin Resolution authorized President Lyndon Johnson to use conventional military force in Vietnam without a congressional declaration of war. This resolution increased presidential power, as the president was thus empowered to intervene militarily in foreign affairs without legislative approval. Therefore, choice (C) is correct. (A) is incorrect because the Louisiana Purchase increased presidential power over foreign policy, as President Jefferson authorized a land purchase even though doing so was not specifically listed in the Constitution as a presidential power. (B) is incorrect because presidential power has generally increased over time, regardless of political party. (D) is incorrect because the Senate voted down the Treaty of Versailles, which President Wilson had championed, thereby undermining presidential authority in foreign affairs.

### 24. A

Kohlberg's moral development theories include a description of different stages individuals attain. Students at the preconventional stage of moral reasoning may unquestioningly follow rules simply to avoid punishment. However, individuals at the postconventional stage recognize that rules are created and followed to benefit society. Participants in rule making are more likely to follow the rules they create, making (A) correct. Kohlberg believed that even same-aged individuals might be at different levels of moral development. Therefore, (C) is incorrect. (B) and (D) are false because at the postconventional stage level, individuals recognize that enforcement of rules should be done flexibly to fit the circumstances.

## 25. D

*Gross national product* (GNP) is a macroeconomic term for the total market value of all the goods and services produced by a nation during a specified period. (C) can be eliminated because the word *gross* means the whole amount of something, so only profits and only activity of large corporations do not match. (A) refers to debt, and (B) refers to natural resources, neither of which are products, so these choices can be eliminated.

## 26. C

Most supporters of Roosevelt's New Deal believed that the government should come to the aid of those in need, particularly during the economic circumstances of the Great Depression. This meant a move away from the government's rather laissez-faire attitude toward the economy. Laissez-faire policies of the 19th century meant that the government left businesses and the economy alone. Progressive legislation at the end of the 19th and beginning of the 20th century began a retreat away from laissez-faire policies that the New Deal accelerated greatly, as in choice (C). (A) is incorrect because speculation remains an integral part of the stock market. (B) is incorrect because the New Deal produced huge deficits and not a balanced budget; the government borrowed money to pay for the New Deal programs. (D) is incorrect because while the expansion of the government bureaucracy happened to be a consequence of the reforms instituted, it was not a goal of New Deal supporters.

## 27. B

Because workers are producing at a higher rate, the union could use this as a justification for shortening the workweek (while maintaining pay rates). Having an apprenticeship program (A) and increasing membership dues (D) are within the purview of

unions under all circumstances and are not related to using increased productivity as a bargaining tool. (C) is a cause that a union might support, but it would not be related to higher worker productivity.

## 28. A

The Act of Supremacy granted King Henry VIII of England authority over the Church of England. This effectively created the Anglican Church, which was separate from the Roman Catholic Church. The other three choices all established limits on the monarch's power. The Magna Carta (1215) guaranteed that freeborn Englishmen could not be fined or imprisoned except according to the laws of the land. During the Glorious Revolution (1688–89), King James II was overthrown in favor of his daughter and her husband, who were invited by the leaders of Parliament to take his place under certain conditions. The Petition of Right (1628) significantly limited the crown's authority, particularly with regard to justice and taxation.

## 29. B

This charter (1683) granted limited self-government to the New York colony. Slavery was never limited in the colonies by Britain, and no colony was given representation in either house of the British Parliament during the colonial period. Indeed, representation became an important issue in the independence struggle. The mercantilist system of the British did not allow American colonists to trade with foreign nations without specific permission.

## 30. B

Costs for shipping were lowered with the construction of the Erie Canal, which runs from the Hudson River at Albany to Lake Erie and Lake Ontario. However, the Albany–to–New York route is along the Hudson River and would not involve use of the canal. The other three answer choices were results of building the canal. The Erie Canal greatly facilitated the transport of agricultural products from the Ohio Valley to the East Coast and international markets (C), especially through the port of New York City (D). It also provided an alternative to the St. Lawrence River, which ran through Canada, then under British rule (A).

# PRAXIS RESOURCES

# State Certification Information

| State | Teacher Certification Division | Praxis State Requirements Link |
|---|---|---|
| Alabama | Office of Teaching and Leading<br>Alabama State Department of Education<br>50 North Ripley St<br>P.O. Box 302101<br>Montgomery, AL 36130-2101<br>Phone: 1-334-242-9983<br>Email: edassessment@alsde.edu<br>Website: **alsde.edu** | **ets.org/praxis/al** |
| Alaska | Alaska Department of Education & Early Development<br>ATTN: Teacher Certification<br>801 West 10th Street, Suite 200<br>P.O. Box 110500<br>Juneau, AK 99811-0500<br>Phone: 1-907-465-2831<br>Fax: 1-907-465-2441<br>Email: tcwebmail@alaska.gov<br>Website: **education.alaska.gov/teachercertification** | **ets.org/praxis/ak** |
| Arkansas | Office of Educator Licensure<br>Arkansas Department of Education<br>Four Capitol Mall<br>Room 106-B<br>Little Rock, AR 72201<br>Phone: 1-501-682-4342<br>Fax: 1-501-683-4898<br>Email: ade.educatorlicensure@arkansas.gov<br>Website: **arkansased.gov/divisions/human-resources-educator-effectiveness-and-licensure/educator-licensure-unit** | **ets.org/praxis/ar** |
| California | California Commission on Teacher Credentialing (CTC)<br>Information Services<br>1900 Capitol Avenue<br>Sacramento, CA 95811-4213<br>Email: credentials@ctc.ca.gov<br>(note: include postal address in correspondence)<br>Website: **ctc.ca.gov** | **ets.org/praxis/ca** |

| State | Teacher Certification Division | Praxis State Requirements Link |
|---|---|---|
| Colorado | Office of Educator Preparation, Licensing and Educator Effectiveness<br>Colorado Department of Education<br>6000 E. Evans Ave., Bldg. #2, Ste. 100<br>Denver, CO 80222<br>Phone: 1-303-866-6628<br>Fax: 1-303-866-6722<br>Email: CDELicensing@cde.state.co.us<br>Website: **cde.state.co.us/cdeprof** | **ets.org/praxis/co** |
| Connecticut | Connecticut State Department of Education<br>Bureau of Educator Standards and Certification<br>P.O. Box 150471<br>Hartford, CT 06115-0471<br>Phone: 1-860-713-6969<br>Fax: 1-860-713-7017<br>Email: teacher.cert@ct.gov<br>Website: **ct.gov/sde/cert** | **ets.org/praxis/ct** |
| Delaware | Delaware Department of Education<br>Collette Education Resource Center<br>35 Commerce Way, Suite 1<br>Dover, DE 19904<br>ATTN: Certification<br>Phone: 1-302-857-3388<br>Website: **deeds.doe.k12.de.us** | **ets.org/praxis/de** |
| District of Columbia | Educator Credentialing<br>OSSE-Division of Elementary, Secondary and Specialized Education<br>Educator Quality and Effectiveness, Teaching and Learning Unit<br>5th Floor<br>810 First Street, NE<br>Washington, DC 20002<br>Phone: 1-202-741-5881<br>Email: osse.asklicensure@dc.gov<br>Website: **osse.dc.gov/ed-credentials** | **ets.org/praxis/dc** |

| State | Teacher Certification Division | Praxis State Requirements Link |
|-------|-------------------------------|-------------------------------|
| Georgia | The Georgia Professional Standards Commission<br>200 Piedmont Avenue SE<br>Suite 1702, West Tower<br>Atlanta, GA 30334-9032<br>Phone: 1-404-232-2500 in metro Atlanta area or outside GA<br>Toll-free: 1-800-869-7775 (in GA, but outside metro Atlanta)<br>Email: mail@gapsc.com<br>Website: **gapsc.com** | **ets.org/praxis/ga** |
| Hawaii | Hawaii Teacher Standards Board<br>ATTN: Licensing Section<br>650 Iwilei Road, Suite 201<br>Honolulu, HI 96817<br>Phone: 1-808-586-2600<br>Fax: 1-808-586-2606<br>Email: htsb@hawaii.gov<br>Website: **htsb.org** | **ets.org/praxis/hi** |
| Idaho | Idaho State Department of Education<br>P.O. Box 83720<br>Boise, Idaho 83720-0027<br>Phone: 1-208-332-6800<br>Fax: 1-208-334-2228<br>Email: info@sde.idaho.gov<br>Website: **sde.idaho.gov/cert-psc/cert/** | **ets.org/praxis/idaho** |
| Indiana | Office of Educator Effectiveness and Licensing<br>Indiana Department of Education<br>151 W. Washington Street<br>South Tower, Suite 600<br>Indianapolis, Indiana 46204<br>Phone: 1-317-232-9010<br>Fax: 1-317-232-9023<br>Email: licensinghelp@doe.in.gov<br>Website: **www.doe.in.gov/licensing** | **ets.org/praxis/in** |

| State | Teacher Certification Division | Praxis State Requirements Link |
|-------|-------------------------------|-------------------------------|
| Iowa | Iowa Board of Educational Examiners<br>Grimes State Office Building<br>400 East 14th Street<br>Des Moines, IA 50319<br>Website: **www.iowa.gov/boee** | **ets.org/praxis/ia** |
| Kansas | Kansas State Department of Education<br>Teacher Licensure and Accreditation<br>Landon State Office Building<br>900 SW Jackson St., Suite 106<br>Topeka, KS 66612-1212<br>Phone: 1-785-296-2288<br>Fax: 1-785-296-7933<br>Email: shelbert@ksde.org<br>Website: **ksde.org/Agency/Division-of-Learning-Services/Teacher-Licensure-and-Accreditation** | **ets.org/praxis/ks** |
| Kentucky | Kentucky Education Professional Standards Board<br>100 Airport Road, 3rd Floor<br>Frankfort, Kentucky 40601<br>Phone: 1-502-564-4606<br>Fax: 1-502-564-7080<br>Toll-free: 1-888-598-7667<br>Website: **epsb.ky.gov** | **ets.org/praxis/ky** |
| Louisiana | Louisiana Department of Education<br>Division of Certification, Preparation and Recruitment<br>P.O. Box 94064<br>Baton Rouge, LA 70804-9064<br>Phone: 1-877-453-2721<br>Fax: 225-342-0193<br>Website: **louisianabelieves.com/teaching/certification** | **ets.org/praxis/la** |

| State | Teacher Certification Division | Praxis State Requirements Link |
|-------|-------------------------------|-------------------------------|
| Maine | State of Maine Department of Education<br>Certification Office<br>23 State House Station<br>Augusta, ME 04333-0023<br>Phone: 1-207-624-6603<br>Fax: 1-207-624-6604<br>Email: cert.doe@maine.gov<br>Website: **maine.gov/doe/cert** | **ets.org/praxis/me** |
| Maryland | Maryland State Department of Education<br>ATTN: Certification Branch<br>200 W. Baltimore Street<br>Baltimore, Maryland 21201<br>Phone: 1-410-767-0412<br>Toll-free: 1-866-772-8922<br>TTY/TDD: 1-410-333-6442<br>Email: info.msde@maryland.gov<br>Website: **marylandpublicschools.org/about/Pages/DEE/Certification/index.aspx** | **ets.org/praxis/md** |
| Minnesota | Minnesota Department of Education<br>Personnel Licensing Team<br>1500 Highway 36 West<br>Roseville, MN 55113-4266<br>Phone: 1-651-582-8691<br>Email: mde.educator-licensing@state.mn.us<br>Website: **education.state.mn.us** | **ets.org/praxis/mn** |
| Mississippi | Mississippi Department of Education<br>P.O. Box 771<br>Jackson, MS 39205-0771<br>Attn: Demetrice Watts<br>Phone: 1-601-359-3483<br>Email: dwatts@mdek12.org<br>Website: **mde.k12.ms.us** | **ets.org/praxis/ms** |

| State | Teacher Certification Division | Praxis State Requirements Link |
|---|---|---|
| Missouri | Missouri Department of Elementary & Secondary Education<br>Educator Certification<br>P.O. Box 480<br>Jefferson City, MO 65102-0480<br>Phone: 1-573-751-0051<br>Email: certification@dese.mo.gov<br>Website: **dese.mo.gov/educator-quality/certification** | **ets.org/praxis/mo** |
| Nebraska | Nebraska Department of Education<br>Teacher Certification<br>301 Centennial Mall South<br>P.O. Box 94987<br>Lincoln, NE 68509<br>Phone: 1-402-471-0739<br>Fax: 1-402-742-2359<br>E-mail: nde.tcertweb@nebraska.gov<br>Website: **www.education.ne.gov/TCERT** | **ets.org/praxis/ne** |
| Nevada | Nevada Department of Education<br>Office of Educator Licensure<br>9890 S. Maryland Parkway, Ste 221<br>Las Vegas, NV 89183<br>Phone: 1-702-486-6458<br>Website: **www.doe.nv.gov/Educator_Licensure** | **ets.org/praxis/nv** |
| New Hampshire | New Hampshire Department of Education<br>101 Pleasant Street<br>Concord, NH 03301-3860<br>Phone: 1-603-271-2409<br>Fax: 1-603-271-4134<br>TDD Access: Relay NH: 711<br>Email: Cert.Info@doe.nh.gov<br>Website: **education.nh.gov/certification** | **ets.org/praxis/nh** |
| New Jersey | New Jersey Department of Education<br>Office of Certification and Induction<br>PO Box 500<br>Trenton, NJ 08625-0500<br>Phone: 1-609-292-2070<br>Website: **state.nj.us/education/educators/license** | **ets.org/praxis/nj** |

| State | Teacher Certification Division | Praxis State Requirements Link |
|---|---|---|
| New Mexico | New Mexico Public Education Department<br>Jerry Apodaca Education Building<br>300 Don Gaspar<br>Santa Fe, NM 87501<br>Phone: 1-505-827-1436 (licensure help desk)<br>1-505-827-5800<br>Email: LicensureUnit@state.nm.us<br>Website: **ped.state.nm.us** | **ets.org/praxis/nm** |
| New York | Office of Teaching Initiatives<br>New York State Education Department<br>89 Washington Ave, 5N EB<br>Albany, New York 12234<br>Phone: 1-518-474-3901<br>TTY: 1-800-421-1220 (within NY), 1-800-855-2880 (nationwide)<br>Website: **www.highered.nysed.gov/tcert** | **ets.org/praxis/ny** |
| North Carolina | North Carolina Department of Public Instruction<br>Licensure Section<br>6365 Mail Service Center<br>Raleigh, NC 27699-6365<br>Phone: 1-800-577-7994 (within NC), 1-919-807-3310 (outside NC)<br>Email: asklicensure@dpi.nc.gov<br>(include full name and last 4 of SSN or application number)<br>Website: **www.ncpublicschools.org/licensure** | **ets.org/praxis/nc** |
| North Dakota | North Dakota Education Standards and Practices Board<br>2718 Gateway Avenue, Suite 204<br>Bismarck, ND 58503-0585<br>Phone: 1-701-328-9641<br>Fax: 1-701-328-9647<br>Email: espbinfo@nd.gov<br>Website: **nd.gov/espb** | **ets.org/praxis/nd** |
| Ohio | Ohio Department of Education<br>Office of Educator Licensure<br>25 South Front Street, Mail Stop 504<br>Columbus, OH 43215-4183<br>Phone: 1-614-466-3593<br>Toll-free: 1-877-644-6338<br>Email: Educator.Licensure@education.ohio.gov<br>Website: **education.ohio.gov/Topics/Teaching/Licensure** | **ets.org/praxis/oh** |

| State | Teacher Certification Division | Praxis State Requirements Link |
|---|---|---|
| Oklahoma | Oklahoma State Department of Education<br>Teacher Certification<br>2500 North Lincoln Boulevard, #212<br>Oklahoma City, Oklahoma 73105-4599<br>Phone: 1-405-525-3337<br>Website: **sde.ok.gov/sde/teacher-certification** | **ets.org/praxis/ok** |
| Oregon | Oregon Teacher Standards and Practices Commission<br>250 Division Street NE<br>Salem, OR 97301<br>Phone: 1-503-378-3586<br>Fax: 1-503-378-4448<br>Email: contact.tspc@oregon.gov<br>Website: **oregon.gov/TSPC** | **ets.org/praxis/or** |
| Pennsylvania | Bureau of School Leadership and Teacher Quality<br>Pennsylvania Department of Education<br>333 Market Street, 12th Floor<br>Harrisburg, PA 17126-0333<br>Phone: 1-717-728-3224<br>TTY/TDD: 1-717-783-8445<br>Fax: 1-717-783-6736<br>Website: **education.pa.gov/Teachers%20-%20 Administrators/Certifications** | **ets.org/praxis/pa** |
| Rhode Island | Rhode Island Department of Education<br>255 Westminster Street<br>Providence, RI 02903<br>Phone: 1-401-222-4600<br>Email: eqac@ride.ri.gov<br>Website: **ride.ri.gov/teachersadministrators/ educatorcertification** | **ets.org/praxis/ri** |

| State | Teacher Certification Division | Praxis State Requirements Link |
|---|---|---|
| South Carolina | Division of Federal, State, & Community Resources<br>Office of Educator Services<br>8301 Parklane Road<br>Columbia, SC 29223<br>Phone: 1-803-896-0325<br>Fax: 1-803-896-0368<br>Email: certification@ed.sc.gov<br>Website: **ed.sc.gov/educators/certification/certification-resources/required-examinations/** | **ets.org/praxis/sc** |
| South Dakota | South Dakota Department of Education<br>Office of Certification and Teacher Quality<br>800 Governors Drive<br>Pierre, SD 57501<br>Phone: 1-605-773-3426<br>(Roxie Thielen and Jane Cronin)<br>Email: certification@state.sd.us<br>Website: **doe.sd.gov/oatq/praxis.aspx** | **ets.org/praxis/sd** |
| Tennessee | > Office of Educator Licensing<br>Tennessee State Department of Education<br>Andrew Johnson Tower, 12th Floor<br>710 James Robertson Parkway<br>Nashville, TN 37243-0377<br>Phone: 1-615-532-4885<br>Fax: 1-615-532-1448<br>Email: Education.Licensing@tn.gov<br>Website: **tennessee.gov/education/section/licensing** | **ets.org/praxis/tn** |
| Utah | Utah State Board of Education<br>Teaching and Learning Licensing<br>250 East 500 South<br>P.O. Box 144200<br>Salt Lake City, UT 84114-4200<br>Phone: 1-801-538-7740<br>Website: **schools.utah.gov/cert** | **ets.org/praxis/ut** |

| State | Teacher Certification Division | Praxis State Requirements Link |
|-------|-------------------------------|-------------------------------|
| Vermont | Vermont Agency of Education<br>219 North Main St., Suite 402<br>Barre, VT 05641<br>Phone: 1-802-479-1700<br>Fax: 1-802-479-4313<br>Email: aoe.edinfo@vermont.gov<br>Website: **education.vermont.gov/educator-quality/ become-a-vermont-educator** | **ets.org/praxis/vt** |
| Virginia | Virginia Department of Education<br>Division of Teacher Education and Licensure<br>P.O. Box 2120<br>Richmond, VA 23218-2120<br>Email: licensure@doe.virginia.gov<br>Website: **doe.virginia.gov/teaching/licensure** | **ets.org/praxis/va** |
| Washington | Professional Educator Standards Board<br>P.O. Box 47236<br>Olympia, WA 98504-7236<br>Email: PESB@k12.wa.us<br>Phone: 1-360-725-6275<br>Fax: 1-360-586-4548<br>Website: **pesb.wa.gov** | **ets.org/praxis/wa** |
| West Virginia | West Virginia Department of Education<br>Office of Professional Preparation<br>1900 Kanawha Blvd. East, Building 6, Room 722<br>Charleston, WV 25305-0330<br>Phone: 1-304-558-7010<br>Toll-free: 1-800-982-2378<br>Website: **wvde.state.wv.us/certification** | **ets.org/praxis/wv** |

| State | Teacher Certification Division | Praxis State Requirements Link |
|---|---|---|
| Wisconsin | Teacher Education, Professional Development, and Licensing<br>Wisconsin Department of Public Instruction<br>125 South Webster Street<br>Madison, WI 53703<br>Phone: 1-800-266-1027<br>Email: licensing@dpi.wi.gov<br>Website: **dpi.wi.gov/tepdl** | **ets.org/praxis/wi** |
| Wyoming | Wyoming Professional Teaching Standards Board<br>Professional Teaching Standards Board<br>1920 Thomes Avenue, Suite 400<br>Cheyenne, WY 82002<br>Phone: 1-307-777-7291<br>Toll-free: 1-800-675-6893<br>Fax: 1-307-777-8718<br>Website: **ptsb.state.wy.us/Licensure/ TestingRequirements/tabid/73/Default.aspx** | **ets.org/praxis/wy** |
| The states represented in the table use one or more tests in the Praxis Series for teacher certification. If your state is not listed, it does not currently use the Praxis exams. Information included here is current as this book goes to print but may have changed; always check with your state's certification division for the most definitive guidance. | | |

# Getting Started: Advice for New Teachers

So you've passed the Praxis with flying colors and fulfilled all the requirements for becoming a teacher in your state. Now it's time to put all of your learning into practice!

## Finding the Right Position

It is common knowledge that more good teachers are needed across the country. But finding the right job can be a daunting process. Luckily, there are some simple best practices that you can prepare to help stand out, such as following professionalism and ethics guidelines to distinguish yourself from other amateur teachers, making sure your license is up to date, and having ready examples of strategies and methods for instruction. Use the following tips to help narrow your focus and streamline your applications.

### 1. Do Your Research

First, determine the grade levels and/or subjects you are most interested in teaching. Make sure you have fulfilled all the qualifications for the state in which you wish to teach. Keep in mind that different states may have different requirements for licensure, while others have license reciprocity. Some schools may even give you a provisional license to start teaching while you complete the necessary test or coursework.

Check the testing requirements for your state at **ets.org/praxis** or by contacting the governing body directly using the *State Certification Information* that we provided in the prior section of this book.

### 2. Identify Where You Would Like to Work

Make a list of the districts and/or schools where you would most prefer to work. Many school districts have websites on which they post job openings. In addition, you should call the district office to find out whether there are any positions open that may not have been listed yet and what the district's application procedures are.

Use the Internet as a resource. In addition to the many general websites for job hunters, there are websites devoted solely to teaching jobs. A few websites will ask you for a subscription fee, but there are many others with free listings. A list of some of these sites is included at the end of this section.

### 3. Attend Job Fairs

While many regional schools may not attend job fairs, they are still a good way to learn about openings and to network with other education professionals. Several of the websites for job-seekers listed at the end of this section also have job fair listings by state. Having a resume and broad cover letter in-hand is a good idea in general, and can make you stand out from the crowd.

Remember that you are assessing potential employers as much as they are assessing you. Consider asking the following:

- What is the first professional development opportunity offered to new teachers?
- What additional duties outside the classroom are expected of teachers?
- What is your teacher retention rate?
- When can I expect to meet my mentor? And how long is the probationary/observational period?
- What is the top school-wide priority this year? Countywide? Statewide?
- What kinds of materials or resources would be available in my classroom? (if applicable)
- What is your policy on lesson planning?

You may also want to ask about the demographics of the student population, the kinds of unique challenges they present, and what supports the school has in place.

### 4. Sign Up for Substitute Teaching

Substitute teaching can be another good strategy for getting your foot in the door in a particular school or district, even if there are no permanent jobs available. Think of this as an opportunity to impress principals and to learn from other teachers about possible openings. You can even submit your resume to the principals in the schools where you are substitute teaching and give them the chance to observe you in the classroom. While substitute teaching can be one of the most difficult jobs, it allows you to network and prove yourself in the classroom.

## Your Resume and the Interview

For many people, writing down all of their accolades and crafting a thoughtful resume can be tedious and stressful. If you find a fulfilling position, though, this may be something that you'll need to update only once or twice a decade. Remember, not everything has to be in the resume and cover letter: you'll have the chance to fill in any additional details during the interview. Our recommendations below are designed to help you focus on these two aspects of landing your teaching job.

### *Building Your Best Cover Letter*

The cover letter should let prospective employers have a glimpse into your character beyond the numbers and scores and snippets from the resume. Keep it professional, but don't be afraid to use a few colloquial words or expressions that let your voice shine through.

- Read about the school you are applying to. What are their current programs, policies, and mission? Specifically mention the experience you have with those programs directly, how your related experience can translate, or how excited you are to learn more about them.

- Use educational buzz-words, list other educational programs that you have used, and try to cover as many of the job description points as possible.
- Don't be afraid to name-drop. If you have been networking in the school, use your connections.
- Remember, many schools accept hundreds of applications for a teaching position. Keep your cover letter as brief and punchy as possible. Avoid formulaic phrasing or drawn-out sentences.

## The Resume

There are many excellent templates to build your resume. Choose one that is clear, easy to follow, and isn't overly artsy or cutesy. The resume should be essentially a cheat-sheet for your school to use and get an instant snapshot of what your training and experience is.

- Use active words that tell exactly what you did, rather than simply listing the item. "Developed and Implemented a Writing Center Training Program to 15 tutors," is more precise and impressive than "Participated in Writing Center Training Program."
- Narrow down accomplishments to 3–4 per job/position if you have many. Stay focused on the job you're applying to and which of your accolades will be most impressive/applicable.
- Remove the fluff. If that summer wait staff position didn't impact your ability to teach directly, it doesn't belong in this resume! Similarly, long-winded explanations of the programs you participated in, or language that's unnecessarily verbose, is off-putting to someone who may be reading hundreds of these.
- Try to stick to the two-pages rule. If your resume can't fit on one page (this would be ideal), cut back where possible to make it a maximum of two pages so that the hiring team isn't flipping through a half-dozen pages to find what school you went to.

## Your Interview

So you made it through the first round and they want you to come in and speak with their team. Whether this is a one-on-one, or group, or a series of short interviews, the general recommendations are the same. Be natural and true to yourself, and be confident and clear in your answers. Remember, we are all just people; the person interviewing you was once in your shoes too.

- Project a relaxed confidence, no matter how you may feel inside. Smile, look them in the eyes, sit up straight, don't fidget, say their name when responding, talk clearly.
- When answering direct questions, such as who you worked with at your last substitute teaching job, answer quickly to reinforce your preparedness. If the questions are more broad or conceptual, pause for a count of 2–3 seconds to show that you're putting real thought into each answer, even if this is a question you were already prepared for.
- Be ready to give specific examples of the teaching you have done. It's a good idea to bring a teaching portfolio, but don't be surprised if they don't want to review it. Schools may ask for sample lesson plans and newsletters, or ask you to teach a lesson as part of the interview process.
- You are interviewing them just as much as they are interviewing you. Ask directed questions about the culture of the school, retention rate, and support systems for new teachers. Having no questions at all may seem like you aren't invested in learning about the school, and fluff questions that could have been answered by simply visiting the website comes off as amateur.

# Starting in the Classroom

Don't get disillusioned if you're not immediately comfortable in your role as a teacher. Give yourself time to adjust, and don't hesitate to ask for advice from others. Be persistent about finding a mentor who can provide support during your first year and beyond. Try to find one in your subject area and determine how much experience you would like that person to have. For the sake of convenience, it's a good idea to find someone who has a similar class schedule or daily routine.

### *Teach Rules and Respect*

With students, be friendly but firm. Establish clear routines and consistent disciplinary measures starting on Day One. This way, the students will have a firm understanding of what is expected of them and when certain behaviors are appropriate. If there is a school-wide behavior program such as PBiS, RtI, or Responsive Classroom, make sure to follow that through in your classroom for consistency. Be aware of how cliques and social hierarchies impact classroom dynamics, avoid power struggles, and don't underestimate the power of your own advice.

Although disciplinary issues vary according to grade level, there are some general tips you may find helpful in setting rules in the classroom:

- Often, misbehavior is an attempt to get your attention or avoid uncomfortable situations on work. Reduce this negative behavior by paying the least amount of attention when a student is acting out and giving that child your full attention when he is behaving.

- When it comes to establishing classroom rules, allow your students to have some input. This will increase their sense of empowerment and respect for the rules.

- Convince all of your students that they are worthwhile and capable. It is easy to assume that struggling students are lazy or beyond help; do not allow yourself to fall into this trap.

- When disciplining students, absolutely avoid embarrassing them in any way, shape, or form, especially in front of their peers. Behaviors are bad, not students.

- Double standards and favoritism will lose you the respect of all your students; always be firm, fair, and consistent. Never talk down to your students.

- Avoid becoming too chummy with your students. Young teachers often feel that they must make "friends" with students, particularly in the older grades. However, it's important to maintain some professional distance and to establish yourself as an authority figure.

- Admit your mistakes. If you wrongly accuse a student of doing something she did not do, make an inappropriate joke, or reprimand a student more harshly than necessary, be sure to apologize and explain. If a parent or administrator criticizes you for your mistake, calmly explain how you felt at that moment and why. Also, explain how you plan on handling that kind of situation in the future.

- Communicate with parents regularly. Help parents see that you are working with them and with the students to help the students succeed at the highest possible level. Parents are more likely to help address problems with students when the parents see that you are sincerely working for the students' academic success.

### Do Your Homework

Any veteran teacher will tell you that you will spend almost as many hours working outside the classroom as you do with your students. Preparing lessons and grading homework and tests can take an enormous amount of time, so it's a good idea to be as organized as possible and thoughtful about the lessons and tests that you assign.

Also, consider what your expectations will be:

- Will you grade every homework assignment or just some of them?
- Will you give students an opportunity to earn extra credit?
- What kind of system will you use for grading tests?

### Design Lesson Plans Early

Before you start planning, be aware of holidays off, assemblies, and similar interruptions. Design your lessons accordingly. Similarly, be sure you know your content, your state's standards, your school's expectations, and the ins and outs of child development. Be prepared with multiple learning styles and differentiated teaching strategies. Try to include some variety of activities in every lesson with valid alternate choices for completion.

Develop time-saving strategies. Saving your lesson plan outline as a template on the computer can be very helpful. Instead of rewriting the whole plan every day, you can just fill in the blanks.

### Establish Rules for Grading Homework

Along with establishing a consistent disciplinary policy early on, it's important to know your school's grading policy or develop grading guidelines. Some teachers set the bar high at the beginning of the year by grading a little tougher than they normally would. Just as many students will underachieve if they think you are a soft grader, they will work hard to meet your expectations if your standards are high. However, it's important to assess your students' abilities and set realistic standards.

Use formative and summative assessment types. Grading every single assignment can get overwhelming; sometimes verbally assessing comprehension is enough. Rubrics are another useful tool for outlining expectations and scoring, as well as making sure you cater to the needs of all your students. Rubrics are also effective when students grade each other.

Returning graded assignments as soon as possible sets a good example, keeps your workload manageable, and prevents students' interest from waning. However, you should never use a student's work as an example of what not to do.

Consider sending grades home on a regular basis and getting them signed by parents in order to keep everyone aware of students' progress. This prevents students and parents from being blindsided by poor grades.

Don't confuse quietness for comprehension. Check in with all students because some may be afraid to admit that they don't understand what's going on. If you feel there is a problem, don't wait to address a student's needs. If you believe that a student may have an undiagnosed disability, let your principal know and follow your school's procedure.

Some teachers find that recognizing students' achievements with tangible rewards can increase students' motivation and positively influence their academic performance. These types of incentive systems work particularly well in the elementary grades.

### Deal with Parents Early On

Establish a relationship with parents from the beginning. Frequent, positive communication is essential to helping the children attain the best education possible, and makes conversations smoother if/when issues arrise. Here are a few tips for keeping in touch with parents:

- Make phone calls, even if you're just going to leave a message. Doing so will allow you to share good news and help guardians become more familiar with you.
- Give students homework folders that frequently travel between school and home, and send personal notes.
- Be ready to deal with breakdowns in communication: it may be necessary to send multiple messages home.
- Send home a short newsletter of things to come.
- Create an email mailing list or a blog, private class social media page or other webpage for families to follow. Be sure to check your school's acceptable online presence standards.

### Set Up Parent-Teacher Conferences

Meeting with parents can often be intimidating for new teachers, particularly if a student is not performing well; just remember that families are your greatest resource and ally for supporting your students outside of the classroom. It's a good idea to seek guidance from experienced teachers, and communicate with administrators if you encounter problems. In addition, try to follow these general guidelines when talking with parents:

- Remain professional. Don't take heated words personally, have good things to say about the student, choose your words carefully, keep examples of the student's work on hand, and document what is said during the meeting.
- Allow parents to ask the first question. This will help you understand their tone and their concerns.
- Be as thick skinned as possible when dealing with problems: some parents want to vent a little before getting to the crux of the issue. Let them vent, try to put them at ease, and then look for a solution or compromise.
- If a parent becomes excessively confrontational, inform an administrator.
- Have documents available to support your statements. For example, if the student has not completed assignments, have gradebook evidence to support your contention.
- Be confident. Listen to what the parents suggest, but also stand up for what you believe is the best course of action.

### Building Relationships with Colleagues

Meet as many teachers in the building as you can; not only will you gain valuable insights about the inner workings of the school, but you'll also make new friends. Don't be afraid to step up and ask questions when information isn't offered. Veteran teachers are a tremendous resource for all kinds of information, ranging from labor contracts to strategies for staying sane under pressure. Also, get to know the other new teachers. These people will be valuable sounding boards and will help you feel less alone.

Earn the respect of your colleagues by stepping up to committee work, and by proving yourself to be a reliable, competent teacher. You should also be polite and friendly with secretaries, custodians, and other school staff; you'll need their help for all sorts of reasons.

Finally, be professional, timely, and unafraid to calmly share your opinions or disagree with administrators. Your professionalism and enthusiasm will earn you their respect and ensure that your needs are met.

### Dealing with Paperwork

Be aware of what kinds of paperwork you need to fill out and file, including the School Improvement Plan, special education forms relating to Individualized Education Plans, budget requests, reading and math benchmarks, and permanent record cards. Consider sitting with fellow teachers when filling out forms. Their companionship will make these tedious tasks more fun.

### Understanding Unions

Depending on your school district, you may be part of a teacher's union. It is important to gain a clear understanding of union requirements. You'll want to know:

- How much money will be deducted from your paycheck for union dues
- How you can obtain a copy of the most recent union contract

### Allow Yourself "Down Time"

Finally, always give yourself time to wind down and distance yourself from the classroom. This is essential to prevent burnout or resentment over a lack of free time, and will allow you to pursue other interests and personal relationships.

## Additional Resources

### Books

Capel, Susan, Marilyn Leask, and Terry Turner, *Learning to Teach in the Secondary School: A Companion to School Experience*, 7th ed. Routledge, 2016.

Codell, Esme. *Educating Esmé: Diary of a Teacher's First Year*. Workman Publishing, 2009.

Dillon, Justin. *Becoming a Teacher*. McGraw Hill, Open University Press, 2001.

Goodnough, Abby. *Ms. Moffett's First Year: Becoming a Teacher in America*. Public Affairs, 2004.

Howe, Randy. *First-Year Teacher: What I Wish I Had Known My First 100 Days on the Job: Wisdom, Tips, and Warnings from Experienced Teachers*. Kaplan, 2009.

Maloy, Robert W., and Irving Seidman. *The Essential Career Guide to Becoming a Middle and High School Teacher*. Bergin & Garvey, 1999.

Parkay, Forrest W., and Beverly Hardcastle Stanford. *Becoming a Teacher,* 10th ed. Prentice Hall, 2015.

Responsive Classroom. *The First Six Weeks of School.* 2nd ed. Center for Responsive Schools, Inc., 2015.

Shalaway, Linda. *Learning to Teach...Not Just for Beginners,* 3rd ed. Teaching Resources, 2005.

Starkey, Lauren. *Change Your Career: Teaching as Your New Profession.* Kaplan, 2007.

Staff of U.S. News and World Report. *U.S. News Ultimate Guide to Becoming a Teacher Sourcebooks,* 2004.

Wilson, Margaret. *Interactive Modeling A Powerful Tool for Teaching Children.* Center for Responsive Schools, Inc., 2012.

Wong, Harry K., and Rosemary T. Wong. *The First Days of School: How to be an Effective Teacher,* 4th ed. Harry K. Wong Publications, 2009.

***Magazines and Journals***

*American Educator*
*The Chronicle of Higher Education*
*Education Week*
*Harvard Educational Review*
*The New York Times* "Education Life"
*The Phi Delta Kappan*
*National Educators Association*

***Internet Resources***

**http://www.pbs.org/education/teacherslounge**
PBS Teachers' Lounge: Resource center

**eric.ed.gov**
Education Resources Information Center; large teaching and education database

**aft.org**
American Federation of Teachers

**proudtoserveagain.com**
Troops to Teachers program—provides opportunities for former members of the U.S. military to become public school teachers

**ed.gov**
U.S. Department of Education

**theteachersguide.com**

**behavioradvisor.com**

**teach-nology.com**
Free and easy-to-use resources for teachers

**kidsource.com**
Site with tips from teachers

**teachingtips.com**
Tips from an experienced teacher

**atozteacherstuff.com**
A teacher-created site listing online resources and tips

*Lesson Plan/Activity Sites*
**abcya.com**
**brainpop.com**
**coolmath-games.com**
**education-world.com**
**enchantedlearning.com**
**gonoodle.com**
**readinga-z.com**
**readwritethink.org**
**scholastic.com/digital/#book**
**teacherspayteachers.com**
**teachnet.com**
**theteacherscorner.net**

*General Teaching Job Sites*
**schoolspring.com**
**teachers-teachers.com**
**job-hunt.com/academia.shtml**
**educationjobs.com**
**k12jobs.com**

**wanttoteach.com/newsite/jobfairs.html**
National teaching job fair website